THE RHETORIC OF NO

THE RHETORIC OF NO

SECOND EDITION

Ray Fabrizio
Edith Karas
Ruth Menmuir

Monterey Peninsula College

Holt, Rinehart and Winston, Inc.

New York   Chicago   San Francisco   Atlanta   Dallas
Montreal   Toronto

Library of Congress Cataloging in Publication Data

Fabrizio, Ray, comp.
  The rhetoric of no.

  1. College readers. I. Karas, Edith, joint
comp. II. Menmuir, Ruth, joint comp. III. Title.
PE1122.F25 1974   808'.04275   73—16247

ISBN: 0–03–089234–1

What is a rebel? A man who says no, but whose refusal does not imply a renunciation. He is also a man who says yes, from the moment he makes his first gesture of rebellion.

ALBERT CAMUS
The Rebel

PREFACE

The second edition of *The Rhetoric of NO*, like the first edition, centers on issues which echo student concerns and sympathies, focusing on dissent as an expression of the dignity of man and a search for the just life.

After the confrontations of the Sixties and their concomitant demand that the classroom deal directly with the issues of the time—war, racism, violence, corruption—it seemed for a while that everyone had had enough of controversy and dissent. The years of protest and reaction had left the nation apparently dazed and exhausted. But recent events have dramatically forced the nation once again to recognize the constructive nature of dissent. If the spirit of totalitarianism requires a constant diet of official dogma and neatly wrapped theory, then the spirit of democracy depends upon diversity of opinion—the freedom from the obligation to conform, the right to say *no*. Not only do many old issues remain, but there are new issues to examine—new injustices, new corruption, new real dangers and imaginary demons. *The Rhetoric of NO* concentrates on contemporary dissent. The essays, each with its own distinctive voice, say *no* to the "unexamined lives" of people and the blind assumptions of a fearful and violent age.

The second edition broadens the range of subjects to include ecology, political power, freedom of the press, monopoly control, sexual freedom, women's liberation, welfare, and amnesty. In addition to selections by more recent writers, we have added essays by such firmly established authors as Orwell, Beauvoir, and Tocqueville. Taken together, the collection shows that there is a tradition of dissent which sheds light on and lends eloquence to the dissent of today. An exposure to some of the best examples can help students evaluate and write about the current problems which often seem so remote, confusing, or threatening.

Dissent, by definition, is "unpopular," and so any collection of protest cannot avoid expressing unpopular positions. However, we have tried to refrain from making ideological judgments of our own both in the selections of material and in the accompanying questions. Furthermore, recognizing that the nature of the material may offend some readers, we can only hope that such stimulation will challenge the readers to question and analyze their responses to the material.

Finally, dissent has its own rhetoric in a full range of tones—resentful or resigned, angry or agonized, irate or ironic, furious or downright funny—varying in intensity, purpose, and effect. With this rhetorical consideration in mind, we have grouped the essays under four "voices": *The Impassioned NO, The Discursive NO, The Reflective NO,* and *The Ironic NO,* according to each author's tone and purpose. An introduction to each of the sections discusses more completely the rationale for such a grouping, and the questions that follow each essay explore in more detail the relationship between style and content. Furthermore, the essays themselves constitute rhetorical models for student writing, containing excellent examples of development by definition, comparison and contrast, analysis, cause and effect, illustration, narration, and description. An appendix arranges the essays into three alternate tables of contents according to theme, subject, and rhetoric.

Acknowledgments

The editors wish to thank Ms. Allye Fabrizio, Dr. Ronald Menmuir, and Sam Karas for their suggestions and loving encouragement.

R.F.
E.K.
R.M.

Monterey, California
November, 1973

CONTENTS

THE IMPASSIONED NO   1

THE DISCURSIVE **NO**   107

THE REFLECTIVE **NO**   241

THE IRONIC NO   349

THE RHETORIC OF NO

THE
IMPASSIONED
NO

*You taught me language; and my profit on't
Is, I know how to curse.*

CALIBAN
in *The Tempest*

The voiceless Caliban could only feel; the articulate Caliban could now curse, and in his curse express an impassioned *no* to his condition of slavery. Like Caliban, each writer in this section speaks with strong emotion and reveals the depth of his feeling in the way he approaches his subject—and his reader.

When a writer is emotionally close to his subject, all of the things that constitute his style—his choice of words, the rhythm of his sentences, the comparisons he makes—convey his emotion and shape his ideas. With the good writer this is not chance or luck but the result of a conscious act. The good writer is able to move far enough away from his feelings to form his ideas and control his writing. When he does, he communicates not only ideas but also the convictions that make those ideas vital to him.

The same emotions which lend force to these ideas often impel the

1

writer to reach out to the reader in some way. He may plead with him, cajole him, or even attack him. He may flatter him or call him names. But whatever he does, he tries to make the reader understand that he is feeling something and that his feeling is a part of what he is trying to say.

Some may say that a person should not attempt to be emotional and logical at the same time. But if we think about this, we see that it is perfectly natural and right for us to "feel" what we "think." Emotion does not necessarily cancel out reason, nor does reason exclude emotion. The only danger comes when a writer, intentionally or unintentionally, disguises emotion as logic. Then the result is *propaganda*, and the unperceptive reader is led to accept pseudologic as truthful communication. (In "The Ironic NO" we will see how writers can intentionally disguise feelings in other ways for different purposes.)

The rhetorical relationship between reason and emotion can be more clearly illustrated through a specific example. Consider the following way of making an argument:

> All men are mortal.
> Socrates is a man.
> Therefore, Socrates is mortal.

This is an example of deductive reasoning, stated without emotion. What happens if we make the argument another way?

> I love old man Socrates very much. At certain times, though, the sudden realization hits me that all men must die. And then I know with desperate certainty that I will lose him.

The second statement is no less logical than the first. But it is different in that its logic is not the total content; it also communicates the author's feeling about his subject. Furthermore, the reader reacts differently to the second statement because of the added dimension of feeling which the writer has chosen to reveal. The feeling, then, becomes part of the communication, shaping both it and the reader's response.

All of the essays in this section are strongly emotional. The emotion each expresses is an essential ingredient of its subject and must be "listened to" as such. Some selections are more passionate than others, some more logical; but all say *no* in a voice which speaks with conviction.

Matthew 23

The Gospel of Matthew, written about 75 A.D., was addressed to a Jewish audience, probably in Antioch. The unknown author's purpose was: (1) to declare to the Jews of his day that Jesus was the Messiah, even though he was rejected by the religious establishment—the scribes, the Pharisees, and the Sadducees; and (2) to justify the turning of the Messiah from the Jews to the Gentiles with His Gospel of "righteousness" —the religion of the free spirit. The rejection of Jesus, as well as the failure by the establishment to respond to the spiritual vision, occasions and justifies the "woes" reproduced here. Chapters 19–25 should be read as a unit to give the full apocalyptic flavor of this Gospel.

Then spake Jesus to the multitudes and to his disciples, saying, The scribes and the Pharisees sit on Moses' seat: all things therefore whatsoever they bid you, *these* do and observe: but do not ye after their works; for they say, and do not. Yea, they bind heavy burdens and grievous to be borne, and lay them on men's shoulders; but they themselves will not move them with their finger. But all their works they do to be seen of men: for they make broad their phylacteries, and enlarge the borders *of their garments*, and love the chief place at feasts, and the chief seats in the synagogues, and the salutations in the market-places, and to be called of men, Rabbi. But be not ye called Rabbi: for one is your teacher, and all ye are brethren. And call no man your father on the earth: for one is your Father, *even* he who is in heaven. Neither be ye called masters: for one is your master, *even* the Christ. But he that is greatest among you shall be your servant. And whosoever shall exalt himself shall be humbled; and whosoever shall humble himself shall be exalted.

But woe unto you, scribes and Pharisees, hypocrites! because ye shut the kingdom of heaven against men: for ye enter not in yourselves, neither suffer ye them that are entering in to enter.

Woe unto you, scribes and Pharisees, hypocrites! for ye compass sea and land to make one proselyte; and when he is become so, ye make him twofold more a son of hell than yourselves.

Woe unto you, ye blind guides, that say, Whosoever shall swear by the temple, it is nothing; but whosoever shall swear by the gold of the temple, he is a debtor. Ye fools and blind: for which is greater, the gold, or the temple that hath sanctified the gold? And, Whosoever shall swear by the altar, it is nothing; but whosoever shall swear by the gift that is upon it, he is a debtor. Ye blind: for which is greater, the gift, or the altar that sanctifieth the gift? He therefore that sweareth by the altar, sweareth by it, and by all things thereon. And he that sweareth by the temple, sweareth by it, and by him that dwelleth therein. And he that sweareth by the heaven, sweareth by the throne of God, and by him that sitteth thereon.

Woe unto you, scribes and Pharisees, hypocrites! for ye tithe mint and anise and cummin, and have left undone the weightier matters of the law, justice, and mercy, and faith: but these ye ought to have done, and not to have left the other undone. Ye blind guides, that strain out the gnat, and swallow the camel!

Woe unto you, scribes and Pharisees, hypocrites! for ye cleanse the outside of the cup and of the platter, but within they are full from extortion and excess. Thou blind Pharisee, cleanse first the inside of the cup and of the platter, that the outside thereof may become clean also.

Woe unto you, scribes and Pharisees, hypocrites! for ye are like unto whited sepulchres, which outwardly appear beautiful, but inwardly are full of dead men's bones, and of all uncleanness. Even so ye also outwardly appear righteous unto men, but inwardly ye are full of hypocrisy and iniquity.

Woe unto you, scribes and Pharisees, hypocrites! for ye build the sepulchres of the prophets, and garnish the tombs of the righteous, and say, If we had been in the days of our fathers, we should not have been partakers with them in the blood of the prophets. Wherefore ye witness to yourselves, that ye are sons of them that slew the prophets. Fill ye up then the measure of your fathers. Ye serpents, ye offspring of vipers, how shall ye escape the judgment of hell? Therefore, behold, I send unto you prophets, and wise men, and scribes: some of them shall ye kill and crucify; and some of them shall ye scourge in your synagogues, and persecute from city to city: that upon you may come all the righteous blood shed on the earth, from the blood of Abel the righteous unto the blood of Zachariah son of Barachiah, whom ye slew between the sanctuary and the altar. Verily I say unto you, All these things shall come upon this generation.

O Jerusalem, Jerusalem, that killeth the prophets, and stoneth them that are sent unto her! how often would I have gathered thy children together, even as a hen gathereth her chickens under her wings, and ye would not! Behold, your house is left unto you desolate. For I say unto you, Ye shall not see me henceforth, till ye shall say, Blessed is he that cometh in the name of the Lord.

For Discussion

1. What general criticism does Jesus make of the scribes and Pharisees? Who would be their modern counterparts?
2. To what exent are the criticisms Jesus makes valid for the church today? For the world?
3. What other descriptions in this selection have modern equivalents?
4. Locate several metaphors and discuss their effectiveness.
5. Discuss the emotional content of the language. Point out those words with the strongest feeling.
6. Epithet and invective are universal weapons of persuasion. In this respect, compare the style of Matthew 23 to that of Miller and Farber (in "The Ironic NO").
7. What change of tone is evident in the last paragraph?

MARK TWAIN

Reflections on Religion

Samuel L. Clemens (1835–1910), perhaps America's most famous author and humorist, took the pen name of "Mark Twain" while a reporter in Virginia City in 1862. His many novels, short stories, essays, and lectures drew upon his varied experiences as a tramp printer, riverboat pilot, prospector, lecturer, traveler, and unsuccessful financial investor. Although they are philosophically consistent with his early humorous works, his later writings are more profoundly cynical and more bitterly satiric. The following "reflections" were dictated by Twain in June 1906; but at the request of his daughter, they were not released for publication until 1960, the 125th anniversary of Clemens' birth, when Mrs. Samossoud lifted the ban on all of his previously unpublished works.

1

Tuesday, June 19, 1906

Our Bible reveals to us the character of our God with minute and remorseless exactness. The portrait is substantially that of a man—if one can imagine a man charged and overcharged with evil impulses far beyond the human limit; a personage whom no one, perhaps, would desire to associate with now that Nero and Caligula are dead. In the Old Testament His acts expose His vindictive, unjust, ungenerous, pitiless and vengeful nature constantly. He is always punishing—punishing trifling misdeeds with thousandfold severity; punishing innocent children for the misdeeds of their parents; punishing unoffending populations for the misdeeds of their rulers; even descending to wreak bloody vengeance upon harmless calves and lambs and sheep and bullocks as punishment for inconsequential trespasses committed by their proprietors. It is perhaps the most damnatory biography that exists in print anywhere. It makes Nero an angel of light and leading by contrast.

It begins with an inexcusable treachery, and that is the keynote of the entire biography. That beginning must have been invented in a pirate's nursery, it so malign and so childish. To Adam is forbidden the fruit of a certain tree—and he is gravely informed that if he disobeys he shall die. How could that be expected to impress Adam? Adam was merely a man in stature; in knowledge and experience he was in no way the superior of a baby of two years of age; he could have no idea of what the word death meant. He had never seen a dead thing; he had never heard of a dead thing before. The word meant nothing to him. If the Adam child had been warned that if he ate of the apples he would be transformed into a meridian of longitude, that threat would have been the equivalent of the other, since neither of them could mean anything to him.

The watery intellect that invented the memorable threat could be depended on to supplement it with other banalities and low grade notions of justice and fairness, and that is what happened. It was decreed that all of Adam's descendants, to the latest day, should be punished for the baby's trespass against a law of his nursery fulminated against him before he was out of his diapers. For thousands and thousands of years his posterity, individual by individual, has been unceasingly hunted and harried with afflictions in punishment of the juvenile misdeameanor which is grandiloquently called Adam's Sin. And during all that vast lapse of time there has been no lack of rabbins and popes and bishops and priests and parsons and lay slaves eager to applaud this infamy, maintain the unassailable justice and righteousness of it, and praise its Author in terms of flattery so gross and extravagant that none but a God could listen to it and not hide His face in disgust and embarrassment. Hardened to flattery as our Oriental potentates are through long experience, not even they would be able to endure the rank quality of it which our God endures with complacency and satisfaction from our pulpits every Sunday.

We brazenly call our God the source of mercy, while we are aware all the time that there is not an authentic instance in history of His ever having exercised that virtue. We call Him the source of morals, while we know by His history and by His daily conduct as perceived with our own senses that He is totally destitute of anything resembling morals. We call Him Father, and not in derision, although we would detest and denounce any earthly father who should inflict upon his child a thousandth part of the pains and miseries and cruelties which our God deals out to His children every day, and has dealt out to them daily during all the centuries since the crime of creating Adam was committed.

We deal in a curious and laughable confusion of notions concerning God. We divide Him in two, bring half of Him down to an obscure and infinitesimal corner of the world to confer salvation upon a little colony of Jews—and only Jews, no one else—and leave the other half of Him throned in Heaven and looking down and eagerly and anxiously watching for results. We reverently study the history of the earthly half and deduce from it the conviction that the earthly half has reformed, is equipped with morals and virtues, and in no way resembles the abandoned, malignant half that abides upon the throne. We conceive that the earthly half is just, merciful, charitable, benevolent, forgiving and full of sympathy for the sufferings of mankind and anxious to remove them. Apparently we deduce this character not by examining facts but by diligently declining to search them, measure them and weigh them. The earthly half requires us to be merciful and sets us an example by inventing a lake of fire and brimstone in which all of us who fail to recognize and worship Him as God are to be burned through all eternity. And not only *we*, who are offered these terms, are to be thus burned if we neglect them, but also the earlier billions of human beings are to suffer this awful fate, although they all lived and died without ever having heard of Him or the terms at all. This exhibition of mercifulness may be called gorgeous. We have nothing approaching it among human savages, nor among the wild beasts of the jungle. We are required to forgive our brother seventy times seven times and be satisfied and content if on our deathbed, after a pious life, our soul escape from our body before the hurrying priest can get to us and furnish it a pass with his mumblings and candles and incantations. This example of the forgiving spirit may also be pronounced gorgeous.

We are told that the two halves of our God are only seemingly disconnected by their separation; that in very fact the two halves remain one, and equally powerful, notwithstanding the separation. This being the case, the earthly half—who mourns over the sufferings of mankind and would like to remove them, and is quite competent to remove them at any moment He may choose—satisfies Himself with restoring sight to a blind person here and there instead of restoring it to all the blind; cures a cripple here and there instead of curing all the cripples; furnishes to five thousand famishing persons a meal and lets the rest of the millions that are hungry remain hungry—and all the time He admonishes inefficient man to cure these ills which God Himself inflicted upon him, and which He could extinguish with a word if He chose to do it, and thus do a plain duty which He had neglected from the beginning and always will neglect while time shall last. He raised several dead persons to life. He manifestly regarded this as a kindness. If it was a kindness it was not just to confine it to half-a-dozen persons. He should have raised the rest of the dead. I would not do it myself, for I think the dead are the only human beings who are really well off—but I merely mention it in passing as one of those curious incongruities with which our Bible history is heavily overcharged.

Whereas the God of the Old Testament is a fearful and repulsive character He is at least consistent. He is frank and outspoken. He makes no pretense to the possession of a moral or a virtue of any kind—except with His mouth. No such thing is anywhere discoverable in His conduct. I think He comes infinitely nearer to being respectworthy than does His reformed self as guilelessly exposed in the New Testament. Nothing in all history—nor even His massed history combined—remotely approaches in atrocity the invention of Hell.

His heavenly self, His Old Testament self, is sweetness and gentleness and respectability, compared with His reformed earthly self. In Heaven he claims not a single merit and hasn't one—outside of those claimed by His mouth—whereas in the earth He claims every merit in the entire catalogue of merits, yet practised them only now and then, penuriously, and finished by conferring Hell upon us, which abolished all His fictitious merits in a body.

2

Wednesday, June 20, 1906

There are one or two curious defects about Bibles. An almost pathetic poverty of invention characterizes them all. That is one striking defect. Another is that each pretends to originality without possessing any. Each borrows from the others and gives no credit, which is a distinctly immoral act. Each in turn confiscates decayed old stage-properties from the others and with naïve confidence puts them forth as fresh new inspirations from on high. We borrow the Golden Rule from Confucius after it has seen service for centuries and copyright it without a blush. When we want a Deluge we go away back to hoary Babylon and borrow it, and are as proud of it and as satisfied with it as if it had been worth the trouble. We still revere it and admire it to-day and claim that it came to us direct from the mouth of the Deity; whereas we know that Noah's flood never happened, and couldn't have happened. The flood is a favorite with Bible makers. If there is a Bible—or even a tribe of savages—that lacks a General Deluge it is only because the religious scheme that lacks it hadn't any handy source to borrow it from.

Another prime favorite with the authors of sacred literature and founders of religions is the Immaculate Conception. It had been worn threadbare before we adopted it as a fresh new idea—and we admire it as much now as did the original conceiver of it when his mind was delivered of it a million years ago. The Hindus prized it ages ago when they acquired Krishna by the Immaculate process. The Buddhists were happy when they acquired Gautama by the same process twenty-five hundred years ago. The Greeks of the same period had great joy in it when their Supreme Being and his cabinet used to come down and people Greece with mongrels half human and half divine. The Romans borrowed the idea from Greece and found great happiness in Jupiter's Immaculate Conception products. We got it direct from Heaven, by way of Rome. We are still charmed with it. And only a fortnight ago, when an Episcopal clergyman in Rochester was summoned before the governing body of his church to answer the charge of intimating that he did not believe that the Savior was miraculously conceived, the Rev. Dr. Briggs, who is perhaps the most daringly broad-minded religious person now occupying an American pulpit, took up the cudgels in favor of the Immaculate Conception in an article in the *North American Review*, and from the tone of that article it seemed apparent that he believed he had settled that vexed question once and for all.[1] His idea was that there could be no doubt about it, for the reason that the Virgin Mary knew it was authentic because the Angel of the Annunciation told her so. Also, it must have been so, for the additional reason that Jude—a later son of Mary, the Virgin, and born in wedlock—was still living and associating with the adherents of the early church many years after the event, and that he said quite decidedly that it was a case of Immaculate Conception; therefore it must be true, for Jude was right there in the family and in a position to know.

If there is anything more amusing than the Immaculate Conception doctrine it is the quaint reasonings whereby ostensibly intelligent human beings persuade themselves that the impossible fact is proven.

If Dr. Briggs were asked to believe in the Immaculate Conception process as exercised in the cases of Krishna, Osiris, Buddha and the rest of the tribe he would decline with thanks and probably be offended. If pushed, he would probably say that it would be childish to believe in those cases, for the reason that they were supported by none but human testimony and that it would be impossible to prove such a thing by human testimony, because if the entire human race were present at a case of Immaculate Conception they wouldn't be able to tell when it happened, nor whether it happened at all—and yet this bright man with

---

[1] Dr. Briggs's article discusses the Virgin Birth and not the Immaculate Conception. The latter refers to the conception of Mary, while the former refers to the birth of Jesus. However, Twain's misuse of the term "Immaculate Conception," common even among Catholics, does not affect the substance of his argument. [Ed.]

the temporarily muddy mind is quite able to believe an impossibility whose authenticity rests entirely upon human testimony—the testimony of but one human being, the Virgin herself, a witness not disinterested, but powerfully interested; a witness incapable of knowing the fact as a fact, but getting all that she supposed she knew about it at second hand —at second hand from an entire stranger, an alleged angel, who could have been an angel, perhaps, but also could have been a tax collector. It is not likely that she had ever seen an angel before or knew their trademarks. He was a stranger. He brought no credentials. His evidence was worth nothing at all to anybody else in the community. It is worth nothing to-day to any but minds which are like Dr. Briggs's—which have lost their clarity through mulling over absurdities in the pious wish to dig something sane and rational out of them. The Immaculate Conception rests wholly upon the testimony of a single witness—a witness whose testimony is without value—a witness whose very existence has nothing to rest upon but the assertion of the young peasant wife whose husband needed to be pacified. Mary's testimony satisfied him but that is because he lived in Nazareth instead of New York. There isn't any carpenter in New York that would take the testimony at par. If the Immacuate Conception could be repeated in New York to-day there isn't a man, woman or child of those four millions who would believe in it—except perhaps some addled Christian Scientists. A person who can believe in Mother Eddy wouldn't strain at an Immaculate Conception, or six of them in a bunch. The Immaculate Conception could not he repeated successfully in New York in our day. It would produce laughter, not reverence and adoration.

To a person who doesn't believe in it, it seems a most puerile invention. It could occur to nobody but a god that it was a large and ingenious arrangement and had dignity in it. It could occur to nobody but a god that a divine Son procured through promiscuous relations with a peasant family in a village could improve the purity of the product, yet that is the very idea. The product acquires purity—purity absolute—purity from all stain or blemish—through a gross violation of both human and divine law, as set forth in the constitution and by-laws of the Bible. Thus the Christian religion, which requires everybody to be moral and to obey the laws, has its very beginning in immorality and in disobedience to law. You couldn't purify a tomcat by the Immaculate Conception process.

Apparently as a pious stage-property it is still useful, still workable, although it is so bent with age and so nearly exhausted by overwork. It is another case of begats. What's-his-name begat Krishna, Krishna begat Buddha, Buddha begat Osiris, Osiris begat the Babylonian deities, they begat God, He begat Jesus, Jesus begat Mrs. Eddy. If she is going to continue the line and do her proper share of the begatting, she must get at it, for she is already an antiquity.

There is one notable thing about our Christianity: bad, bloody, merciless, money-grabbing and predatory as it is—in our country particularly, and in all other Christian countries in a somewhat modified degree—it is still a hundred times better than the Christianity of the Bible, with its prodigious crime—the invention of Hell. Measured by our Christianity of to-day, bad as it is, hypocritical as it is, empty and hollow as it is, neither the Deity nor His Son is a Christian, nor qualified for that moderately high place. Ours is a terrible religion. The fleets of the world could swim in spacious comfort in the innocent blood it has spilt.

3

Friday, June 22, 1906

. . .

The Gospel of Peace is always making a good deal of noise with its mouth; always rejoicing in the progress it is making toward final perfection, and always diligently neglecting to furnish the statistics. George the Third reigned sixty years, the longest reign in English history up to his time. When his revered successor, Victoria, turned the sixty-year corner—thus scoring a new long-reign record—the event was celebrated with great pomp and circumstance and public rejoicing in England and her colonies. Among the statistics fetched out for general admiration were these: that for each year of the sixty of her reign Victoria's Christian soldiers had fought in a separate and distinct war. Meantime the possessions of England had swollen to such a degree by depredations committed upon helpless and godless pagans that there were not figures enough in Great Britain to set down the stolen acreage and they had to import a lot from other countries.

There are no peaceful nations now except those unhappy ones whose borders have not been invaded by the Gospel of Peace. All Christendom is a soldier-camp. During all the past generation the Christian poor have been taxed almost to starvation-point to support the giant armaments which the Christian Governments have built up, each to protect itself from the rest of the brotherhood and, incidentally, to snatch any patch of real estate left exposed by its savage owner. King Leopold II of Belgium—probably the most intensely Christian monarch, except Alexander the Sixth,[2] that has escaped Hell thus far—has stolen an entire kingdom in Africa, and in the fourteen years of Christian endeavor there has reduced the population of thirty millions to fifteen by murder, mutilation, overwork, robbery, rapine—confiscating the helpless native's very labor

---

[2] The reigning Russian monarch was Nicholas II, the son of Alexander III. It is not clear whether Twain has someone in particular in mind or whether he is being ironic. [Ed.]

and giving him nothing in return but salvation and a home in Heaven, furnished at the last moment by the Christian priest.

Within this last generation each Christian power has turned the bulk of its attention to finding out newer and still newer and more and more effective ways of killing Christians—and, incidentally, a pagan now and then—and the surest way to get rich quickly in Christ's earthly kingdom is to invent a gun that can kill more Christians at one shot than any other existing gun.

Also, during the same generation each Christian Government has played with its neighbors a continuous poker game in the naval line. In this game France puts up a battleship; England sees that battleship and goes it one battleship better; Russian comes in and raises it a battleship or two—*did*, before the untaught stranger entered the game and reduced her stately pile of chips to a damaged ferryboat and a cruiser that can't cruise. We are in it ourselves now. This game goes on and on and on. There is never a new shuffle; never a new deal. No player ever calls another's hand. It is merely an unending game of put up and put up and put up; and by the law of probabilities a day is coming when no Christians will be left on the land, except the women. The men will all be at sea, manning the fleets.

This singular game, which is so costly and so ruinous and so silly, is called statesmanship—which is different from assmanship on account of the spelling. Anybody but a statesman could invent some way to reduce these vast armaments to rational and sensible and safe police proportions, with the result that thenceforth all Christians could sleep in their beds unafraid, and even the Savior could come down and walk on the seas, foreigner as He is, without dread of being chased by Christian battleships.

Has the Bible done something still worse than drench the planet with innocent blood? To my mind it has—but this is only an opinion, and it may be a mistaken one. There has never been a Protestant boy or a Protestant girl whose mind the Bible has not soiled. No Protestant child ever comes clean from association with the Bible. This association cannot be prevented. Sometimes the parents try to prevent it by not allowing the children to have access to the Bible's awful obscenities, but this only whets the child's desire to taste that forbidden fruit, and it does taste it—seeks it out secretly and devours it with a strong and grateful appetite. The Bible does its baleful work in the propagation of vice among children, and vicious and unclean ideas, daily and constantly, in every Protestant family in Christendom. It does more of this deadly work than all the other unclean books in Christendom put together; and not only more, but a thousandfold more. It is easy to protect the young from those other books, and they are protected from them. But they have no protection against the deadly Bible.

Is it doubted that the young people hunt out the forbidden passages privately and study them with pleasure? If my reader were here present —let him be of either sex or any age, between ten and ninety—I would make him answer this question himself—and he could answer in only one way. He would be obliged to say that by his own knowledge and experience of the days of his early youth he knows positively that the Bible defiles all Protestant children, without a single exception.

Do I think the Christian religion is here to stay? Why should I think so? There had been a thousand religions before it was born. They are all dead. There had been millions of gods before ours was invented. Swarms of them are dead and forgotten long ago. Ours is by long odds the worst God that the ingenuity of man has begotten from his insane imagination—and shall He and His Christianity be immortal against the great array of probabilities furnished by the theological history of the past? No. I think that Christianity and its God must follow the rule. They must pass on in their turn and make room for another God and a stupider religion. Or perhaps a better than this? No. That is not likely. History shows that in the matter of religions we progress backward and not the other way. No matter, there will be a new God and a new religion. They will be introduced to popularity and accepted with the only arguments that have ever persuaded any people in this earth to adopt Christianity, or any other religion that they were not born to: the Bible, the sword, the torch and the axe—the only missionaries that have ever scored a single victory since gods and religions began in the world. After the new God and the new religion have become established in the usual proportions—one-fifth of the world's population ostensible adherents, the four-fifths pagan missionary field, with the missionary scratching its continental back complacently and inefficiently—will the new converts believe in them? Certainly they will. They have always believed in the million gods and religions that have been stuffed down their midriffs. There isn't anything so grotesque or so incredible that the average human being can't believe it. . . .

4

Saturday, June 23, 1906

.   .   .

We know that the real God, the Supreme God, the actual Maker of the universe, made everything that is in it. We know that He made all the creatures, from the microbe and the brontosaur down to man and the monkey, and that He knew what would happen to each and every one of them from the beginning of time to the end of it. In the case of each creature, big or little, He made it an unchanging law that that creature should suffer wanton and unnecessary pains and miseries every day of its life—that by that law these pains and miseries could not be avoided by any diplomacy exercisable by the creature; that its way, from birth to death, should be beset by traps, pitfalls and gins, ingeniously planned and ingeniously concealed; and that by another law every transgression of a law of Nature, either ignorantly or wittingly committed, should in every instance be visited by a punishment ten-thousandfold out of proportion to the transgression. We stand astonished at the all-comprehensive malice which could patiently descend to the contriving of elaborate tortures for the meanest and pitifulest of the countless kinds of creatures that were to inhabit the earth. The spider was so contrived that she would not eat grass but must catch flies and such things and inflict a slow and horrible death upon them, unaware that her turn would come next. The wasp was so contrived that he also would decline grass and stab the spider, not conferring upon her a swift and merciful death, but merely half-paralyzing her, then ramming her down into the wasp den, there to live and suffer for days while the wasp babies should chew her legs off at their leisure. In turn, there was a murderer provided for the wasp, and another murderer for the wasp's murderer, and so on throughout the whole scheme of living creatures in the earth. There isn't one of them that was not designed and appointed to inflict misery and murder on some fellow creature and suffer the same in turn from some other murderous fellow creature. In flying into the web the fly is merely guilty of an indiscretion—not a breach of any law—yet the fly's punishment is ten-thousandfold out of proportion to that little indiscretion.

The ten-thousandfold law of punishment is rigorously enforced against every creature, man included. The debt, whether made innocently or guiltily, is promptly collected by Nature—and in this world, without waiting for the ten-billionfold additional penalty appointed—in the case of man—for collection in the next.

This system of atrocious punishments for somethings and nothings begins upon the helpless baby on its first day in the world and never ceases until its last one. Is there a father who would persecute his baby with unearned colics and the unearned miseries of teething, and follow these with mumps, measles, scarlet-fever and the hundred other persecutions appointed for the unoffending creature? And then follow these, from youth to the grave, with a multitude of ten-thousandfold punishments for laws broken either by intention or indiscretion? With a fine sarcasm we ennoble God with the title of Father—yet we know quite well that we should hang His style of father wherever we might catch him. . . .

In His destitution of one and all of the qualities which could grace a God and invite respect for Him and reverence and worship, the real God, the genuine God, the Maker of the mighty universe is just like all the other gods in the list. He proves every day that He takes no interest in man, nor in the other animals, further than to torture them, slay them and get out of this pastime such entertainment as it may afford—and do what He can not to get weary of the eternal and changeless monotony of it.

5

Monday, June 25, 1906

. . .

As to the human race. There are many pretty and winning things about the human race. It is perhaps the poorest of all the inventions of all the gods but it has never suspected it once. There is nothing prettier than its naïve and complacent appreciation of itself. It comes out frankly and proclaims without bashfulness or any sign of a blush that it is the noblest work of God. It has had a billion opportunities to know better, but all signs fail with this ass. I could say harsh things about it but I cannot bring myself to do it—it is like hitting a child.

Man is not to blame for what he is. He didn't make himself. He has no control over himself. All the control is vested in his temperament—which he did not create—and in the circumstances which hedge him round from the cradle to the grave and which he did not devise and cannot change by any act of his will, for the reason that he has no will. He is as purely a piece of automatic mechanism as is a watch, and can no more dictate or influence his actions than can the watch. He is a subject for pity, not blame—and not contempt. He is flung head over heels into this world without ever a chance to decline, and straightway he conceives and accepts the notion that he is in some mysterious way under obligations to the unknown Power that inflicted this outrage upon him —and thenceforth he considers himself responsible to that Power for every act of his life, and punishable for such of his acts as do not meet with the approval of that Power—yet that same man would argue quite differently if a human tyrant should capture him and put chains upon him of any kind and require obedience; that the tyrant had no right to do that; that the tyrant had no right to put commands upon him of any kind and require obedience; that the tyrant had no right to compel him to commit murder and then put the responsibility for the murder upon him. Man constantly makes a most strange distinction between man and his Maker in the matter of morals. He requires of his fellow man obedience to a very creditable code of morals but he observes without shame or disapproval his God's utter destitution of morals.

God ingeniously contrived man in such a way that he could not escape obedience to the laws of his passions, his appetites and his various unpleasant and undesirable qualities. God has so contrived him that all his goings out and comings in are beset by traps which he cannot possibly avoid and which compel him to commit what are called sins—and then God punishes him for doing these very things which from the beginning of time He had always intended that he should do. Man is a machine and God made it—without invitation from any one. Whoever makes a machine here below is responsible for that machine's performance. No one would think of such a thing as trying to put the responsibility upon the machine itself. We all know perfectly well—though we all conceal it, just as I am doing, until I shall be dead and out of reach of public opinion—we all know, I say, that God, and God alone, is responsible for every act and word of a human being's life between cradle and grave. We know it perfectly well. In our secret hearts we haven't the slightest doubt of it. In our secret hearts we have no hesitation in proclaiming as an unthinking fool anybody who thinks he believes that he is by any possibility capable of committing a sin against God—or who thinks he thinks he is under obligations to God and owes Him thanks, reverence and worship.

For Discussion

1. Paraphrase Twain's argument that the first part of Genesis is an "inexcusable treachery." What do you think of this argument? Comment on Twain's use of it as a recurring theme throughout the whole piece.
2. What differences does Twain see between the Old and the New Testaments?
3. Name the striking defects in the Bible, according to Twain.
4. How does Twain discredit the doctrine of the Immaculate Conception? Do you agree or disagree?
5. What does Twain see as the basic dangers of belief in the biblical God? How does he support his argument?
6. What is Twain objecting to in the discussion of the Gospel of Peace? What is your opinion?
7. Describe the "real God" as Twain sees him.
8. Twain says that man's difficulties arise from his "moral sense." What does he mean?
9. What is Twain's religious philosophy? Would you call him an atheist? What is his personal philosophy regarding man's relationship to nature?
10. What universal human follies are being satirized in this piece?
11. Twain uses phrases such as "watery intellect" and "celestial bandits" to describe both the authors of the Bible and the biblical God. Locate at least one similar use of invective on each page and discuss its effect. (Also see Mencken and Miller in "The Ironic NO" for use of invective.)
12. What is the central irony that Twain wants us to see in Christianity?

CHIEF JOSEPH

I Will Speak with a Straight Tongue

The Nez Percés lived at peace with the whites and neighboring tribes in the mountains of the Northwest until the infiltration of settlers into their land became unbearable. Joseph (In-mut-too-yah-lat-lat), born in 1840, became chief at the age of thirty-one and achieved fame as the brilliant military tactician and leader of the Nez Percés' attempt to escape into Canada in 1877. In eleven weeks and 1600 miles of flight, the tribe engaged ten separate United States military commands in thirteen battles, winning most of them. However, after many hardships, and within only thirty miles of the Canadian border, Chief Joseph surrendered to Generals Howard and Miles on October 5, 1877. The following speech was delivered in January, 1879, to the Department of Indian Affairs in Washington, D.C., where Joseph was permitted to go in order to plead for the relief of his people.

My friends, I have been asked to show you my heart. I am glad to have a chance to do so. I want the white people to understand my people. Some of you think an Indian is like a wild animal. This is a great mistake. I will tell you all about our people, and then you can judge whether an Indian is a man or not. I believe much trouble and blood would be saved if we opened our hearts more. I will tell you in my way how the Indian sees things. The white man has more words to tell you how they look to him, but it does not require many words to speak the truth. What I have to say will come from my heart, and I will speak with a straight tongue. Ah-cum-kin-i-ma-me-hut (the Great Spirit) is looking at me, and will hear me.

My name is In-mut-too-yah-lat-lat (Thunder traveling over the Mountains). I am chief of the Wal-lam-wat-kin band of Chute-pa-lu, or Nez Percés (nose-pierced Indians). I was born in eastern Oregon, thirty-eight winters ago. My father was chief before me. When a young man, he was called Joseph by Mr. Spaulding, a missionary. He died a few years ago. He left a good name on earth. He advised me well for my people.

Our fathers gave us many laws, which they had learned from their fathers. These laws were good. They told us to treat all men as they treated us; that we should never be the first to break a bargain; that it was a disgrace to tell a lie; that we should speak only the truth; that it was a shame for one man to take from another his wife, or his property without paying for it. We were taught to believe that the Great Spirit sees and hears everything, and that he never forgets; that hereafter he will give every man a spirit-home according to his deserts: if he has been a good man, he will have a good home; if he has been a bad man, he will have a bad home. This I believe, and all my people believe the same.

We did not know there were other people besides the Indian until about one hundred winters ago, when some men with white faces came to our country. They brought many things with them to trade for furs and skins. They brought tobacco, which was new to us. They brought guns with flint stones on them, which frightened our women and children. Our people could not talk with these white-faced men, but they used signs which all people understand. These men were Frenchmen, and they called our people "Nez Percés," because they wore rings in their noses for ornaments. Although very few of our people wear them now, we are still called by the same name. These French trappers said a great many things to our fathers, which have been planted in our hearts. Some were good for us, but some were bad. Our people were divided in opinion about these men. Some thought they taught more bad than good. An Indian respects a brave man, but he despises a coward. He loves a straight tongue, but he hates a forked tongue. The French trappers told us some truths and some lies.

The first white men of your people who came to our country were named Lewis and Clark. They also brought many things that our people had never seen. They talked straight, and our people gave them a great feast, as a proof that their hearts were friendly. These men were very kind. They made presents to our chiefs and our people made presents to them. We had a great many horses, of which we gave them what they needed, and they gave us guns and tobacco in return. All the Nez Percés made friends with Lewis and Clark, and agreed to let them pass through their country, and never to make war on white men. This promise the Nez Percés have never broken. No white man can accuse them of bad faith, and speak with a straight tongue. It has always been the pride of the Nez Percés that they were the friends of the white men. When my father was a young man there came to our country a white man (Rev. Mr. Spaulding) who talked spirit law. He won the affections of our people because he spoke good things to them. At first he did not say anything about white men wanting to settle on our lands. Nothing was said about that until about twenty winters ago, when a number of white people came into our country and built houses and made farms. At first our people made no complaint. They thought there was room enough for all to live in peace, and they were learning many things from the white men that seemed to be good. But we soon found that the white men were growing rich very fast, and were greedy to possess everything the Indian had. My father was the first to see through the schemes of the white men, and he warned his tribe to be careful about trading with them. He had suspicion of men who seemed anxious to make money. I was a boy then, but I remember well my father's caution. He had sharper eyes than the rest of our people.

Next there came a white officer (Governor Stevens), who invited all the Nez Percés to a treaty council. After the council was opened he made known his heart. He said there were a great many white people in our country, and many more would come; that he wanted the land marked out so that the Indians and white men could be separated. If they were to live in peace it was necessary, he said, that the Indians should have a country set apart for them, and in that country they must stay. My father, who represented his band, refused to have anything to do with the council, because he wished to be a free man. He claimed that no man owned any part of the earth, and a man could not sell what he did not own.

Mr. Spaulding took hold of my father's arm and said, "Come and sign the treaty." My father pushed him away, and said: "Why do you ask me to sign away my country? Is it your business to talk to us about spirit matters and not to talk to us about parting with our land." Governer Stevens urged my father to sign his treaty, but he refused. "I will not sign your paper," he said; "you go where you please, so do I; you are not a child, I am no child; I can think for myself. No man can think for me. I have no other home than this. I will not give it up to any man. My people would have no home. Take away your paper. I will not touch it with my hand."

My father left the council. Some of the chiefs of the other bands of the Nez Percés signed the treaty, and then Governor Stevens gave them presents of blankets. My father cautioned his people to take no presents, for "after a while," he said, "they will claim that you have accepted pay for your country." Since that time four bands of the Nez Percés have received annuities from the United States. My father was invited to many councils, and they tried hard to make him sign the treaty, but he was firm as the rock, and would not sign away his home. His refusal caused a difference among the Nez Percés.

Eight years later (1863) was the next treaty council. A chief called Lawyer, because he was a great talker, took the lead in this council, and sold nearly all the Nez Percés country. My father was not there. He said to me: "When you go into council with the white man, always remember your country. Do not give it away. The white man will cheat you out of your home. I have taken no pay from the United States. I have never sold our land." In this treaty Lawyer acted without authority from our band. He had no right to sell the Wallowa[1] (winding water) country. That had always belonged to my father's own people, and the other bands had never disputed our right to it. No other Indians ever claimed Wallowa.

In order to have all people understand how much land we owned, my father planted poles around it and said:

"Inside is the home of my people—the white man may take the land outside. Inside this boundary all our people were born. It circles around the graves of our fathers, and we will never give up these graves to any man."

The United States claimed they had bought all the Nez Percés' country outside the Lapwai Reservation, from Lawyer and other chiefs, but we continued to live on this land in peace until eight years ago, when white men began to come inside the bounds my father had set. We warned them against this great wrong, but they would not leave our land, and some bad blood was raised. The white men represented that we were going upon the warpath. They reported many things that were false.

The United States Government again asked for a treaty council. My father had become blind and feeble. He could no longer speak for his people. It was then that I took my father's place as chief. In this council I made my first speech to white men. I said to the agent who held the council:

"I did not want to come to this council, but I came hoping that we could save blood. The white man has no right to come here and take our country. We have never accepted any presents from the Government. Neither Lawyer nor any other chief had authority to sell this land. It has always belonged to my people. It came unclouded to them from our fathers, and we will defend this land as long as a drop of Indian blood warms the hearts of our men."

The agent said he had orders, from the Great White Chief at Washington, for us to go upon the Lapwai Reservation, and that if we obeyed

[1] The Wallowa River (winding water) was in the northeastern part of Oregon, in the area near Idaho.

he would help us in many ways. "You must move to the agency," he said. I answered him: "I will not. I do not need your help; we have plenty, and we are contented and happy if the white man will let us alone. The reservation is too small for so many people with all their stock. You can keep your presents; we can go to your towns and pay for all we need; we have plenty of horses and cattle to sell, and we won't have any help from you; we are free now; we can go where we please. Our fathers were born here. Here they lived, here they died, here are their graves. We will never leave them." The agent went away, and we had peace for a little while.

Soon after this my father sent for me. I saw he was dying. I took his hand in mine. He said: "My son, my body is returning to my mother earth, and my spirit is going very soon to see the Great Spirit Chief. When I am gone, think of your country. You are the chief of these people. They look to you to guide them. Always remember that your father never sold this country. You must stop your ears whenever you are asked to sign a treaty selling your home. A few years more, and white men will be all around you. They have their eyes on this land. My son, never forget my dying words. This country holds your father's body. Never sell the bones of your father and your mother." I pressed my father's hand and told him I would protect his grave with my life. My father smiled and passed away to the spirit land.

I buried him in that beautiful valley of winding waters. I love that land more than all the rest of the world. A man who would not love his father's grave is worse than a wild animal.

For a short time we lived quietly. But this could not last. White men had found gold in the mountains around the land of winding water. They stole many horses from us, and we could not get them back because we were Indians. The white men told lies for each other. They drove off a great many of our cattle. Some white men branded our young cattle so they could claim them. We had no friend who would plead our cause before the law councils. It seemed to me that some of the white men in Wallowa were doing these things on purpose to get up a war. They knew that we were not strong enough to fight them. I labored hard to avoid trouble and bloodshed. We gave up some of our country to the white men, thinking that then we could have peace. We were mistaken. The white man would not let us alone. We could have avenged our wrongs many times, but we did not. Whenever the Government has asked us to help them against other Indians, we have never refused. When the white men were few and we were strong we could have killed them all off, but the Nez Percés wished to live at peace.

If we have not done so, we have not been to blame. I believe that the old treaty has never been correctly reported. If we ever owned the land we own it still, for we never sold it. In the treaty councils the commissioners have claimed that our country had been sold to the Government. Suppose a white man should come to me and say, "Joseph, I like your horses, and I want to buy them." I say to him, "No, my horses suit me, I will not sell them." Then he goes to my neighbor, and says to him: "Joseph has some good horses. I want to buy them, but he refuses to sell." My neighbor answers, "Pay me the money, and I will sell you Joseph's horses." The white man returns to me, and says, "Joseph, I have bought your horses, and you must let me have them." If we sold our lands to the Government, this is the way they were bought.

On account of the treaty made by the other bands of the Nez Percés, the white men claimed my lands. We were troubled greatly by white men crowding over the line. Some of these were good men, and we lived on peaceful terms with them, but they were not all good.

Nearly every year the agent came over from Lapwai and ordered us on to the reservation. We always replied that we were satisfied to live in Wallowa. We were careful to refuse presents or annuities which he offered.

Through all the years since the white men came to Wallowa we have been threatened and taunted by them and the treaty Nez Percés. They have given us no rest. We have had a few good friends among white men, and they have always advised my people to bear these taunts without fighting. Our young men were quick-tempered, and I have had great trouble in keeping them from doing rash things. I have carried a heavy load on my back ever since I was a boy. I learned then that we were but few, while the white men were many, and that we could not hold our own with them. We were like deer. They were like grizzly bears. We had a small country. Their country was large. We were contented to let things remain as the Great Spirit Chief made them. They were not; and would change the rivers and mountains if they did not suit them.

Year after year we have been threatened, but no war was made upon my people until General Howard came to our country two years ago and told us he was the white war-chief of all that country. He said: "I have a great many soldiers at my back. I am going to bring them up here, and then I will talk to you again. I will not let white men laugh at me the next time I come. The country belongs to the Government, and I intend to make you go upon the reservation."

I remonstrated with him against bringing more soldiers to the Nez Percés' country. He had one house full of troops all the time at Fort Lapwai.

The next spring the agent at Umatilla agency sent an Indian runner to tell me to meet General Howard at Walla Walla. I could not go myself, but I sent my brother and five other head men to meet him, and they had a long talk.

General Howard said: "You have talked straight, and it is all right.

You can stay in Wallowa." He insisted that my brother should go with him to Fort Lapwai. When the party arived there General Howard sent out runners and called all the Indians in to a grand council. I was in that council. I said to General Howard, "We are ready to listen." He answered that he would not talk then, but would hold a council next day, when he would talk plainly. I said to General Howard: "I am ready to talk today. I have been in a great many councils, but I am no wiser. We are all sprung from a woman, although we are unlike in many things. We can not be made over again. You are as you were made, and as you were made you can remain. We are just as we were made by the Great Spirit, and you can not change us; then why should children of one mother and one father quarrel—why should one try to cheat the other? I do not believe that the Great Spirit Chief gave one kind of men the right to tell another kind of men what they must do."

General Howard replied: "You deny my authority, do you? You want to dictate to me, do you?"

Then one of my chiefs—Too-hool-hool-suit—rose in the council and said to General Howard: "The Great Spirit Chief made the world as it is, and as he wanted it, and he made a part of it for us to live upon. I do not see where you get authority to say that we shall not live where he placed us."

General Howard lost his temper and said: "Shut up! I don't want to hear any more of such talk. The law says you shall go upon the reservation to live, and I want you to do so, but you persist in disobeying the law" (meaning the treaty). "If you do not move, I will take the matter into my own hand, and make you suffer for your disobedience."

Too-hool-hool-suit answered: "Who are you, that you ask us to talk, and then tell me I sha'n't talk? Are you the Great Spirit? Did you make the world? Did you make the sun? Did you make the rivers to run for us to drink? Did you make the grass to grow? Did you make all these things, that you talk to us as though we were boys? If you did, then you have the right to talk as you do."

General Howard replied, "You are an impudent fellow, and I will put you in the guard house," and then ordered a soldier to arrest him.

Too-hool-hool-suit made no resistance. He asked General Howard: "Is that your order? I don't care. I have expressed my heart to you. I have nothing to take back. I have spoken for my country. You can arrest me, but you can not change me or make me take back what I have said."

The soldiers came forward and seized my friend and took him to the guard house. My men whispered among themselves whether they should let this thing be done. I counseled them to submit. I knew if we resisted that all the white men present, including General Howard, would be killed in a moment, and we would be blamed. If I had said nothing, General Howard would never have given another unjust order against my men. I saw the danger, and, while they dragged Too-hool-hool-suit to prison, I arose and said: "I am going to talk now. I don't care whether you arrest me or not." I turned to my people and said: "The arrest of Too-hool-hool-suit was wrong, but we will not resent the insult. We were invited to this council to express our hearts, and we have done so." Too-hool-hool-suit was a prisoner for five days before he was released.

The council broke up for that day. On the next morning General Howard came to my lodge, and invited me to go with him and White-Bird and Looking-Glass, to look for land for my people. As we rode along we came to some good land that was already occupied by Indians and white people. General Howard, pointing to this land, said: "If you will come on to the reservation, I will give you these lands and move these people off."

I replied: "No. It would be wrong to disturb these people. I have no right to take their homes. I have never taken what did not belong to me. I will not now."

We rode all day upon the reservation, and found no good land unoccupied. I have been informed by men who do not lie that General Howard sent a letter that night, telling the soldiers at Walla Walla to go to Wallowa Valley, and drive us out upon our return home.

In the council, next day, General Howard informed me, in a haughty spirit, that he would give my people thirty days to go back home, collect all their stock, and move on to the reservation, saying, "If you are not here in that time, I shall consider that you want to fight, and will send my soldiers to drive you on."

I said: "War can be avoided, and it ought to be avoided. I want no war. My people have always been the friends of the white man. Why are you in such a hurry? I can not get ready to move in thirty days. Our stock is scattered, and Snake River is very high. Let us wait until fall, then the river will be low. We want time to hunt up our stock and gather supplies for winter."

General Howard replied: "If you let the time run over one day, the soldiers will be there to drive you on to the reservation, and all your cattle and horses outside of the reservation at that time will fall into the hands of the white men."

I knew I had never sold my country, and that I had no land in Lapwai; but I did not want bloodshed. I did not want my people killed. I did not want anybody killed. Some of my people had been murdered by white men, and the white murderers were never punished for it. I told General Howard about this, and again said I wanted no war. I wanted the people who lived upon the lands I was to occupy at Lapwai to have time to gather their harvest.

I said in my heart that, rather than have war, I would give up my country. I would give up my father's grave. I would give up everything rather than have the blood of white men upon the hands of my people.

General Howard refused to allow me more than thirty days to move my people and their stock. I am sure that he began to prepare for war at once.

When I return to Wallowa I found my people very much excited upon discovering that the soldiers were already in the Wallowa Valley. We held a council and decided to move immediately, to avoid bloodshed.

Too-hool-hool-suit, who felt outraged by his imprisonment, talked for war, and made many of my young men willing to fight rather than be driven like dogs from the land where they were born. He declared that blood alone would wash out the disgrace General Howard had put upon him. It required a strong heart to stand up against such talk, but I urged my people to be quiet, and not to begin a war.

We gathered all the stock we could find, and made an attempt to move. We left many of our horses and cattle in Wallowa, and we lost several hundred in crossing the river. All of my people succeeded in getting across in safety. Many of the Nez Percés came together in Rocky Cañon to hold a grand council. I went with all my people. This council lasted ten days. There was a great deal of war talk, and a great deal of excitement. There was one young brave present whose father had been killed by a white man five years before. This man's blood was bad against white men, and he left the council calling for revenge.

Again I counseled peace, and I thought the danger was past. We had not complied with General Howard's order because we could not, but we intended to do so as soon as possible. I was leaving the council to kill beef for my family, when news came that the young man whose father has been killed had gone out with several other hot-blooded young braves and killed four white men. He rode up to the council and shouted: "Why do you sit here like women? The war has begun already." I was deeply grieved. All the lodges were moved except my brother's and my own. I saw clearly that the war was upon us when I learned that my young men had been secretly buying ammunition. I heard then that Too-hool-hool-suit, who had been imprisoned by General Howard, had succeeded in organizing a war party. I knew that their acts would involve all my people. I saw that the war could not be prevented. The time had passed. I counseled peace from the beginning. I knew that we were too weak to fight the United States. We had many grievances, but I knew that war would bring more. We had good white friends, who advised us against taking the war path. My friend and brother, Mr. Chapman, who has been with us since the surrender, told us just how the war would end. Mr. Chapman took sides against us, and helped General Howard. I do not blame him for doing so. He tried hard to prevent bloodshed. We hoped the white settlers would not join the soldiers. Before the war commenced we had discussed this matter all over, and many of my people were in favor of warning them that if they took no part against us they should not be molested in the event of war being begun by General Howard. This plan was voted down in the war council.

There were bad men among my people who had quarreled with white men, and they talked of their wrongs until they roused all the bad hearts in the council. Still I could not believe that they would begin the war. I know that my young men did a great wrong, but I ask, Who was first to blame? They had been insulted a thousand times; their fathers and brothers had been killed; their mothers and wives had been disgraced; they had been driven to madness by whisky sold to them by white men; they had been told by General Howard that all their horses and cattle which they had been unable to drive out of Wallowa were to fall into the hands of white men; and, added to all this, they were homeless and desperate.

I would have given my own life if I could have undone the killing of white men by my people. I blame my young men and I blame the white men. I blame General Howard for not giving my people time to get their stock away from Wallowa. I do not acknowledge that he had the right to order me to leave Wallowa at any time. I deny that either my father or myself ever sold that land. It is still our land. It may never again be our home, but my father sleeps there, and I love it as I love my mother. I left there, hoping to avoid bloodshed.

If General Howard had given me plenty of time to gather up my stock, and treated Too-hool-hool-suit as a man should be treated, there would have been no war.

My friends among white men have blamed me for the war. I am not to blame. When my young men began the killing, my heart was hurt. Although I did not justify them, I remembered all the insults I had endured, and my blood was on fire. Still I would have taken my people to the buffalo country without fighting, if possible.

I could see no other way to avoid a war. We moved over to White Bird Creek, sixteen miles away, and there encamped, intending to collect our stock before leaving; but the soldiers attacked us, and the first battle was fought. We numbered in that battle sixty men, and the soldiers a hundred. The fight lasted but a few minutes, when the soldiers retreated before us for twelve miles. They lost thirty-three killed, and had seven wounded. When an Indian fights, he only shoots to kill; but soldiers shoot at random. None of the soldiers were scalped. We do not believe in scalping, nor in killing wounded men. Soldiers do not kill many Indians unless they are wounded and left upon the battle field. Then they kill Indians.

Seven days after the first battle, General Howard arrived in the Nez Percés' country, bringing seven hundred more soldiers. It was now war in earnest. We crossed the Salmon River, hoping General Howard would follow. We were not disappointed. He did follow us, and we got back between him and his supplies, and cut him off for three days. He sent out two companies to open the way. We attacked them, killing one officer, two guides, and ten men.

We withdrew, hoping the soldiers would follow, but they had got fighting enough for that day. They entrenched themselves, and next day we attacked them again. The battle lasted all day, and was renewed next morning. We killed four and wounded seven or eight.

About this time General Howard found out that we were in his rear. Five days later he attacked us with three hundred and fifty soldiers and settlers. We had two hundred and fifty warriors. The fight lasted twenty-seven hours. We lost four killed and several wounded. General Howard's loss was twenty-nine men killed and sixty wounded.

The following day the soldiers charged upon us, and we retreated with our families and stock a few miles, leaving eighty lodges to fall into General Howard's hands.

Finding that we were outnumbered, we retreated to Bitter Root Valley. Here another body of soldiers came upon us and demanded our surrender. We refused. They said, "You can not get by us." We answered, "We are going by you without fighting if you will let us, but we are going by you anyhow." We then made a treaty with these soldiers. We agreed not to molest any one, and they agreed that we might pass through the Bitter Root country in peace. We bought provisions and traded stock with white men there.

We understood that there was to be no more war. We intended to go peaceably to the buffalo country, and leave the question of returning to our country to be settled afterward.

With this understanding we traveled on for four days, and, thinking that the trouble was all over, we stopped and prepared tent poles to take with us. We started again, and at the end of two days we saw three white men passing our camp. Thinking that peace had been made, we did not molest them. We could have killed them or taken them prisoners, but we did not suspect them of being spies, which they were.

That night the soldiers surrounded our camp. About daybreak one of my men went out to look after his horses. The soldiers saw him and shot him down like a coyote. I have since learned that these soldiers were not those we had left behind. They had come upon us from another direction. The new white war chief's name was Gibbon. He charged upon us while some of my people were still asleep. We had a hard fight. Some of my men crept around and attacked the soldiers from the rear. In this battle we lost nearly all our lodges, but we finally drove General Gibbon back.

Finding that he was not able to capture us, he sent to his camp a few miles away for his big guns (cannons), but my men had captured them and all the ammunition. We damaged the big guns all we could, and carried away the powder and lead. In the fight with General Gibbon we lost fifty women and children and thirty fighting men. We remained long enough to bury our dead. The Nez Percés never make war on women and children; we could have killed a great many women and children while the war lasted, but we would feel ashamed to do so cowardly an act.

We never scalp our enemies, but when General Howard came up and joined General Gibbon, their Indian scouts dug up our dead and scalped them. I have been told that General Howard did not order this great shame to be done.

We retreated as rapidly as we could toward the buffalo country. After six days General Howard came close to us, and we went out and attacked him, and captured nearly all his horses and mules (about two hundred and fifty head). We then marched on to the Yellowstone Basin.

On the way we captured one white man and two white women. We released them at the end of three days. They were treated kindly. The women were not insulted. Can the white soldiers tell me of one time when Indian women were taken prisoners, and held three days and then released without being insulted? Were the Nez Percés' women who fell into the hands of General Howard's soldiers treated with as much respect? I deny that a Nez Percé was ever guilty of such a crime.

A few days later we captured two more white men. One of them stole a horse and escaped. We gave the other a poor horse and told him he was free.

Nine days' march brought us to the mouth of Clark's Fork of the Yellowstone. We did not know what had become of General Howard, but we supposed that he had sent for more horses and mules. He did not come up, but another new war chief (General Sturgis) attacked us. We held him in check while we moved all our women and children and stock out of danger, leaving a few men to cover our retreat.

Several days passed, and we heard nothing of General Howard, or Gibbon, or Sturgis. We had repulsed each in turn, and began to feel secure, when another army, under General Miles, struck us. This was the fourth army, each of which outnumbered our fighting force, that we had encountered within sixty days.

We had no knowledge of General Miles' army until a short time before he made a charge upon us, cutting our camp in two, and capturing nearly all of our horses. About seventy men, myself among them, were cut off. My little daughter, twelve years old, was with me. I gave her a rope, and told her to catch a horse and join the others who were cut off from the camp. I have not seen her since, but I have learned that she is alive and well.

I thought of my wife and children, who were now surrounded by soldiers, and I resolved to go to them or die. With a prayer in my mouth to the Great Spirit Chief who rules above, I dashed unarmed through the line of soldiers. It seemed to me that there were guns on every side, before and behind me. My clothes were cut to pieces and my horse was wounded, but I was unhurt. As I reached the door of my lodge, my wife handed me my rifle, saying: "Here's your gun. Fight!"

The soldiers kept up a continuous fire. Six of my men were killed in one spot near me. Ten or twelve soldiers charged into our camp and got possession of two lodges, killing three Nez Percés and losing three of their men, who fell inside our lines. I called my men to drive them back. We fought at close range, not more than twenty steps apart, and drove the soldiers back upon their main line, leaving their dead in our hands. We secured their arms and ammunition. We lost, the first day and night, eighteen men and three women. General Miles lost twenty-six killed and forty wounded. The following day General Miles sent a messenger into my camp under protection of a white flag. I sent my friend Yellow Bull to meet him.

Yellow Bull understood the messenger to say that General Miles wished me to consider the situation; that he did not want to kill my people unnecessarily. Yellow Bull understood this to be a demand for me to surrender and save blood. Upon reporting this message to me, Yellow Bull said he wondered whether General Miles was in earnest. I sent him back with my answer, that I had made up my mind, but would think about it and send word soon. A little later he sent some Cheyenne scouts with another message. I went out to meet them. They said they believed that General Miles was sincere and really wanted peace. I walked on to General Miles' tent. He met me and we shook hands. He said, "Come, let us sit down by the fire and talk this matter over." I remained with him all night; next morning Yellow Bull came over to see if I was alive, and why I did not return.

General Miles would not let me leave the tent to see my friend alone.

Yellow Bull said to me: "They have got you in their power, and I am afraid they will never let you go again. I have an officer in our camp, and I will hold him until they let you go free."

I said: "I do not know what they mean to do with me, but if they kill me you must not kill the officer. It will do no good to avenge my death by killing him."

Yellow Bull returned to my camp. I did not make any agreement that day with General Miles. The battle was renewed while I was with him. I was very anxious about my people. I knew that we were near Sitting Bull's camp in King George's land, and I thought maybe the Nez Percés who had escaped would return with assistance. No great damage was done to either party during the night.

On the following morning I returned to my camp by agreement, meeting the officer who had been held a prisoner in my camp at the flag of truce. My people were divided about surrendering. We could have escaped from Bear Paw Mountain if we had left our wounded, old women, and children behind. We were unwilling to do this. We had never heard of a wounded Indian recovering while in the hands of white men.

On the evening of the fourth day General Howard came in with a small escort, together with my friend Chapman. We could now talk understandingly. General Miles said to me in plain words, "If you will come out and give up your arms, I will spare your lives and send you to your reservation." I do not know what passed between General Miles and General Howard.

I could not bear to see my wounded men and women suffer any longer; we had lost enough already. General Miles had promised that we might return to our own country with what stock we had left. I thought we could start again. I believed General Miles, or I never would have surrendered. I have heard that he has been censured for making the promise to return us to Lapwai. He could not have made any other terms with me at that time. I would have held him in check until my friends came to my assistance, and then neither of the generals nor their soldiers would have ever left Bear Paw Mountain alive.

On the fifth day I went to General Miles and gave up my gun, and said, "From where the sun now stands I will fight no more."[2] My people needed rest—we wanted peace.

I was told we could go with General Miles to Tongue River and stay there until spring, when we would be sent back to our country. Finally it was decided that we were to be taken to Tongue River. We had nothing to say about it. After our arrival at Tongue River, General Miles received orders to take us to Bismarck. The reason given was, that subsistence would be cheaper there.

General Miles was opposed to this order. He said: "You must not blame me. I have endeavored to keep my word, but the chief who is over me has given the order, and I must obey it or resign. That would do you no good. Some other officer would carry out the order."

I believe General Miles would have kept his word if he could have

[2] Chief Joseph surrendered on October 5, 1877, with these words: "Tell General Howard I know his heart. What he told me before, I have in my heart. I am tired of fighting. Our chiefs are killed. Looking Glass is dead. Too-hool-hool-suit is dead. The old men are all dead. It is the young men who say yes and no. He who led on the young men is dead. It is cold and we have no blankets. The little children are freezing to death. My people, some of them, have run away to the hills and have no blankets, no food; no one knows where they are—perhaps freezing to death. I want to have time to look for my children and see how many I can find. Maybe I shall find them among the dead. Hear me, my chiefs. I am tired; my heart is sick and sad. From where the sun now stands I will fight no more forever." [Ed.]

done so. I do not blame him for what we have suffered since the surrender. I do not know who is to blame. We gave up all our horses—over eleven hundred—and all our saddles—over one hundred—and we have not heard from them since. Somebody has got our horses.

General Miles turned my people over to another soldier, and we were taken to Bismarck. Captain Johnson, who now had charge of us, received an order to take us to Fort Leavenworth. At Leavenworth we were placed on a low river bottom, with no water except river water to drink and cook with. We had always lived in a healthy country, where the mountains were high and the water was cold and clear. Many of my people sickened and died, and we buried them in this strange land. I can not tell how much my heart suffered for my people while at Leavenworth. The Great Spirit Chief who rules above seemed to be looking some other way, and did not see what was being done to my people.

During the hot days (July 1878) we received notice that we were to be moved farther away from our own country. We were not asked if we were willing to go. We were ordered to get into railroad cars. Three of my people died on the way to Baxter Springs. It was worse to die there than to die fighting in the mountains.

We were moved from Baxter Springs (Kansas) to the Indian Territory, and set down without our lodges. We had but little medicine, and we were nearly all sick. Seventy of my people have died since we moved there.

·   ·   ·

At last I was granted permission to come to Washington and bring my friend Yellow Bull and our interpreter with me. I am glad we came. I have shaken hands with a great many friends, but there are some things I want to know which no one seems able to explain. I can not understand how the Government sends a man out to fight us, as it did General Miles, and then breaks his word. Such a government has something wrong about it. I can not understand why so many chiefs are allowed to talk so many different ways, and promise so many different things. I have seen the Great Father Chief (the President), the next Great Chief (Secretary of the Interior), the Commissioner Chief (Hayt), the Law Chief (General Butler), and many other law chiefs (Congressmen), and they all say they are my friends, and that I shall have justice, but while their mouths all talk right I do not understand why nothing is done for my people. I have heard talk and talk, but nothing is done. Good words do not last long unless they amount to something. Words do not pay for my dead people. They do not pay for my country, now overrun by white men. They do not protect my father's grave. They do not pay for all my horses and cattle. Good words will not give me back my children. Good words will not make good the promise of your War Chief General Miles. Good words will not give my people good health and stop them from dying. Good words will not get my people a home where they can live in peace and take care of themselves. I am tired of talk that comes to nothing. It makes my heart sick when I remember all the good words and all the broken promises. There has been too much talking by men who had no right to talk. Too many misrepresentations have been made, too many misunderstandings have come up between the white men about the Indians. If the white man wants to live in peace with the Indian he can live in peace. There need be no trouble. Treat all men alike. Give them the same law. Give them all an even chance to live and grow. All men were made by the same Great Spirit Chief. They are all brothers. The earth is the mother of all people, and all people should have equal rights upon it. You might as well expect the rivers to run backward as that any man who was a free man should be contented when penned up and denied liberty to go where he pleases. If you tie a horse to a stake, do you expect he will grow fat? If you pen an Indian up on a small spot of earth, and compel him to stay there, he will not be contented, nor will he grow and prosper. I have asked some of the great white chiefs where they get their authority to say to the Indian that he shall stay in one place, while he sees white men going where they please. They can not tell me .

I only ask of the Government to be treated as all other men are treated. If I can not go to my own home, let me have a home in some country where my people will not die so fast. I would like to go to Bitter Root Valley. There my people would be healthy; where they are now they are dying. Three have died since I left my camp to come to Washington.

When I think of our condition my heart is heavy. I see men of my race treated as outlaws and driven from country to country, or shot down like animals.

I know that my race must change. We can not hold our own with the white men as we are. We only ask an even chance to live as other men live. We ask to be recognized as men. We ask that the same law shall work alike on all men. If the Indian breaks the law, punish him by the law. If the white man breaks the law, punish him also.

Let me be a free man—free to travel, free to stop, free to work, free to trade where I choose, free to choose my own teachers, free to follow the religion of my fathers, free to think and talk and act for myself—and I will obey every law, or submit to the penalty.

Whenever the white man treats an Indian as they treat each other, then we will have no more wars. We shall all be alike—brothers of one father and one mother, with one sky above us and one country around us, and one government for all. Then the Great Spirit Chief who rules above will smile upon this land, and send rain to wash out the bloody spots made by brothers' hands from the face of the earth. For this time the Indian race are waiting and praying. I hope that no more groans of wounded men and women will ever go to the ear of the Great Spirit Chief above, and that all people may be one people.

In-mut-too-yah-lat-lat has spoken for his people.

For Discussion

1. What traits does Chief Joseph reveal about himself that are different from those often dramatized in the popular mind? What qualities do you admire in him? What are his weaknesses, if any?
2. Discuss Joseph's concept of religion and nature. How do the passages about Joseph's father illustrate this concept?
3. Discuss the treatment of the Nez Percés by the various white leaders, beginning with Lewis and Clark.
4. How would you characterize the government's tactics in the Nez Percés' treaties? What contemporary parallels to this kind of "diplomacy" can you cite?
5. How was Too-hool-hool-suit different from Chief Joseph?
6. Defend or reject Chief Joseph's conviction that war could have been avoided had General Howard given the Nez Percés more time to move to the reservation. What does the "agreement" with the soldiers reveal about the difficulties of negotiation in times of conflict? Mention some contemporary parallels.
7. Chief Joseph finds it difficult to lay the blame on anyone. Do you agree or disagree? Explain.
8. Discuss and evaluate the social and ethical implications of the last two paragraphs.
9. Examine the passage in which Joseph denounces "good words." Describe how the emotion is conveyed through sentence structure, word choice, and other elements of style.

EMMA GOLDMAN

What I Believe

Born in Lithuania in 1869, Emma Goldman immigrated to the United States in 1885 and by 1889 had become an avowed anarchist. For the next thirty years she advocated anarchism from the lecture platform, in the strike line, and on the printed page. Opposed to America's entry into World War I, she and Alexander Berkman, a long-time associate, were arrested for obstructing the military draft. After two years' imprisonment, they were deported to Russia in 1919. However, Goldman became disillusioned by Lenin and Trotsky and left Russia for England; she later went to Canada and Spain. She died in 1940 on a trip to Toronto. Goldman wrote the following essay in 1908 in an attempt to clear up false impressions of herself and her ideas.

"What I believe" has many times been the target of hack writers. Such blood-curdling and incoherent stories have been circulated about me, it is no wonder that the average human being has palpitation of the heart at the very mention of the name Emma Goldman. It is too bad that we no longer live in the times when witches were burned at the stake or tortured to drive the evil spirit out of them. For, indeed, Emma Goldman is a witch! True, she does not eat little children, but she does many worse things. She manufactures bombs and gambles in crowned heads. B-r-r-r!

Such is the impression the public has of myself and my beliefs. It is therefore very much to the credit of *The World* that it gives its readers at least an opportunity to learn what my beliefs really are.

The student of the history of progressive thought is well aware that every idea in its early stages has been misrepresented and the adherents of such ideas have been maligned and persecuted. One need not go back two thousand years to the time when those who believed in the gospel of Jesus were thrown into the arena or hunted into dungeons to realize how little great beliefs or earnest believers are understood. The history of progress is written in the blood of men and women who have dared to espouse an unpopular cause, as, for instance, the black man's right to his body, or woman's right to her soul. If, then, from time immemorial, the New has met with opposition and condemnation, why should my beliefs be exempt from a crown of thorns?

"What I believe" is a process rather than a finality. Finalities are for gods and governments, not for the human intellect. While it may be true that Herbert Spencer's formulation of liberty is the most important on the subject, as a political basis of society, yet life is something more than formulas. In the battle for freedom, as Ibsen has so well pointed out, it is the struggle for, not so much the attainment of, liberty, that develops all that is strongest, sturdiest and finest in human character.

Anarchism is not only a process, however, that marches on with "somber steps," coloring all that is positive and constructive in organic development. It is a conspicuous protest of the most militant type. It is so absolutely uncompromising, insisting and permeating a force as to overcome the most stubborn assault and to withstand the criticism of those who really constitute the last trumpets of a decaying age.

Anarchists are by no means passive spectators in the theater of social development; on the contrary, they have some very positive notions as regards aims and methods.

That I may make myself as clear as possible without using too much space, permit me to adopt the topical mode of treatment of "What I Believe."

I.   AS TO PROPERTY

"Property" means dominion over things and the denial to others of the use of those things. So long as production was not equal to the normal demand, institutional property may have had some *raison d'être*. One has only to consult economics, however, to know that the productivity of labor within the last few decades has increased so tremendously as to exceed normal demand a hundred-fold, and to make property not only a hindrance to human well-being, but an obstacle, a deadly barrier, to all progress. It is the private dominion over things that condemns millions of people to be mere nonentities, living corpses without originality or power of initiative, human machines of flesh and blood, who pile up mountains of wealth for others and pay for it with a gray, dull and wretched existence for themselves. I believe that there can be no real wealth, social wealth, so long as it rests on human lives—young lives, old lives and lives in the making.

It is conceded by all radical thinkers that the fundamental cause of this terrible state of affairs is (1) that man must sell his labor; (2) that his inclination and judgment are subordinated to the will of a master.

Anarchism is the only philosophy that can and will do away with this humiliating and degrading situation. It differs from all other theories inasmuch as it points out that man's development, his physical well-being, his latent qualities and innate disposition alone must determine the character and conditions of his work. Similarly will one's physical and mental appreciations and his soul cravings decide how much he shall consume. To make this a reality will, I believe, be possible only in a society based on voluntary cooperation of productive groups, communities and societies loosely federated together, eventually developing into a free communism, actuated by a solidarity of interests. There can be no freedom in the large sense of the word, no harmonious development, so long as mercenary and commercial considerations play an important part in the determination of personal conduct.

II. AS TO GOVERNMENT

I believe Government, organized authority, or the State, is necessary only to maintain or protect property and monopoly. It has proven efficient in that function only. As a promoter of individual liberty, human well-being and social harmony, which alone constitute real order, government stands condemned by all the great men of the world.

I therefore believe, with my fellow-Anarchists, that the statutory regulations, legislative enactments, constitutional provisions, are invasive. They never yet induced man to do anything he could and would not do by virtue of his intellect or temperament, nor prevented anything that man was impelled to do by the same dictates. Millet's pictorial description of "The Man with the Hoe," Meunier's masterpieces of the miners that have aided in lifting labor from its degrading position, Gorki's descriptions of the underworld, Ibsen's psychological analysis of human life, could never have been induced by government any more than the spirit which impels a man to save a drowning child or a crippled woman from a burning building has ever been called into operation by statutory regulations or the policeman's club. I believe—indeed, I know—that whatever is fine and beautiful in the human, expresses and asserts itself in spite of government, and not because of it.

The Anarchists are therefore justified in assuming that anarchism—the absence of government—will insure the widest and greatest scope for unhampered human development, the cornerstone of true social progress and harmony.

As to the stereotyped argument that government acts as a check on crime and vice, even the makers of law no longer believe it. This country spends millions of dollars for the maintenance of her "criminals" behind prison bars, yet crime is on the increase. Surely this state of affairs is not owing to an insufficiency of laws! Ninety percent of all crimes are property crimes, which have their root in our economic iniquities. So long as these latter continue to exist we might convert every lamp-post into a gibbet without having the least effect on the crime in our midst. Crimes resulting from heredity can certainly never be cured by law. Surely we are learning even today that such crimes can effectively be treated only by the best modern medical methods at our command, and, above all, by the spirit of a deeper sense of fellowship, kindness and understanding.

III. AS TO MILITARISM

I should not treat of this subject separately since it belongs to the paraphernalia of government, if it were not for the fact that those who are most vigorously opposed to my beliefs on the ground that the latter stand for force are the advocates of militarism.

The fact is that Anarchists are the only true advocates of peace, the only people who call a halt to the growing tendency of militarism, which is fast making of this erstwhile free country an imperialistic and despotic power.

The military spirit is the most merciless, heartless and brutal in existence. It fosters an institution for which there is not even a pretense of justification. The soldier, to quote Tolstoi, is a professional man-killer. He does not kill for the love of it, like a savage, or in a passion, like a homicide. He is a cold-blooded, mechanical, obedient tool of his military superiors. He is ready to cut throats or scuttle a ship at the command of his ranking officer, without knowing or, perhaps, caring how, why or wherefore. I am supported in this contention by no less a military light than General Funston. I quote from the latter's communication to *The New York Evening Post* of June 30 [1908], dealing with the case of Private William Buwalda, which caused such a stir all through the Northwest. "The first duty of an officer or enlisted man," says our noble warrior, "is unquestioning obedience and loyalty to the Government to which he has sworn allegiance; it makes no difference whether he approves of that Government or not."

How can we harmonize the principle of "unquestioning obedience" with the principle of "life, liberty and the pursuit of happiness"? The deadly power of militarism has never before been so effectually demonstrated in this country as in the recent condemnation by court-martial of William Buwalda, of San Francisco, Company A, Engineers, to five years in military prison. Here was a man who had a record of fifteen years of continuous service. "His character and conduct were unimpeachable," we are told by General Funston, who, in consideration of it, reduced Buwalda's sentence to three years. Yet the man is thrown suddenly out of the army, dishonored, robbed of his chances of a pension and sent to prison. What was his crime? Just listen, ye free-born Americans! William Buwalda attended a public meeting, and after the lecture he shook hands with the speaker. General Funston, in his letter to *The Post*, to which I have already referred above, asserts that Buwalda's action was a "great military offense, infinitely worse than desertion." In another public statement, which the General made in Portland, Oregon, he said that "Buwalda's was a serious crime, equal to treason."

It is quite true that the meeting had been arranged by Anarchists. Had the Socialists issued the call, General Funston informs us, there would have been no objection to Buwalda's presence. Indeed, the General says, "I would not have the slightest hesitancy about attending a Socialist meeting myself." But to attend an Anarchist meeting with Emma Goldman as speaker—could there be anything more "treasonable"?

For this horrible crime a man, a free-born American citizen, who has given this country the best fifteen years of his life, and whose character and conduct during that time were "unimpeachable," is now languishing in a prison, dishonored, disgraced and robbed of a livelihood.

Can there be anything more destructive of the true genius of liberty than the spirit that made Buwalda's sentence possible—the spirit of unquestioning obedience? Is it for this that the American people have in the last few years sacrificed four hundred million dollars and their hearts' blood?

I believe that militarism—a standing army and navy in any country—is indicative of the decay of liberty and of the destruction of all that is best and finest in our nation. The steadily growing clamor for more battleships and an increased army on the ground that these guarantee us peace is as absurd as the argument that the peaceful man is he who goes well armed.

The same lack of consistency is displayed by those peace pretenders who oppose anarchism because it supposedly teaches violence, and who would yet be delighted over the possibility of the American nation soon being able to hurl dynamite bombs upon defenseless enemies from flying machines.

I believe that militarism will cease when the liberty-loving spirits of the world say to their masters: "Go and do your own killing. We have sacrificed ourselves and our loved ones long enough fighting your battles. In return you have made parasites and criminals of us in times of peace and brutalized us in times of war. You have separated us from our brothers and have made of the world a human slaughterhouse. No, we will not do your killing or fight for the country that you have stolen from us."

Oh, I believe with all my heart that human brotherhood and solidarity will clear the horizon from the terrible red streak of war and destruction.

IV.   AS TO FREE SPEECH AND PRESS

The Buwalda case is only one phase of the larger question of free speech, free press and the right of free assembly.

Many good people imagine that the principles of free speech or press can be exercised properly and with safety within the limits of constitutional guarantees. That is the only excuse, it seems to me, for the terrible apathy and indifference to the onslaught upon free speech and press that we have witnessed in this country within the last few months.

I believe that free speech and press means that I may say and write what I please. This right, when regulated by constitutional provisions, legislative enactments, almighty decisions of the Postmaster-General or the policeman's club, becomes a farce. I am well aware that I will be warned of consequences if we remove the chains from speech and press. I believe, however, that the core of consequences resulting from the unlimited exercise of expression is to allow more expression.

Mental shackles have never yet stemmed the tide of progress, whereas premature social explosions have only too often been brought about through a wave of repression.

Will our governors never learn that countries like England, Holland, Norway, Sweden and Denmark, with the largest freedom of expression, have been freest from "consequences"? Whereas Russia, Spain, Italy, France and, alas! even America, have raised these "consequences" to the most pressing political factor. Ours is supposed to be a country ruled by the majority, yet every policeman who is not vested with power by the majority can break up a meeting, drag the lecturer off the platform and club the audience out of the hall in true Russian fashion. The Postmaster-General, who is not an elective officer, has the power to suppress publications and confiscate mail. From his decision there is no more appeal than from that of the Russian Czar. Truly, I believe we need a new Declaration of Independence. Is there no modern Jefferson or Adams?

V.   AS TO THE CHURCH

At the recent convention of the political remnants of a once revolutionary idea it was voted that religion and vote getting have nothing to do with each other. Why should they? So long as man is willing to delegate to the devil the care of his soul, he might with the same consistency delegate to the politician the care of his rights. That religion is a private affair has long been settled by the Bis-Marxian Socialists of Germany. Our American Marxians, poor of blood and originality, must needs go to Germany for their wisdom. That wisdom has served as a capital whip to lash the several millions of people into the well disciplined army of Socialism. It might do the same here. For goodness' sake, let's not offend respectability, let's not hurt the religious feelings of the people.

Religion is a superstition that originated in man's mental inability to solve natural phenomena. The Church is an organized institution that has always been a stumbling block to progress.

Organized churchism has stripped religion of its naiveté and primitiveness. It has turned religion into a nightmare that oppresses the human soul and holds the mind in bondage. "The Dominion of Darkness," as the last true Christian, Leo Tolstoi, calls the Church, has been a foe of human development and free thought, and as such it has no place in the life of a truly free people.

VI.   AS TO MARRIAGE AND LOVE

I believe these are probably the most tabooed subjects in this country. It is almost impossible to talk about them without scandalizing the cherished propriety of a lot of good folk. No wonder so much ignorance prevails relative to these questions. Nothing short of an open, frank and intelligent discussion will purify the air from the hysterical, sentimental rubbish that is shrouding these vital subjects, vital to individual as well as social well-being.

Marriage and love are not synonymous; on the contrary, they are often antagonistic to each other. I am aware of the fact that some marriages are actuated by love, but the narrow, material confines of marriage, as it is, speedily crush the tender flower of affection.

Marriage is an institution which furnishes the State and Church with a tremendous revenue and the means of prying into that phase of life which refined people have long considered their own, their very own most sacred affair. Love is that most powerful factor of human relationship which from time immemorial has defied all man-made laws and broken through the iron bars of conventions in church and morality. Marriage is often an economic arrangement purely, furnishing the woman with a life long insurance policy and the man with a perpetuator of his kind or a pretty toy. That is, marriage, or the training thereto, prepares the woman for the life of a parasite, a dependent, helpless servant, while it furnishes to man the right of a chattel mortgage over a human life.

How can such a condition of affairs have anything in common with love?—with the element that would forego all the wealth of money and power and live in its own world of untrammeled human expression? But this is not the age of romanticism, of Romeo and Juliet, Faust and Marguerite, of moonlight ecstasies, of flowers and songs. Ours is a practical age. Our first consideration is an income. So much the worse for us if we have reached the era when the soul's highest flights are to be checked. No race can develop without the love element.

But if two people are to worship at the shrine of love, what is to become of the golden calf, marriage? "It is the only security for the woman, for the child, the family, the State." But it is no security to love; and without love no true home can or does exist. Without love no child should be born; without love no true woman can be related to a man. The fear that love is not sufficient material safety for the child is out of date. I believe when woman signs her own emancipation, her first declaration of independence will consist in admiring and loving a man for the qualities of his heart and mind and not for the quantities in his pocket. The second declaration will be that she has the right to follow that love without let or hindrance from the outside world. The third and most important declaration will be the absolute right to free motherhood.

In such a mother and in an equally free father rests the safety of the child. They have the strength, the sturdiness, the harmony to create an atmosphere wherein alone the human plant can grow into an exquisite flower.

VII. AS TO ACTS OF VIOLENCE

And now I have come to that point in my beliefs about which the greatest misunderstanding prevails in the minds of the American public. "Well, come, now, don't you propagate violence, the killing of crowned heads and Presidents?" Who says that I do? Have you heard me, has any one heard me? Has any one seen it printed in our literature? No, but the papers say so, everybody says so; consequently it must be so. Oh, for the accuracy and logic of the dear public!

I believe that anarchism is the only philosophy of peace, the only theory of a social relationship that values human life above everything else. I know that some Anarchists have committed acts of violence, but it is the terrible economic inequality and great political injustice that prompt such acts, not anarchism. Every institution to-day rests on violence, our very atmosphere is saturated with it. So long as such a state exists we might as well strive to stop the rush of Niagara as hope to do away with violence. I have already stated that countries with some measure of freedom of expression have had few or no acts of violence. What is the moral? Simply this: No act committed by an Anarchist has been for personal gain, aggrandizement or profit, but rather a conscious protest against some repressive, arbitrary, tyrannical measure from above.

President Carnot of France was killed by Caserio in response to Carnot's refusal to commute the death sentence of Vaillant, for whose life the entire literary, scientific and humanitarian world of France had pleaded.

Bresel went to Italy on his own money earned in the silk weaving mills at Paterson to call King Humbert to the bar of justice for his order to shoot defenseless women and children during a bread riot. Angelino executed Prime Minister Canovas for the latter's resurrection of the Spanish inquisition at Montjuich Prison. Alexander Berkman attempted the life of Henry C. Frick during the Homestead strike only because of his intense sympathy for the eleven strikers killed by Pinkertons and for the widows and orphans evicted by Frick from their wretched little homes that were owned by Mr. Carnegie.

Every one of these men not only made their reasons known to the world in spoken or written statements, showing the causes that led to their acts, proving that the unbearable economic and political pressure, the suffering and despair of their fellowmen [sic], women and children prompted their acts, and not the philosophy of anarchism. They came openly, frankly and ready to stand the consequences, ready to give their own lives.

In diagnosing the true nature of our social disease I cannot condemn those who through no fault of their own are suffering from a widespread malady.

I do not believe that these acts can or ever have been intended to bring about the social reconstruction. That can only be done, first, by a broad and wide education as to man's place in society and his proper relation to his fellows; and, second, through example. By example I mean the actual living of a truth once recognized, not the mere theorizing of its life element. Lastly, and the most powerful weapon, is the conscious, intelligent, organized, economic protest of the masses through direct action and the general strike.

It is the harmony of organic growth which produces variety of color and form—the complete whole we admire in the flower. Analogously will the organized activity of free human beings endowed with the spirit of solidarity result in the perfection of social harmony—which is anarchism. Indeed, only anarchism makes non-authoritarian organization a reality, since it abolishes the existing antagonism between individuals and classes.

For Discussion

1. What is an anarchist?
2. What are your feelings about Goldman as reflected in her writing?
3. What view of human nature underlies Goldman's comments about society?

4. Which of the attitudes toward marriage and love expressed by Goldman are evident in today's women's liberation movement?

5. What other concerns of Goldman find popular expression today? Give examples.

6. Reconcile Goldman's attack on the military—which employs violence—with her defense of anarchists who use violence.

7. Which of Goldman's beliefs are most compelling to you? Which are least acceptable? Why?

8. Examine one of Goldman's topics and comment upon the method she uses to develop it.

9. What effect is created by the opening paragraphs? What do they reveal about her attitude toward her audience?

ADOLF HITLER

Nation and Race

The spectacular ascent to power of Adolf Hitler was the result of numerous causes, not the least of which was his appeal to a national sense of racial superiority. Book I of *Mein Kampf* (1925), from which the following selection is taken, was written while Hitler, a member of the National Socialist party, was in jail after an aborted attempt to overthrow the state government of Bavaria in 1923. Together with Book II (1926), it eventually became the creed of millions of Germans. Within eight years of its publication, Hitler had been elected Führer for life, and the decade that followed saw him conquer most of Europe. The combined strength of the Allies finally defeated the Axis powers, and Hitler is believed to have committed suicide in Berlin on April 20, 1945.

There are some truths which are so obvious that for this very reason they are not seen or at least not recognized by ordinary people. They sometimes pass by such truisms as though blind and are most astonished when someone suddenly discovers what everyone really ought to know. Columbus's eggs lie around by the hundreds of thousands, but Columbuses are met with less frequently.

Thus men without exception wander about in the garden of Nature; they imagine that they know practically everything and yet with few exceptions pass blindly by one of the most patent principles of Nature's rule: the inner segregation of the species of all living beings on this earth.

Even the most superficial observation shows that Nature's restricted

From "Nation and Race" by Adolf Hitler from Vol. I, Chapter 11, of *Mein Kampf*, trans. by Ralph Manheim. Copyright 1943, copyright © 1971 renewed, by Houghton Mifflin Company. Reprinted by permission of Houghton Mifflin Company.

form of propagation and increase is an almost rigid basic law of all the innumerable forms of expression of her vital urge. Every animal mates only with a member of the same species. The titmouse seeks the titmouse, the finch the finch, the stork the stork, the field mouse the field mouse, the dormouse the dormouse, the wolf the she-wolf, etc.

Only unusual circumstances can change this, primarily the compulsion of captivity or any other cause that makes it impossible to mate within the same species. But then Nature begins to resist this with all possible means, and her most visible protest consists either in refusing further capacity for propagation to bastards or in limiting the fertility of later offspring; in most cases, however, she takes away the power of resistance to disease or hostile attacks.

This is only too natural.

Any crossing of two beings not at exactly the same level produces a medium between the level of the two parents. This means: the offspring will probably stand higher than the racially lower parent, but not as high as the higher one. Consequently, it will later succumb in the struggle against the higher level. Such mating is contrary to the will of Nature for a higher breeding of all life. The precondition for this does not lie in associating superior and inferior, but in the total victory of the former. The stronger must dominate and not blend with the weaker, thus sacrificing his own greatness. Only the born weakling can view this as cruel, but he after all is only a weak and limited man; for if this law did not prevail, any conceivable higher development of organic living beings would be unthinkable.

The consequence of this racial purity, universally valid in Nature, is not only the sharp outward delimitation of the various races, but their uniform character in themselves. The fox is always a fox, the goose a goose, the tiger a tiger, etc., and the difference can lie at most in the varying measure of force, strength, intelligence, dexterity, endurance, etc., of the individual specimens. But you will never find a fox who in his inner attitude might, for example, show humanitarian tendencies toward geese, as similarly there is no cat with a friendly inclination toward mice.

Therefore, here, too, the struggle among themselves arises less from inner aversion than from hunger and love. In both cases, Nature looks on calmly, with satisfaction, in fact. In the struggle for daily bread all those who are weak and sickly or less determined succumb, while the struggle of the males for the female grants the right or opportunity to propagate only to the healthiest. And struggle is always a means for improving a species' health and power of resistance and, therefore, a cause of its higher development.

If the process were different, all further and higher development would cease and the opposite would occur. For, since the inferior always predominates numerically over the best, if both had the same possibility of preserving life and propagating, the inferior would multiply so much more rapidly that in the end the best would inevitably be driven into the background, unless a correction of this state of affairs were undertaken. Nature does just this by subjecting the weaker part to such severe living conditions that by them alone the number is limited, and by not permitting the remainder to increase promiscuously, but making a new and ruthless choice according to strength and health.

No more than Nature desires the mating of weaker with stronger individuals, even less does she desire the blending of a higher with a lower race, since, if she did, her whole work of higher breeding, over perhaps hundreds of thousands of years, might be ruined with one blow.

Historical experience offers countless proofs of this. It shows with terrifying clarity that in every mingling of Aryan blood with that of lower peoples the result was the end of the cultured people. North America, whose population consists in by far the largest part of Germanic elements who mixed but little with the lower colored peoples, shows a different humanity and culture from Central and South America, where the predominantly Latin immigrants often mixed with the aborigines on a large scale. By this one example, we can clearly and distinctly recognize the effect of racial mixture. The Germanic inhabitant of the American continent, who has remained racially pure and unmixed, rose to be master of the continent; he will remain the master as long as he does not fall a victim to defilement of the blood.

The result of all racial crossing is therefore in brief always the following:

(a) Lowering of the level of the higher race;
(b) Physical and intellectual regression and hence the beginning of a slowly but surely progressing sickness.

To bring about such a development is, then, nothing else but to sin against the will of the eternal creator.

And as a sin this act is rewarded.

When man attempts to rebel against the iron logic of Nature, he comes into struggle with the principles to which he himself owes his existence as a man. And this attack must lead to his own doom.

Here, of course, we encounter the objection of the modern pacifist, as truly Jewish in its effrontery as it is stupid! "Man's rôle is to overcome Nature!"

Millions thoughtlessly parrot this Jewish nonsense and end up by really imagining that they themselves represent a kind of conqueror of Nature; though in this they dispose of no other weapon than an idea, and at that such a miserable one, that if it were true no world at all would be conceivable.

But quite aside from the fact that man has never yet conquered Nature in anything, but at most has caught hold of and tried to lift one or another corner of her immense gigantic veil of eternal riddles and secrets, that in reality he invents nothing but only discovers everything, that he does not dominate Nature, but has only risen on the basis of his knowledge of various laws and secrets of Nature to be lord over those other living creatures who lack this knowledge—quite aside from all this, an idea cannot overcome the preconditions for the development and being of humanity, since the idea itself depends only on man. Without human beings there is no human idea in this world, therefore, the idea as such is always conditioned by the presence of human beings and hence of all the laws which created the precondition for their existence.

And not only that! Certain ideas are even tied up with certain men. This applies most of all to those ideas whose content originates, not in an exact scientific truth, but in the world of emotion, or, as it is so beautifully and clearly expressed today, reflects an "inner experience." All these ideas, which have nothing to do with cold logic as such, but represent only pure expressions of feeling, ethical concepts, etc., are chained to the existence of men, to whose intellectual imagination and creative power they owe their existence. Precisely in this case the preservation of these definite races and men is the precondition for the existence of these ideas. Anyone, for example, who really desired the victory of the pacifistic idea in this world with all his heart would have to fight with all the means at his disposal for the conquest of the world by the Germans; for, if the opposite should occur, the last pacifist would die out with the last German, since the rest of the world has never fallen so deeply as our own people, unfortunately, has for this nonsense so contrary to Nature and reason. Then, if we were serious, whether we liked it or not, we would have to wage wars in order to arrive at pacifism. This and nothing else was what Wilson, the American world savior, intended, or so at least our German visionaries believed—and thereby his purpose was fulfilled.

In actual fact the pacifist-humane idea is perfectly all right perhaps when the highest type of man has previously conquered and subjected the world to an extent that makes him the sole ruler of this earth. Then this idea lacks the power of producing evil effects in exact proportion as its practical application becomes rare and finally impossible. Therefore, first struggle and then we shall see what can be done. Otherwise mankind has passed the high point of its development and the end is not the domination of any ethical idea but barbarism and consequently chaos. At this point someone or other may laugh, but this planet once moved through the ether for millions of years without human beings and it can do so again some day if men forget that they owe their higher existence, not to the ideas of a few crazy ideologists, but to the knowledge and ruth-less application of Nature's stern and rigid laws.

Everything we admire on this earth today—science and art, technology and inventions—is only the creative product of a few peoples and origi-nally perhaps of *one* race. On them depends the existence of this whole culture. If they perish, the beauty of this earth will sink into the grave with them.

However much the soil, for example, can influence men, the result of the influence will always be different depending on the races in question. The low fertility of a living space may spur the one race to the highest achievements; in others it will only be the cause of bitterest poverty and final undernourishment with all its consequences. The inner nature of peo-ples is always determining for the manner in which outward influences will be effective. What leads the one to starvation trains the other to hard work.

All great cultures of the past perished only because the originally crea-tive race died out from blood poisoning.

The ultimate cause of such a decline was their forgetting that all cul-ture depends on men and not conversely; hence that to preserve a cer-tain culture the man who creates it must be preserved. This preservation is bound up with the rigid law of necessity and the right to victory of the best and strongest in this world.

Those who want to live, let them fight, and those who do not want to fight in this world of eternal struggle do not deserve to live.

Even if this were hard—that is how it is! Assuredly, however, by far the harder fate is that which strikes the man who thinks he can over-come Nature, but in the last analysis only mocks her. Distress, misfor-tune, and diseases are her answer.

The man who misjudges and disregards the racial laws actually for-feits the happiness that seems destined to be his. He thwarts the tri-umphal march of the best race and hence also the precondition for all human progress, and remains, in consequence, burdened with all the sensibility of man, in the animal realm of helpless misery.

. . .

It is idle to argue which race or races were the original representative of human culture and hence the real founders of all that we sum up under the word "humanity." It is simpler to raise this question with regard to the present, and here an easy, clear answer results. All the human culture, all the results of art, science, and technology that we see before us today, are almost exclusively the creative product of the Aryan. This very fact admits of the not unfounded inference that he alone was the founder of all higher humanity, therefore representing the prototype of all that we understand by the word "man." He is the Prometheus of mankind from whose bright forehead the divine spark of genius has sprung at all times, forever kindling anew that fire of knowledge which illumined the night of silent mysteries and thus caused man to climb the path to mastery over the other beings of this earth. Exclude him—and perhaps after a few thousand years darkness will again descend on the earth, human culture will pass, and the world turn to a desert.

For Discussion

1. Discuss the logic of the analogy Hitler uses to introduce his argument for racial purity.
2. How scientifically accurate are Hitler's assertions regarding Nature and its laws?
3. In deductive argument, if the premises are false, the conclusions are false. What unsupported assumptions does Hitler use as premises?
4. Hitler's mastery of propaganda is well known. Discuss the connotations of the following "glittering generalities":
   a. racial progress
   b. highest type of man
   c. will of nature
   d. will of the eternal order
   e. racial laws
5. Hitler frequently pairs words like "higher-lower," "superior-inferior," and "stronger-weaker." What kind of thinking is reflected in these value judgments?
6. Discuss the reasoning that links warfare with the will of nature, with pacifism, and with culture.
7. Hitler was one of the world's most powerful speakers, shouting passionately at his audience and whipping them into a frenzy of patriotism. Find passages which lend themselves to this kind of oratory.

ROBERT McAFEE BROWN

In Conscience, I Must Break the Law

Robert McAfee Brown, born in 1920, is both an educator and a clergyman. He was ordained to the ministry of the Presbyterian Church, received his Ph.D. from Columbia University, and has studied in the United States, England, and Scotland. Active in achieving better relations between Protestants and Catholics, Brown was invited to attend Vatican Council II during 1963 and 1964 as a Protestant observer and to contribute a regular column to the Catholic weekly, *Commonweal.* He demonstrated his belief in social equality by taking part in a Freedom Ride in July 1961, which resulted in his spending twenty-four hours in a Tallahassee, Florida, jail. Since 1963, he has been a professor of religion at Stanford University.

"Vietnam? I've got other things to worry about." There was a time when it was easy for me to say that. I was worried about the California battle over Proposition 14, in which the real estate interests were trying to palm off on the California voters legislation designed to discriminate against minority groups, a measure later declared unconstitutional by the United States Supreme Court. I was worried about the plight of the migrant workers in the San Joaquin Valley, who were striking for the right to bargain collectively. I was also, if truth be told, worried about other things as well: getting tomorrow's lecture finished, scrounging up the extra dollars I was going to need when state income-tax time rolled

By permission of the editors. From the October 31, 1967, issue of *Look* Magazine. Copyright 1967 by Cowles Communications, Inc.

around, finding time to get acquainted with my kids, recouping some of the losses on the writing project on which I was currently so far behind.

In this, I was like many millions of Americans. In addition, also like many millions of Americans, I was probably afraid to face the issue of Vietnam, afraid that if I learned enough about it, I would have to join those radical, far-out types who two or three years ago were saying in such lonely fashion what many middle-class people are saying now: that our policy in Vietnam is wrong, that it is callous and brutalizing to those who must implement it, that it cannot be supported by thinking or humane people and that if one comes to feel this way, he has to engage in the uncomfortable and annoying and possibly threatening posture of putting his body where his words are.

In the interval since I discovered that I couldn't duck Vietnam any longer, I have tried to do my homework, read some history, examine the Administration's position, listen to its critics and come to a stand of my own. I've come to a stand, all right. And I only regret, not just for the sake of my own conscience, but for the sake of the thousands of Americans and the hundreds of thousands of Asians who have died in Vietnam, that I did not come to it with much greater speed. For I have now gone the full route—from unconcern

> to curiosity
> to study
> to mild concern
> to deep concern
> to signing statements
> to genteel protest
> to marching
> to moral outrage
> to increasingly vigorous protest
> to . . . civil disobedience.

The last step, of course, is the crucial one, the one where I part company with most of my friends in the liberal groups where I politic, with most of my friends in the academic community where I work and with most of my friends in the church where I worship. And since I am a reasonable man, not given to emotive decisions, one who by no stretch of the imagination could be called far-out, one who is not active in the New Left, one who still shaves and wears a necktie—a typical Establishment-type middle-class American WASP—I feel it important to record why it is that such a person as myself finds it impossible to stop merely at the level of vigorous protest of our policy in Vietnam and feels compelled to step over the line into civil disobedience.

My basic reason is also my most judgmental: I have utterly lost confidence in the Johnson Administration. Those who do not share that premise may shrink from the consequences I draw from it. All I can say by way of reply is that I tried for many months to work from the pre-supposition that the Administration was genuinely seeking peace and that it was trying to conduct foreign policy in honorable terms. But the record now makes patently clear to me that our Government is not will-ing to negotiate seriously save on terms overwhelmingly favorable to it and that it has refused to respond to many feelers that have come from the other side. I can no longer trust the spokesmen for the administration when they engage in their customary platitudes about a desire to negoti-ate. What they do belies what they say, and at the moment they express willingness to talk with Hanoi, they engage in further frantic acts of escalation that bring us closer to the brink of World War III and a nuclear holocaust. I do not believe that they are any longer reachable in terms of modifying their senseless policy of systematically destroying a small nation of dark-skinned people so that American prestige can emerge unscathed. All of us who have written, spoken, marched, peti-tioned, reasoned and organized must surely see that in the moments when Mr. Johnson is not calling us unpatriotic, he is simply ignoring a mounting chorus of moral horror with benign disdain and proceeding day by day, week by week, month by month, to escalate the war far past the point of no return.

This means that if one believes that what we are doing in Southeast Asia is immoral, he has no effective way of seeking to change such a policy, for the policy, in the face of two or three years of increasing criticism, is only becoming more hard-nosed, more irrational, more insane. The procedures through which change can normally be brought about in a democracy are increasingly futile. Mr. Johnson emasculated Congress in August 1964 with the Gulf of Tonkin agreement, which he now uses to justify air war over China. Public protests are written off as examples of lack of patriotism or lack of fidelity to the Americans now in Vietnam or even, by members of the House Armed Services Committee, as trea-sonable. With each act of military escalation, the moral horror of the war is escalated. We have been killing women and children all along; now, we kill more of them. We have been destroying the villages of civilians all along; now, we destroy more of them. We have been break-ing almost every one of the rules that civilized men have agreed consti-tute the minimal standards of decency men must maintain in the inde-cency of war; now, we break them more often.

This escalation of military power demands the escalation of moral protest. Those of us who condemn this war, who are repulsed by it and who realize that history is going to judge our nation very harshly for its part in it, must see more and more clearly that it is not enough any longer to sign another advertisement or send another telegram or give another speech—or write another article. The ways of genteel, legal pro-test have shown themselves to be ineffective. During the time of their impact, escalation has not lessened, it has increased. (I leave as a purely academic matter the question of whether escalation would have been worse without the genteel protests. Undoubtedly, it would have been. But it is too easy a rationalization to argue that we might have killed 500,000 Vietnamese, whereas, thanks to the protests, we may have only killed 100,000. Howard Zinn has remarked that World War II furnished us with a very convenient moral calculus: it is not permitted to kill 6,000,000 Jews, but anything short of that number can be justified in comparison.)

Military escalation has become our Government's stock response to every problem, and in its exercise, our leaders have demonstrated themselves incapable of change. Their only response, now no more than a conditioned reflex, is to hit a little harder. They become prisoners of their own propaganda. Their rationalizations of their policy become more frantic, their attacks on their critics more strident, their defense of their actions more removed from the realm of reality. In justifying the decision to bomb within ten miles of the China border, Mr. Johnson, in a not-untypical burst of omniscience, assured us that he knew the mind of the Peking government and that the Peking government would not interpret our action as a widening of the war. But who, even in Peking, can predict how that government will respond? Such acts and gestures and declarations on our part indicate the awful temptation of using power irresponsibly and the way in which our blithe self-confidence may sow the seeds of our—and everybody else's—destruction. I do not know which is more terrifying to contemplate: the possibility that Administration leaders really believe the reasons they give to defend their policy or the possibility that behind their public reasons, there lies another set of motivations and justifications that they dare not share with the rest of us. On either count, their right to lead the most powerful nation on earth is faulted.

I have already suggested that history will judge them harshly. But such a statement is a little too smug, however true it may be. History will judge *us* harshly, that is to say, those of us who continue to support our present policy makers, either overtly by echoing their tattered clichés or covertly by our silence. He who is not against them is for them.

In the face of such conclusions, one is counseled, "Work for '68. Wait for '68." I will, of course, work for '68, just as, inevitably, being a child of time, I must wait for it. But I am no longer content to throw all my energies in that direction, and for the following reasons: (1) It seems clear that no Democrat will have either the courage or the power to challenge Mr. Johnson. In the face of his virtually certain nomination, it is important that millions of persons like myself get on record as indicating that under no circumstances whatsoever would we vote for him. (2) There is little indication that the Republican party will offer a real choice.

Nixon and Reagan are more hawkish than Johnson, and Romney has displayed an indecisiveness about Vietnam seldom matched in the history of American politics. (3) The vacuum within the two major parties leaves voters opposed to our Vietnam policy with rather bleak alternatives. The decision to cast no vote at all cannot be justified by those who believe in the democratic process. All that is left, then, is to vote for a protest candidate who will not win. Several million voters so acting might serve notice on whoever wins that there is a body of opposition that cannot be discounted. But serving notice is a far cry from influencing policy. (4) All of this remains desperately abstract, however, because 1968 is a full year off. What is not in the least abstract is that in the meantime, men and women and children are dying. They are dying horrible deaths, inflicted not only by the Vietcong but also by our own soldiers. As our casualty rate increases in the next 12 months, the casualty rate of the enemy will increase perhaps ten times as fast. Meanwhile, our escalation will be bringing us closer and closer to war with China and possibly with Russia.

In the face of such facts, an informed conscience does not have the luxury of waiting 12 months to see what the political machinery may or may not produce. Therefore, I find myself forced, by the exclusion of alternatives as well as by an increasing sense of moral imperative, to escalate my own protest to the level of civil disobedience. The war is so wrong, and ways of registering concern about it have become so limited, that civil disobedience seems to me the only honorable route left.

I make this judgment, foreseeing two possible consequences.

First, there is always the remote possibility (on which it is not wise to count too heavily) that civil disobedience might make a significant enough impact on the nation as a whole that the policy makers could not any longer ignore the voice and act of protest. If engaged in by significant enough numbers of people (and significant enough people) it could conceivably shock the nation and the world into a recognition that our actions in Vietnam are so intolerable that a drastic shift in our policy could no longer be avoided. There is the further remote possibility that others, not yet ready to escalate their protest to civil disobedience, might at least escalate somewhere in the spectrum and thus produce a total yield noticeably higher than in the past.

I would like to believe that such things might happen. I see little likelihood that they will. Why, then, protest by breaking the law, if such protest is not going to do any discernible good? Because there comes a time when the issues are so clear and so crucial that a man does not have the choice of waiting until all the possible consequences can be charted. There comes a time when a man must simply say, "Here I stand, I can do no other, God help me." There comes a time when it is important for the future of a nation that it be recorded that in an era of great folly, there were at least some within that nation who recognized the folly for what it was and were willing, at personal cost, to stand against it. There comes a time when, in the words of Father Pius-Raymond Régamey, one has to oppose evil even if one cannot prevent it, when one has to choose to be a victim rather than an accomplice. There comes a time when thinking people must give some indication for their children and their children's children that the national conscience was not totally numbed by Washington rhetoric into supporting a policy that is evil, vicious and morally intolerable.

If such language sounds harsh and judgmental, it is meant precisely to be such. The time is past for gentility, pretty speeches and coy evasions of blunt truths. Evil deeds must be called evil. Deliberate killing of civilians—by the tens of thousands—must be called murder. Forcible removal of people from their homes must be called inhumane and brutal. A country that permits such things to be done in its name deserves to be condemned, not only by the decent people of other countries but particularly by the decent people who are its citizens, who will call things what they are and who recognize finally and irrevocably that the most evil deed of all is not to do bestial things but to do bestial things and call them humane.

In light of this, I no longer have any choice but to defy those laws of our land that produce such rotten fruits. I believe with Martin Luther King that such civil disobedience as I engage in must be done nonviolently, and that it must be done with a willingness to pay the penalties that society may impose upon me. I recognize the majesty of Law and its impregnable quality as a bulwark of a free society, and it is in the name of Law that I must defy given laws that are an offense against morality, making this witness wherever need be—in the churches, on the streets, in the assembly halls, in the courts, in jails.

Each person who takes this route must find the level at which his own conscience comes into conflict with laws relating to American presence in Vietnam, and the cardinal rule for those engaging in civil disobedience must be a respect for the consciences of those who choose a different point along the spectrum at which to make their witness; words like "chicken" or "rash" must have no place in their lexicon. Some will refuse to pay that portion of their Federal income tax directly supporting the war. Others will engage in "unlawful assembly" in front of induction centers. For myself, it is clear what civil disobedience will involve. I teach. I spend my professional life with American youth of draft age. And while I will not use the classroom for such purposes, I will make clear that from now on my concerns about Vietnam will be explicitly focused on counseling, aiding and abetting all students who declare that out of moral conviction they will not fight in Vietnam. I will "counsel, aid and abet" such students to find whatever level of moral protest is consonant with their consciences, and when for them this means refusing service in the armed forces, I will support them in that stand. In doing so, I am committing a Federal offense, for the Military Selective Service Act of 1967 specifically states that anyone who "knowingly counsels, aids or abets another to refuse or evade registration or service in the armed forces" opens himself to the same penalties as are visited upon the one he so counsels, aids and abets, namely up to five years in jail or up to $10,000 in fines, or both.

I will continue to do this until I am arrested. As long as I am not arrested, I will do it with increasing intensity, for I am no longer willing that 18- or 19-year-old boys should pay with their lives for the initially bumbling but now deliberate folly of our national leaders. Nor am I willing to support them in action that may lead them to jail, from a safe preserve of legal inviolability for myself. I must run the same risks as they, and therefore I break the law on their behalf, so that if they are arrested, I too must be arrested. If this means jail, I am willing to go with them, and perhaps we can continue there to think and learn and teach and reflect and emerge with a new set of priorities for American life. If, as is far more likely, this means merely public abuse or ridicule, then perhaps a minority of us can be disciplined, chastened and strengthened by that kind of adversity.

But whatever it means, the time has come when some of us can no longer afford the luxury of gentility or the luxury of holding "moderate" positions. The issue must be joined. Our country is committing crimes so monstrous that the only thing more monstrous would be continuing silence or inaction in the face of them.

For Discussion

1. How does the author characterize himself in relation to other Americans?
2. What in principle is Brown's objection to the Vietnam conflict?
3. Why does Brown finally advocate civil disobedience? What reasons does he offer to support his view?
4. What is Brown's rationale for increased protest?
5. Discuss the author's concept of responsibility of the individual as a member of society. (Also see Wald later in this section and Thoreau and Egendorf in "The Reflective NO.")
6. Discuss the form of Brown's civil disobedience. What other avenues of protest exist?
7. Buffon said, "Style is the man himself." If this is true, what kind of man is Brown? How does he qualify as impassioned?

STOKELY CARMICHAEL

Black Power

Stokely Carmichael was born in Trinidad in 1941 and came to the United States in 1952. A graduate of New York City's Bronx High School of Science and of Howard University, Carmichael took part in the civil rights movement in Lowndes County, Alabama, and was one of the first "freedom riders" to be arrested. Voicing the position of the intellectual black militant, Carmichael was elected chairman of the Student Nonviolent Coordinating Committee (SNCC) in 1966. After serving for one year, he traveled to Cuba. He has since spent time in England, appearing in Peter Brook's controversial motion picture *Tell Me Lies*, as well as writing and lecturing. Presently, he resides in Conakry, Guinea, with his wife, the well-known singer Miriam Makeba. The following speech was delivered at the Congress on the Dialectics of Liberation in London in July 1967.

We had intended to prepare a written speech for this Congress, and had started to prepare it three weeks before the trip, but the U.S. government thought that as I was starving it would be better if they saw to it that I got some meals every day, so they confined me to their prison system, and I lost all the notes. So I tried to get another one together.

Now since I've been at the Congress from Saturday I've been very confused, because I'm not a psychologist or a psychiatrist, I'm a political activist and I don't deal with the individual. I think it's a cop out when people talk about the individual. What we're talking about around the U.S. today, and I believe around the Third World, is the system of international white supremacy coupled with international capitalism. And we're out to smash that system. And people who see themselves as part of that system are going to be smashed with it—or we're going to be smashed.

From *To Free a Generation: The Dialectics of Liberation*, ed. David Cooper (New York: Collier Books, 1968), pp. 150–174. Reprinted by permission of the Institute of Phenomenological Studies.

So that I'm not going to center on the individual—I'm not even going to talk about him at all. I want to talk about the system. I want to use some quotes to back up my feeling about talking of the system, and the first one comes from one of my patron saints: Frantz Fanon. His quote is that

> Freud insisted that the individual factor be taken into account through psychoanalysis. It will be seen that the black man's alienation is not an individual question. It is a question of socio-diagnostics. The Negro problem does not resolve itself into the problem of Negroes living among white men, but rather of Negroes exploited, enslaved, despised by the colonialist, capitalist society that is only accidently white.

But since it is accidentally white, that's what we talk about—white western society.

Now the other reason that I don't talk about the individual is that I feel that whenever you raise questions about racial problems to white western society, each white man says "Well don't blame me, I'm only one person and I really don't feel that way. Actually I have nothing against you, I see you as an equal. You're just as good as I am—almost." And to try and clear that up I want to point out the difference between individual racism as opposed to institutionalized racism.

It is important to this discussion of racism to make a distinction between the two types: individual racism and institutional racism. The first type consists of overt acts by individuals, with usually the immediate result of the death of victims, or the traumatic and violent destruction of property. This type can be recorded on TV cameras and can frequently be observed in the process of commission.

The second type is less overt, far more subtle, less identifiable in terms of specific individuals committing the acts, but is no less destructive of human life. The second type is more the overall operation of established and respected forces in the society, and does not receive the condemnation that the first type receives.

Let me give you an example of the first type: When unidentified white terrorists bomb a black church and kill five black children, that is an act of individual racism, widely deplored by most segments of the world. But when in that same city, Birmingham, Alabama, not five but 500 black babies die each year because of lack of proper food, shelter and medical facilities; and thousands more are destroyed and maimed physically, emotionally and intellectually because of conditions of poverty and discrimination in the black community, that is a function of institutionalized racism. When a black family moves into a home in a white neighborhood, and it is stoned, burned or routed out, the latter is an overt act of individual racism, and many people condemn that, in words at least. But it is institutionalized racism that keeps the black people locked in dilapidated slums, tenements, where they must live out their daily lives subject to the prey of exploiting slum landlords, merchants, loan-sharks and the restrictive practices of real-estate agents. We're talking now about the U.S., but I think you can apply a little of it to London. But the society either pretends it does not know of institutionalized racism, or is incapable of doing anything meaningful about the conditions of institutionalized racism. And the resistance to doing anything meaningful about institutionalized racism stems from the fact that western society enjoys its luxury from institutionalized racism, and therefore, were it to end institutionalized racism, it would in fact destroy itself.

O.K. then, now I want to talk about de-mystifying human beings, and I'm talking about the Third World, I'm not talking about the white West. I think that the Third World are the people whom, at least in the U.S., black people are concerned with. The white West has been able to do very well for itself. I want to talk, then, very specifically about a number of things under that.

The first is the importance of definitions. The second: we want to talk about cultural integrity versus cultural imposition. And then we want to talk about the U.S., specifically the cities and the rebellions (as opposed to "riots" as they are called by the white press) that are occurring in the U.S., which are going to lead to guerrilla warfare. And we want to talk about violence because the West is always upset by violence when a black man uses it. Yeah.

I want to start off with definitions by using a quote from one of my favorite books, which is *Alice in Wonderland*, by Lewis Carroll. In the book there's a debate between Humpty Dumpty and Alice around the question of definitions. It goes like this:

> "When I use a word," Humpty Dumpty said, in a rather scornful tone, "it means just what I choose it to mean. Neither more nor less."
> "The question is," said Alice, "whether you can make words mean so many different things."
> "The question is," said Humpty Dumpty, "who is to be master. That is all."

Now I think that Lewis Carroll is correct. Those who can define are the masters. And white western society has been able to define, and that's why she has been the master. And we want to follow up with a lot of those examples, because I think that the white youth of my generation in the West today does not understand his own subconscious racism, because he accepts the writings of the West, which has destroyed, distorted and lied about history, so that he starts off with a basic assumption of superiority which is not even recognizable.

Frederick Douglass, the great black leader of the 1800s, said that when a slave stops obeying a master, then and only then does he seek his liberation. Camus said the same thing 100 years later on the first page of *The Rebel*, when he said that when a slave stops accepting definitions imposed upon him by his master, then and only then does he begin to move and create a life for himself. That's very important, because what the people of the Third World are going to have to do today is to stop accepting the definitions imposed on them by the West. Let's give some examples.

The first one is that the history book tells you that nothing happens until a white man comes along. If you ask any white person who discovered America, they'll tell you "Christopher Columbus." And if you ask them who discovered China, they'll tell you "Marco Polo." And if you ask them, as I used to be told in the West Indies, I was not discovered until Sir Walter Raleigh needed pitch lake for his ship, and he came along and found me and said "Whup—I have discovered you." And my history began.

But let us examine the racism in that statement. Let us examine it very closely. Columbus did not discover America. Columbus may be the first recorded white man to have set foot in America. That is all. There were people there before Columbus. Unfortunately, those people were not white—unfortunately for the white West, fortunately for us, they weren't white. But what happens is that white western society never recognizes the existence of non-white people, either consciously or subconsciously. So that all around the world, the peoples of the Third World never did anything until some white man came along—and that's why China's nonexistent, because Mao won't let no white folk in there. Yeah. And pretty soon Hong Kong is going to be nonexistent because they're going to kick them out.

So that the situation you have is that history has been written—but indeed it has been so distorted. One of the biggest lies, I think, that western society could have told was to name itself Western Civilization. And now all through history we were studying Western Civilization, and that meant that all else was uncivilized. And white kids who read that today never recognize that they're being told that they are superior to everybody else because they have produced civilization. At best, that's a misnomer, at worst, and more correctly it's a damn lie. Western Civilization has been anything but civilized. It has been most barbaric, as a matter of fact. We are told that Western Civilization begins with the Greeks, and the epitome of that is Alexander the Great. The only thing that I can remember about Alexander the Great was that at age twenty-six he wept because there were no other people to kill, murder and plunder. And that is the epitome of Western Civilization. And if you're not satisfied with that, you could always take the Roman Empire. Their favorite pastime was watching men kill each other or lions eating up men. They were a civilized people. The fact is that their civilization, as they called it, stemmed from the fact that they oppressed other peoples. And that the oppression of other people allowed them a certain luxury, at the expense of those other people. That has been interpreted as "civilization" for the West, and that is precisely what it has done. The only difference is that after the Roman Empire, when the British Empire—on which the sun never used to set, but today it sets, sometimes it don't even rise—began to exploit non-white people, what they did was they let color be the sole choice of the people they would exploit.

Now that's very important because as we go along you can see one of the best examples you can see today. You see, because you've been able to lie about terms, you've been able to call people like Cecil Rhodes a philanthropist, when in fact he was a murderer, a rapist, a plunderer and a thief. But you call Cecil Rhodes a philanthropist because what he did was that after he stole our diamonds and our gold, he gave us some crumbs so that we can go to school and become just like you. And that was called philanthropy. But we are renaming it: the place is no longer called Rhodesia, it is called Zimbabwe, that's its proper name. And Cecil Rhodes is no longer a philanthropist, he's known to be a thief—you can keep your Rhodes Scholars, we don't want the money that came from the sweat of our people.

Now let us move on to present times. I'm always appalled when some white person tells me that "progress is being made." I always ask him "progress for whom? And from whom?" Progress for white people might be made, because I would say that since World War II they have learned a little about how to get along with people of color. But I don't think there's been progress for the black people, there's not been progress for the people of color around the Third World. And progress will not be measured for us by white people. We will have to tell you when progress is being made. You cannot tell us when progress is being made, because progress for us means getting you off our backs, and that's the only progress that we can see.

Now then, we want to talk about cultural integrity versus cultural imposition, because that stems from definitions. Because the white West felt somehow that it was better than everybody else—I remember when I was a young man in the West Indies, I had to read Rudyard Kipling's *The White Man's Burden*. I thought the best thing the white man could do for me was to leave me alone, but Rudyard Kipling told them to come and save me because I was half savage, half child. It was very white of him. What has happened is that the West has used force to impose its culture on the Third World wherever it has been. If a few settlers left England to go to Zimbabwe, there was no reason for them to rename that country after themselves, Rhodesia, and then force everybody to speak their language, English. If they had respect for the cultures of other people, they would have spoken the language of those people and adopted their religions. But what in fact happened was because the West was so powerful—that's the word nobody wants to talk about, power. It was only power that made people bow their heads to the West, you know. They didn't bow it because they liked Jesus Christ, or because they liked white folks. No, Machiavelli said a long time ago that "people obey masters for one of two reasons. Either they love them, or they fear them." I often ask myself whether or not the West believes the Third World really loves them and that's why they've obeyed them. But it's clear that they feared them. The West with its guns and its power and its might came into Africa, Asia, Latin America and the U.S.A. and raped it. And while they raped it they used beautiful terms. They told the Indians "We're civilizing you, and we're taming the West. And if you won't be civilized, we'll kill you." So they committed genocide and stole the land, and put the Indians on reservations, and they said that they had civilized the country.

They weren't satisfied with that. They came to Africa and stole Africans and brought them to the U.S.A., and we were being brought there to be "civilized," because we were cannibals and we ate each other, and they were going to give us a better life, which was, of course, slavery.

Now I want to make just one clear distinction, before I move on, in terms of cultural integrity. Inside the countries of the West there was democracy for the whites, at least some form of it. But that democracy was at the expense of non-white people. While Britain surely enjoyed her papers, and her Parliamentary nonsense about constitutionality, she was suppressing all of Africa. The same thing holds true for France, and De Gaulle still suppresses Somaliland, I would like to inform him; and the same thing, of course, is true today for the U.S.

White people are very funny, you know. De Gaulle got out of Vietnam a few years ago, and now he's gotten very broad-minded. But he's still in Somaliland.

So what the West was able to do is impose its culture and it told everyone "we are better, we are civilized." And because of its force, all of the non-white countries began to try to imitate Europe and to imitate its ways, and to try and copy it because nobody wanted to be uncivilized. . . . Our ancestors had recognized that they knew what civilization was long before Europeans even got out of their caves, and that they should have stuck to their way of life. Had they done that, perhaps we shouldn't be in the shape we are in today.

So that all other non-western people have been stripped of their own culture. They have been forced to accept a culture that does not belong to them. And so messed up are the minds of people of color around the world, that in certain sections of Vietnam today, and in Japan certainly, women who have slanted eyes are cutting their eyes so that they can get round eyes to look like the West. Needless to say what black people have been doing to their hair, especially females: they have been putting hot combs in their hair, straightening it, attempting to look like white people, because the West has defined beauty as that which was theirs—the white woman, who was supposed to be taboo.

And so the non-white world began to copy and to imitate, began to do all the things of the West. I think what is happening in the world today is that there's a fight for cultural integrity. Each group of people wants to retain its own integrity, and say "To Hell with the West and its culture. Let it keep it. We want ours." I don't propose to speak for the Red Guards, but I would assume that that's part of the fight that they're waging. It's a healthy fight and it needs to be waged. I know in the U.S. that one of the fights that we're waging is the fight for our own cultural integrity. We want to be able to recognize the contributions that the non-white peoples of the world have made. It's amazing that, when you do some reading, you find out that they did most of what the white people claim that they did. They just distorted history. Pythagoras didn't give you geometry, the Egyptians gave it to you.

I have something against England, I really do. Because when I was young I had to read all that rot about how good England was to Trinidad, while she was raping us left and right. And all I used to read about London when I was small was the beauty of London, and how peacefully everybody lived, and how nice life was—at my expense. And I used to say "I sure would like to get to London and burn it down to the ground." But that's violence!

Now the trouble with the West is that it feels it has the right to *give* everybody their independence. That's totally absurd. You can never *give* anyone their independence. All men are born free. They are enslaved by other men. So that the only act that the men who enslaved them can do is, not give them their independence, but stop oppressing them. There's a very important difference, and I don't think people make that distinction all the time. I'm amazed when I pick up the paper and read that "England today decided to give independence to the West Indies." Who the hell is England to give me my independence? All they can do is stop oppressing me, get off my back. But it sounds so much nicer when they say, "We're giving you your independence. You're ready for it now." Rather than for them to admit to themselves "We're going to stop oppressing you because we're becoming a little bit more civilized; or because you're making it uncomfortable for us and we can no longer afford to oppress you at the price that you're asking us to pay." Which is correct. But you wouldn't expect self-condemnation.

So that you cannot grant anybody independence, they just take it. And that is what White America is going to learn. They cannot *give* us anything. No white liberal can give me anything. The only thing a white liberal can do for me is to help civilize other whites, because they need to be civilized.

Now in order to move on to the U.S.—because I know what's on everybody's mind is the rebellions and the guerrilla warfare that is taking place inside the U.S.—I'd just like to read some of the notes that I jotted down, so that you can maybe get a clearer picture, because you don't live in the States. However, I don't think you really need that much of a clearer picture, because England isn't far behind.

It is estimated that in another five to ten years two thirds of the 20 million black people that inhabit the U.S. will be living in the ghettos, in the heart of the cities. Joining us are going to be hundreds of thousands of Puerto Ricans, Mexican Americans, and people of the American Indian population. The American city, in essence, is going to be populated by the peoples of the Third World while the white middle classes will flee to the suburbs. Now the black people do not control, nor do we own, the resources—we do not control the land, the houses or the stores. These are all owned by whites who live outside the community. These are very real colonies, in the sense that there is cheap labor exploited by those who live outside the cities. It is white power that makes the laws, and enforces those laws with guns and sticks in the hands of white racist policemen and their black mercenaries. It does not seem that at any point the men who control the power and resources of the U.S. ever sat down and designed those black enclaves, and formally articulated the terms of their colonial and dependent status, as was done, for example, by the Apartheid government of South Africa which both Britain and the U.S. and France backs. Yet one cannot distinguish between one ghetto and another as one moves around the U.S. It appears as if each ghetto is the same. Note that the U.S. has, within its continental borders, forty-eight states, and each of these states has a ghetto in all of its major cities. As one moves from city to city it is as though some malignant, racist, planning unit has done precisely this: designed each one from the same master blue-print. And indeed, if the ghetto had been formally and deliberately planned, instead of growing spontaneously and inevitably from the racist functionings of the various institutions that combine to make the society, it would somehow be less frightening. The situation would be less frightening, because if these ghettos were the result of design and conspiracy, one could understand their similarity as being artificially and consciously imposed, rather than the result of identical patterns of white racism which repeat themselves in cities as far apart as Boston is from Watts—that is, 3000 miles.

We understand that a capitalist system automatically contains within itself racism, whether by design or not. Capitalism and racism seem to go hand in hand. The struggle for Black Power in the U.S., and certainly the world, is the struggle to free these colonies from external domination. But we do not seek merely to create communities where, in place of white rulers, black rulers control the lives of black masses, and where black money goes into a few black pockets. We want to see it go into the communal pocket. The society we seek to build among black people is not an oppressive capitalist society. Capitalism, by its very nature, cannot create structures free from exploitation.

The question may be asked, how does the struggle to free these internal colonies relate to the struggle against imperialism all around the world? We realistically survey our numbers and know that it is not possible for black people to take over the whole country militarily. In a highly industrialized nation the struggle is different. The heart of production and the heart of trade is in the cities. *We* are in the cities. We can become, and are becoming, a disruptive force in the flow of services, goods and capital. While we disrupt internally and aim for the eye of the octopus, we are hoping that our brothers are disrupting externally to sever the tentacles of the U.S.

That's very important, because Newark, New Jersey, is where Engelhart has his capital—and for the last five days he couldn't do any work. Good move for the Africans. You know who Engelhart is, don't you—you don't—you should read about South Africa, he controls most of it, along with Rockefeller, the liberal from the U.S.

It is sometimes said that the African-American movement in the U.S. does not understand the true nature of the struggle in the world today; that the movement is involved in fighting only racial discrimination, and only with the weapon of non-violence. It used to be. As you know, the Black Power movement which SNCC initiated moved away from the movement for integration. This was not only because the movement's goals were middle class—such as job opportunities for college graduates, equal public facilities—and not only because white Americans' concept of integration was based on the assumption that there was nothing of value in the black community and that little value would ever come from the black community—and that's very important, because the West doesn't understand its own racism when they talk about integration. When they talk about integration, they talk about accepting black people—isn't that ridiculous? I have to talk about whether or not I want to accept *them*, and they're never willing to talk about that, because they know they'll come up losing. So that integration is absolutely absurd unless you can talk about it on a two-way streak, where black people sit down and decide about integration. That means if you're really going to talk about integration, you don't talk about black people moving into white neighborhoods, you talk about white people moving into black neighborhoods.

Because of the middle-class orientation of the integration movement, and because of its subconscious racism, and because of its non-violent approach, it has never been able to involve the black proletariat. It could never attract and hold the young bloods who clearly understood the savagery of white America, and who were ready to meet it with armed resistance. It is the young bloods who contain especially the hatred Che Guevera speaks of when he says, and I quote:

"Hatred is an element of the struggle, relentless hatred of the enemy that impels us over and beyond the natural limitations of man, and transforms us into effective, violent, selected and cold killing machines."

The Black Power movement has been the catalyst for the bringing together of these young bloods—the real revolutionary proletariat, ready to fight by any means necessary for the liberation of our people.

The Black Power movement in the U.S. is exposing the extent of the racism and exploitation which permeates all the institutions in the country. It has unique appeal to young black students on campuses across the U.S. These students have been deluded by the fiction in white America that if the black man would educate himself and behave himself, he would be acceptable enough to leave the ranks of the oppressed and have tea with the Queen. However, this year, when provoked by savage white policemen, students on many campuses fought back, whereas before they had accepted these incidents without rebellion. As students are a part of these rebellions, they begin to acquire a resistance-consciousness. They begin to realize that white America might let a very few of them escape, one by one, into the mainstream of a society, but as soon as blacks move in concert around their blackness she will reply with the fury which reveals her true racist nature.

It is necessary, then, to understand that our analysis of the U.S. and international capitalism is one that begins in race. Color and culture were, and are, key factors in our oppression. Therefore our analysis of history and our economic analysis are rooted in these concepts. Our historical analysis for example views the U.S. as being conceived in racism. Although the first settlers themselves were escaping from oppression, and although their armed uprising against their mother country was around the aggravation of colonialism, and their slogan was "no taxation without representation," the white European settlers could not extend their lofty theories of democracy to the red men, whom they systematically exterminated as they expanded into the territory of the country which belonged to the red men. Indeed, in the same town in which the settlers set up their model of government based on the theory of representative democracy, the first slaves were brought from Africa. In the writings of the glorious Constitution, guaranteeing "life, liberty, the pursuit of happiness" and all that other garbage, these were rights for white men only, for the black man was counted only as three fifths of a person. If you read the U.S. Constitution, you will see that this clause is still in there to this very day—that the black man was three fifths of a man.

It was because white America needed cheap or free labor that she raped our African homeland of millions of black people. Because we were black and considered inferior by white Americans and Europeans, our enslavement was justified and rationalized by the so-called white Christians, who attempted to explain their crimes by spouting lies about civilizing the heathens, pagans, savages from Africa, whom they portrayed as being "better off" in the Americas than they were in their homeland. These circumstances laid the systematic base and framework for the racism which has become institutionalized in white American society.

In our economic analysis, our interpretation of Marx comes not only from his writing, but, as we see it, from the relationship of capitalistic countries to people of color around the world. Now I'm going to use the Labor Movement as an example to show what happens when people in a white country in the West organize themselves when they're being oppressed. I want to use the Labor Movement in the U.S. because it's always quoted around the world as the real movement, or friend, of the black man, who is going to be able to help him. This is true for all other little white countries when the white workers organize—here's how they get out of the bind.

The Labor Movement of the U.S.—while in the beginning certainly some of their great leaders in the struggle were against the absolute control of the economy by the industrial lords—essentially fought only for money. And that has been the fight of white workers in the West. The fight for one thing—more money. Those few who had visions of extending the fight for workers' control of production never succeeded in transmitting their entire vision to the rank and file. The Labor Movement found itself asking the industrial lords, not to give up their control, but merely to pass out a few more of the fruits of this control. Thereby did the U.S. anticipate the prophecy of Marx, and avoided the inevitable class struggle within the country by expanding into the Third World and exploiting the resources and slave labor of people of color. Britain, France, did the same thing. U.S. capitalists never cut down on their domestic profits to share with the workers. Instead, they expanded internationally, and threw the bones of their profits to the American working class, who lapped them up. The American working class enjoys the fruits of the labors of the Third World workers. The proletariat has become the Third World, and the bourgeoisie is white western society.

And to show how that works—and not only how it works just in terms of the bourgeoisie—I've watched the relationships of whites to whites who are communist, and whites to non-whites whom they call communist. Now every time the U.S. wants to take somebody's country, they get up and say "Communists are invading them and terrorist guerrilla warfare is on the way, and we must protect democracy, so send thousands of troops to Vietnam to kill the Communists." Italy is a white country. Over one third of its population is communist. Why doesn't the U.S. invade Italy? Tito is an acknowledged communist. The U.S. gives him aid. Why don't they invade Tito's country, if they really care about stopping communism? The U.S. is not kidding anybody. When they want to take over somebody's land who is non-white, they talk about communist aggression—that's what they did in Cuba, in Santo Domingo, and it's what they're doing in Vietnam. They're always telling people how they're going to stop them from going communist. And don't talk about dictatorship. Franco is perhaps the worst dictator in the world today, but the U.S. gives him aid.

So that it is clear it is not a question of communist invasion; it's really a question of being able to take the countries they want most from the people, and the countries they want most are obviously the non-white countries because that is where the resources of the world are today. That's where they have been for the last few centuries. And that's why white western society has to be there.

Now we want to make two distinctions, because when rebellions break out in the large cities of America, the first thing that people say is that they're riots. And white western society is very good, the first thing they want is order; law and order. "We must have law and order." They never talk about justice, because they're incapable of talking about it. Hitler had the most efficient system of law and order I've ever seen. He happened to have been a fascist. He did not have justice coupled with his law and order. The U.S. knows about law and order, it doesn't know about justice. It is for white western society to talk about law and order. It is for the Third World to talk about justice.

Now we want to talk just a little about violence. For God's sake, I don't understand how the white West can ever talk against violence. They are the most violent people on the face of the earth. They have used violence to get everything they have. And yet they're the first to talk against violence. The armed rebellions and the guerrilla warfare going on in the U.S. today is not the most violent thing going on in the world. Vietnam, South Africa, Zimbabwe, Hong Kong, Aden, Somaliland—that's where your violence really is. For violence takes many forms. It can take the form of physical warfare, or it can take the form of a slow death.

The Jews in the Warsaw ghetto were suffering from violence. It didn't take an actual physical form until they were put in the gas chambers, but they were suffering from mental violence. Wherever you go in Africa today, the Africans are suffering from violence, violence inflicted on them by the white West, be it that they are stripped of their culture, of their human dignity, or of the resources of their very land.

And it is crystal clear to the peoples of the Third World today that it's time out for talk. There can be no talk about how to stop violence. That's clear because even Camus talks about that, even though he cops out. Camus talks about executioner/victim. He says, well, there's executioner/victim relationships in society, and the executioner uses force to keep his victim down. But the victim gets tired of that. And what happens is that when the victim moves either to a position of equality or to try to conquer the executioner, he uses the force and the means and the methods that his oppressor used to keep him down. That happens to be violence. I never get caught up with violence. As a matter of fact, one of my favorite quotes on that, to stop all the talk about it, is a quote from Sartre, which my patron saint used. Sartre says:

> What then did you expect when you unbound the gag that had muted those black mouths? That they would chant your praises? Did you think that when those heads that our fathers had forcefully bowed down to the ground were raised again, you would find adoration in their eyes?

That's Jean-Paul Sartre, not me.

We are working to increase the revolutionary consciousness of black people in America to join with the Third World. Whether or not violence is used is not decided by us, it is decided by the white West. We are fighting a political warfare. Politics is war without violence. War is politics with violence. The white West will make the decision on how they want the political war to be fought. We are not any longer going to bow our heads to any white man. If he touches one black man in the U.S., he is going to go to war with every black man in the U.S.

We are going to extend our fight internationally and we are going to hook up with the Third World. It is the only salvation—we are fighting to save our humanity. We are indeed fighting to save the humanity of the world, which the West has failed miserably in being able to preserve. And the fight must be waged from the Third World. There will be new speakers. They will be Che, they will be Mao, they will be Fanon. You can have Rousseau, you can have Marx, you can even have the great libertarian John Stuart Mill.

I want to tell you why violence is important in terms of building a resistance-consciousness in the U.S. Now I want to use a quote which we learned from Germany:

> The triumph of the Storm Troopers required that the tortured victim allow himself to be led to the gallows without protesting, that he repudiate and abandon himself to the point where he ceases to affirm his identity.

There is nothing more terrible than these processions of human beings going to their deaths like human beings. I'm afraid black Americans cannot afford to march to the gallows the way Jews did. If the U.S., white America, decides to play Nazis, we're going to let them know the black Americans are not Jews, we're going to fight back to the death. And in case you think that sounds very violent, let me remind you of a poem that your great, great Prime Minister, Sir Winston Churchill, read when you were getting ready to attack Germany, even though you were told that you were a minority. He read a poem, incidentally, I don't know if he told you, which was written by a black man named Claude McKay from Jamaica, and he wrote it for black people. It is called "If We Must Die." It is our poem today in the U.S. Its message goes something like this:

"We will nobly die, fighting back, and for each of the thousand blows we will deal one death blow. But we're going to die like men. We are not going to take the oppression of white society any longer. That is clear in our minds. How it is in white society's mind is another question, but they are not defining for us any longer our struggle. We will define our struggle and we will carry it out as we see fit."

We have to extend our fight internationally, not only because such a consciousness would destroy within black communities the minority complex so carefully calculated by the American press, but also because we know that if the black man realizes that the counter-insurgency efforts of the U.S. are directed against his brothers, he will not fight in any of their wars. He will not go. Then it will become crystal clear to the world that the imperialist wars of the U.S. are nothing less than racist wars. During the past year we have initiated a black resistance movement to the Draft, which is being led by our hero, the World Champion, Mr. Mohammed Ali. Not only because we're against black men fighting their brothers in Vietnam, but also because we're certain that the next Vietnam will either be in the Congo, in South Africa, in Zimbabwe, Bolivia, in Guatemala, in Brazil, in Peru, or indeed in the West Indies. And we are not going to fight our brothers.

And to answer your question about violence, the African-American has tried for the past 400 years to peacefully coexist inside the U.S. It has been to no avail. We have never lynched a white man, we have never burned their churches, we have never bombed their houses, we have never beaten them in the streets. I wish we could say the same for white people around the world. Our history demonstrates that the reward for trying to peacefully coexist has been the physical and psychological murder of our peoples. We have been lynched, our houses have been bombed, and our churches burned. We are now being shot down like dogs in the streets by white racist policemen. We can no longer accept this oppression without retribution. We understand that as we expand our resistance, and internationalize the consciousness of our people, as our martyred brother Malcolm X did, we will get retaliation from the government, as he did. As the resistance struggle escalates we are well aware of the reality of Che's words, when he says:

"The struggle will not be a mere street fight, but it will be a long and harsh struggle."

And to the end, we are going to work with our common brothers and sisters in the Third World to fight this oppression.

I would like to conclude, then, by telling you just precisely what black people in America are going to do, and when we're going to do it, and how we're going to do it, and why we're going to do it. This is your only chance to hear it clear, because you'll be hearing it from the BBC next time.

Black people in the U.S. have no time to play nice polite parlor games, especially when the lives of our children are at stake. Some white Americans can afford to speak softly, tread lightly, employ the soft sell and put-off—or is it put-down?—because they own the society. For black people to adopt their methods of relieving our oppression is certainly ludicrous. We blacks must respond in our own way, on our own terms, in a manner which fits our temperaments. The definition of ourselves, the road we pursue, the goals we seek are our responsibility. It is crystal clear that society is capable of, and willing to, reward those individuals who do not forcefully condemn it—to reward them with prestige, status and material benefits. But these crumbs of corruption will be rejected. The plain fact is that as a people we have absolutely nothing to lose by refusing to play such games. Anything less than clarity, honesty and forcefulness perpetuates the centuries of sliding over, dressing up and soothing down the true feelings, hopes and demands of an oppressed black people. Mild demands and hypocritical smiles mislead white America into thinking that all is fine and peaceful; they lead white America into thinking that the path and pace chosen to deal with racial problems are acceptable to the masses of black Americans. It is far better to speak forcefully and truthfully. Only when one's true self, black or white, is exposed can society proceed to deal with the problems from a position of clarity, and not from one of misunderstanding.

Thus we have no intention of engaging in the rather meaningless language so common to discussions of race in the world today. They say:

"Things were and are bad, but we are making progress. Granted, your demands are legitimate, but we cannot move hastily. Stable societies are best built slowly. Be careful that you do not anger or alienate your white allies. Remember, after all, you are only ten per cent of the population."

We reject the language and these views, whether expressed by blacks or by whites. We leave them to others to mouth, because we don't feel that this rhetoric is either relevant or useful. Rather we suggest a more meaningful language—that of Frederick Douglass, a great black man who understood the nature of protest in society. He said:

> Those who profess to favor freedom, yet deprecate agitation, are men who want crops without ploughing up the ground. They want rain without thunder and lightning. They want the ocean without the awful wrath of its many waters. Power concedes nothing without demands—it never did and it never will. Find out just what any people will quietly submit to, and you have found out the exact measure of injustice and wrong which will be imposed upon them. And these will continue until they are resisted with either words or blows, or with both. The limits of tyrants are prescribed by the endurance of those whom they oppress.

He was a slave.

Black Power, to us, means that black people see themselves as a part of a new force, sometimes called the Third World; that we see our struggle as closely related to liberation struggles around the world. We must hook up with these struggles. We must, for example, ask ourselves: when black people in Africa begin to storm Johannesburg, what will be the reaction of the U.S.? What will be the role of the West, and what will be the role of black people living inside the U.S.? It seems inevitable that the U.S. will move to protect its financial interests in South Africa, which means protecting the white rule in South Africa, as England has already done. Black people in the U.S. have the responsibility to oppose, and if not to oppose, certainly to neutralize the effort by white America. This is but one example of many such situations which have already arisen around the world; there are more to come.

There is only one place for Black Americans in these struggles and that is on the side of the Third World.

Now I want to draw two conclusions. I want to give a quote from Fanon. Frantz Fanon in *The Wretched of the Earth* puts forth clearly the reasons for this, and the relationships of the concept called Black Power to the concept of a new force in the world. This is Mr. Fanon's quote:

> Let us decide not to imitate Europe. Let us try to create the whole man, whom Europe has been incapable of bringing to triumphant birth. Two centuries ago a former European colony decided to catch up with Europe. It succeeded so well that the U.S.A. became a monster in which the taints, the sickness and the inhumanity of Europe have grown to appalling dimensions. The Third World today faces Europe like a colossal mass, whose aim should be to try to resolve the problems to which Europe has not been able to find the answers. It is a question of the Third World starting a new history of man, a history which will have regard to the sometimes prodigious thesis which Europe has put forward, but which will also not forget Europe's crimes, of which the most horrible was committed in the heart of man and

consisted of the pathological tearing apart of his functions and the crumbling away of his unity.

No, there is no question of a return to nature. It is simply a very concrete question of not dragging men towards mutilation, of not imposing upon the brain rhythms which very quickly obliterate it and wreck it. The pretext of catching up must not be used for pushing men around, to tear him away from himself or from his privacy, to break and to kill him.

No, we do not want to catch up with anyone. What we want to do is go forward all the time, night and day, in the company of man, in the company of all men.

Since there's been a lot of talk about psychology, I've thought up a psychological problem. White liberals are always saying "What can we do?" I mean they're always coming to help black people. And I thought of an analogy. If you were walking down the street and a man had a gun on another man—let's say both of them were white—and you had to help somebody, whom would you help? It's obvious to me that if I were walking down the street, and a man had a gun on another man, and I was going to help, I'd help the man who didn't have the gun, if the man who had the gun was just pulling the gun on the other man for no apparent reason—if he was just going to rob him or shoot him because he didn't like him. The only way I could help is either to get a gun and shoot the man with the gun, or join the fellow who doesn't have a gun and both of us gang up on the man with the gun. But white liberals never do that. When the man has the gun, they walk around him and they come to the victim, and they say "Can I help you?" And what they mean is "help you adjust to the situation with the man who has the gun on you."

So that if indeed white liberals are going to help, their own job is to get the gun from the man and talk to him, because he is in fact the sick man. The black man is not the sick man, it is the white man who is sick, he's the one who picked up the gun first.

So the psychologists ought to stop investigating and examining people of color, they ought to investigate and examine their own corrupt society. That's where they belong. And once they are able to do that, then maybe we can move on to build in the Third World.

I want to conclude, then, by reading a poem that was written by a young man who works in SNCC, the organization for which I work. His name is Worth Long. It's called "Arson and Cold Grace, or How I Yearn To Burn, Baby, Burn."

We have found you out, four faced Americans, we have found you out.
We have found you out, false faced farmers, we have found you out.
The sparks of suspicion are melting your waters
And waters can't drown them, the fires are burning

And firemen can't calm them with falsely appeasing
And preachers can't pray with hopes for deceiving
Nor leaders deliver a lecture on losing
Nor teachers inform them the chosen are choosing
For now is the fire and fires won't answer
To logical reason and hopefully seeming
Hot flames must devour the kneeling and feeling
And torture the masters whose idiot pleading
Gets lost in the echoes of dancing and bleeding.
We have found you out, four faced farmers, we have found you out.
We have found you out, four faced America, we have found you out.[1]

[1] Reprinted by permission of the Student National Coordinating Committee.

For Discussion

1. What is the Third World?
2. What distinction does Carmichael make between individual and institutionalized racism? Why does he make a point of this?
3. How does Carmichael connect Western civilization with racism?
4. Compare Carmichael's ideas on the white liberal with those of other black leaders. (Also see King and Baldwin in "The Reflective NO.")
5. Explain Carmichael's idea of independence in relation to imperialism.
6. How does the new colonialism operate in the United States? Can you recognize any trends working against it?
7. Carmichael popularized the phrase "black power," which was the title of a book by Richard Wright published in 1954. How is the concept of black power incompatible with integration?
8. What relationship does Carmichael establish between capitalism and racism?
9. What ironies does Carmichael point out in discussing U.S. opposition to communism?
10. How does violence relate to politics? To war?
11. What are the advantages for the black American in becoming a part of the Third World movement? What might be the disadvantages?
12. Describe Carmichael's attitude toward his specific audience. How does it influence his treatment of his argument?
13. What is Carmichael's outlook toward the future?

JAMES KUNEN

Why We're Against the Biggees

James Kunen was nineteen years old and a student at Columbia
University when the student protest erupted there in 1968.
Sparked by Columbia's plans to build a gym in Morningside
Park (which separates Columbia from Harlem) without consult-
ing the community, the revolt became a protest against all the
ills the university had come to represent. Subsequently the
revolt had counterparts in colleges and universities across the
United States and Europe. Although Kunen denied any importance for his writing, the following essay begins to make clear
what much of student dissent was all about. *The Strawberry
Statement*, his chronicle of the events at Columbia, was published in 1969 and was subsequently made into a movie.

I have surveyed the opinions of the well-intentioned American middle
class regarding Columbia. That is, I have spoken to my mother about it.
She's been reading the *New Republic*, and is currently fond of saying
that the Columbia rebellion was set up in advance by people who are
not students at Columbia, and who do not have its interests at heart.
This is entirely true.

The Columbia rebellion was set in motion by a nebulous group of outsiders who are variously known as the corporate power elite, the military-
industrial complex, the Establishment. A friend of mine refers to them
as the Biggees.

The Biggees are a small group of men. Little else about them is known.

They are probably old. They possess wealth surpassing the bounds of imagination. They have no real needs or desires, but cultivate avarice as a sort of obsessive hobby. They sit in smoke-filled rooms, so it may be presumed that they smoke cigars. In the councils of the Biggees, one might hear decisions that one thought no one could make. Buy Uruguay. Sell Bolivia. Hold India. Pollute New York. The decisions are of incomprehensible variety, but they have in common the fact that they are swiftly implemented and invariably soak the Little Man.

Sometimes the Biggees slug it out with each other, as in the gold market, where they get down to the nitty-gritty of buying and selling *money* (a commerce that no one else can understand, let alone participate in), but more often they are after *our* coin.

The Biggees lie. They shout up and down that Vitalis has V₇, but they don't say what V₇ *is*. They say that Arrid stops wetness, but they don't explain why wetness should be stopped. (I can think of a lot of things that qualify for stoppage way ahead of wetness.) They lie about little things like that, and big things like Vietnam, the ghetto, Democracy. It's all the same—truth in lending, truth in labeling, truth in government; none of them exist.

The Biggees control. I read a sixth-grader's history paper about the Spanish-American War. The young boy, having put away his Mattel M-16 automatic rifle for the evening to do his homework, wrote that the 1898 war was fought by America to set the poor Cubans free from tyranny. He added that America traditionally fights on the side of right for justice and freedom and therefore always wins, "like in Vietnam today." The Biggees have that kid right where they want him. They've got his mind; when he's eighteen they'll take his body.

Look around you. The Biggees are everywhere. Look in your driveway. They build cars that dissociate in three years, and they make everybody buy them, and they're in on the gas biz too, so you can forget about mileage. And no one can make them change. You get organized and ask them to please just put all bumpers at a standard level so maybe a little less than that 50,000 of us will die on the roads next year, but no, they can't do it. They can't do it because it will *cost* to do it, and anyway, if all bumpers were at the same height, then there wouldn't be any choice, and that's what democracy's all about. If you didn't know that that's what democracy's all about, there are frequent ads to remind you. It seems, for instance, that in socialist countries there are only three colors of lipstick, whereas capitalism provides forty.

And with these forty shades of lipstick the Biggees turn our women into nauga-babes (vinyl girls) who in pre-fab sexiness sit tracing cheap pictures in the air with cigarettes they never made up their minds to start smoking. And, arguing about what to-do to do next, one of these naugas might be heard to say, "It's a free country."

But it isn't a free country. You can't drop out of school because you'd be drafted, and you have to study certain things to get a degree, and you have to have a degree to make it, and you have to make it to get what you want, and you can't even decide what you want, because it's all pro-grammed into you beforehand. You can *say* whatever you want, but you won't be heard because the media control that, but if you do manage to be heard, the People won't like it, because the people have been told what to like. And if they don't like you, they might even kill you, because the government endorses killing by exemplification.

All of which brings us to Columbia, because at Columbia we're all together and we teach each other and feel strong. The Biggees are kill-ing people in Vietnam and keeping the blacks down at home, because they have to keep some people at the bottom for their system to work, or so they thought. Now they're finding out that the downs can really screw them up bad, so they'd like to raise them just a bit, but that would certainly cost, so for the moment they'll try to keep them down by promising them rewards if they behave.

So here we all are at Columbia not comprehending this great money motivation because we didn't grow up in a depression and have always had coin and therefore don't value it as highly as we might. We're right at Harlem, so we see how it is. And we've got the draft right on us, so we know how that is. And we don't like it.We don't like it at all, because we've got a lot of life ahead of us and we're for it. Killing and dying just don't make it with us.

And lo and behold, right here at Columbia where all we young angries are seething, who should be president but Grayson Kirk, a Biggee if ever there was one. Consolidated Edison, IBM, Socony Mobil, Asia Founda-tion, I.D.A.—he's got an iron in every fire that's consuming us. And it turns out that Military Intelligence has offices at the university, and Electronic Research Laboratories is raking in about $5 million per annum on radar, and we're in the Institute for Defense Analysis in a big way, and the School of International Affairs is hitting it off really well with the CIA. All the while the university is systematically desiccating the integrated community of Morningside Heights, and has its eyes on land all the way over to Seventh Avenue, so that some fine day there'll be a nice white suburban buffer zone in the middle of Manhattan, which people will know, by the inevitable iron gates around it, to be Columbia.

Seeing all this, we decided to change it. Of course, if you don't like it you can leave, but if you leave you're going to run into something else you don't like, and you can't go on leaving forever because you'll run out of places to go. So we decided to change it. We petitioned, we dem-onstrated, we wrote letters, and we got nowhere. We weren't refused; we were ignored. So one day we went into the buildings, and one day somewhat later we were pulled out and arrested and many people were beaten. In the intervening days we were widely accused of having our-selves a good time in the buildings. We did have a good time. We had a good time because for six days we regulated our own lives and were free.

But Dr. Kirk and his associates saw that we were free and they knew of course that that sort of thing must not be permitted. They knew also that they could not deal with our demands, because that would mean a breakdown of their law and a violation of their order. So they called in the police. And they expressed regret that the police injured 150 people, and they really did regret it, because the brutal bust showed everybody how far the powerful will go to retain their power, how far they will go rather than answer a single question, rather than admit that questions can be asked.

As I write this and as you read it people are dying. So you see it isn't really a topic for suburban conversation or magazine articles. It's some-thing that must be dealt with. That's what's happening at Columbia, not a revolution but a counterattack. We are fighting to recapture a school from business and war and rededicate it to learning and life. Right now nobody controls Columbia, but if we get it, we will never give it back. And there are 5 million college students in the country watching us. And a lot of them have just about had it with the Biggees.

For Discussion

1. Logically, the term "Biggees" is an oversimplification which relies upon individual connotation for its specific meaning. Name your own Biggees.
2. Kunen sometimes combines great and small ills. Find an example of this combination and analyze its effect.
3. Discuss the idea that what happened at Columbia was a counterattack rather than a revolution.
4. How might Columbia be considered a symbol of other protest movements? What elements would they share?
5. Argue for or against Kunen's contention that this is not a free country.
6. Do you think that Kunen speaks for the majority of college students today? What do you think the purpose of the university should be?
7. Reread the first and last paragraphs. Explain how and why the tone changes.
8. How does Kunen's style reveal his attitude toward his subject?

GEORGE WALD

A Generation in Search of a Future

Dr. George Wald, Harvard biologist and 1967 Nobel Prize winner in physiology and medicine, delivered the following talk extemporaneously to a meeting of students and faculty at the Massachusetts Institute of Technology on March 4, 1969, to protest the misuses of science. Dr. Wald's speech created a strong, immediate response and has continued to impress young and old alike. It has received wide circulation through readings on FM radio and distribution in pamphlet form, and has been hailed as one of the most important speeches of our time.

All of you know that in the last couple of years there has been student unrest breaking at times into violence in many parts of the world: in England, Germany, Italy, Spain, Mexico and needless to say, in many parts of this country. There has been a great deal of discussion as to what it all means. Perfectly clearly it means something different in Mexico from what it does in France, and something different in France from what it does in Tokyo, and something different in Tokyo from what it does in this country. Yet unless we are to assume that students have gone crazy all over the world, or that they have just decided that it's the thing to do, there must be some common meaning.

I don't need to go so far afield to look for that meaning. I am a teacher, and at Harvard, I have a class of about 350 students—men and women—most of them freshmen and sophomores. Over these past few years I have felt increasingly that something is terribly wrong—and this year ever so much more than last. Something has gone sour, in teaching and

Reprinted by permission of the author.

80

in learning. It's almost as though there were a widespread feeling that education has become irrelevant.

A lecture is much more of a dialogue than many of you probably appreciate. As you lecture, you keep watching the faces; and information keeps coming back to you all the time. I began to feel, particularly this year, that I was missing much of what was coming back. I tried asking the students, but they didn't or couldn't help me very much.

But I think I know what's the matter, even a little better than they do. I think that this whole generation of students is beset with a profound uneasiness. I don't think that they have yet quite defined its source. I think I understand the reasons for their uneasiness even better than they do. What is more, I share their uneasiness.

What's bothering those students? Some of them tell you it's the Vietnam War. I think the Vietnam War is the most shameful episode in the whole of American history. The concept of War Crimes is an American invention. We've committed many War Crimes in Vietnam; but I'll tell you something interesting about that. We were committing War Crimes in World War II, even before the Nuremburg trials were held and the principle of war crimes started. The saturation bombing of German cities was a War Crime. Dropping atom bombs on Hiroshima and Nagasaki was a War Crime. If we had lost the war, some of our leaders might have had to answer for those actions.

I've gone through all of that history lately, and I find that there's a gimmick in it. It isn't written out, but I think we established it by precedent. That gimmick is that if one can allege that one is repelling or retaliating for an *aggression*—after that everything goes. And you see we are living in a world in which all wars are wars of defense. All War Departments are now Defense Departments. This is all part of the double talk of our time. The aggressor is always on the other side. And I suppose this is why our ex-Secretary of State, Dean Rusk—a man in whom repetition takes the place of reason, and stubbornness takes the place of character—went to such pains to insist, as he still insists, that in Vietnam we are repelling an aggression. And if that's what we are doing —so runs the doctrine—anything goes. If the concept of war crimes is ever to mean anything, they will have to be defined as categories of acts, regardless of alleged provocation. But that isn't so now.

I think we've lost that war, as a lot of other people think, too. The Vietnamese have a secret weapon. It's their willingness to die, beyond our willingness to kill. In effect they've been saying, you can kill us, but you'll have to kill a lot of us, you may have to kill all of us. And thank heavens, we are not yet ready to do that.

Yet we have come a long way—far enough to sicken many Americans, far enough even to sicken our fighting men. Far enough so that our national symbols have gone sour. How many of you can sing about "the rockets' red glare, bombs bursting in air" without thinking, those are *our* bombs and *our* rockets bursting over South Vietnamese villages? When those words were written, we were a people struggling for freedom against oppression. Now we are supporting real or thinly disguised military dictatorships all over the world, helping them to control and repress peoples struggling for their freedom.

But that Vietnam War, shameful and terrible as it is, seems to me only an immediate incident in a much larger and more stubborn situation.

Part of my trouble with students is that almost all the students I teach were born since World War II. Just after World War II, a series of new and abnormal procedures came into American life. We regarded them at the time as temporary aberrations. We thought we would get back to normal American life some day. But those procedures have stayed with us now for more than 20 years, and those students of mine have never known anything else. They think those things are normal. Students think we've always had a Pentagon, that we have always had a big army, and that we always had a draft. But those are all new things in American life; and I think that they are incompatible with what America meant before.

How many of you realize that just before World War II the entire American army including the Air Force numbered 139,000 men? Then World War II started, but we weren't yet in it; and seeing that there was great trouble in the world, we doubled this army to 268,000 men. Then in World War II it got to be 8 million. And then World War II came to an end, and we prepared to go back to a peacetime army somewhat as the American army had always been before. And indeed in 1950—you think about 1950, our international commitments, the Cold War, the Truman Doctrine, and all the rest of it—in 1950 we got down to 600,000 men.

Now we have 3.5 million men under arms: about 600,000 in Vietnam, about 300,000 more in "support areas" elsewhere in the Pacific, about 250,000 in Germany. And there are a lot at home. Some months ago we were told that 300,000 National Guardsmen and 200,000 reservists—so half a million men—had been specially trained for riot duty in the cities.

I say the Vietnam War is just an immediate incident, because so long as we keep that big army, it will always find things to do. If the Vietnam War stopped tomorrow, with that big a military establishment, the chances are that we would be in another such adventure abroad or at home before you knew it.

As for the draft: Don't reform the draft—get rid of it.

A peacetime draft is the most un-American thing I know. All the time I was growing up I was told about oppressive Central European countries and Russia, where young men were forced into the army; and I was told what they did about it. They chopped off a finger, or shot off a couple of toes; or better still, if they could manage it, they came to this country. And we understood that, and sympathized, and were glad to welcome them.

Now by present estimates four to six thousand Americans of draft age have left this country for Canada, another two or three thousand have gone to Europe, and it looks as though many more are preparing to emigrate.

A few months ago I received a letter from the Harvard Alumni Bulletin posing a series of questions that students might ask a professor involving what to do about the draft. I was asked to write what I would tell those students. All I had to say to those students was this: If any of them had decided to evade the draft and asked my help, I would help him in any way I could. I would feel as I suppose members of the underground railway felt in pre-Civil War days, helping runaway slaves to get to Canada. It wasn't altogether a popular position then, but what do you think of it now?

A bill to stop the draft was recently introduced in the Senate (S. 503), sponsored by a group of senators that ran the gamut from McGovern and Hatfield to Barry Goldwater. I hope it goes through; but any time I find that Barry Goldwater and I are in agreement, that makes me take another look.

And indeed there are choices in getting rid of the draft. I think that when we get rid of the draft, we must also cut back the size of the armed forces. It seems to me that in peacetime a total of one million men is surely enough. If there is an argument for American military forces of more than one million men in peacetime, I should like to hear that argument debated.

There is another thing being said closely connected with this: that to keep an adequate volunteer army, one would have to raise the pay considerably. That's said so positively and often that people believe it. I don't think it is true.

The great bulk of our present armed forces are genuine volunteers. Among first-term enlistments, 49 percent are true volunteers. Another 30 percent are so-called "reluctant volunteers," persons who volunteer under pressure of the draft. Only 21 percent are draftees. All re-enlistments, of course, are true volunteers.

So the great majority of our present armed forces are true volunteers. Whole services are composed entirely of volunteers: the Air Force for example, the Navy, almost all the Marines. That seems like proof to me that present pay rates are adequate. One must add that an Act of Congress in 1967 raised the base pay throughout the services in three installments, the third installment still to come, on April 1, 1969. So it is hard to understand why we are being told that to maintain adequate armed services on a volunteer basis will require large increases in pay;

that they will cost an extra $17 billion per year. It seems plain to me that we can get all the armed forces we need as volunteers, and at present rates of pay.

But there is something ever so much bigger and more important than the draft. That bigger thing, of course, is the militarization of our country. Ex-President Eisenhower warned us of what he called the military-industrial complex. I am sad to say that we must begin to think of it now as the military-industrial-labor union complex. What happened under the plea of the Cold War was not alone that we built up the first big peacetime army in our history, but we institutionalized it. We built, I suppose, the biggest government building in our history to run it, and we institutionalized it.

I don't think we can live with the present military establishment and its $80-100 billion a year budget, and keep America anything like we have known it in the past. It is corrupting the life of the whole country. It is buying up everything in sight: industries, banks, investors, universities; and lately it seems also to have bought up the labor unions.

The Defense Department is always broke; but some of the things they do with that $80 billion a year would make Buck Rogers envious. For example: the Rocky Mountain Arsenal on the outskirts of Denver was manufacturing a deadly nerve poison on such a scale that there was a problem of waste disposal. Nothing daunted, they dug a tunnel two miles deep under Denver, into which they have injected so much poisoned water that beginning a couple of years ago Denver began to experience a series of earth tremors of increasing severity. Now there is a grave fear of a major earthquake. An interesting debate is in progress as to whether Denver will be safer if that lake of poisoned water is removed or left in place. (N.Y. *Times*, July 4, 1968; *Science*, Sept. 27, 1968.)

Perhaps you have read also of those 6000 sheep that suddenly died in Skull Valley, Utah, killed by another nerve poison—a strange and, I believe, still unexplained accident, since the nearest testing seems to have been 30 miles away.

As for Vietnam, the expenditure of fire power has been frightening. Some of you may still remember Khe Sanh, a hamlet just south of the Demilitarized Zone, where a force of U.S. Marines was beleaguered for a time. During that period we dropped on the perimeter of Khe Sanh more explosives than fell on Japan throughout World War II, and more than fell on the whole of Europe during the years 1942 and 1943.

One of the officers there was quoted as having said afterward, "It looks like the world caught smallpox and died." (N.Y. *Times*, Mar. 28, 1968.)

The only point of government is to safeguard and foster life. Our government has become preoccupied with death, with the business of killing and being killed. So-called Defense now absorbs 60 percent of the national budget, and about 12 percent of the Gross National Product.

A lively debate is beginning again on whether or not we should deploy antiballistic missiles, the ABM. I don't have to talk about them, everyone else here is doing that. But I should like to mention a curious circumstance. In September, 1967, or about 1½ years ago, we had a meeting of M.I.T. and Harvard people, including experts on these matters, to talk about whether anything could be done to block the Sentinel system, the deployment of ABM's. Everyone present thought them undesirable; but a few of the most knowledgeable persons took what seemed to be the practical view, "Why fight about a dead issue? It has been decided, the funds have been appropriated. Let's go on from there."

Well, fortunately, it's not a dead issue.

An ABM is a nuclear weapon. It takes a nuclear weapon to stop a nuclear weapon. And our concern must be with the whole issue of nuclear weapons.

There is an entire semantics ready to deal with the sort of thing I am about to say. It involves such phrases as "those are the facts of life." No—they are the facts of death. I don't accept them, and I advise you not to accept them. We are under repeated pressure to accept things that are presented to us as settled—decisions that have been made. Always there is the thought: let's go on from there! But this time we don't see how to go on. We will have to stick with those issues.

We are told that the United States and Russia between them have by now stockpiled in nuclear weapons approximately the explosive power of 15 tons of TNT for every man, woman and child on earth. And now, it is suggested that we must make more. All very regrettable, of course; but those are "the facts of life." We really would like to disarm; but our new Secretary of Defense has made the ingenious proposal that now is the time to greatly increase our nuclear armaments so that we can disarm from a position of strength.

I think all of you know there is no adequate defense against massive nuclear attack. It is both easier and cheaper to circumvent any known nuclear defense system than to provide it. It's all pretty crazy. At the very moment we talk of deploying ABM's, we are also building the MIRV, the weapon to circumvent ABM's.

So far as I know, the most conservative estimates of Americans killed in a major nuclear attack, with everything working as well as can be hoped and all foreseeable precautions taken, run to about 50 millions. We have become callous to gruesome statistics, and this seems at first to be only another gruesome statistic. You think, Bang!—and next morning, if you're still there, you read in the newspapers that 50 million people were killed.

But that isn't the way it happens. When we killed close to 200,000 people with those first little, old-fashioned uranium bombs that we dropped on Hiroshima and Nagasaki, about the same number of persons were maimed, blinded, burned, poisoned and otherwise doomed. A lot of them took a long time to die.

That's the way it would be. Not a bang, and a certain number of corpses to bury; but a nation filled with millions of helpless, maimed, tortured and doomed persons, and the survivors of a nuclear holocaust will be huddled with their families in shelters, with guns ready to fight off their neighbors, trying to get some uncontaminated food and water.

A few months ago Sen. Richard Russell of Georgia ended a speech in the Senate with the words: "If we have to start over again with another Adam and Eve, I want them to be Americans, and I want them on this continent and not in Europe." That was a United States senator holding a patriotic speech. Well, here is a Nobel Laureate who thinks that those words are criminally insane.

How real is the threat of full-scale nuclear war? I have my own very inexpert idea, but realizing how little I know and fearful that I may be a little paranoid on this subject, I take every opportunity to ask reputed experts. I asked that question of a very distinguished professor of government at Harvard about a month ago. I asked him what sort of odds he would lay on the possibility of full-scale nuclear war within the foreseeable future. "Oh," he said comfortably, "I think I can give you a pretty good answer to that question. I estimate the probability of full-scale nuclear war, provided that the situation remains about as it is now, at 2 percent per year." Anybody can do the simple calculation that shows that 2 percent per year means that the chance of having that full-scale nuclear war by 1990 is about one in three, and by 2000, it is about 50-50.

I think I know what is bothering the students. I think that what we are up against is a generation that is by no means sure that it has a future.

I am growing old, and my future so to speak is already behind me. But there are those students of mine who are in my mind always; and there are my children, two of them now 7 and 9, whose future is infinitely more precious to me than my own. So it isn't just their generation; it's mine too. We're all in it together.

Are we to have a chance to live? We don't ask for prosperity, or security; only for a reasonable chance to live, to work out our destiny in peace and decency. Not to go down in history as the apocalyptic generation.

And it isn't only nuclear war. Another overwhelming threat is the population explosion. That has not yet even begun to come under control. There is every indication that the world population will double before the year 2000; and there is a widespread expectation of famine on an unprecedented scale in many parts of the world. The experts tend to differ only in the estimates of when those famines will begin. Some think by 1980, others think they can be staved off until 1990, very few expect that they will not occur by the year 2000.

That is the problem. Unless we can be surer than we now are that this generation has a future, nothing else matters. It's not good enough to give it tender loving care, to supply it with breakfast foods, to buy it expensive educations. Those things don't mean anything unless this generation has a future. And we're not sure that it does.

I don't think that there are problems of youth, or student problems. All the real problems I know are grown-up problems.

Perhaps you will think me altogether absurd, or "academic," or hopelessly innocent—that is, until you think of the alternatives—if I say as I do to you now: we have to get rid of those nuclear weapons. There is nothing worth having that can be obtained by nuclear war: nothing material or ideological, no tradition that it can defend. It is utterly self-defeating. Those atom bombs represent an unusable weapon. The only use for an atom bomb is to keep somebody else from using one. It can give us no protection, but only the doubtful satisfaction of retaliation. Nuclear weapons offer us nothing but a balance of terror; and a balance of terror is still terror.

We have to get rid of those atomic weapons, here and everywhere. We cannot live with them.

I think we've reached a point of great decision, not just for our nation, not only for all humanity, but for life upon the Earth. I tell my students, with a feeling of pride that I hope they will share, that the carbon, nitrogen and oxygen that make up 99 percent of our living substance, were cooked in the deep interiors of earlier generations of dying stars. Gathered up from the ends of the universe, over billions of years, eventually they came to form in part the substance of our sun, its planets and ourselves. Three billion years ago life arose upon the Earth. It seems to be the only life in the solar system. Many a star has since been born and died.

About two million years ago, man appeared. He has become the dominant species on the Earth. All other living things, animal and plant, live by his sufferance. He is the custodian of life on Earth. It's a big responsibility.

The thought that we're in competition with Russians or with Chinese is all a mistake, and trivial. Only mutual destruction lies that way. We are one species, with a world to win. There's life all over this universe, but in all the universe we are the only men.

Our business is with life, not death. Our challenge is to give what account we can of what becomes of life in the solar system, this corner of the universe that is our home and, most of all, what becomes of men —all men of all nations, colors and creeds. It has beome one world, a world for all men. It is only such a world that now can offer us life and the chance to go on.

For Discussion

1. What accusations does Wald make against the United States government? Defend the government's actions.
2. According to Wald, what should be the only point of government? To what extent would Thoreau (in "The Reflective NO") and Goldman agree?
3. Explore the idea that "all wars are wars of defense."
4. Why does Wald refer to the incidents involving nerve poison?
5. Attack or defend the accusation that Senator Russell's words are "criminally insane."
6. In view of the strength of Wald's argument against nuclear warfare, how do you explain our reluctance to halt nuclear stockpiling?
7. What existing phenomena, other than student unrest, do you think are the result of the fear of an uncertain future?
8. To what extent do you share Wald's fear that *you* are part of a generation without a future?
9. How do you explain the increasing popularity of this essay? How does its force depend upon more than a description of specific grievances?
10. Wald documents his generalizations with statistics and facts—a discursive method—and yet his voice is not discursive. What qualities do you find in his voice that make his argument impassioned? (It will help to read the last paragraph aloud.)

ANATOLI KUZNETSOV

I Could No Longer Breathe

In August 1968, the Soviet writer Anatoli Kuznetsov defected to the West, declaring that he had "arrived at the complete rejection of Marxism-Leninism" and had "come to realize the utter falsity, stupidity and reactionary nature of 'Socialist' realism." One of the Soviet Union's most celebrated young writers, Kuznetsov had been a member of the Communist Party since 1955. The following selection, originally printed in the *London Daily Telegraph and Morning Post*, explains his defection and asserts his belief that literature can flourish only when the artist is free to write as his conscience dictates.

You will say it's hard to understand. Why should a writer whose books have sold millions of copies, and who is extremely popular and well-off in his own country, suddenly decide not to return to that country, which, moreover, he loves?

The loss of hope: I simply cannot live there any longer. This feeling is something stronger than me. I just can't go on living there. If I were now to find myself again in the Soviet Union, I should go out of my mind. If I were not a writer, I might have been able to bear it. But, since I am a writer, I can't. Writing is the only occupation in the world that seriously appeals to me. When I write, I have the illusion that there is some sort of sense in my life. Not to write is for me roughly the same as for a fish not to swim. I have been writing as long as I can remember. My first work was published twenty-five years ago.

In those twenty-five years, not a single one of my works has been printed in the Soviet Union as I wrote it. For political reasons, the Soviet censorship and the editors shorten, distort and violate my works to the

Reprinted by permission of The Daily Telegraph, Ltd., London, from the Sunday *Telegraph*, August 3, 1969.

point of making them completely unrecognizable. Or they do not permit them to be published at all. So long as I was young, I went on hoping for something. But the appearance of each new work of mine was not a cause for rejoicing but for sorrow. Because my writing appears in such an ugly, false and misshapen form, and I am ashamed to look people in the face. To write a good book in the Soviet Union, that is still the simplest thing to do. The real trouble begins only later, when you try to get it published. For the past ten years, I have been living in a state of constant, unavoidable and irresolvable contradiction. Finally, I have simply given up.

I wrote my last novel, *The Fire*, with no feeling left in my heart, without faith and without hope. I knew in advance for certain that, even if they published it, they would ruthlessly cut everything human out of it, and that at best it would appear as just one more "ideological" potboiler. (And that is, incidentally, exactly what happens.)

I came to the point where I could no longer write, no longer sleep, no longer breathe.

A writer is above all an artist who is trying to penetrate into the unknown. He must be honest and objective, and be able to do his creative work in freedom. These are all obvious truths. These are the very things that writers are forbidden in the Soviet Union.

Artistic freedom in the Soviet Union has been reduced to the "freedom" to praise the Soviet system and the Communist Party and to urge people to fight for Communism. The theoretical basis for this is an article that Lenin wrote sixty years ago on "The Party Organization and Party Literature," which laid it down that every writer is a propagandist for the party. His job is to receive slogans and orders from the party and make propaganda out of them.

This means that writers in Russia are faced with the following choices:

(a) Simply to go along with this idiocy—to let their brains and their consciences have no effect on their actions. If Stalin is on top, then praise Stalin. If they order people to plant maize, then write about maize. If they decide to expose Stalin's crimes, then expose Stalin. And when they stop criticizing him, you stop too. There are so very many Soviet "writers" who are just like that.

But real life will not forgive a man who violates his conscience. Those writers have all become such cynics and spiritual cripples and their hidden regret for their wasted talent eats away at them to such an extent that their wretched existence cannot be called life but rather a caricature of life. It would probably be difficult to think up a worse punishment for oneself than to have to spend one's whole life trembling, cringing, trying fearfully to get the sense of the latest order and fearing to make the slightest mistake. Oh, God!

(b) To write properly, as their ability and consciences dictate.

It is then 100-to-1 that what they write will not be published. It will simply be buried. It may even be the cause of the author's physical destruction. It is a sad thought that Russia has long and deep "traditions" in this connection. The best Russian writers were always persecuted, dragged before the courts, murdered or reduced to suicide.

(c) To try and write honestly "as far as possible." To choose subjects that are not dangerous. To write in allegories. To seek out cracks in the censorship. To circulate your works from hand to hand in manuscript form. To do at least something: a sort of compromise solution. I was one of those who chose this third way. But it didn't work for me. The censors always managed to bring me to my knees. My anxiety to save at least something from what I had written, so that something would reach the reader, meant only that in the end all my published writings were neither genuine literature nor utterly contemptible but something in between.

However much I protested or tried to prove some point, it was like beating my head against a wall. Literature in the Soviet Union is controlled by people who are ignorant, cynical, and themselves very remote from literature. But they are people with excellent knowledge of the latest instructions from the men at the top of the prevailing Party dogmas. I could not force my way through their ranks. [Evgeny] Evtushenko managed to achieve a little in this way. [Alexander] Solzhenitsyn managed a little more, but even that is all over now. The cracks were noticed and cemented up. Russian writers go on writing and keep hoping for something. It is a nightmare.

My mania: So for a quarter of a century I went on dreaming about a happy state of affairs, which is unthinkable for a Soviet writer—to be able to write and publish his writings without restriction and without fear. Not to choke off his own song. To have no thought for party instructions, government-appointed editors and political censors. Not to start trembling at every knock on the door. Not to be hiding his manuscripts away in a hole in the ground almost before the ink on them is dry.

Oh, the number of holes I have dug in the ground to conceal my jam jars full of "dangerous" and "doubtful" manuscripts. I couldn't keep them in my desk because whenever I wasn't there my flat could be broken into and searched and my manuscripts confiscated, as happened with Solzhenitsyn and many others. My writing desk, in fact, had no drawers at all. The Russian earth itself served as my desk and my safe. It became a real mania for me to be able to see my writing published in the form in which I had written it. I wanted to see it just once, and then they could do what they liked with me. Yes, in that sense I was a sick man. I was a maniac.

As a boy I saw books being burned in Russia in 1937, under Stalin. I saw books being burned in 1942 in occupied Kiev, under Hitler, and now it has pleased God to let me know in my lifetime that my own books are being burned. Because now that I have left the Soviet Union, my books will, of course, be destroyed there too. In fact, I pray that my published works should be destroyed down to the very last one. Since they are not what I actually wrote and wanted to say to my readers, that means, after all, that they are not my books! I disassociate myself from them.

And so: I hereby, publicly and definitively, disassociate myself from everything that has been published under the name of "Kuznetsov" in the USSR or has appeared in translation from Soviet editions in other countries of the world. I solemnly declare that Kuznetsov is a dishonest, conformist, cowardly author. I renounce this name. I want to be, at last, an honest man and an honest writer. All my writings published from this day onward will bear the signature "A. Anatol." I request you to regard only such works as being mine.

What do I hope for? In recent years I have, from time to time, locked securely in my room, permitted myself a treat: I wrote as I pleased. It was a painful and unusual experience. It was as if, in a world where everybody went on all fours, somebody, shut in a cellar, had stood up and walked upright.

Then for some months, I dug my manuscripts up from their hiding places in the ground, photographed them and buried them again. I have succeeded in bringing those films across the frontier with me—thousands of pages on film, everything I have ever written in my life. They include my known works, such as *Babi Yar*, but in its true form. They also include things that could not be published in Russia. And some that I doubt whether I shall be able to publish in the West.

But now I have hope, at least. In any case, these are not the words of Kuznetsov but of a quite different author. Not a Soviet author and not a Western author, not a Red one and not a White one, but just an author living in this twentieth century on this earth. And what is more, a writer who has made a desperate effort to be in this century, an honest writer who wants to associate himself with those who strive for humanity in the present wild, wild, wild life of this mad, mad world.

For Discussion

1. What caused Kuznetsov's disillusionment as a writer in Soviet Russia?
2. Consider the three choices that Russian writers face, and argue for one over the other two.
3. Why does Kuznetsov wish his works to be destroyed?
4. Argue for or against society's right to censor the artist.
5. Identify the passages which most strongly convey the impassioned tone of this essay.

JOHNNIE TILLMON

Welfare Is a Women's Issue

The first paragraph of this essay establishes Johnnie Tillmon's credentials as a spokeswoman for those on welfare. Spurred by her own experience, she organized the nation's first welfare rights group in the Watts area of Los Angeles in 1963 and is presently chairwoman of the National Welfare Rights Organization. Encouraging every woman to "be honest about where your own head is," she advocates action based upon knowledge. The following essay is a first step toward acquiring that knowledge.

I'm a woman. I'm a black woman. I'm a poor woman. I'm a fat woman. I'm a middle-aged woman. And I'm on welfare.

In this country, if you're any one of those things—poor, black, fat, female, middle-aged, on welfare—you count less as a human being. If you're all those things, you don't count at all. Except as a statistic.

I am a statistic.

I am 45 years old. I have raised six children.

I grew up in Arkansas, and I worked there for fifteen years in a laundry, making about $20 or $30 a week, picking cotton on the side for carfare. I moved to California in 1959 and worked in a laundry there for nearly four years. In 1963, I got too sick to work anymore. My husband and I had split up. Friends helped me to go on welfare.

They didn't call it welfare. They called it A.F.D.C.—Aid to Families with Dependent Children. Each month I get $363 for my kids and me. I pay $128 a month rent; $30 for utilities, which include gas, electricity, and water; $120 for food and non-edible household essentials; $50 for school lunches for the three children in junior and senior high school who are not eligible for reduced-cost meal programs. This leaves exactly

Reprinted by permission of *Ms.* Magazine, Spring, 1972.

$5 per person per month for everything else—clothing, shoes, recreation, incidental personal expenses and transportation. This check allows $1 a month for transportation for me but none for my children. That's how we live.

There are millions of statistics like me. Some on welfare. Some not. And some, really poor, who don't even know they're entitled to welfare. Not all of them are black. Not at all. In fact, the majority—about two-thirds—of all the poor families in the country are white.

Welfare's like a traffic accident. It can happen to anybody, but especially it happens to women.

And that's why welfare is a women's issue. For a lot of middle-class women in this country, Women's Liberation is a matter of concern. For women on welfare it's a matter of survival.

Survival. That's why we had to go on welfare. And that's why we can't get off welfare now. Not us women. Not until we do something about liberating poor women in this country.

Because up until now we've been raised to expect to work, all our lives, for nothing. Because we are the worst-educated, the least-skilled, and the lowest-paid people there are. Because we have to be almost totally responsible for our children. Because we are regarded by everybody as dependents. That's why we are on welfare. And that's why we stay on it.

Welfare is all about dependency.

Welfare is the most prejudiced institution in this country, even more than marriage, which it tries to imitate. Let me explain that a little.

Forty-four percent of all poor families are headed by women. That's bad enough. But the *families* on A.F.D.C. aren't really families. Because 99 percent of them are headed by women. That means there is no man around. In half the states there really can't be men around because A.F.D.C. says if there is an "able-bodied" man around, then you can't be on welfare. If the kids are going to eat, and the man can't get a job, then he's got to go. So his kids can eat.

The truth is that A.F.D.C. is like a super-sexist marriage. You trade in *a* man for *the* man. But you can't divorce him if he treats you bad. He can divorce you, of course, cut you off anytime he wants. But in that case, *he* keeps the kids, not you.

The man runs everything. In ordinary marriage, sex is supposed to be for your husband. On A.F.D.C., you're not supposed to have any sex at all. You give up control of your own body. It's a condition of aid. You may even have to agree to get your tubes tied so you can never have more children just to avoid being cut off welfare.

The man, the welfare system, controls your money. He tells you what to buy, what not to buy, where to buy it, and how much things cost. If things—rent, for instance—really cost more than he says they do, it's just too bad for you. He's always right. Everything is budgeted down to the last penny; and you've got to make your money stretch.

The man can break into your house any time he wants to and poke into your things. You've got no right to protest. You've got no right to privacy when you go on welfare.

Like I said, welfare's a super-sexist marriage. In fact, welfare was invented mostly for women. It grew out of something called the Mother's Pension Laws. To be eligible, you had to be female, you had to be a mother, you had to be "worthy." "Worthy" meant were your kids "legitimate," was your home "suitable," were you "proper"?

In 1935, the Mother's Pension Laws became part of the Social Security system. And they changed the name of the program to Aid to Families with Dependent Children.

Of course now there are other welfare programs, other kinds of people on welfare—the blind, the disabled, the aged. (Many of them are women, too, especially the aged.) Those others make up just over a third of all the welfare caseloads. We A.F.D.C.'s are two-thirds. But when the politicians talk about the "welfare cancer eating at our vitals," they're not talking about the aged, blind and disabled. Nobody minds them. They're the "deserving poor." Politicians are talking about A.F.D.C. Politicians are talking about us—the women who head up 99 percent of the A.F.D.C. families—and our kids. We're the "cancer," the "undeserving poor." Mothers and children.

In fact, welfare isn't even for mothers. It's for the children. It's like a bonus for reproducing the race. Some bonus—all of $720 a year or $60 a month for a family of four if you live in Mississippi. It's more in other places—up to $346 a month for a family of four in New Jersey. But nowhere, nohow, is it enough to live on.

In this country, we believe in something called the "work ethic." That means that your work is what gives you human worth. But the work ethic itself is a double standard. It applies to men, and to women on welfare. It doesn't apply to all women. If you're a society lady from Scarsdale and you spend all your time sitting on your prosperity paring your nails, well, that's okay. Women aren't supposed to work. They're supposed to be married.

But if you don't have a man to pay for everything, particularly if you have kids, then everything changes. You've "failed" as a woman, because you've failed to attract and keep a man. There's something wrong with you. It can't possibly be the man's fault, his lack of responsibility. It must be yours. That's why Governor Reagan can get away with slandering A.F.D.C. recipients, calling them "lazy parasites," "pigs at the trough," and such. We've been trained to believe that the only reason people are on welfare is because there's something wrong with their character. If people have "motivation," if people only *want* to work, they can, and they will be able to support themselves and their kids in decency.

If this were true, we wouldn't have the working poor. Right now, 66 percent of the "employable" mothers are already employed—many full time—but at such pitifully low wages that we still need, and are entitled to, public assistance to survive.

The truth is a job doesn't necessarily mean an adequate income. A woman with three kids—not twelve kids, mind you, just three kids—that woman, earning the full Federal minimum wage of $1.60 an hour, is still stuck in poverty. She is below the Government's own official poverty line. There are some ten million jobs that now pay less than the minimum wage, and if you're a woman, you've got the best chance of getting one. Why would a 45-year-old woman work all day in a laundry ironing shirts at 90-some cents an hour? Because she knows there's some place lower she could be. She could be on welfare. Society needs women on welfare as "examples" to let every woman, factory workers and housewife workers alike, know what will happen if she lets up, if she's laid off, if she tries to go it alone without a man. So these ladies stay on their feet or on their knees all their lives instead of asking *why* they're only getting 90-some cents an hour, instead of daring to fight and complain.

And still, 33 percent of the employable mothers are looking for work.

We are this country's source of cheap labor. But we can't, some of us, get any jobs.

The President keeps repeating the "dignity of work" idea. What dignity? Wages are the measure of dignity that society puts on a job. Wages and nothing else. There is no dignity in starvation. Nobody denies, least of all poor women, that there is dignity and satisfaction in being able to support your kids through honest labor.

We wish we could do it.

The problem is that our country's economic policies deny the dignity and satisfaction of self-sufficiency to millions of people—the millions who suffer every day in underpaid dirty jobs—and still don't have enough to survive.

People still believe that old lie that A.F.D.C. mothers keep on having kids just to get a bigger welfare check. On the average, another baby means another $35 a month—barely enough for food and clothing. Having babies for profit is a lie that only men could make up, and only men could believe. Men, who never have to bear the babies or have to raise them and maybe send them to war.

There are a lot of other lies that male society tells about welfare mothers: That A.F.D.C. mothers are immoral. That A.F.D.C. mothers are lazy, misuse their welfare checks, spend it all on booze and are stupid and incompetent. If people are willing to believe these lies, it's partly because they're just special versions of the lies that society tells about *all* women.

For instance, the notion that all A.F.D.C. mothers are lazy: that's just a negative version of the idea that women don't work and don't want to. It's a way of rationalizing the male policy of keeping women as domestic slaves.

The notion that A.F.D.C. mothers are immoral is another way of saying that all women are likely to become whores unless they're kept under control by men and marriage.

A.F.D.C. mothers misuse their welfare checks? That's simply a justification for harassment. It comes from the male theory that women have no head for money, that they're naturally frivolous. In fact, an A.F.D.C. mother's probably got a better head for money than Rockefeller. She has to. She has so little to begin with that she's got to make every penny count, if she and her kids are even going to survive.

A.F.D.C. mothers are stupid, incompetent? That allows welfare officials to feel good about being paternalistic and justifies their policy of preventing A.F.D.C. mothers from making decisions about their own lives. It even explains why people are on welfare in the first place: because they're dumb, because there's something wrong with them.

A.F.D.C. mothers are the cause of slums and high taxes? Well, what's that but a special version of the notion that Eve, and Eve only, brought sin into the world? Welfare isn't the cause of high taxes. War is. Plus a lot of other things that poor women would like to see changed.

Society can continue to believe these lies only so long as women themselves believe them, as long as women sit still for them. Even many of my own sisters on welfare believe these things about themselves. Many ladies on welfare never get over their shame. But those of us who get beyond it are some of the strongest, most liberated women in this country.

To understand how this can be, you've got to remember that women on welfare are subject to all the same phony "female" ideals as all other women. But at the same time they're denied any opportunity to live up to those ideals.

On TV, a woman learns that human worth means beauty and that beauty means being thin, white, young and rich. She learns that her body is really disgusting the way it is, and that she needs all kinds of expensive cosmetics to cover it up. She learns that a "real woman" spends her time worrying about how her bathroom bowl smells; that being important means being middle class, having two cars, a house in the suburbs, and a minidress under your maxicoat. In other words, an A.F.D.C. mother learns that being a "real woman" means being all the things she isn't and having all the things she can't have.

Either it breaks you, and you start hating yourself, or you break it.

There's one good thing about welfare. It kills your illusions about yourself, and about where this society is really at. It's laid out for you straight. You have to learn to fight, to be aggressive, or you just don't make it. If you can survive being on welfare, you can survive anything. It gives you a kind of freedom, a sense of your own power and together-ness with other women.

Maybe it is we poor welfare women who will really liberate women in this country. We've already started on our own welfare plan.

Along with other welfare recipients, we have organized together so we can have some voice. Our group is called the National Welfare Rights Organization (N.W.R.O.). We put together our own welfare plan, called Guaranteed Adequate Income (G.A.I.), which would eliminate sexism from welfare. There would be no "categories"—men, women, children, single, married, kids, no kids—just poor people who need aid. You'd get paid according to need and family size only—$6,500 for a family of four (which is the Department of Labor's estimate of what's adequate), and that would be upped as the cost of living goes up.

Of course, nobody in power—and that means rich, white men—wants anything to do with G.A.I. It's too "radical." The President has his own plan, the Family Assistance Plan (F.A.P.), before Congress now. The President says we've got a "welfare crisis" in this country and that F.A.P.'s going to solve it. What he really means is that he's got a politi-cal problem, and that F.A.P.'s going to solve *it*. Because that's what F.A.P. is, really, politics. The President calls F.A.P. a reform. It's not. It's a nice intellectual-sounding principle of an "income floor," but it won't help poor people a bit. Under F.A.P., a family of four would get $2,400 a year. Right now, 45 states and the District of Columbia are paying A.F.D.C. recipients over $2,400 a year in benefits and food stamps, and food stamps would be eliminated under F.A.P. That means that nine out of ten of all A.F.D.C. recipients—women and their children—would be even worse off under F.A.P. than they are now.

And that's not all.

First. There's a built-in "family maximum." If you've got seven kids you get $3,600 a year. If you've got ten kids, you still get $3,600 a year. If you have that eighth kid, by choice or by chance—maybe because you couldn't get birth control devices from the public clinic or because there was no clinic—then it's just too bad. That kid's invisible, as far as the Government is concerned.

Second. That $2,400 applies only to A.F.D.C.—to women and children. They've got a whole *different* schedule for the "deserving poor"—the aged, blind and disabled. A better schedule. For instance, an aged couple —just two people—will get almost exactly the same as an A.F.D.C. family of *four*.

Third. A single woman—not aged, not disabled, not a mother—gets nothing at all from F.A.P., no matter how hard up and desperate and unable to get work she is. If you don't have kids, you're not a person.

Fourth. If a mother refuses a job or job-training recommended for her by the welfare officials, she can be cut off and payments due her children are made to a "third party," someone outside her own family, someone she doesn't even choose. This brings up the most important point about F.A.P.: forced work.

Under F.A.P., a woman has to take any job offered her. She doesn't decide whether the job is suitable and pays a living wage. In fact, the job can pay as little as $1.20 an hour, or less, if "prevailing wages" are less. She doesn't decide whether child care facilities are good enough. The welfare people make these decisions for her. If she doesn't go along, her check is cut off.

"We can only put people in jobs that exist," the F.A.P. people say. We all know what kinds of jobs those are—maids get as low as $20 a week in Mississippi, living in five or six days, and only seeing their kids on weekends. And even these kinds of jobs, low as they are, are few and far between.

Child care provisions in F.A.P. don't make any sense either. They're just decorations to make it seem okay to force women with little children to work. In fact, the way it looks now, A.F.D.C. mothers may have to pay for all or part of their child care out of their own earnings, even though they only need child care because of the forced-work law.

There is an important point for women to remember when they fight for quality universal child care. Be careful that your enthusiasm doesn't get used to create a reservoir of cheap female labor. Because that's who's going to be working in those child care centers—poor women. If we don't watch it, an A.F.D.C. mother can end up paying a child-care center, which in turn will pay her less than the minimum wage to watch her children—and your children, too. Institutionalized, partially self-employed Mammies—that's what can happen to us.

A woman should be able to *choose* whether to work outside her home or in it, to choose whether she wants to care for her own children all the time or part-time. And the people who work in child care centers have to be paid decent wages or our kids won't get decent care.

The same thing goes for the birth control and abortion movements. Nobody realizes more than poor women that all women should have the right to control their own reproduction. But we also know how easily the lobby for birth control can be perverted into a weapon against poor women. The word is choice. Birth control as a right, not an obligation. A personal decision, not the condition of a welfare check.

As far as I'm concerned, the ladies of N.W.R.O. are the front-line troops of women's freedom. Both because we have so few illusions and because our issues are so important to all women—the right to a living wage for women's work, the right to life itself.

If I were President, I would solve this so-called welfare crisis in a minute and go a long way toward liberating every woman. I'd just issue a proclamation that women's work is *real* work. In other words, I'd start paying women a living wage for doing the work we are already doing—child-raising and housekeeping. And the welfare crisis would be over, just like that. Housewives would be getting wages, too—a legally determined percentage of their husband's salary—instead of having to ask for and account for money they've already earned.

For me, Women's Liberation is simple. No woman in this country can feel dignified, no woman can be liberated, until all women get off their knees. That's what N.W.R.O. is all about—women standing together, on their feet.

For Discussion

1. What requirements of a good opening are met in the first paragraph of this essay?
2. Why is welfare a women's issue?
3. Tillmon compares welfare to a sexist marriage. What makes this an effective analogy?
4. How does the work ethic penalize welfare women both financially and psychologically?
5. What lies about women in general—and welfare mothers in particular—does Tillmon expose?
6. According to Tillmon, what positive effects can being on welfare produce?
7. What prejudices does the Family Assistance Plan reflect?
8. What basic principle is at the heart of the Guaranteed Adequate Income? What do you think of this plan?
9. How does Tillmon take the welfare issue beyond the limits of her personal experience?
10. Analyze the language and sentence structure of this essay. Find examples of words and constructions which are uncommon in formal writing. What effect do they have upon you as audience?

RAMSEY CLARK

Watergate: A Brush with Tyranny

Ramsey Clark, former Attorney General of the United States, has consistently taken a liberal stance toward the administration of justice. He has urged stricter laws on firearms, federal support to upgrade local law enforcement agencies, and rehabilitation programs to replace damaging prison systems. Clark opposes wiretapping and other police actions that might tend to infringe on the civil rights of a suspected offender. He is the author of *Crime in America: Observations on Its Nature, Causes, Prevention and Control* (1970). The essay which follows was published in June 1973, during the early weeks of the Senate Select Committee's investigation into Watergate.

Watergate is more than a sordid affair; it exposes a set of values. Values permeate conduct and, beyond the vast domain of chance and necessity which chiefly determine our fate, are the principal factors in the exercise of free will.

The values manifested by Watergate are many: power above law; ends above means; deception above truth; self-interest above public service. The central assumption is that the world is divided into good people and bad people. The good people may, under varying circumstances, be all Americans, all Republicans, all persons in the Administration, all on the White House staff, or in the Department of Justice, all within a particular clique, the President, you and me, or finally only me. The values justify bombing in Cambodia, bugging the Watergate, or causing a special investigation of Daniel Ellsberg.

Reprinted by permission of *The Nation* Magazine from the June 4, 1973, issue.

In his speech of April 30 on Watergate, President Nixon said, ". . . like any other calling, politics has good people and bad people." He described Mr. Ehrlichman and Mr. Haldeman as ". . . two of the finest public servants it has been my privilege to know." Of Watergate, he asked, "How could it have happened?" Because these good people, ". . . whose zeal exceeded their judgment . . . may have done wrong in a cause they deeply believed to be right." By this explanation, the good people are still right, just imprudent.

What then of the rule of law? How can it hope to achieve freedom, justice, equality, peace? The rule of law applies alike to friend and foe, rich and poor, loved and hated, feared and trusted. Under a value system that divides nations and societies into good and bad, law and government are simply means of power to be used to further the interests of the "good" people, to control the "bad" people.

This value system has tended to guide the Nixon Administration in all its activities. There need be no legal justification for bombing in Cambodia. Lon Nol today is among the good people, so for the present it is in our interest to bomb his fellow citizens to protect him. A civilized world with a rule of law would call that murder.

The result is to politicize the conduct of government and the use of law. A politicized law is will, not law. Law and government are then used for the political ends of those who wield their power. At the end of this road lies tyranny. To analyze the phenomena adequately, you must look at both what is said and what is done.

While illustrations abound throughout the executive branch, and into regulatory agencies and such independent activities as the Corporation for Public Broadcasting, the Department of Justice offers the prime example. Here is the seat of law in the executive branch: its name, and presumably its purpose, is justice; equal justice under law. President Nixon has staffed the Department of Justice with politicians: Mitchell, Kleindienst, Wilson, Gray, Leonard, Ruckelshaus, Frizell, Mardian, Rehnquist, Kashiwa. Six had previously sought election to or served in statewide political office. Elliot Richardson, just confirmed as Attorney General, makes the seventh of eleven. Politicians can make extraordinary contributions to law and government even in the management of the bureaucracy. But when professional legal discipline is infected by political consideration, we are a government of men, not laws. When politicians are placed in key legal positions, the appearance of infection is immediate and the probability of its actuality high. No Presidential appointee at Justice during the Kennedy and Johnson administrations had sought or served in elective office. As a matter of policy, men known primarily as lawyers, not as politicians, were chosen for lawyers' jobs.

Political people have brought political judgments to the Department of

Justice under President Nixon. In crime control, civil rights enforcement and First Amendment areas, among others, the department took political actions.

President Nixon espouses wiretapping. For the first time in history an Attorney General, John Mitchell, contended for an inherent power in the President to tap without Congressional or judicial approval in domestic security cases. This view was later rejected by the U.S. Supreme Court but we do not yet know who was tapped as a result. Mr. Nixon's first assistant attorney general for the Criminal Division, Will Wilson, took a hard political line on law enforcement, but resigned under a cloud. He had been the private attorney for a man under federal investigation for fraud from whom he borrowed tens of thousands of dollars after becoming Chief Prosecutor of the United States. Mr. Wilson signed a check payable to a private investigator indicted for wiretapping—the bad person tapped was a federal bank examiner, assigned to investigate Mr. Wilson's client. Attorney General Mitchell met in his office in the Department of Justice with political campaign officials, listened to suggestions that the Democratic National Committee be wiretapped—a federal crime —and never admonished them of the law, or threatened prosecution. (At least, John Ehrlichman, also a lawyer, when told, he says, of the burglarizing of Daniel Ellsberg's psychiatrist's files—a crime—said, "Don't do it again.")

To demonstrate strong commitment to tough law enforcement, the first Nixon Chief Marshal of the United States was recruited from the military; he was Provost Marshal Gen. Carl Turner. The Chief Marshal is the highest civilian law-enforcement officer in the federal establishment, just as the Attorney General is the ranking lawyer and the director of the FBI heads the major investigative office. The Provost Marshal General commands the Military Police of the United States, numbering several hundred thousand. A paramilitary concept of civilian police is foreign to the spirit of a free, democratic society. General Turner was soon to be behind prison bars for stealing guns forfeited by persons apprehended by U.S. Marshals. General Turner appropriated the guns for good people, his personal collection and his bank account, ironically paralleling the Administration's view of gun control; take them from bad people, give them to good people.

Soon the Administration's value patterns emerged. While abandoning social programs promising relief from poverty, legal services for the poor and the quest for equal justice, government acted to keep people in their place, to make them behave. "Law and order" meant control by force. Tough cops meant bully power.

Sometimes the philosophy claimed was "strict construction," but neither acts nor words could meet this test. A more sweeping and unfounded claim of executive privilege has never been expounded than that espoused by Attorney General Kleindienst. The privilege could pull the curtain of secrecy over all executive activity.

No Justice on the Supreme Court appointed by President Nixon has agreed with Justice Black's strict construction of the First Amendment. Black believed that because the Amendment provided "Congress shall make no law . . . abridging the freedom . . . of the press . . . ," Congress could make no law abridging freedom of the press.

Invoking the symbolism of the death penalty, preventive detention and a no-knock law, while attacking Supreme Court rulings enforcing the rights of defendants, the Department of Justice slowly abandoned, then opposed, enforcement of the equal protection clause. In October 1969, when young attorneys in the Civil Rights Division began the first employee protest in the department's history over the failure to enforce the law, some resigning, Atty. Gen. John Mitchell said, "I couldn't care less." In a major case involving school desegregation in Mississippi in 1970, the U.S. Court of Appeals for the Fifth Circuit, using unprecedented language, referred to the "obtuse, patronizing failure" of the department to "do its duty." And when the department failed to enforce a court order it had sought requiring removal of the Vietnam Veterans Against the War from the Capitol grounds in Washington, Judge George L. Hart said in open court to Asst. Atty. Gen. L. Patrick Gray, you have "degraded the court."

The President followed the standard by politicizing the Calley trial, telling the world and the military courts he would be the final judge. A brave young army prosecutor, Capt. Aubrey Daniel, stood up for the rule of law and criticized his Commander in Chief for demeaning it.

By political actions, the Administration reassured the good people, supporting the largest, most lawless sweep arrests in our history—those of 7,000 persons protesting the war in Vietnam in May 1971. The Department of Justice protected the good people who acted violently in its interest by refusing to convene a grand jury to investigate the deaths of students at Kent State. Following a police raid on the Black Panthers in Chicago in 1969, the Department of Justice first promised a private commission of inquiry that indictments would be returned, itself an improper act, then released a grand jury report which Sen. John L. McClellan criticized as without authority in law. The report blamed everyone, but indicted no one in the death of Fred Hampton and Mark Clark and the wounding of four Black Panthers in the Chicago police raid. FBI ballistics found that one shot, at most, had been fired by Panthers, while scores were fired by police.

In the operation of the Department of Justice, numerous political and lawless acts have come to light. U.S. Attorney Stewart, in San Diego, interfered with a grand jury that was investigating a major Nixon contributor who supported Stewart for a judgeship. Deputy Attorney General Kleindienst sat in his office and listened while the administrative assistant to a Republican Senator pleaded for a constituent and suggested a large political contribution. Kleindienst did nothing, saying later that he did not recognize the conduct as an attempt to bribe. The person was later convicted of attempting to bribe Mr. Kleindienst in that very meeting. ITT officials held private conversations, unscheduled and outside the presence of staff attorneys working on ITT cases, with Attorney General Mitchell and Deputy Attorney General Kleindienst.

James R. Hoffa was granted parole swiftly and separately by a law-and-order Administration that did not pretend to give equal consideration to other applications. (One might ask what lesson tens of thousands of offenders take from this single act.) Attorney General Mitchell directly interceded in a matter for Robert Vesco, then under investigation. Vesco gave $200,000 as a political contribution, later returned.

L. Patrick Gray became the second head of a federal bureau that had never had an agent charged with corruption in office. As acting director of the FBI, he accepted, and destroyed without reading, he says, a file that might have contained evidence of crime. Agents in a new federal drug agency that was set up in the Department of Justice for political visibility—thus destroying morale among professionals in career service enforcement of laws controlling dangerous drugs—without obtaining search warrants required by the fourth Amendment or facts to support their actions, smashed into private homes in Illinois, terrorized the families, threatened death, used force, destroyed property—and found nothing.

For the first time in history the U.S. Government, acting through the Department of Justice, sought to restrain a free press prior to publication, and a federal grand jury sought to force a newspaper reporter to appear before it bringing notes and answering questions about his sources. The illustrations already known seem endless. How many more are yet to come to light?

We should concede, with Felix Cohen, that "for most judges, for most lawyers, for most human beings, we are as unconscious of our value patterns as we are of the oxygen that we breathe." Perhaps those involved in Watergate fall into the majority who are unconscious of their value patterns. But the patterns are clear. They are lawless, truthless and violent values that seek to seize power, to curb opposition, to have their way. They are the values of Richard M. Nixon, President of the United States.

We should strive for a leadership guided by a philosophy that stands for something decent, that is passionately devoted to the quest for truth, realizing that only if we see the truth can we in time overcome the problems. There is a desperate need for reaffirmation of the American ideals of Freedom, Equality and Justice. But these things will not be possible in a society whose government leaders hold law in contempt. We must, in the words of a 29-year-old Abraham Lincoln, make reverence for law "the political religion of the nation."

For Discussion

1. What values are manifested by Watergate? What activities do they justify, according to Clark?
2. What drawbacks does Clark see in dividing the world into good and bad people?
3. Discuss the irresponsible actions of the Nixon administration in the name of "law and order."
4. What do you think is Clark's view of citizen protest? Of wiretapping? Of freedom of the press?
5. How have succeeding events affected the impact of this essay?
6. How does Clark's impassioned tone influence the quality of his argument?

THE
DISCURSIVE
NO

*...a decent respect to the opinions of mankind requires that
they should declare the causes which impel them to the separation.*
Declaration of Independence

Whereas the impassioned writer expresses strong feeling and makes an
appeal for the reader's total involvement, the discursive writer minimizes
the expression of his feelings and asks the reader to judge his ideas on
their own merit. This means that, insofar as he is able, he does not allow
his emotions to dominate his argument. This is not to say that the discursive writer does not feel strongly, but rather that he prefers to express
his argument as dispassionately as possible. Any emotion that the reader
might feel comes from the persuasiveness of the writer's facts and logic.

That reason and logic are the chief concerns of the discursive writer
is apparent from a glance at the derivation of the word *discursive*. It is
the adjective form of *discourse*, meaning an extended treatment of a
subject in an organized and logical manner. It emphasizes orderly pro-
gression of evidence and ideas in support of reasonable judgments. The
success or failure of discursive writing rests mainly upon the force of its

objectivity—its logic, its appeal to our minds—rather than upon the force of its feeling.

The discursive writer, therefore, makes special demands upon his reader. He trusts him to think, to be receptive to reason. He has "a decent respect to the opinions of mankind," to use Jefferson's words— meaning that he assumes the reader has an open mind, is capable of changing his opinion despite any personal leanings he may already have, and is intelligent and interested enough to follow an argument and evaluate it.

This is expecting a great deal from the reader. In fact, the discursive writer expects more from his reader than does the reflective or impassioned writer. He relies upon him to participate fully in the discussion, to continually evaluate and judge. In short, he expects him to be what Mark Twain called the "athletic reader." The discursive writer wants his reader's understanding—not of himself but of his subject. This means that the reader's involvement is primarily intellectual and not emotional.

The essays that follow are predominantly discursive. The degree of their persuasiveness depends upon the degree of their responsibility in presenting ideas for our responsible judgment. Every essay, in its own way, "declares the causes which impel" its author to dissent.

PLATO

Apology

The *Apology* means the "Defense," and the dialogue so-named
was written by Plato and contains an account of Socrates' trial
and defense, made by himself. Because Socrates believed that
right action for men was action based on rational principle, he
spent a good part of his life exposing the ignorance and the
unsoundness of thought in his political contemporaries. The
enmity he thus produced was finally responsible for his being
brought to trial on charges of atheism and corrupting youth,
charges which carried a possible death penalty. He was found
guilty, though it is commonly believed that he was not, and
was executed in 399 B.C. This selection is the latter part of the
Apology in which Socrates enunciates the philosophical-moral
principles by which he had conducted his life.

I have said enough in answer to the charge of Meletus: any elaborate
defense is unnecessary; but I know only too well how many are the
enmities which I have incurred, and this is what will be my destruction
if I am destroyed;—not Meletus, nor yet Anytus, but the envy and
detraction of the world, which has been the death of many good men,
and will probably be the death of many more; there is no danger of my
being the last of them.

Some one will say: And are you not ashamed, Socrates, of a course
of life which is likely to bring you to an untimely end? To him I may
fairly answer: There you are mistaken: a man who is good for anything
ought not to calculate the chance of living or dying; he ought only to consider whether in doing anything he is doing right or wrong—acting the
part of a good man or of a bad. Whereas, upon your view, the heroes
who fell at Troy were not good for much, and the son of Thetis above all,
who altogether despised danger in comparison with disgrace; and when
he was so eager to slay Hector, his goddess mother said to him, that if
he avenged his companion Patroclus, and slew Hector, he would die himself—"Fate," she said, in these or the like words, "waits for you next

after Hector"; he, receiving this warning, utterly despised danger and death, and instead of fearing them, feared rather to live in dishonor, and not to avenge his friend. "Let me die forthwith," he replies, "and be avenged of my enemy, rather than abide here by the beaked ships, a laughing stock and a burden of the earth." Had Achilles any thought of death and danger? For wherever a man's place is, whether the place which he has chosen or that in which he has been placed by a commander, there he ought to remain in the hour of danger; he should not think of death or of anything but of disgrace. And this, O men of Athens, is a true saying.

Strange, indeed, would be my conduct, O men of Athens, if I, who, when I was ordered by the generals whom you chose to command me at Potidaea and Amphipolis and Delium, remained where they placed me, like any other man, facing death—if now, when, as I conceive and imagine, God orders me to fulfill the philosopher's mission of searching into myself and other men, I were to desert my post through fear of death, or any other fear; that would indeed be strange, and I might justly be arraigned in court for denying the existence of the gods, if I disobeyed the oracle because I was afraid of death, fancying that I was wise when I was not wise. For the fear of death is indeed the pretense of wisdom, and not real wisdom, being a pretense of knowing the unknown; and no one knows whether death, which men in their fear apprehend to be the greatest evil, may not be the greatest good. Is not this ignorance of a disgraceful sort, the ignorance which is the conceit that a man knows what he does not know? And in this respect only I believe myself to differ from men in general, and may perhaps claim to be wiser than they are:—that whereas I know but little of the world below, I do not suppose that I know: but I do know that injustice and disobedience to a better, whether God or man, is evil and dishonorable, and I will never fear or avoid a possible good rather than a certain evil. And therefore if you let me go now, and are not convinced by Anytus, who said that since I had been prosecuted I must be put to death; (or if not that I ought never to have been prosecuted at all); and that if I escape now, your sons will all be utterly ruined by listening to my words—if you say to me, Socrates, this time we will not mind Anytus, and you shall be let off, but upon one condition, that you are not to enquire and speculate in this way any more, and that if you are caught doing so again you shall die;—if this was the condition on which you let me go, I should reply: Men of Athens, I honor and love you; but I shall obey God rather than you, and while I have life and strength I shall never cease from the practice and teaching of philosophy, exhorting any one whom I meet and saying to him after my manner: You, my friend—a citizen of the great and mighty and wise city of Athens—are you not ashamed of heaping up the greatest amount of money and honor and reputation, and caring so little about wisdom and truth and the greatest improvement of the soul, which you never regard or heed at all? And if the person with whom I am arguing, says: Yes, but I do care; then I do not leave him or let him go at once; but I proceed to interrogate and examine and cross-examine him, and if I think that he has no virtue in him, but only says that he has, I reproach him with undervaluing the greater, and overvaluing the less. And I shall repeat the same words to every one whom I meet, young and old, citizen and alien, but especially to the citizens, inasmuch as they are my brethren. For know that this is the command of God; and I believe that no greater good has ever happened in the State than my service to the God. For I do nothing but go about persuading you all, old and young alike, not to take thought for your persons or your properties, but first and chiefly to care about the greatest improvement of the soul. I tell you that virtue is not given by money, but that from virtue comes money and every other good of man, public as well as private. This is my teaching, and if this is the doctrine which corrupts the youth, I am a mischievous person. But if any one says that this is not my teaching, he is speaking an untruth. Wherefore, O men of Athens, I say to you, do as Anytus bids or not as Anytus bids, and either acquit me or not; but whichever you do, understand that I shall never alter my ways, not even if I have to die many times.

Men of Athens, do not interrupt, but hear me; there was an understanding between us that you should hear me to the end: I have something more to say, at which you may be inclined to cry out; but I believe that to hear me will be good for you, and therefore I beg that you will not cry out. I would have you know, that if you kill such an one as I am, you will injure yourselves more than you will injure me. Nothing will injure me, not Meletus nor yet Anytus—they cannot, for a bad man is not permited to injure a better than himself. I do not deny that Anytus may, perhaps, kill him, or drive him into exile, or deprive him of civil rights; and he may imagine, and others may imagine, that he is inflicting a great injury upon him: but there I do not agree. For the evil of doing as he is doing—the evil of unjustly taking away the life of another—is greater far.

And now, Athenians, I am not going to argue for my own sake, as you may think, but for yours, that you may not sin against the God by condemning me, who am his gift to you. For if you kill me you will not easily find a successor to me, who, if I may use such a ludicrous figure of speech, am a sort of gadfly,[1] given to the State by God; and the State is a great and noble steed who is tardy in his motions owing to his very size, and requires to be stirred into life. I am that gadfly which God has

[1] A biting insect; a person who repeatedly and persistently annoys others with schemes, ideas, demands, and requests.

attached to the State, and all day long and in all places am always fastening upon you, arousing and persuading and reproaching you. You will not easily find another like me, and therefore I would advise you to spare me. I dare say that you may feel out of temper (like a person who is suddenly awakened from sleep), and you think that you might easily strike me dead as Anytus advises, and then you would sleep on for the remainder of your lives, unless God in his care of you sent you another gadfly. When I say that I am given to you by God, the proof of my mission is this:—if I had been like other men, I should not have neglected all my own concerns or patiently seen the neglect of them during all these years, and have been doing yours, coming to you individually like a father or elder brother, exhorting you to regard virtue; such conduct, I say, would be unlike human nature. If I had gained anything, or if my exhortations had been paid, there would have been some sense in my doing so; but now, as you will perceive, not even the impudence of my accusers dares to say that I have ever exacted or sought pay of any one; of that they have no witness. And I have a sufficient witness to the truth of what I say—my poverty.

Some one may wonder why I go about in private giving advice and busying myself with the concerns of others, but do not venture to come forward in public and advise the State. I will tell you why. You have heard me speak at sundry times and in divers places of an oracle or sign which comes to me, and is the divinity which Meletus ridicules in the indictment. This sign, which is a kind of voice, first began to come to me when I was a child; it always forbids but never commands me to do anything which I am going to do. This is what deters me from being a politician. And rightly, as I think. For I am certain, O men of Athens, that if I had engaged in politics, I should have perished long ago, and done no good either to you or to myself. And do not be offended at my telling you the truth: for the truth is, that no man who goes to war with you or any other multitude, honestly striving against the many lawless and unrighteous deeds which are done in a State, will save his life; he who will fight for the right, if he would live even for a brief space, must have a private station and not a public one.

I can give you convincing evidence of what I say, not words only, but what you value far more—actions. Let me relate to you a passage of my own life which will prove to you that I should never have yielded to injustice from any fear of death and that "as I should have refused to yield" I must have died at once. I will tell you a tale of the courts, not very interesting perhaps, but nevertheless true. The only office of State which I ever held, O men of Athens, was that of senator: the tribe Antiochis, which is my tribe, had the presidency at the trial of the generals who had not taken up the bodies of the slain after the battle of Arginusae; and you proposed to try them in a body, contrary to law, as you all thought afterward; but at the time I was the only one of the Prytanes who was opposed to the illegality, and I gave my vote against you; and when the orators threatened to impeach and arrest me, and you called and shouted, I made up my mind that I would run the risk, having law and justice with me, rather than take part in your injustice because I feared imprisonment and death. This happened in the days of the democracy. But when the oligarchy of the Thirty was in power, they sent for me and four others into the rotunda, and bade us bring Leon the Salaminian from Salamis, as they wanted to put him to death. This was a specimen of the sort of commands which they were always giving with the view of implicating as many as possible in their crimes; and then I showed, not in word only but in deed, that, if I may be allowed to use such an expression, I cared not a straw for death, and that my great and only care was lest I should do an unrighteous or unholy thing. For the strong arm of that oppressive power did not frighten me into doing wrong; and when we came out of the rotunda the other four went to Salamis and fetched Leon, but I went quietly home. For which I might have lost my life, had not the power of the Thirty shortly afterwards come to an end. And many will witness to my words.

Now, do you really imagine that I could have survived all these years, if I had led a public life, supposing that like a good man I had always maintained the right and had made justice, as I ought, the first thing? No, indeed, men of Athens, neither I nor any other man. But I have been always the same in all my actions, public as well as private, and never have I yielded any base compliance to those who are slanderously termed my disciples, or to any other. Not that I have any regular disciples. But if any one likes to come and hear me while I am pursuing my mission, whether he be young or old, he is not excluded. Nor do I converse only with those who pay; but any one, whether he be rich or poor, may ask and answer me and listen to my words; and whether he turns out to be a bad man or a good one, neither result can be justly imputed to me; for I never taught or professed to teach him anything. And if any one says that he has ever learned or heard anything from me in private which all the world has not heard, let me tell you that he is lying.

But I shall be asked, Why do people delight in continually conversing with you? I have told you already, Athenians, the whole truth about this matter: they like to hear the cross-examination of the pretenders to wisdom; there is amusement in it. Now, this duty of cross-examining other men has been imposed upon me by God; and has been signified to me by oracles, visions, and in every way in which the will of divine power was ever intimated to any one. This is true, O Athenians; or, if not true, would be soon refuted. If I am or have been corrupting the youth, those of them who are now grown up and have become sensible that I gave them bad advice in the days of their youth should come forward as accusers, and take their revenge; or if they do not like to come themselves, some of their relatives, fathers, brothers or other kinsmen, should say what evil their families have suffered at my hands. Now is their time. Many of them I see in the court. There is Crito, who is of the same age and of the same deme[2] with myself, and there is Critobulus, his son, whom I also see. Then again there is Lysanias of Sphettus, who is the father of Aeschines—he is present; and also there is Antiphon of Cephisus, who is the father of Epigenes; and there are the brothers of several who have associated with me. There is Nicostratus the son of Theosdotides, and the brother of Theodotus (now Theodotus himself is dead, and therefore he, at any rate, will not seek to stop him); and there is Paralus the son of Demodocus, who had a brother Theages; and Adeimantus the son of Ariston, whose brother Plato is present; and Aeantodorus, who is the brother of Apollodorus, whom I also see. I might mention a great many others, some of whom Meletus should have produced as witnesses in the course of his speech; and let him still produce them, if he has forgotten—I will make way for him. And let him say, if he has any testimony of the sort which he can produce. Nay, Athenians, the very opposite is the truth. For all these are ready to witness on behalf of the corrupter, of the injurer of their kindred, as Meletus and Anytus call me; not the corrupted youth only—there might have been a motive for that—but their uncorrupted elder relatives. Why should they too support me with their testimony? Why, indeed, except for the sake of truth and justice, and because they know that I am speaking the truth, and that Meletus is a liar.

Well, Athenians, this and the like of this is all the defense which I have to offer. Yet a word more. Perhaps there may be some one who is offended at me, when he calls to mind how he himself on a similar, or even a less serious occasion, prayed and entreated the judges with many tears, and how he produced his children in court, which was a moving spectacle, together with a host of relations and friends; whereas I, who am probably in danger of my life, will do none of these things. The contrast may occur to his mind, and he may be set against me, and vote in anger because he is displeased at me on this account. Now, if there be such a person among you—mind, I do not say that there is—to him I may fairly reply: My friend, I am a man, and like other men, a creature of flesh and blood, and not "of wood or stone," as Homer says; and I have a family, yes, and sons, O Athenians, three in number, one almost a man, and two others who are still young; and yet I will not bring any of them hither in order to petition you for an acquittal. And why not? Not from any self-assertion or want of respect for you. Whether I am or am not afraid of death is another question, of which I will not now

---

[2] A district.

speak. But, having regard to public opinion, I feel that such conduct would be discreditable to myself, and to you, and to the whole State. One who has reached my years, and who has a name for wisdom, ought not to demean himself. Whether this opinion of me be deserved or not, at any rate the world has decided that Socrates is in some way superior to other men. And if those among you who are said to be superior in wisdom and courage, and any other virtue, demean themselves in this way, how shameful is their conduct! I have seen men of reputation, when they have been condemned, behaving in the strangest manner: they seemed to fancy that they were going to suffer something dreadful if they died and that they could be immortal if you only allowed them to live; and I think that such are a dishonor to the State and that any stranger coming in would have said of them that the most eminent men of Athens, to whom the Athenians themselves give honor and command, are no better than women. And I say that these things ought not to be done by those of us who have a reputation; and if they are done, you ought not to permit them; you ought rather to show that you are far more disposed to condemn the man who gets up a doleful scene and makes the city ridiculous, than him who holds his peace.

But, setting aside the question of public opinion, there seems to be something wrong in asking a favor of a judge, and thus procuring an acquittal, instead of informing and convincing him. For his duty is, not to make a present of justice, but to give judgment; and he has sworn that he will judge according to the laws, and not according to his own good pleasure; and we ought not to encourage you, nor should you allow yourselves to be encouraged, in this habit of perjury—there can be no piety in that. Do not then require me to do what I consider dishonorable and impious and wrong, especially now, when I am being tried for impiety on the indictment of Meletus. For if, O men of Athens, by force of persuasion and entreaty I could overpower your oaths, then I should be teaching you to believe that there are no gods, and in defending should simply convict myself of the charge of not believing in them. But that is not so—far otherwise. For I do believe that there are gods, and in a sense higher than that in which any of my accusers believe in them. And to you and to God I commit my cause, to be determined by you as is best for you and me.

There are many reasons why I am not grieved, O men of Athens, at the vote of condemnation. I expected it, and am only surprised that the votes are so nearly equal; for I had thought that the majority against me would have been far larger; but now, had thirty votes gone over to the other side, I should have been acquitted. And I may say, I think, that I have escaped Meletus. I may say more; for without the assistance of Anytus and Lycon, any one may see that he would not have had a fifth part of the votes, as the law requires, in which case he would have incurred a fine of a thousand drachmae.

And so he proposes death as the penalty. And what shall I propose on my part, O men of Athens? Clearly that which is my due. And what is my due? What returns shall be made to the man who has never had the wit to be idle during his whole life; but has been careless of what the many care for—wealth, and family interests, and military offices, and speaking in the assembly, and magistracies, and plots, and parties. Reflecting that I was really too honest a man to be a politician and live, I did not go where I could do no good to you or to myself; but where I could do the greatest good privately to every one of you, thither I went, and sought to persuade every man among you that he must look to himself, and seek virtue and wisdom before he looks to his private interests, and look to the State before he looks to the interests of the State; and that this should be the order which he observes in all his actions. What shall be done to such an one? Doubtless some good thing, O men of Athens, if he has his reward; and the good should be of a kind suitable to him. What would be a reward suitable to a poor man who is your benefactor, and who desires leisure that he may instruct you? There can be no reward so fitting as maintenance in the Prytaneum,[3] O men of Athens, a reward which he deserves far more than the citizen who has won the prize at Olympia in the horse or chariot race, whether the chariots were drawn by two horses or by many. For I am in want, and he has enough; and he only gives you the appearance of happiness, and I give you the reality. And if I am to estimate the penalty fairly, I should say that maintenance in the Prytaneum is the just return.

Perhaps you think that I am braving you in what I am saying now, as in what I said before about the tears and prayers. But this is not so. I speak rather because I am convinced that I never intentionally wronged any one, although I cannot convince you—the time has been too short: if there were a law at Athens, as there is in other cities, that a capital cause should not be decided in one day, then I believe that I should have convinced you. But I cannot in a moment refute great slanders; and, as I am convinced that I never wronged another, I will assuredly not wrong myself. I will not say of myself that I deserve any evil, or propose any penalty. Why should I? Because I am afraid of the penalty of death which Meletus proposes? When I do not know whether death is a good or an evil, why should I propose a penalty which would certainly be an evil? Shall I say imprisonment? And why should I live in prison, and be the slave of the magistrate of the year—of the Eleven? Or shall the penalty be a fine, and imprisonment until the fine is paid? There is the same

[3] A public building used as a meeting place for the administrative body of the community.

objection. I should have to lie in prison, for money I have none, and cannot pay. And if I say exile (and this may possibly be the penalty which you will affix), I must indeed be blinded by the love of life, if I am so irrational as to expect that when you, who are my own citizens, cannot endure my discourses and words, and have found them so grievous and odious that you will have no more of them, others are likely to endure me. No indeed, men of Athens, that is not very likely. And what a life should I lead, at my age, wandering from city to city, ever changing my place of exile, and always being driven out! For I am quite sure that wherever I go, there, as here, the young men will flock to me; and if I drive them away, their elders will drive me out at their request; and if I let them come, their fathers and friends will drive me out for their sakes.

Some one will say: Yes, Socrates, but cannot you hold your tongue, and then you may go into a foreign city, and no one will interfere with you? Now, I have great difficulty in making you understand my answer to this. For if I tell you that to do as you say would be a disobedience to the God, and therefore that I cannot hold my tongue, you will not believe that I am serious; and if I say again that daily to discourse about virtue, and of those other things about which you hear me examining myself and others, is the greatest good of man, and that the unexamined life is not worth living, you are still less likely to believe me. Yet I say what is true, although a thing of which it is hard for me persuade you. Also, I have never been accustomed to think that I deserve to suffer any harm. Had I money I might have estimated the offense at what I was able to pay, and not have been much the worse. But I have none, and therefore I must ask you to proportion the fine to my means. Well, perhaps I could afford a mina, and therefore I propose that penalty: Plato, Crito, Critobulus, and Apollodorus, my friends here, bid me say thirty minae, and they will be the sureties. Let thirty minae be the penalty; for which sum they will be ample security to you.

Not much time will be gained, O Athenians, in return for the evil name which you will get from the detractors of the city, who will say that you killed Socrates, a wise man; for they will call me wise, even though I am not wise, when they want to reproach you. If you had waited a little while, your desire would have been fulfilled in the course of nature. For I am far advanced in years, as you may perceive, and not far from death. I am speaking now not to all of you, but only to those who have condemned me to death. And I have another thing to say to them: You think that I was convicted because I had no words of the sort which would have procured my acquittal—I mean, if I had thought fit to leave nothing undone or unsaid. Not so; the deficiency which led to my conviction was not of words—certainly not. But I had not the boldness or impudence or inclination to address you as you would have liked me to do, weeping and wailing and lamenting, and saying and doing many things which you have been accustomed to hear from others, and which, as I maintain, are unworthy of me. I thought at the time that I ought not to do anything common or mean when in danger: nor do I now repent of the style of my defense; I would rather die having spoken after my manner, than speak in your manner and live. For neither in war nor yet at law ought I or any man to use every way of escaping death. Often in battle there can be no doubt that if a man will throw away his arms, and fall on his knees before his pursuers, he may escape death; and in other dangers there are other ways of escaping death, if a man is willing to say and do anything. The difficulty, my friends, is not to avoid death, but to avoid unrighteousness; for that runs faster than death. I am old and move slowly, and the slower runner has overtaken me, and my accusers are keen and quick, and the faster runner, who is unrighteousness, has overtaken them. And now I depart hence condemned by you to suffer the penalty of death,—they too go their ways condemned by the truth to suffer the penalty of villainy and wrong; and I must abide by my award—let them abide by theirs. I suppose that these things may be regarded as fated,—and I think that they are well.

And now, O men who have condemned me, I would fain prophesy to you; for I am about to die, and in the hour of death men are gifted with prophetic power. And I prophesy to you who are my murderers, that immediately after my departure punishment far heavier than you have inflicted on me will surely await you. Me you have killed because you wanted to escape the accuser, and not to give an account of your lives. But that will not be as you suppose: far otherwise. For I say that there will be more accusers of you than there are now; accusers whom hitherto I have restrained: and as they are younger they will be more inconsiderate with you, and you will be more offended at them. If you think that by killing men you can prevent some one from censuring your evil lives, you are mistaken; that is not a way of escape which is either possible or honorable; the easiest and the noblest way is not to be disabling others, but to be improving yourselves. This is the prophecy which I utter before my departure to the judges who have condemned me.

Friends, who would have acquitted me, I would like also to talk with you about the thing which has come to pass, while the magistrates are busy, and before I go to the place at which I must die. Stay then a little, for we may as well talk with one another while there is time. You are my friends, and I should like to show you the meaning of this event which has happened to me. O my judges—for you I may truly call judges—I should like to tell you of a wonderful circumstance. Hitherto the divine faculty of which the internal oracle is the source has constantly been in the habit of opposing me even about trifles, if I was going to make a slip or error in any matter; and now as you see there has come upon me that which may be thought, and is generally believed to be, the last and worst evil. But the oracle made no sign of opposition, either when I was leaving my house in the morning, or when I was on my way to the court, or while I was speaking, at anything which I was going to say; and yet I have often been stopped in the middle of a speech, but now in nothing I either said or did touching the matter in hand has the oracle opposed me. What do I take to be the explanation of this silence? I will tell you. It is an intimation that what has happened to me is a good, and that those of us who think that death is an evil are in error. For the customary sign would surely have opposed me had I been going to evil and not to good.

Let us reflect in another way, and we shall see that there is great reason to hope that death is a good; for one of two things—either death is a state of nothingness and utter unconsciousness, or, as men say, there is a change and migration of the soul from this world to another. Now, if you suppose that there is no consciousness, but a sleep like the sleep of him who is undisturbed even by dreams, death will be an unspeakable gain. For if a person were to select the night in which his sleep was undisturbed even by dreams, and were to compare with this the other days and nights of his life, and then were to tell us how many days and nights he had passed in the course of his life better and more pleasantly than this one, I think that any man, I will not say a private man, but even the great king will not find many such days or nights, when compared with the others. Now, if death be of such a nature, I say that to die is gain; for eternity is then only a single night. But if death is the journey to another place, and there, as men say, all the dead abide,[4] what good, O my friends and judges, can be greater than this? If, indeed, when the pilgrim arrives in the world below, he is delivered from the professors of justice in this world, and finds the true judges who are said to give judgment there, Minos and Rhadamanthus and Aeacus and Triptolemus, and other sons of God who were righteous in their own life, that pilgrimage will be worth making. What would not a man give if he might converse with Orpheus and Musaeus and Hesiod and Homer? Nay, if this be true, let me die again and again. I myself, too, shall have a wonderful interest in there meeting and conversing with Palamedes, and Ajax the son of Telamon, and any other ancient hero who has suffered death through an unjust judgment; and there will be no small pleasure, as I think, in comparing my own sufferings with theirs. Above

---

[4] A reference to Hades, for the Greeks not a place of punishment but the dwelling place for all souls after death.

all, I shall then be able to continue my search into true and false knowledge; as in this world, so also in the next; and I shall find out who is wise, and who pretends to be wise, and is not. What would not a man give, O judges, to be able to examine the leader of the great Trojan expedition; or Odysseus or Sisyphus, or numberless others, men and women too! What infinite delight would there be in conversing with them and asking them questions! In another world they do not put a man to death for asking questions: assuredly not. For besides being happier than we are, they will be immortal, if what is said is true.

Wherefore, O judges, be of good cheer about death, and know of a certainty, that no evil can happen to a good man, either in life or after death. He and his are not neglected by the gods; nor has my own approaching end happened by mere chance. But I see clearly that the time had arrived when it was better for me to die and be released from trouble; wherefore the oracle gave no sign. For which reason, also, I am not angry with my condemners, or with my accusers; they have done me no harm, although they did not mean to do me any good; and for this I may gently blame them.

Still, I have a favor to ask of them. When my sons are grown up, I would ask you, O my friends, to punish them; and I would have you trouble them, as I have troubled you, if they seem to care about riches, or anything, more than about virtue; or if they pretend to be something when they are really nothing,—then reprove them, as I have reproved you, for not caring about that for which they ought to care, and thinking that they are something when they are really nothing. And if you do this, both I and my sons will have received justice at your hands.

The hour of departure has arrived, and we go our ways—I to die, and you to live. Which is better God only knows.

For Discussion

1. What are the charges Socrates answers in the *Apology?*
2. How should a man live, according to Socrates? (How does his ethical philosophy compare with Thoreau's?)
3. How valid is Socrates' contention that the taker of life injures himself more than he injures his victim? Discuss his rationale in terms of capital punishment today.
4. What is Socratic wisdom?
5. What explanation does Socrates give for his failure to engage in politics? Apply this to today.
6. Why wouldn't Socrates plead for his life or accept exile?
7. Examine the nature of Socrates' self-criticism. How is it consistent with his philosophy?

8. In what ways can you defend the Athenians' attack against Socrates?
9. Discuss the metaphor of the gadfly.
10. Discursive argumentation is usually supported by facts. On what does Socrates base his defense?
11. What argument can you make for including the *Apology* in "The Reflective NO"?
12. Consider Socrates' special audience. Find examples of language—impassioned, ironic, or otherwise—which reveal his attitude toward this audience.

THOMAS JEFFERSON

Declaration of Independence

Thomas Jefferson, the third President of the United States, was born into an aristocratic Virginia family in 1743. One of the most educated men of his time and class, Jefferson was only thirty-three years old when he was chosen chairman of the committee to frame the Declaration of Independence. Jefferson was genuinely devoted to the idea of the elimination of tyranny of all types, including "the tyranny of the majority." He was a friend of Thomas Paine, whose liberal influence can be seen in Jefferson's writing, notably on slavery and religion. Jefferson died in 1826.

The unanimous declaration of the thirteen
United States of America, in Congress, July 4, 1776

When, in the course of human events, it becomes necessary for one people to dissolve the political bands which have connected them with another, and to assume among the powers of the earth the separate and equal station to which the laws of nature and of nature's God entitle them, a decent respect to the opinions of mankind requires that they should declare the causes which impel them to the separation.

We hold these truths to be self-evident: That all men are created equal; that they are endowed by their Creator with certain inalienable rights; that among these are life, liberty, and the pursuit of happiness. That, to secure these rights, governments are instituted among men, deriving their just powers from the consent of the governed; that, whenever any form of government becomes destructive of these ends, it is the right of the people to alter or to abolish it, and to institute a new government, laying its foundation on such principles, and organizing its powers in such form, as to them shall seem most likely to effect their safety and happiness. Prudence, indeed, will dictate that governments long established should not be changed for light and transient causes; and accordingly all experience hath shown that mankind are more disposed to suffer, while evils are sufferable, than to right themselves by abolishing the forms to which they are accustomed. But when a long train of abuses and usurpations, pursuing invariably the same object, evinces a design to reduce them under absolute despotism, it is their right, it is their duty, to throw off such government and to provide new guards for their future security. Such has been the patient suffering of these colonies, and such is now the necessity which constrains them to alter their former systems of government. The history of the present king of Great Britain is a history of repeated injuries and usurpations, all having in direct object the establishment of an absolute tyranny over these states. To prove this, let facts be submitted to a candid world.

He has refused his assent to laws the most wholesome and necessary for the public good.

He has forbidden his governors to pass laws of immediate and pressing importance, unless suspended in their operation till his assent should be obtained, and, when so suspended, he has utterly neglected to attend to them.

He has refused to pass other laws for the accommodation of large districts of people, unless those people would relinquish the right of representation in the legislature—a right inestimable to them and formidable to tyrants only.

He has called together legislative bodies, at places unusual, uncomfortable, and distant from the repository of their public records, for the sole purpose of fatiguing them into compliance with his measures.

He has dissolved representative houses repeatedly for opposing with manly firmness his invasions on the rights of the people.

He has refused for a long time after such dissolutions to cause others to be elected; whereby the legislative powers, incapable of annihilation, have returned to the people at large for their exercise: the state remaining, in the meantime, exposed to all the dangers of invasion from without and convulsions within.

He has endeavored to prevent the population of these states; for that purpose obstructing the laws for naturalization of foreigners; refusing to pass others to encourage their migration hither, and raising the conditions of new appropriations of lands.

He has obstructed the administration of justice by refusing his assent to laws for establishing his judiciary powers.

He has made judges dependent on his will alone for the tenure of their offices and the amount and payment of their salaries.

He has erected a multitude of new offices and sent hither swarms of officers to harass our people and eat out their substance.

He has kept among us, in times of peace, standing armies without the consent of our legislatures.

He has affected to render the military independent of and superior to the civil power.

He has combined with others to subject us to a jurisdiction foreign to our constitutions and unacknowledged by our laws, giving his assent to their acts of pretended legislation:

For quartering large bodies of armed troops among us;

For protecting them by a mock trial from punishment for any murders which they should commit on the inhabitants of these states;

For cutting off our trade with all parts of the world;

For imposing taxes on us without our consent;

For depriving us in many cases of the benefits of trial by jury;

For transporting us beyond seas to be tried for pretended offenses;

For abolishing the free system of English laws in a neighboring province, establishing therein an arbitrary government, and enlarging its boundaries so as to render it at once an example and fit instrument for introducing the same absolute rule into these colonies;

For taking away our charters, abolishing our most valuable laws, and altering fundamentally the forms of our government;

For suspending our own legislatures and declaring themselves invested with power to legislate for us in all cases whatsoever.

He has abdicated government here by declaring us out of his protection and waging war against us.

He has plundered our seas, ravaged our coasts, burnt our towns and destroyed the lives our our people.

He is at this time transporting large armies of foreign mercenaries to complete the work of death, desolation, and tyranny already begun, with circumstances of cruelty and perfidy scarcely parallelled in the most barbarous ages and totally unworthy of the head of a civilized nation.

He has constrained our fellow citizens taken captive upon the high seas to bear arms against their country, to become the executioners of their friends and brethren, or to fall themselves by their hands.

He has excited domestic insurrection amongst us, and has endeavored to bring on the inhabitants of our frontiers the merciless Indian savages, whose known rule of warfare is an undistinguished destruction of all ages, sexes, and conditions.

In every stage of these oppressions we have petitioned for redress, in the most humble terms; our repeated petitions have been answered only by repeated injury. A prince whose character is thus marked by every act which may define a tyrant is unfit to be the ruler of a free people.

Nor have we been wanting in attention to our British brethren. We have warned them, from time to time, of attempts by their legislature to extend an unwarrantable jurisdiction over us. We have reminded them of the circumstances of our emigration and settlement here. We have appealed to their native justice and magnanimity; and we have conjured them by the ties of our common kindred, to disavow these usurpations, which would inevitably interrupt our connections and correspondence. They, too, have been deaf to the voice of justice and consanguinity. We must, therefore, acquiesce in the necessity which denounces our separation, and hold them, as we hold the rest of mankind, enemies in war; in peace, friends.

We, therefore, the representatives of the United States of America, in general congress assembled, appealing to the Supreme Judge of the World for the rectitude of our intentions, do, in the name and by the authority of the good people of these colonies, solemnly publish and declare that these united colonies are, and of right ought to be, free and independent states; that they are absolved from all allegiance to the British crown, and that all political connection between them and the state of Great Britain is, and ought to be, totally dissolved; and that as free and independent states they have full power to levy war, conclude peace, contract alliances, establish commerce, and to do all other acts and things which independent states may of right do. And for the support of this declaration, with a firm reliance on the protection of Divine Providence we mutually pledge to each other our lives, our fortunes, and our sacred honor.

For Discussion

1. The Declaration of Independence is a good example of deductive argument, moving from general assumptions to specific conclusions and using supporting examples along the way. Discuss the assumptions which are "self-evident."
2. When is revolution justified? Do you agree?
3. Discuss the rationale for the sequence in which the grievances are listed.
4. In what way does the Declaration go beyond its historical boundaries and apply to events today? Look at both the underlying principles and the specific grievances.
5. In earlier drafts of the Declaration, the language was much more impassioned. How does the formal language of the present version affect its meaning?

FIRST U. S. CONGRESS

Bill of Rights

The authors of the Constitution had a healthy distrust of governments, even of the new one they were then formulating. When it became apparent, in 1789, that the Constitution could not be ratified unless a bill of rights was assured, the First Congress proposed twelve amendments, ten of which were speedily adopted. (The other two, dealing with matters of representation and compensation of Congressmen, were dropped because they had nothing to do with civil rights.) Reflecting the eighteenth-century belief in inherent natural rights, the Bill of Rights spells out safeguards against destruction of individual liberty by governmental power.

Article I. Congress shall make *no* law respecting an establishment of religion, or prohibiting the free exercise thereof; or abridging the freedom of speech or of the press; or the right of the people peaceably to assemble, and to petition the Government for a redress of grievances.

Article II. A well-regulated militia being necessary to the security of a free state, the right of the people to keep and bear arms shall *not* be infringed.

Article III. *No* soldier shall, in time of peace, be quartered in any house, without the consent of the owner, *nor* in the time of war, but in a manner to be prescribed by law.

Article IV. The right of the people to be secure in their persons, houses, papers, and effects, against unreasonable searches and seizures, shall *not* be violated, and *no* warrants shall issue, but upon probable cause, supported by oath or affirmation, and particularly describing the place to be searched, and the persons or things to be seized.

Article V. *No* person shall be held to answer for a capital, or otherwise infamous crime, unless on a presentment or indictment of a grand jury, except in cases arising in the land or naval forces, or in the militia, when in actual service in time of war or public danger; *nor* shall any person be subject for the same offense to be twice put in jeopardy of life or limb; *nor* shall be compelled in any criminal case to be a witness against himself, *nor* be deprived of life, liberty, or property, without due process of law; *nor* shall private property be taken for public use, without just compensation.

Article VI. In all criminal prosecutions, the accused shall enjoy the right to a speedy and public trial, by an impartial jury of the state and district wherein the crime shall have been committed, which district shall have been previously ascertained by law, and to be informed of the nature and cause of the accusation; to be confronted with the witnesses against him; to have compulsory process for obtaining witnesses in his favor, and to have the assistance of counsel for his defense.

Article VII. In suits at common law, where the value in controversy shall exceed twenty dollars, the right of trial by jury shall be preserved, and *no* fact tried by a jury shall be otherwise re-examined in any court of the United States than according to the rules of the common law.

Article VIII. Excessive bail shall *not* be required, *nor* excessive fines imposed, *nor* cruel and unusual punishments inflicted.

Article IX. The enumeration in the Constitution, of certain rights, shall *not* be construed to deny or disparage others retained by the people.

Article X. The powers *not* delegated to the United States by the Constitution, *nor* prohibited by it to the States, are reserved to the States respectively, or to the people.

For Discussion

1. What do you understand each article to mean? What precise limits, if any, do you think each imposes on governmental power? Which are clear, and which are vague?
2. Assume that the amendments were adopted in a sequence of priority, and argue for or against this ranking.
3. Which amendments do you think need changing or eliminating? What new ones would you add? Why?
4. What inherent natural rights are embodied in the Bill of Rights?
5. A recent survey revealed that more than 80 percent of those polled would reject the Bill of Rights if it were presented today. Supply an explanation for this apparent paradox.
6. Give examples of situations you see today in which government has trespassed against one or more of the amendments.

ALEXIS de TOCQUEVILLE

The Tyranny of the Majority

Alexis de Tocqueville, French historian and political scientist, was born in 1805. Bored with his duties as a magistrate, he came to the United States to study penal methods, and, as a result of his travels, wrote his famous analysis of American politics, *Democracy in America*, in 1835. The book, from which the following material is excerpted, brought him immediate recognition and, ultimately, the position of Minister of Foreign Affairs in the Second Republic.

I hold it to be an impious and an execrable maxim that, politically speaking, a people has a right to do whatsoever it pleases; and yet I have asserted that all authority originates in the will of the majority. Am I, then, in contradiction with myself?

A general law—which bears the name of Justice—has been made and sanctioned, not only by a majority of this or that people, but by a majority of mankind. The rights of every people are consequently confined within the limits of what is just. A nation may be considered in the light of a jury which is empowered to represent society at large, and to apply the great and general law of Justice. Ought such a jury, which represents society, to have more power than the society in which the laws it applies originate?

When I refuse to obey an unjust law, I do not contest the right which the majority has of commanding, but I simply appeal from the sovereignty of the people to the sovereignty of mankind. It has been asserted that a people can never entirely outstep the boundaries of justice and of reason in those affairs which are more peculiarly its own; and that consequently full power may fearlessly be given to the majority by which it is represented. But this language is that of a slave.

A majority taken collectively may be regarded as a being whose opinions, and most frequently whose interests, are opposed to those of another being, which is styled a minority. If it be admitted that a man, possessing absolute power, may misuse that power by wronging his adversaries, why should a majority not be liable to the same reproach? Men are not apt to change their characters by agglomeration; nor does their patience in the presence of obstacles increase with the consciousness of their strength.[1] And for these reasons I can never willingly invest any number of my fellow-creatures with that unlimited authority which I should refuse to any one of them.

I do not think that it is possible to combine several principles in the same government, so as at the same time to maintain freedom, and really to oppose them to one another. The form of government which is usually termed *mixed* has always appeared to me to be a mere chimera. Accurately speaking there is no such thing as a mixed government (with the meaning usually given to that word), because in all communities some one principle of action may be discovered, which preponderates over the others. England in the last century, which has been more especially cited as an example of this form of government, was in point of fact an essentially aristocratic state, although it comprised very powerful elements of democracy: for the laws and customs of the country were such, that the aristocracy could not but preponderate in the end, and subject the direction of public affairs to its own will. The error arose from too much attention being paid to the actual struggle which was going on between the nobles and the people, without considering the probable issue of the contest, which was in reality the important point. When a community really has a mixed government, that is to say, when it is equally divided between two adverse principles, it must either pass through a revolution, or fall into complete dissolution.

I am therefore of the opinion that some one social power must always be made to predominate over the others; but I think that liberty is endangered when this power is checked by no obstacles which may retard its course, and force it to moderate its own vehemence.

Unlimited power is in itself a bad and dangerous thing; human beings are not competent to exercise it with discretion; and God alone can be omnipotent, because his wisdom and his justice are always equal to his power. But no power upon earth is so worthy of honor for itself, or of reverential obedience to the rights which it represents, that I would consent to admit its uncontrolled and all-predominant authority. When I see the right and the means of absolute command are conferred on a

---

[1] No one will assert that a people cannot forcibly wrong another people: but parties may be looked upon as lesser nations within a greater one, and they are aliens to each other: if therefore it be admitted that a nation can act tyrannically towards another nation, it cannot be denied that a party may do the same towards another party.

people or upon a king, upon an aristocracy or a democracy, a monarchy or a republic, I recognize the germ of tyranny, and I journey onward to a land of more hopeful institutions.

In my opinion the main evil of the present democratic institutions of the United States does not arise, as is often asserted in Europe, from their weakness, but from their overpowering strength; and I am not so much alarmed at the excessive liberty which reigns in that country, as at the very inadequate securities which exist against tyranny.

When an individual or a party is wronged in the United States, to whom can he apply for redress? If to public opinion, public opinion constitutes the majority; if to the legislature, it represents the majority, and implicitly obeys its injunctions; if to the executive power, it is appointed by the majority and remains a passive tool in its hands; the public troops consist of the majority under arms; the jury is the majority invested with the right of hearing judicial cases; and in certain States even the judges are elected by the majority. However iniquitous or absurd the evil of which you complain may be, you must submit to it as well as you can.[2]

If, on the other hand, a legislative power could be so constituted as to

---

[2] A striking instance of the excesses which may be occasioned by the despotism of the majority occurred at Baltimore in the year 1812. At that time the war was very popular in Baltimore. A journal which had taken the other side of the question excited the indignation of the inhabitants by its opposition. The populace assembled, broke the printing-presses, and attacked the houses of the newspaper-editors. The militia was called out, but no one obeyed the call; and the only means of saving the poor wretches who were threatened by the frenzy of the mob, was to throw them into prison as common malefactors. But even this precaution was ineffectual; the mob collected again during the night; the magistrates again made a vain attempt to call out the militia; the prison was forced, one of the newspaper-editors was killed upon the spot, and the others were left for dead; the guilty parties were acquitted by the jury when they were brought to trial.

I said one day to an inhabitant of Pennsylvania, "Be so good as to explain to me how it happens, that in a State founded by Quakers, and celebrated for its toleration, freed Blacks are not allowed to exercise civil rights. They pay the taxes; is it not fair that they should have a vote?"

"You insult us," replied my informant, "if you imagine that our legislators could have committed so gross an act of injustice and intolerance."

"What, then, the Blacks possess the right of voting in this country?"

"Without the smallest doubt."

"How comes it, then, that at the polling-booth this morning I did not perceive a single Negro in the whole meeting?"

"This is not the fault of the law: the Negroes have an undisputed right of voting; but they voluntarily abstain from making their appearance."

"A very pretty piece of modesty on their parts!" rejoined I.

"Why, the truth is that they are not disinclined to vote, but they are afraid of being maltreated; in this country the law is sometimes unable to maintain its authority, without the support of the majority. But in this case the majority entertains very strong prejudices against the Blacks, and the magistrates are unable to protect them in the exercise of their legal privileges."

"What, then, the majority claims the right not only of making the laws, but of breaking the laws it has made?"

represent the majority without necessarily being the slave of its passions; an executive, so as to retain a certain degree of uncontrolled authority; and a judiciary, so as to remain independent of the two other powers; a government would be formed which would still be democratic without incurring any risk of tyrannical abuse.

I do not say that tyrannical abuses frequently occur in America at the present day; but I maintain that no sure barrier is established against them, and that the causes which mitigate the government are to be found in the circumstances and the manners of the country more than in its laws.

A distinction must be drawn between tyranny and arbitrary power. Tyranny may be exercised by means of the law, and in that case it is not arbitrary: arbitrary power may be exercised for the good of the community at large, in which case it is not tyrannical. Tyranny usually employs arbitrary means, but, if necessary, it can rule without them.

In the United States the unbounded power of the majority, which is favorable to the legal despotism of the legislature, is likewise favorable to the arbitrary authority of the magistrate. The majority has an entire control over the law when it is made and when it is executed; and as it possesses an equal authority over those who are in power, and the community at large, it considers public officers as its passive agents, and readily confides the task of serving its designs to their vigilance. The details of their office and the privileges which they are to enjoy are rarely defined beforehand; but the majority treats them, as a master does his servants, when they are always at work in his sight, and he has the power of directing or reprimanding them at every instant.

In general the American functionaries are far more independent than the French civil officers within the sphere which is prescribed to them. Sometimes, even, they are allowed by the popular authority to exceed those bounds; and as they are protected by the opinion, and backed by the cooperation, of the majority, they venture upon such manifestations of their power as astonish a European. By this means habits are formed in the heart of a free country which may some day prove fatal to its liberties.

It is in the examination of the display of public opinion in the United States, that we clearly perceive how far the power of the majority surpasses all the powers with which we are acquainted in Europe. Intellectual principles exercise an influence which is so invisible and often so inappreciable, that they baffle the toils of oppression. At the present time the most absolute monarchs in Europe are unable to prevent certain notions, which are opposed to their authority, from circulating in secret throughout their dominions, and even in their courts. Such is not the case in America; as long as the majority is still undecided, discussion is carried on; but as soon as its decision is irrevocably pronounced, a submissive silence is observed; and the friends, as well as the opponents, of the measure, unite in assenting to its propriety. The reason of this is perfectly clear: no monarch is so absolute as to combine all the powers of society in his own hands, and to conquer all opposition, with the energy of a majority, which is invested with the right of making and of executing the laws.

The authority of a king is purely physical, and it controls the actions of the subject without subduing his private will; but the majority possesses a power which is physical and moral at the same time; it acts upon the will as well as upon the actions of men, and it represses not only all contest, but all controversy.

I know no country in which there is so little true independence of mind and freedom of discussion as in America. In any constitutional state in Europe every sort of religious and political theory may be advocated and propagated abroad; for there is no country in Europe so subdued by any single authority, as not to contain citizens who are ready to protect the man who raises his voice in the cause of truth, from the consequences of his hardihood. If he is unfortunate enough to live under an absolute government, the people is upon his side; if he inhabits a free country, he may find a shelter behind the authority of the throne, if he require one. The aristocratic part of society supports him in some countries, and the democracy in others. But in a nation where democratic institutions exist, organized like those of the United States, there is but one sole authority, one single element of strength and of success, with nothing beyond it.

In America, the majority raises very formidable barriers to the liberty of opinion: within these barriers an author may write whatever he pleases, but he will repent it if he ever step beyond them. Not that he is exposed to the terrors of an *auto-da-fé*, but he is tormented by the slights and persecutions of daily obloquy. His political career is closed for ever, since he has offended the only authority which is able to promote his success. Every sort of compensation, even that of celebrity, is refused to him. Before he published his opinions, he imagined that he held them in common with many others; but no sooner has he declared them openly, than he is loudly censured by his overbearing opponents, whilst those who think, without having the courage to speak, like him, abandon him in silence. He yields at length, oppressed by the daily efforts he has been making, and he subsides into silence, as if he was tormented by remorse for having spoken the truth.

Fetters and headsmen were the coarse instruments which tyranny formerly employed; but the civilization of our age has refined the arts of despotism, which seemed however to have been sufficiently perfected before. The excesses of monarchical power had devised a variety of physical means of oppression: the democratic republics of the present day have rendered it as entirely an affair of the mind, as that will which it is intended to coerce. Under the absolute sway of an individual despot, the body was attacked in order to subdue the soul; and the soul escaped the blows which were directed against it, and rose superior to the attempt; but such is not the course adopted by tyranny in democratic republics; there the body is left free, and the soul is enslaved. The sovereign can no longer say, "You shall think as I do on pain of death;" but he says, "You are free to think differently from me, and to retain your life, your property, and all that you possess; but if such be your determination, you are henceforth an alien among your people. You may retain your civil rights, but they will be useless to you, for you will never be chosen by your fellow-citizens if you solicit their suffrages; and they will affect to scorn you, if you solicit their esteem. You will remain among men, but you will be deprived of the rights of mankind. Your fellow-creatures will shun you like an impure being; and those who are most persuaded of your innocence will abandon you too, lest they should be shunned in their turn. Go in peace! I have given you your life, but it is an existence incomparably worse than death."

Monarchical institutions have thrown an odium upon despotism; let us beware lest democratic republics should restore oppression, and should render it less odious and less degrading in the eyes of the many, by making it still more onerous to the few.

Works have been published in the proudest nations of the Old World, expressly intended to censure the vices and deride the follies of the times: Labruyère inhabited the palace of Louis XIV when he composed his chapter upon the Great, and Molière criticized the courtiers in the very pieces which were acted before the Court. But the ruling power in the United States is not to be made game of; the smallest reproach irritates its sensibility, and the slightest joke which has any foundation in truth renders it indignant; from the style of its language to the more solid virtues of its character, everything must be made the subject of encomium. No writer, whatever be his eminence, can escape from this tribute of adulation to his fellow-citizens. The majority lives in the perpetual practice of self-applause; and there are certain truths which the Americans can only learn from strangers or from experience.

If great writers have not at present existed in America, the reason is very simply given in these facts; there can be no literary genius without freedom of opinion, and freedom of opinion does not exist in America. The Inquisition has never been able to prevent a vast number of antireligious books from circulating in Spain. The empire of the majority succeeds much better in the United States, since it actually removes the wish of publishing them. Unbelievers are to be met with in America, but, to say the truth, there is no public organ of infidelity. Attempts have been made by some governments to protect the morality of nations by prohibiting licentious books. In the United States no one is punished for this sort of works, but no one is induced to write them; not because all the citizens are immaculate in their manners, but because the majority of the community is decent and orderly.

In these cases the advantages derived from the exercise of this power are unquestionable; and I am simply discussing the nature of the power itself. This irresistible authority is a constant fact, and its judicious exercise is an accidental occurrence.

For Discussion

1. Discuss the paradox in the opening paragraph.
2. What criterion does Tocqueville use to determine when a majority, as well as a minority, becomes tyrannical?
3. What reason does Tocqueville give to support his assertion that "one social power" should predominate?
4. Give reasons for agreeing or disagreeing with Tocqueville's preference for excessive liberty over excessive security.
5. Why does Tocqueville see the United States as being in danger of exercising too much power? What does he pose as an alternative to such a tyranny?
6. What danger does Tocqueville see in the independence of American functionaries?
7. How does freedom of discussion in America contrast with that in Europe?
8. Comment on the difference between the kind of oppression exercised by the older monarchial powers and that of present-day democracies.
9. Defend or reject the argument, stated in the last two paragraphs, concerning the lack of great controversial writing in America.
10. Look at the second footnote. What stylistic purpose is served by providing such information in footnote form rather than in the text itself?

CLARENCE DARROW

Address to the Prisoners in Cook County Jail

Although his eloquence in the courtroom earned him the title of The Great Defender, Clarence Darrow was a controversial figure because of his atheism, his socialism, his opposition to capital punishment, and his frequent support of other unpopular causes. After Darrow delivered the following lecture to the prisoners at Cook County Jail in Chicago in 1902, he was criticized by friends who thought the talk inappropriate for its audience. Darrow then had it printed in rather expensive pamphlet form and sold it for five cents, expressly because he believed the truth should be spoken to all people.

If I looked at jails and crimes and prisoners in the way the ordinary person does, I should not speak on this subject to you. The reason I talk to you on the question of crime, its cause and cure, is that I really do not in the least believe in crime. These is no such thing as a crime as the word is generally understood. I do not believe there is any sort of distinction between the real moral conditions of the people in and out of jail. One is just as good as the other. The people here can no more help being here than the people outside can avoid being outside. I do not believe that people are in jail because they deserve to be. They are in jail simply because they cannot avoid it on account of circumstances which are entirely beyond their control and for which they are in no way responsible.

I suppose a great many people on the outside would say I was doing you harm if they should hear what I say to you this afternoon, but you cannot be hurt a great deal anyway, so it will not matter. Good people outside would say that I was really teaching you things that were calculated to injure society, but it's worth while now and then to hear something different from what you ordinarily get from preachers and the like. These will tell you that you should be good and then you will get rich and be happy. Of course we know that people do not get rich by being good, and that is the reason why so many of you people try to get rich some other way, only you do not understand how to do it quite as well as the follow outside.

There are people who think that everything in this world is an accident. But really there is no such thing as an accident. A great many folks admit that many of the people in jail ought to be there, and many who are outside ought to be in. I think none of them ought to be here. There ought to be no jails; and if it were not for the fact that the people on the outside are so grasping and heartless in their dealings with the people on the inside, there would be no such institution as jails.

I do not want you to believe that I think all you people here are angels. I do not think that. You are people of all kinds, all of you doing the best you can—and that is evidently not very well. You are people of all kinds and conditions and under all circumstances. In one sense everybody is equally good and equally bad. We all do the best we can under the circumstances. But as to the exact things for which you are sent here, some of you are guilty and did the particular act because you needed the money. Some of you did it because you are in the habit of doing it, and some of you because you are born to it, and it comes to be as natural as it does, for instance, for me to be good.

Most of you probably have nothing against me, and most of you would treat me the same way as any other person would, probably better than some of the people on the outside would treat me, because you think I believe in you and they know I do not believe in them. While you would not have the least thing against me in the world, you might pick my pockets. I do not think all of you would, but I think some of you would. You would not have anything against me, but that's your profession, a few of you. Some of the rest of you, if my doors were unlocked, might come in if you saw anything you wanted—not out of any malice to me, but because that is your trade. There is no doubt there are quite a number of people in this jail who would pick my pockets. And still I know this—that when I get outside pretty nearly everybody picks my pocket. There may be some of you who would hold up a man on the street, if you did not happen to have something else to do, and needed the money; but when I want to light my house or my office the gas company holds me up. They charge me one dollar for something that is worth twenty-five cents. Still all these people are good people; they are pillars of society and support the churches, and they are respectable.

When I ride on the streetcars I am held up—I pay five cents for a ride that is worth two and a half cents, simply because a body of men have bribed the city council and the legislature, so that all the rest of us have to pay tribute to them.

If I do not want to fall into the clutches of the gas trust and choose to burn oil instead of gas, then good Mr. Rockefeller holds me up, and he uses a certain portion of his money to build universities and support churches which are engaged in telling us how to be good.

Some of you are here for obtaining property under false pretenses— yet I pick up a great Sunday paper and read the advertisements of a merchant prince—"Shirtwaists for 39 cents, marked down from $3.00."

When I read the advertisements in the paper I see they are all lies. When I want to get out and find a place to stand anywhere on the face of the earth, I find that it has all been taken up long ago before I came here, and before you came here, and somebody says, "Get off, swim into the lake, fly into the air; go anywhere, but get off." That is because these people have the police and they have the jails and the judges and the lawyers and the soldiers and all the rest of them to take care of the earth and drive everybody off that comes in their way.

A great many people will tell you that all this is true, but that it does not excuse you. These facts do not excuse some fellow who reaches into my pocket and takes out a five-dollar bill. The facts that the gas company bribes the members of the legislature from year to year, and fixes the law, so that all you people are compelled to be "fleeced" whenever you deal with them; the fact that the streetcar companies and the gas companies have control of the streets; and the fact that the landlords own all the earth—this, they say, has nothing to do with you.

Let us see whether there is any connection between the crimes of the respectable classes and your presence in the jail. Many of you people are in jail because you have really committed burglary; many of you, because you have stolen something. In the meaning of the law, you have taken some other person's property. Some of you have entered a store and carried off a pair of shoes because you did not have the price. Possibly some of you have committed murder. I cannot tell what all of you did. There are a great many people here who have done some of these things who really do not know themselves why they did them. I think I know why you did them—every one of you; you did these things because you were bound to do them. It looked to you at the time as if you had a chance to do them or not, as you saw fit; but still, after all, you had no choice. There may be people here who had some money in their pockets and who still went out and got some more money in a way society forbids. Now, you may not yourselves see exactly why it was you did this thing, but if you look at the question deeply enough and carefully enough you will see that there were circumstances that drove you to do exactly the thing which you did. You could not help it any more than we outside can help taking the positions that we take. The reformers who tell you to be good and you will be happy, and the people on the outside who have property to protect—they think that the only way to do it is by building jails and locking you up in cells on weekdays and praying for you Sundays.

I think that all of this has nothing whatever to do with right conduct. I think it is very easily seen what has to do with right conduct. Some so-called criminals—and I will use this word because it is handy, it means nothing to me—I speak of the criminals who get caught as distinguished from the criminals who catch them—some of these so-called criminals are in jail for their first offenses, but nine tenths of you are in jail because you did not have a good lawyer and, of course, you did not have a good lawyer because you did not have enough money to pay a good lawyer. There is no very great danger of a rich man going to jail.

. . .

First and last, people are sent to jail because they are poor. Sometimes, as I say, you may not need money at the particular time, but you wish to have thrifty forehanded habits, and do not always wait until you are in absolute want. Some of you people are perhaps plying the trade, the profession, which is called burglary. No man in his right senses will go into a strange house in the dead of night and prowl around with a dark lantern through unfamiliar rooms and take chances of his life, if he has plenty of the good things of the world in his own home. You would not take any such chances as that. If a man had clothes on his clothes-press and beefsteak in his pantry and money in the bank, he would not navigate around nights in houses where he knows nothing about the premises whatever. It always requires experience and education for this profession, and people who fit themselves for it are no more to blame than I am for being a lawyer. A man would not hold up another man on the street if he had plenty of money in his own pocket. He might do it if he had one dollar or two dollars, but he wouldn't if he had as much money as Mr. Rockefeller has. Mr. Rockefeller has a great deal better hold-up game than that.

The more that is taken from the poor by the rich, who have the chance to take it, the more poor people there are who are compelled to resort to these means for a livelihood. They may not understand it, they may not think so at once, but after all they are driven into that line of employment.

. . .

There is one way to cure all these offenses, and that is to give the people a chance to live. There is no other way, and there never was any other way since the world began; and the world is so blind and stupid that it will not see. If every man and woman and child in the world had a chance to make a decent, fair, honest living, there would be no jails and no lawyers and no courts. There might be some persons here or there with some peculiar formation of their brain, like Rockefeller, who would do these things simply to be doing them; but they would be very, very few, and those should be sent to a hospital and treated, and not sent to jail; and they would entirely disappear in the second generation, or at least in the third generation.

I am not talking pure theory. I will just give you two or three illustrations.

The English people once punished criminals by sending them away. They would load them on a ship and export them to Australia. England was owned by lords and nobles and rich people. They owned the whole earth over there, and the other people had to stay in the streets. They could not get a decent living. They used to take their criminals and send them to Australia—I mean the class of criminals who got caught. When these criminals got over there, and nobody else had come, they had the whole continent to run over, and so they could raise sheep and furnish their own meat, which is easier than stealing it. These criminals then became decent, respectable people because they had a chance to live. They did not commit any crimes. They were just like the English people who sent them there, only better. And in the second generation the descendants of those criminals were as good and respectable a class of people as there were on the face of the earth, and then they began building churches and jails themselves.

A portion of this country was settled in the same way, landing prisoners down on the southern coast; but when they got here and had a whole continent to run over and plenty of chances to make a living, they became respectable citizens, making their own living just like any other citizen in the world. But finally the descendants of the English aristocracy who sent the people over to Australia found out they were getting rich, and so they went over to get possession of the earth as they always do, and they organized land syndicates and got control of the land and ores, and then they had just as many criminals in Australia as they did in England. It was not because the world had grown bad; it was because the earth had been taken away from the people.

· · ·

Everybody makes his living along the lines of least resistance. A wise man who comes into a country early sees a great undeveloped land. For instance, our rich men twenty-five years ago saw that Chicago was small and knew a lot of people would come here and settle, and they readily saw that if they had all the land around here it would be worth a good deal, so they grabbed the land. You cannot be a landlord because somebody has got it all. You must find some other calling. In England and Ireland and Scotland less than five percent own all the land there is, and the people are bound to stay there on any kind of terms the landlords give. They must live the best they can, so they develop all these various professions—burglary, picking pockets, and the like.

Again, people find all sorts of ways of getting rich. These are diseases like everything else. You look at people getting rich, organizing trusts and making a million dollars, and somebody gets the disease and he starts out. He catches the mumps or the measles; he is not to blame, it is in the air. You will find men speculating beyond their means, because the mania of money-getting is taking possession of them. It is simply a disease—nothing more, nothing less. You cannot avoid catching it; but the fellows who have control of the earth have the advantage of you. See what the law is: when these men get control of things, they make the laws. They do not make the laws to protect anybody; courts are not instruments of justice. When your case gets into court it will make little difference whether you are guilty or innocent, but it's better if you have a smart lawyer. And you cannot have a smart lawyer unless you have money. First and last it's a question of money. Those men who own the earth make the laws to protect what they have. They fix up a sort of fence or pen around what they have, and they fix the law so the fellow on the outside cannot get in. The laws are really organized for the protection of the men who rule the world. They were never organized or enforced to do justice. We have no system for doing justice, not the slightest in the world.

Let me illustrate: Take the poorest person in this room. If the community had provided a system of doing justice, the poorest person in this room would have as good a lawyer as the richest, would he not? When you went into court you would have just as long a trial and just as fair a trial as the richest person in Chicago. Your case would not be tried in fifteen or twenty minutes, whereas it would take fifteen days to get through with a rich man's case.

Then if you were rich and were beaten, your case would be taken to the Appellate Court. A poor man cannot take his case to the Appellate Court; he has not the price. And then to the Supreme Court. And if he were beaten there he might perhaps go to the United States Supreme Court. And he might die of old age before he got into jail. If you are poor, it's a quick job. You are almost known to be guilty, else you would not be there. Why should anyone be in the criminal court if he were not guilty? He would not be there if he could be anywhere else. The officials have no time to look after all these cases. The people who are on the outside, who are running banks and building churches and making jails, they have no time to examine 600 or 700 prisoners each year to see whether they are guilty or innocent. If the courts were organized to promote justice the people would elect somebody to defend all these criminals, somebody as smart as the prosecutor—and give him as many detectives and as many assistants to help, and pay as much money to defend you as to prosecute you. We have a very able man for state's attorney, and he has many assistants, detectives, and policemen without end, and judges to hear the cases—everything handy.

Most all of our criminal code consists in offenses against property. People are sent to jail because they have committed a crime against property. It is of very little consequence whether one hundred people more or less go to jail who ought not to go—you must protect property, because in this world property is of more importance than anything else.

How is it done? These people who have property fix it so they can protect what they have. When somebody commits a crime it does not follow that he has done something that is morally wrong. The man on the outside who has committed no crime may have done something. For instance: to take all the coal in the United States and raise the price two dollars or three dollars when there is no need of it, and thus kill thousands of babies and send thousands of people to the poorhouse and tens of thousands to jail, as is done every year in the United States—this is a greater crime than all the people in our jails ever committed; but the law does not punish it. Why? Because the fellows who control the earth make the laws. If you and I had the making of the laws, the first thing we would do would be to punish the fellow who gets control of the earth. Nature put this coal in the ground for me as well as for them and nature made the prairies up here to raise wheat for me as well as for them, and then the great railroad companies came along and fenced it up.

. . .

I will guarantee to take from this jail, or any jail in the world, five hundred men who have been the worst criminals and lawbreakers who ever got into jail, and I will go down to our lowest streets and take five hundred of the most abandoned prostitutes, and go out somewhere where there is plenty of land, and will give them a chance to make a living, and they will be as good people as the average in the community.

There is a remedy for the sort of condition we see here. The world never finds it out, or when it does find it out it does not enforce it. You may pass a law punishing every person with death for burglary, and it will make no difference. Men will commit it just the same. In England there was a time when one hundred different offenses were punishable with death, and it made no difference. The English people strangely found out that so fast as they repealed the severe penalties and so fast as they did away with punishing men by death, crime decreased instead of increased; that the smaller the penalty the fewer the crimes.

Hanging men in our county jails does not prevent murder. It makes murderers.

And this has been the history of the world. It's easy to see how to do away with what we call crime. It is not so easy to do it. I will tell you how to do it. It can be done by giving the people a chance to live—by destroying special privileges. So long as big criminals can get the coal fields, so long as the big criminals have control of the city council and get the public streets for streetcars and gas rights—this is bound to send thousands of poor people to jail. So long as men are allowed to monopolize all the earth, and compel others to live on such terms as these men see fit to make, then you are bound to get into jail.

The only way in the world to abolish crime and criminals is to abolish the big ones and the little ones together. Make fair conditions of life. Abolish the right of private ownership of land, abolish monopoly, make the world partners in production, partners in the good things of life. Nobody would steal if he could get something of his own some easier way. Nobody will commit burglary when he has a house full. No girl will go out on the streets when she has a comfortable place at home. The man who owns a sweatshop or a department store may not be to blame himself for the condition of his girls, but when he pays them five dollars, three dollars, and two dollars a week, I wonder where he thinks they will get the rest of their money to live. The only way to cure these conditions is by equality. There should be no jails. They do not accomplish what they pretend to accomplish. If you would wipe them out there would be no more criminals than now. They terrorize nobody. They are a blot upon any civilization, and a jail is an evidence of the lack of charity of the people on the outside who make the jails and fill them with the victims of their greed.

For Discussion

1. How is Darrow's view of mankind reflected in his opening remarks?
2. How does Darrow equate the crimes of the respectable classes and those of the prisoners? What differentiates the crimes? What additional examples of respectable crimes can you provide?
3. What evidence does Darrow offer to support his belief that an equitable share of the world's goods will eliminate crime? How would this belief apply to what he calls respectable crime?
4. Discuss Darrow's theory on the inviolability of private property. How does it relate to present conflicts in America?
5. How does Darrow feel about capital punishment? (Also see Gregory in "The Ironic NO.")
6. Discuss the practicability of Darrow's proposal to abolish large and small crimes together.
7. Examine each use of concrete illustration. To what extent would these examples support the same argument today?
8. How would you describe Darrow's manner of speaking? What does it tell you about his attitude toward his audience?

GEORGE ORWELL

Politics and the English Language

Born in India and educated in England, George Orwell (pseudonym of Eric Blair) served five years with the Indian Imperial Police in Burma, until his disgust with imperialism caused him to leave the British Colonial Service. Two books of essays and stories reflect his experiences as a civil servant: *Burmese Days* (1934) and *Shooting an Elephant and Other Essays* (1945). During the early 1930s, Orwell wrote fiction in Paris, an experience he recounted in *Down and Out in London and Paris* (1933), and fought as a common soldier in the Spanish Civil War, which he wrote about in *Homage to Catalonia* (1938). Always politically aware and concerned for the victims of social injustice, Orwell developed into a major satirical force in the 1940s with *Animal Farm* (1945), an animal fable which was clearly an allegory of the Russian Revolution, and *1984* (1949), an anti-Utopian novel that revealed Orwell's fears of a worldwide movement toward totalitarianism. The essay which follows has become a classic and definitive essay on the uses of language.

Most people who bother with the matter at all would admit that the English language is in a bad way, but it is generally assumed that we cannot by conscious action do anything about it. Our civilization is decadent, and our language—so the argument runs—must inevitably share in the general collapse. It follows that any struggle against the abuse of language is a sentimental archaism, like preferring candles to electric light or hansom cabs to airplanes. Underneath this lies the half-conscious belief that language is a natural growth and not an instrument which we shape for our purposes.

Now, it is clear that the decline of a language must ultimately have political and economic causes: it is not due simply to the bad influence of this or that individual writer. But an effect can become a cause, reinforcing the original cause and producing the same effect in an intensified form, and so on indefinitely. A man may take to drink because he feels himself to be a failure, and then fail all the more completely because he drinks. It is rather the same thing that is happening to the English language. It becomes ugly and inaccurate because our thoughts are foolish, but the slovenliness of our language makes it easier for us to have foolish thoughts. The point is that the process is reversible. Modern English, especially written English, is full of bad habits which spread by imitation and which can be avoided if one is willing to take the necessary trouble. If one gets rid of these habits one can think more clearly, and to think clearly is a necessary first step towards political regeneration: so that the fight against bad English is not frivolous and is not the exclusive concern of professional writers. I will come back to this presently, and I hope that by that time the meaning of what I have said here will have become clearer. Meanwhile, here are five specimens of the English language as it is now habitually written.

These five passages have not been picked out because they are especially bad—I could have quoted far worse if I had chosen—but because they illustrate various of the mental vices from which we now suffer. They are a little below the average, but are fairly representative samples. I number them so that I can refer back to them when necessary:

(1) I am not, indeed, sure whether it is not true to say that the Milton who once seemed not unlike a seventeenth-century Shelley had not become, out of an experience ever more bitter in each year, more alien (sic) to the founder of that Jesuit sect which nothing could induce him to tolerate.

Professor Harold Laski (Essay in *Freedom of Expression*)

(2) Above all, we cannot play ducks and drakes with a native battery of idioms which prescribes such egregious collocations of vocables as the Basic *put up with* for *tolerate* or *put at a loss* for *bewilder*.

Professor Lancelot Hogben (*Interglossa*)

(3) On the one side we have the free personality; by definition it is not neurotic, for it has neither conflict nor dream. Its desires, such as they are, are transparent, for they are just what institutional approval keeps in the forefront of consciousness; another institutional pattern would alter their number and intensity; there is little in them that is natural, irreducible, or culturally dangerous. But *on the other side*, the social bond itself is nothing

but the mutual reflection of these self-secure integrities. Recall the definition of love. Is not this the very picture of a small academic? Where is there a place in this hall of mirrors for either personality or fraternity?

Essay on psychology in Politics (New York)

(4) All the "best people" from the gentlemen's clubs, and all the frantic fascist captains, united in common hatred of Socialism and bestial horror of the rising tide of the mass revolutionary movement, have turned to acts of provocation, to foul incendiarism, to medieval legends of poisoned wells, to legalize their own destruction of proletarian organizations, and rouse the agitated petty-bourgeoisie to chauvinistic fervor on behalf of the fight against the revolutionary way out of the crisis.   Communist pamphlet

(5) If a new spirit *is* to be infused into this old country, there is one thorny and contentious reform which must be tackled, and that is the humanization and galvanization of the B.B.C. Timidity here will bespeak canker and atrophy of the soul. The heart of Britain may be sound and of strong beat, for instance, but the British lion's roar at present is like that of Bottom in Shakespeare's *Midsummer Night's Dream*—as gentle as any sucking dove. A virile new Britain cannot continue indefinitely to be traduced in the eyes, or rather ears, of the world by the effete languors of Langham Place, brazenly masquerading as "standard English." When the Voice of Britain is heard at nine o'clock, better far and infinitely less ludicrous to hear aitches honestly dropped than the present priggish, inflated, inhibited, school-ma'amish arch braying of blameless bashful mewing maidens.

Letter in Tribune

Each of these passages has faults of its own, but quite apart from avoidable ugliness, two qualities are common to all of them. The first is staleness of imagery; the other is lack of precision. The writer either has a meaning and cannot express it, or he inadvertently says something else, or he is almost indifferent as to whether his words mean anything or not. This mixture of vagueness and sheer incompetence is the most marked characteristic of modern English prose, and especially of any kind of political writing. As soon as certain topics are raised, the concrete melts into the abstract and no one seems able to think of turns of speech that are not hackneyed: prose consists less and less of *words* chosen for the sake of their meaning, and more and more of *phrases* tacked together like the sections of a prefabricated hen-house. I list below, with notes and examples, various of the tricks by means of which the work of prose-construction is habitually dodged:

Dying metaphors. A newly-invented metaphor assists thought by evoking a visual image, while on the other hand a metaphor which is technically "dead" (e.g., *iron resolution*) has in effect reverted to being an ordinary word and can generally be used without loss of vividness. But in between these two classes there is a huge dump of worn-out metaphors which have lost all evocative power and are merely used because they save people the trouble of inventing phrases for themselves. Examples are: *Ring the changes on, take up the cudgels for, toe the line, ride roughshod over, stand shoulder to shoulder with, play into the hands of, an axe to grind, grist to the mill, fishing in troubled waters, on the order of the day, Achilles' heel, swan song, hotbed.* Many of these are used without knowledge of their meaning (what is a "rift," for instance?), and incompatible metaphors are frequently mixed, a sure sign that the writer is not interested in what he is saying. Some metaphors now current have been twisted out of their original meaning without those who use them even being aware of the fact. For example, *toe the line* is sometimes written *tow the line.* Another example is *the hammer and the anvil,* now always used with the implication that the anvil gets the worst of it. In real life it is always the anvil that breaks the hammer, never the other way about; a writer who stopped to think what he was saying would be aware of this, and would avoid perverting the original phrase.

Operators, or *verbal false limbs.* These save the trouble of picking out appropriate verbs and nouns, and at the same time pad each sentence with extra syllables which give it an appearance of symmetry. Characteristic phrases are: *render inoperative, militate against, prove unacceptable, make contact with, be subjected to, give rise to, give grounds for, have the effect of, playing a leading part* (role) *in, making itself felt, take effect, exhibit a tendency to, serve the purpose of,* etc., etc. The keynote is the elimination of simple verbs. Instead of being a single word, such as *break, stop, spoil, mend, kill,* a verb becomes a phrase, made up of a noun or adjective tacked on to some general-purposes verb such as *prove, serve, form, play, render.* In addition, the passive voice is wherever possible used in preference to the active, and noun constructions are used instead of gerunds (*by examination of* instead of *by examining*). The range of verbs is further cut down by means of the *-ize* and *de-* formations, and banal statements are given an appearance of profundity by means of the *not un-* formation. Simple conjunctions and prepositions are replaced by such phrases as *with respect to, having regard to, the fact that, by dint of, in view of, in the interests of, on the hypothesis that;* and the ends of sentences are saved from anti-climax by such resounding commonplaces as *greatly to be desired, cannot be left out of account, a development to be expected in the near future, deserving of serious consideration, brought to a satisfactory conclusion,* and so on and so forth.

Pretentious diction. Words like *phenomenon, element, individual* (as noun), *objective, categorical, effective, virtual, basis, primary, promote, constitute, exhibit, exploit, utilize, eliminate, liquidate,* are used to dress up simple statements and give an air of scientific impartiality to biased judgments. Adjectives like *epoch-making, epic, historic, unforgettable, triumphant, age-old, inevitable, inexorable, veritable,* are used to dignify the sordid processes of international politics, while writing that aims at glorifying war usually takes on an archaic color, its characteristic words being: *realm, throne, chariot, mailed fist, trident, sword, shield, buckler, banner, jackboot, clarion.* Foreign words and expressions such as *cul de sac, ancien régime, deus ex machina, mutatis mutandis, status quo, gleichschaltung, weltanschauung,* are used to give an air of culture and elegance. Except for the useful abbreviations *i.e., e.g.,* and *etc.,* there is no real need for any of the hundreds of foreign phrases now current in English. Bad writers, and especially scientific, political and sociological writers, are nearly always haunted by the notion that Latin or Greek words are grander than Saxon ones, and unnecessary words like *expedite, ameliorate, predict, extraneous, deracinated, clandestine, subaqueous* and hundreds of others constantly gain ground from their Anglo-Saxon opposite numbers.[1] The jargon peculiar to Marxist writing (*hyena, hangman, cannibal, petty bourgeois, these gentry, lackey, flunky, mad dog, White Guard, etc.*) consists largely of words and phrases translated from Russian, German or French; but the normal way of coining a new word is to use a Latin or Greek root with the appropriate affix and, where necessary, the *-ize* formation. It is often easier to make up words of this kind (*deregionalize, impermissible, extramarital, non-fragmentary* and so forth) than to think up the English words that will cover one's meaning. The result, in general, is an increase in slovenliness and vagueness.

Meaningless words. In certain kinds of writing, particularly in art criticism and literary criticism, it is normal to come across long passages which are almost completely lacking in meaning.[2] Words like *romantic, plastic, values, human, dead, sentimental, natural, vitality,* as used in art criticism, are strictly meaningless, in the sense that they not only do not point to any discoverable object, but are hardly even expected to do so by the reader. When one critic writes, "The outstanding feature of Mr. X's work is its living quality," while another writes, "The immediately striking thing about Mr. X's work is its peculiar deadness," the reader accepts this as a simple difference of opinion. If words like *black* and *white* were involved, instead of the jargon words *dead* and *living,* he would see at once that language was being used in an improper way.

---

[1] An interesting illustration of this is the way in which the English flower names which were in use till very recently are being ousted by Greek ones, *snap-dragon* becoming *antirrhinum, forget-me-not* becoming *myosotis,* etc. It is hard to see any practical reason for this change of fashion: it is probably due to an instinctive turning-away from the more homely word and a vague feeling that the Greek word is scientific.

[2] Example: "Comfort's catholicity of perception and image, strangely Whitmanesque in range, amost the exact opposite in aesthetic compulsion, continues to evoke that trembling atmospheric accumulative hinting at a cruel, an inexorably serene timelessness . . . Wrey Gardiner scores by aiming at simple bullseyes with precision. Only they are not so simple, and through this contented sadness runs more than the surface bittersweet of resignation." (*Poetry Quarterly.*)

Many political words are similarly abused. The word *Fascism* has now no meaning except in so far as it signifies "something not desirable." The words *democracy, socialism, freedom, patriotic, realistic, justice,* have each of them several different meanings which cannot be reconciled with one another. In the case of a word like *democracy,* not only is there no agreed definition, but the attempt to make one is resisted from all sides. It is almost universally felt that when we call a country democratic we are praising it: consequently, the defenders of every kind of régime claim that it is a democracy, and fear that they might have to stop using the word if it were tied down to any one meaning. Words of this kind are often used in a consciously dishonest way. That is, the person who uses them has his own private definition, but allows his hearer to think he means something quite different. Statements like *Marshal Pétain was a true patriot, The Soviet Press is the freest in the world, The Catholic Church is opposed to persecution,* are almost always made with intent to deceive. Other words used in variable meanings, in most cases more or less dishonestly, are: *class, totalitarian, science, progressive, reactionary, bourgeois, equality.*

Now that I have made this catalogue of swindles and perversions, let me give another example of the kind of writing that they lead to. This time it must of its nature be an imaginary one. I am going to translate a passage of good English into modern English of the worst sort. Here is a well-known verse from *Ecclesiastes:*

> I returned, and saw under the sun, that the race is not to the swift, nor the battle to the strong, neither yet bread to the wise, nor yet riches to men of understanding, nor yet favor to men of skill; but time and chance happeneth to them all.

Here it is in modern English:

> Objective consideration of contemporary phenomena compels the conclusion that success or failure in competitive activities exhibits no tendency to be commensurate with innate capacity, but that a considerable element of the unpredictable must invariably be taken into account.

This is a parody, but not a very gross one. Exhibit (3), above, for instance, contains several patches of the same kind of English. It will be seen that I have not made a full translation. The beginning and ending of the sentence follow the original meaning fairly closely, but in the middle the concrete illustrations—race, battle, bread—dissolve into the vague phrase "success or failure in competitive activities." This had to be so, because no modern writer of the kind I am discussing—no one capable of using phrases like "objective consideration of contemporary phenomena"—would ever tabulate his thoughts in that precise and detailed way. The whole tendency of modern prose is away from concreteness. Now analyze these two sentences a little more closely. The first contains 49 words but only 60 syllables, and all its words are those of everyday life. The second contains 38 words of 90 syllables: 18 of its words are from Latin roots, and one from Greek. The first sentence contains six vivid images, and only one phrase ("time and chance") that could be called vague. The second contains not a single fresh, arresting phrase, and in spite of its 90 syllables it gives only a shortened version of the meaning contained in the first. Yet without a doubt it is the second kind of sentence that is gaining ground in modern English. I do not want to exaggerate. This kind of writing is not yet universal, and outcrops of simplicity will occur here and there in the worst-written page. Still, if you or I were told to write a few lines on the uncertainty of human fortunes, we should probably come much nearer to my imaginary sentence than to the one from *Ecclesiastes*.

As I have tried to show, modern writing at its worst does not consist in picking out words for the sake of their meaning and inventing images in order to make the meaning clearer. It consists in gumming together long strips of words which have already been set in order by someone else, and making the results presentable by sheer humbug. The attraction of this way of writing is that it is easy. It is easier—even quicker, once you have the habit—to say *In my opinion it is a not unjustifiable assumption that* than to say *I think*. If you use ready-made phrases, you not only don't have to hunt about for words; you also don't have to bother with the rhythms of your sentences, since these phrases are generally so arranged as to be more or less euphonious. When you are composing in a hurry—when you are dictating to a stenographer, for instance, or making a public speech—it is natural to fall into a pretentious, Latinized style. Tags like *a consideration which we should do well to bear in mind* or *a conclusion to which all of us would readily assent* will save many a sentence from coming down with a bump. By using stale metaphors, similes and idioms, you save much mental effort at the cost of leaving your meaning vague, not only for your reader but for yourself. This is the significance of mixed metaphors. The sole aim of a metaphor is to call up a visual image. When these images clash—as in *The Fascist octopus has sung its swan song, the jackboot is thrown into the melting pot* —it can be taken as certain that the writer is not seeing a mental image of the objects he is naming; in other words he is not really thinking. Look again at the examples I gave at the beginning of this essay. Professor Laski (1) uses five negatives in 53 words. One of these is superfluous, making nonsense of the whole passage, and in addition there is the slip *alien* for *akin*, making further nonsense, and several avoidable pieces of clumsiness which increase the general vagueness. Professor Hogben (2) plays ducks and drakes with a battery which is able to write prescriptions, and, while disapproving of the everyday phrase *put up with*, is unwilling to look *egregious* up in the dictionary and see what it means. (3), if one takes an uncharitable attitude towards it, is simply meaningless: probably one could work out its intended meaning by reading the whole of the article in which it occurs. In (4), the writer knows more or less what he wants to say, but an accumulation of stale phrases chokes him like tea leaves blocking a sink. In (5), words and meaning have almost parted company. People who write in this manner usually have a general emotional meaning—they dislike one thing and want to express solidarity with another—but they are not interested in the detail of what they are saying. A scrupulous writer, in every sentence that he writes, will ask himself at least four questions, thus: What am I trying to say? What words will express it? What image or idiom will make it clearer? Is this image fresh enough to have an effect? And he will probably ask himself two more: Could I put it more shortly? Have I said anything that is avoidably ugly? But you are not obliged to go to all this trouble. You can shirk it by simply throwing your mind open and letting the ready-made phrases come crowding in. They will construct your sentences for you—even think your thoughts for you, to a certain extent—and at need they will perform the important service of partially concealing your meaning even from yourself. It is at this point that the special connection between politics and the debasement of language becomes clear.

In our time it is broadly true that political writing is bad writing. Where it is not true, it will generally be found that the writer is some kind of rebel, expressing his private opinions and not a "party line." Orthodoxy, of whatever color, seems to demand a lifeless, imitative style. The political dialects to be found in pamphlets, leading articles, manifestoes, White Papers and the speeches of under-secretaries do, of course, vary from party to party, but they are all alike in that one almost never finds in them a fresh, vivid, home-made turn of speech. When one watches some tired hack on the platform mechanically repeating the familiar phrases—*bestial atrocities, iron heel, bloodstained tyranny, free peoples of the world, stand shoulder to shoulder*—one often has a curious feeling that one is not watching a live human being but some kind of dummy: a feeling which suddenly becomes stronger at moments when the light catches the speaker's spectacles and turns them into blank discs which seem to have no eyes behind them. And this is not altogether fanciful. A speaker who uses that kind of phraseology has gone some distance toward turning himself into a machine. The appropriate noises are coming out of his larynx, but his brain is not involved as it would be if he were choosing his words for himself. If the speech he is making is one that he is accustomed to make over and over again, he may be almost unconscious of what he is saying, as one is when one utters the responses in church. And this reduced state of consciousness, if not indispensable, is at any rate favorable to political conformity.

In our time, political speech and writing are largely the defense of the indefensible. Things like the continuance of British rule in India, the Russian purges and deportations, the dropping of the atom bombs on Japan, can indeed be defended, but only by arguments which are too brutal for most people to face, and which do not square with the professed aims of political parties. Thus political language has to consist largely of euphemism, question-begging and sheer cloudy vagueness. Defenseless villages are bombarded from the air, the inhabitants driven out into the countryside, the cattle machine-gunned, the huts set on fire with incendiary bullets: this is called *pacification*. Millions of peasants are robbed of their farms and sent trudging along the roads with no more than they can carry: this is called *transfer of population* or *rectification of frontiers*. People are imprisoned for years without trial, or shot in the back of the neck or sent to die of scurvy in Arctic lumber camps: this is called *elimination of unreliable elements*. Such phraseology is needed if one wants to name things without calling up mental pictures of them. Consider for instance some comfortable English professor defending Russian totalitarianism. He cannot say outright, "I believe in killing off your opponents when you can get good results by doing so." Probably, therefore, he will say something like this:

> While freely conceding that the Soviet régime exhibits certain features which the humanitarian may be inclined to deplore, we must, I think, agree that a certain curtailment of the right to political opposition is an unavoidable concomitant of transitional periods, and that the rigors which the Russian people have been called upon to undergo have been amply justified in the sphere of concrete achievement.

The inflated style is itself a kind of euphemism. A mass of Latin words falls upon the facts like soft snow, blurring the outlines and covering up all the details. The great enemy of clear language is insincerity. When there is a gap between one's real and one's declared aims, one turns, as it were instinctively, to long words and exhausted idioms, like a cuttlefish squirting out ink. In our age there is no such thing as "keeping out of politics." All issues are political issues, and politics itself is a mass of lies, evasions, folly, hatred and schizophrenia. When the general atmosphere is bad, language must suffer. I should expect to find—this is a guess which I have not sufficient knowledge to verify—that the German, Russian and Italian languages have all deteriorated in the last ten or fifteen years as a result of dictatorship.

But if thought corrupts language, language can also corrupt thought. A bad usage can spread by tradition and imitation, even among people who should and do know better. The debased language that I have been discussing is in some ways very convenient. Phrases like *a not unjustifiable assumption, leaves much to be desired, would serve no good purpose, a consideration which we should do well to bear in mind*, are a continuous temptation, a packet of aspirins always at one's elbow. Look back through this essay, and for certain you will find that I have again and again committed the very faults I am protesting against. By this morning's post I have received a pamphlet dealing with conditions in Germany. The author tells me that he "felt impelled" to write it. I open it at random, and here is almost the first sentence that I see: "[The Allies] have an opportunity not only of achieving a radical transformation of Germany's social and political structure in such a way as to avoid a nationalistic reaction in Germany itself, but at the same time of laying the foundations of a cooperative and unified Europe." You see, he "feels impelled" to write—feels, presumably, that he has something new to say —and yet his words, like cavalry horses answering the bugle, group themselves automatically into the familiar dreary pattern. This invasion of one's mind by ready-made phrases (*lay the foundations, achieve a radical transformation*) can only be prevented if one is constantly on guard against them, and every such phrase anesthetizes a portion of one's brain.

I said earlier that the decadence of our language is probably curable. Those who deny this would argue, if they produced an argument at all, that language merely reflects existing social conditions, and that we cannot influence its development by any direct tinkering with words and constructions. So far as the general tone or spirit of a language goes, this may be true, but it is not true in detail. Silly words and expressions have often disappeared, not through any evolutionary process but owing to the conscious action of a minority. Two recent examples were *explore every avenue* and *leave no stone unturned*, which were killed by the jeers of a few journalists. There is a long list of fly-blown metaphors which could similarly be got rid of if enough people would interest themselves in the job; and it should also be possible to laugh the *not un-* formation out of existence,[3] to reduce the amount of Latin and Greek in the average sentence, to drive out foreign phrases and strayed scientific words, and, in general, to make pretentiousness unfashionable. But all these are minor points. The defense of the English language implies more than this, and perhaps it is best to start by saying what it does *not* imply.

To begin with, it has nothing to do with archaism, with the salvaging of obsolete words and turns of speech, or with the setting-up of a

---

[3] One can cure oneself of the *not un-* formation by memorizing this sentence: *A not unblack dog was chasing a not unsmall rabbit across a not ungreen field.*

"standard English" which must never be departed from. On the contrary, it is especially concerned with the scrapping of every word or idiom which has outworn its usefulness. It has nothing to do with correct grammar and syntax, which are of no importance so long as one makes one's meaning clear, or with the avoidance of Americanisms, or with having what is called a "good prose style." On the other hand it is not concerned with fake simplicity and the attempt to make written English colloquial. Nor does it even imply in every case preferring the Saxon word to the Latin one, though it does imply using the fewest and shortest words that will cover one's meaning. What is above all needed is to let the meaning choose the word, and not the other way about. In prose, the worst thing one can do with words is to surrender to them. When you think of a concrete object, you think wordlessly, and then, if you want to describe the thing you have been visualizing, you probably hunt about till you find the exact words that seem to fit it. When you think of something abstract you are more inclined to use words from the start, and unless you make a conscious effort to prevent it, the existing dialect will come rushing in and do the job for you, at the expense of blurring or even changing your meaning. Probably it is better to put off using words as long as possible and get one's meaning as clear as one can through pictures or sensations. Afterwards one can choose—not simply *accept*—the phrases that will best cover the meaning, and then switch round and decide what impressions one's words are likely to make on another person. This last effort of the mind cuts out all stale or mixed images, all prefabricated phrases, needless repetitions, and humbug and vagueness generally. But one can often be in doubt about the effect of a word or a phrase, and one needs rules that can rely on when instinct fails. I think the following rules will cover most cases:

(i) Never use a metaphor, simile or other figure of speech which you are used to seeing in print.

(ii) Never use a long word where a short one will do.

(iii) If it is possible to cut a word out, always cut it out.

(iv) Never use the passive where you can use the active.

(v) Never use a foreign phrase, a scientific word or a jargon word if you can think of an everyday English equivalent.

(vi) Break any of these rules sooner than say anything barbarous.

These rules sound elementary, and so they are, but they demand a deep change of attitude in anyone who has grown used to writing in the style now fashionable. One could keep all of them and still write bad English, but one could not write the kind of stuff that I quoted in these five specimens at the beginning of this article.

I have not here been considering the literary use of language, but merely language as an instrument for expressing and not for concealing or preventing thought. Stuart Chase and others have come near to claiming that all abstract words are meaningless, and have used this as a pretext for advocating a kind of political quietism. Since you don't know what Fascism is, how can you struggle against Fascism? One need not swallow such absurdities as this, but one ought to recognize that the present political chaos is connected with the decay of language, and that one can probably bring about some improvement by starting at the verbal end. If you simplify your English, you are freed from the worst follies of orthodoxy. You cannot speak any of the necessary dialects, and when you make a stupid remark its stupidity will be obvious, even to yourself. Political language—and with variations this is true of all political parties, from Conservatives to Anarchists—is designed to make lies sound truthful and murder respectable, and to give an appearance of solidity to pure wind. One cannot change this all in a moment, but one can at least change one's habits, and from time to time one can even, if one jeers loudly enough, send some worn-out and useless phrase—some *jackboot, Achilles' heel, hotbed, melting pot, acid test, veritable inferno* or other lump of verbal refuse—into the dustbin where it belongs.

For Discussion

1. How does Orwell relate the quality of our language to the quality of our thinking?
2. What dangers does Orwell see in using phrases which have already been "set in order by someone else"?
3. What objection does Orwell raise to the use of foreign words and phrases?
4. Why is the choice of an image so important, according to Orwell? Discuss his examples of concreteness.
5. Examine Orwell's list of dying metaphors, operators or verbal false limbs, pretentious diction, and meaningless words. Contribute additional examples of your own to each category.
6. How does politics debase language? How does language debase politics?
7. Discuss the applicability of the following statements to the political situation today:
    a. "In our time it is broadly true that political writing [or speech] is bad writing."
    b. "In our time, political speech and writing are largely the defense of the indefensible."
    c. "All issues are political issues, and politics itself is a mass of lies, evasions, folly, hatred and schizophrenia."
8. Explain the effect of insincerity of meaning upon language.
9. Give some contemporary examples of language which Orwell would throw in the dustbin.
10. Which of Orwell's rules would you find most difficult to follow?
11. Discuss the effectiveness of Orwell's imagery in this essay.

SYLVIA MEAGHER

Accessories After the Fact

Sylvia Meagher lives in New York City and writes for magazines ranging from *Esquire* to *Studies on the Left.* She has worked in the field of international public health and has lectured widely throughout the United States and Canada. Universally considered the most knowledgeable person in the field of published documents relating to the assassination of President Kennedy, she compiled—on her own—the only index to the hastily assembled twenty-six volumes of Hearings and Exhibits of the Warren Commission, which investigated and reported the circumstances surrounding the assassination. *Accessories After the Fact,* from which the following excerpt is taken, is an exhaustive study of the Warren Report in the light of subsequent research by Meagher and others.

During the eight o'clock news that morning the face of Dallas Police Chief Jesse E. Curry filled the television screen with assurances that every possible precaution had been taken to ensure the safety of President John Fitzgerald Kennedy. At two o'clock New York time I sat in my office with white-faced colleagues, listening to news bulletins over a transistor radio. President Kennedy had been shot while riding in a motorcade in Dallas.

We all remembered the indignities suffered by U.N. Ambassador Adlai Stevenson in Dallas less than a month before when a spitting, savage mob of right-wing extremists had subjected him to the hatred and fury they felt for the United Nations, which he represented and symbolized. The screaming insults, the blows, and the spittle were intended for all who believed in the United Nations. They were intended for those who hoped and worked for an end to the cold war and a beginning of genuine peace, for equality and mutual respect among men, for the rule of law and an end to brute violence—aims which had animated President Kennedy's historic speech at American University in June 1963.

At 2:30 P.M. the voice on the radio said with solemn anguish, "The President is dead." Someone in the room screamed with shock and grief. Someone cursed the John Birch Society and its kind. "Don't worry," I said derisively, "you'll see, it was a Communist who did it."

An hour later, back at the television screen on which Curry earlier had reassured the audience, I heard that Lee Harvey Oswald—a man with a Russian wife and a history of pro-Castro activities—had been taken into custody.

This is the personal background for my instantaneous skepticism about the official version of what happened in Dallas on November 22, 1963. In the three years that have followed, intensive study of the evidence against the alleged lone assassin has convinced me, as intuition alone could not, that the truth about Dallas remains unknown and that Lee Harvey Oswald may well have been innocent.

President John Fitzgerald Kennedy arrived at Love Field in Dallas, Texas, on Friday, November 22, 1963, at 11:40 A.M. In his party were his wife Jacqueline Kennedy, Vice-President Lyndon B. Johnson and Mrs. Johnson, Governor of Texas John B. Connally, Jr., and Mrs. Connally, and several prominent members of the Senate and the House. One purpose of the Presidential visit to Texas was to seek a reconciliation between warring factions within the state's Democratic Party. Despite apprehension about the President's safety in this city of right-wing activities, the President proceeded in his open car in a motorcade from the airfield toward the Trade Mart Building, where he was to be guest of honor at a luncheon organized by Dallas civic and business leaders.

At 12:30 P.M. the Presidential car proceeded from Houston Street to Elm Street, approaching a triple underpass. Shots rang out. The President and Governor Connally, who was seated directly in front of him, were hit.

The car raced to Parkland Hospital, where the President was taken to an emergency room and futile attempts were made to save his life. He was declared dead at 1 P.M. Governor Connally was seriously wounded, underwent surgery, and in due course recovered from his bullet wounds.

After President Kennedy was pronounced dead, Vice-President Johnson left Parkland Hospital under heavy security protection, proceeding to Love Field. He boarded the Presidential airplane and at 2:38 P.M. took the oath of office and became the thirty-sixth President of the United States.

As Johnson was sworn into office, Lee Harvey Oswald was undergoing interrogation at the Dallas police headquarters on suspicion of shooting to death a patrolman, J. D. Tippit, who was murdered shortly after 1 P.M. on a street in Oak Cliff, a section of Dallas some distance from the scene of the assassination. Oswald was employed at the Texas School Book Depository on Elm Street, where witnesses had reported a man shooting at the motorcade from the sixth-floor southeast corner window. Within little more than a minute after the President and the Governor were shot, Oswald had been encountered on the second floor of the Book Depository by a motorcycle officer and the Book Depository superintendent; they found in Oswald's demeanor and appearance no cause for suspicion and proceeded immediately to the roof of the building.

Some time later, apparently 30 or 40 minutes after the encounter, the superintendent reported to the Dallas police captain in charge of homicide that Oswald was missing. The captain placed Oswald under suspicion of the assassination but before sending out an alarm for the missing man learned that Oswald was under arrest for the Tippit killing.

Oswald remained in police custody from Friday afternoon until Sunday morning. The Dallas police and district attorney quickly identified him as a defector who had lived in the Soviet Union, returned to the United States with a Russian wife, and became active in pro-Castro activities. While they acknowledged that Oswald steadfastly claimed that he was innocent of both the assassination and the murder of the policeman, the Dallas authorities repeatedly told the press and the public that his guilt was certain, giving a running account of evidence—real and imaginary—which they regarded as conclusive.

The police announced that Oswald would be transferred to the county jail on Sunday morning. Anonymous telephone calls the night before the transfer threatened that Oswald would be seized and killed, yet the plans for a public transfer proceeded.

Handcuffed to a detective and flanked by officers, Oswald was escorted to the police basement to begin the removal to the county jail. Suddenly, a man in the crowd of reporters and plainclothesmen fired a revolver point-blank, felling the prisoner. Oswald was removed to Parkland Hospital, where he died about two hours later. His killer, Jack Ruby, proprietor of a strip-joint, was to die of cancer in the same hospital some three years later.

The police charges that Oswald, a Marxist, had committed the assassination caused public misgivings, for it was a most strange denouement to the widespread assumption immediately after the President's death that he had been killed by the same right-wing fanatics who had abused Adlai Stevenson. The public's anxieties were compounded by the murder of Oswald in the police basement by Ruby, a known police buff. Dallas officials were denounced on every side for their mishandling of events at every stage; not even the authoritative weight of the Federal Bureau of

Investigation sufficed in this instance to make the police version of the assassination credible to the American public or to observers abroad.

No one outside of Dallas was prepared to agree that, as police spokesmen said upon Oswald's death, "the case is closed." One week after the assassination, on November 29, 1963, President Johnson appointed a Commission, chaired by the Chief Justice of the U.S. Supreme Court, to "satisfy itself that the truth is known as far as it can be discovered and to report its findings and conclusions to him [the President], to the American people, and to the world."

The report of the President's Commission—the Warren Report—was published at the end of September 1964. In essence, its conclusions were the same as those of the Dallas authorities: Lee Harvey Oswald, acting alone and unaided, had assassinated the President and murdered a police officer. Two months later, at the end of November 1964, 26 volumes of Hearings and Exhibits were published, assertedly presenting the testimony and evidence upon which the Warren Report was predicated.

This book [*Accessories After the Fact*] examines the correlation, or lack of correlation, between the Report on the one hand and the Hearings and Exhibits on the other. The first pronounces Oswald guilty; the second, instead of corroborating the verdict reached by the Warren Commission, creates a reasonable doubt of Oswald's guilt and even a powerful presumption of his complete innocence of all the crimes of which he was accused.

On the day of the assassination the national climate of arrogance and passivity in the face of relentless violence—beatings, burnings, bombings, and shootings—yielded in some quarters to a sudden hour of humility and self-criticism. The painful moment passed quickly, for the official thesis of the lone, random assassin destroyed the impulse for national self-scrutiny and repentance. Thus, the climate of cruelty and barbaric hatred was restored after what was scarcely an interruption, and it was possible for Cuban *émigrés*—virtually with impunity and without regard for the hundreds of people who might be killed or injured —to fire a bazooka at the United Nations Headquarters building to express displeasure at the presence there of Che Guevara. Thus, it was possible for American Nazi thugs to assault peaceful citizens assembled at a public meeting in Dallas at Christmas 1965. Thus it is possible for Americans to look upon the napalmed children of Vietnam and listen to their terror and agony nightly over the television tubes, and to go about their daily business as usual.

Few people who have followed the events closely—and who are not indentured to the Establishment—conceive of the Kennedy assassination as anything but a political crime. That was the immediate and universal belief on November 22 before the opinion-makers got to work endorsing the official explanation of the complex mystery as Gospel and entreating all good citizens to do the same.

What is noteworthy about the advocates of the Report is that they defend their position largely by rhetoric, asking how anyone can possibly question the probity of Chief Justice Warren or Senator Russell (much as one may disagree with his views on race) or even Allen Dulles. They do not argue on evidence, because frequently they are uninformed, and in preaching their faith in the Warren Commission there is scarcely a platitude they are not willing to use. As a general rule, partisans of the Report have not read it, much less the 26 volumes of Hearings and Exhibits. In discussion and debate, they expose their unfamiliarity with the facts and expound all kinds of irresponsible errors and assumptions. The critics of the Report, on the other hand, have by and large performed arduous labor and taken great pains to master and document the available information with the scrupulousness which was to be expected but is not found in the Warren Report. Only a few of the critics who question or reject the Report have been guilty of careless or incomplete research; and while that is not to be condoned, it is nevertheless the Commission and not the lone critic which had the responsibility of establishing and reporting the truth, with virtually unlimited manpower and funds at its disposal.

It is not the critic's responsibility to explain why the Chief Justice signed such a Report or why Robert Kennedy accepts it or to answer other similar questions posed by the orthodox defenders. As critic Tom Katen has pointed out, instead of evaluating the evidence in terms of Robert Kennedy's acquiescence, his acquiescence should be evaluated in the light of the evidence. Nor is it the critic's responsibility to name the person or persons who committed the assassination if Oswald did not—another characteristic *non sequitur*. It is, on the other hand, clearly the responsibility of the authors and advocates of the Report to explain and justify its explicit documented defects. If they cannot or will not, then let the Government which has given us such a profoundly defective document—at a cost to the people of well over a million dollars—scrap the Report and commission one that will sustain its assertions and conclusions and survive the test of close scrutiny.

One of the most reprehensible actions of the Warren Commission is that it disbanded the moment it handed over its Report, leaving no individual or corporate entity to answer legitimate questions arising from demonstrable misstatements of fact in the Report. On September 27, 1964, the Commission, in effect, attempted to close the case no less firmly than the Dallas police tried to close it on November 25, 1963. Letters to Commission members or counsel posing factual questions on the basis of material cited in the official volumes have gone either completely unanswered, or unanswered in substance. The policy of silence is an affront to concerned citizens and invites the irresistible inference that the authors are unable to defend or justify the points at issue.[1]

The haste with which the Warren Commission closed its case is arresting, because when all is said and done it is the very same case that the Dallas police tried to close before Oswald's corpse grew cold. Chief Jesse E. Curry and Captain J. Will Fritz of the Dallas police and Dallas District Attorney Henry Wade said that Oswald was guilty. The Commission says so. Curry, Fritz, and Wade said that he acted alone and had no accomplices. The Commission says so. Curry, Fritz, and Wade said that he shot Tippit. The Commission says so. The Commission adds the charge that he tried to kill Major General Edwin A. Walker—but that is no tribute to its investigatory skill as opposed to that of the Dallas police. It is merely a story told by Marina Oswald and accepted by the Commission too readily by far, in disregard for the inconsistency between her story and the objective facts recorded contemporaneously or determined later, and in disregard for the doubts which arose about Marina Oswald's credibility when unyielding facts forced the Commission to reject her matching story of an attempt by her husband to assassinate Richard M. Nixon.

The Commission's blatant bias for and against witnesses and its double standard of judging credibility are in themselves beyond belief. Marina Oswald's testimony is treated as impeccable, despite the ludicrous Nixon story and her poor showing under the sole cross-examination (by Senator Russell) to which she was subjected. Helen Markham is another star witness. If Mrs. Markham did not misstate the truth one can only say— as Counsel Joseph Ball said on a public platform—that she is an "utter screwball." It is not necessary to belabor the Commission's desperation in declaring her wild testimony as having "probative value." Having deemed "reliable" the testimony of Marina Oswald and Helen Markham,

---

[1] In mid-1965 I addressed letters to former members of the Warren Commission (Gerald R. Ford, John Sherman Cooper, Earl Warren) and to members of the staff (lawyers J. Lee Rankin, Albert E. Jenner, Jr., Wesley J. Liebeler, and Melvin E. Eisenberg; and historian Alfred Goldberg), requesting clarification on various points of evidence. In four cases (Cooper, Goldberg, Liebeler, and Rankin) no reply was received. In one case, a former assistant counsel agreed to discuss the questions put to him by telephone, on a confidential basis and not for attribution. He was not able to resolve the relevant problems—indeed, he was not even aware of the existence of one piece of evidence (the actual full-page ad of Klein's Sporting Goods in the February 1963 *American Rifleman*, from which it is evident that the rifle ordered by "Hidell" was a different model from the rifle found in the Depository), which I sent to him at his request.

In the remaining cases, I received replies of a purely formal nature, referring me to others for the requested information, only to have the redirected queries go without reply. One such reply promised that the writer would send a substantive response to the questions raised in my letter during the week of July 19, 1965; the promised response has yet to arrive.

how does the Commission deal with witnesses who on the face of it have neither fabricated nor become embroiled in blatant self-contradiction nor raved confusedly? The Commission decided that Seth Kantor was "mistaken." Buell Wesley Frazier and his sister—mistaken. W. W. Litchfield —mistaken or "lying." Wanda Helmick—mistaken or "lying." It dealt in the same way with Gertrude Hunter, Edith Whitworth, Roger Craig, Arnold Rowland, Victoria Adams, William Whaley, Albert Guy Bogard, Dial Ryder, C. A. Hamblen, Wilma Tice, and still others.

All those "mistaken" or "lying" witnesses have one thing in common: they gave evidence which in whole or in part was inconsistent with or antithetical to the official thesis of the lone psychotic assassin and the lone psychotic killer of the lone psychotic assassin. That was the thesis of the Dallas police and district attorney on November 25, 1963, and, with minor and inconsequential variations, the thesis of the Warren Commission a year later.

It has been said jokingly that the Dallas police are not so bad—look how quickly they caught Jack Ruby. Not so bad? They are brilliant. In some 48 hours they solved three murders of unparalleled complexity and mystery with the same conclusions as those reached a year later by the Chief Justice and his six eminent colleagues, the stable of bright young lawyers, the legions of investigators, and the regiment of criminology experts. The Dallas police achieved in a matter of some three days what the Commission achieved after an investigation said to be unprecedented in scope, depth, duration, and, we daresay, expense. Not many police departments can match the Dallas force.

In addition to the crimes and brutalities often committed by police and other officers of the law—not only in the South but in other regions—it is frequently alleged that police officers are found increasingly among the members of right-wing extremist organizations, several of which are known to collect arsenals and plan acts of violence and destruction.

The Dallas police permitted the most important prisoner in the history of Texas to be gunned down in their basement while handcuffed to a detective and flanked by officers. A few months later the Dallas police lost another prisoner, a woman who said she had worked for Ruby once, by suicide in one of their jail cells. Yet the same police solved the mystery of the assassination and the murder of Tippit with enough speed, authority, and skill to make one's mind reel. (Unfortunately they did not do nearly so well in the shooting of Warren Reynolds, a witness at the Tippit scene, a case which has remained unsolved since January 1964). It seems unfair that editorial writers first assailed the Dallas force with contempt, and then wrote dazzling tributes to the Warren Commission without retracting their unkind words about the hapless Dallas police. If one accepts and endorses the Warren Report, one must also commend the Dallas police for their swift, sure work, and vindicate them in their finding that Oswald was the lone assassin and that the case was closed.

The difficulty is that the editorial writers and partisans of the Report rushed into a chorus of superlatives before they could read the 888-page Report with requisite care, and long before the supporting documents and testimony were made available for study and comparison. When the Hearings and Exhibits were issued two months after the Report, there was another concert of praise, equally extravagant and premature. None of the favorable appraisals was conditional on study of the Hearings and Exhibits to see if they corroborated the assertions in the Report (except perhaps for a critique by Professor Herbert Packer) and few have been followed by a restatement, reiterating or modifying the initial appraisal on the basis of such study.

There is much mention of the 26 volumes of the Hearings and Exhibits but little familiarity with their contents, organization, or character. The first 15 volumes consist of transcripts of the testimony of witnesses. Volumes I through V present the testimony of witnesses heard by the Warren Commission itself—not by the full Commission, as a rule, but with two or three members present—in the chronological sequence of their appearances. Volumes VI through XV present the testimony taken in depositions—that is, testimony under oath taken by a Commission lawyer, usually in Dallas, in the presence of a court reporter—arranged not chronologically but in rough approximation of the area of evidence on which a witness testified.

Volumes XVI through XXVI consist of Exhibits. The first three volumes in this group consist of exhibits identified by number (CE 1, CE 2, etc.) which were read into the record during the examination of the witnesses who testified before the Commission and whose testimony is found in Volumes I through V, as mentioned already. The next three volumes (Volumes XIX through XXI) consist of exhibits read into the record during the testimony of witnesses who provided the depositions contained in Volumes VI through XV; these exhibits, unlike the first group, are identified by the name of the witness and then by number (*Armstrong Exhibit No. 1, Paine Exhibit No. 2*, etc.). Finally, the last five volumes (XXII through XXVI) revert to numbered exhibits (*CE 2003, CE 2905*, etc.) selected by an unspecified criterion and not linked with specific testimony or entered on the record during the Hearings. (Thousands of cubic feet of Commission documents, consisting of reports and paper not converted into exhibits or published, are in the custody of the National Archives in Washington, D.C. Still other documents and materials are "classified" and not available for examination even at the Archives.)

Scrutiny of the Hearings and Exhibits, it must be acknowledged, is a monumental undertaking, involving the mastering of 26 thick volumes consisting of some 20,000 pages and more than ten million words. Few people have the time or fortitude for such a task. There are imposing obstacles even to the study of one or two distinct elements of the evidence in their entirety, to determine whether there is fidelity between the raw data and the account given in the Report. Such clearly delimited study would not require exorbitant time or effort if the Commission had included a subject index to make possible the tracing of the relevant testimony and documents to any single item of evidence.[2] The sheer mass of unclassified, unexplored data is enough to discourage an attempt to take inventory. It would be tantamount to a search for information in the *Encyclopedia Britannica* if the contents were untitled, unalphabetized, and in random sequence. It is hard to be unsympathetic to the student who shuddered and declined to read the Hearings and Exhibits word by word; however, it is equally hard to be sympathetic to the apologist for the Report who read the Report superficially without skepticism or notice of its internal contradictions, publicly endorsing the findings and influencing opinion in favor of the Report while not bothering to read the Hearings and Exhibits.

It has been said that the American people are the only jury that Lee Harvey Oswald will ever have. It is our responsibility, then, to examine with utmost care and objectivity the evidence for and against him, and to reach an independent verdict. That responsibility cannot be delegated to others, however exalted their reputations and their honors. The first step must be the patient reading of the Hearings and Exhibits, imposing as the task is. If that reading demonstrates that the Report is an inaccurate, incomplete, or partisan synthesis of the raw material on which it supposedly relies, the authors—the Warren Commission—must account for the discrepancies in a manner that satisfies all doubt about their competence and their motives. If they cannot, or will not, provide such satisfaction, the people are entitled to a new investigation and a new report, by a competent and disinterested body submitting to the adversary procedure and permitting Oswald the maximum defense which can be given an accused man posthumously—an act of justice thus far denied him.

A new investigation utilizing the adversary procedure may theoretically also find that Oswald was the lone assassin. If such a finding is supported by unambiguous evidence which cannot be successfully challenged by the defense and if it is based on procedural decorum and equity, it will be acceptable. If there is a different finding, implicating co-assassins or absolving Oswald entirely, that too must meet the strictest tests of evidence and procedure.

A new investigation is imperative, because study of the Hearings and

[2] Sylvia Meagher, *Subject Index to the Warren Report and Hearings and Exhibits* (New York: Scarecrow Press, 1966).

Exhibits has destroyed the grounds for confidence in the Warren Report. Study has shown the Report to contain (1) statements of fact which are inaccurate and untrue, in the light of the official Exhibits and objective verification; (2) statements for which the citations fail to provide authentication; (3) misrepresentation of testimony; (4) omission of references to testimony inimical to findings in the Report; (5) suppression of findings favorable to Oswald; (6) incomplete investigation of suspicious circumstances which remain unexplained; (7) misleading statements resulting from inadequate attention to the contents of Exhibits; (8) failure to obtain testimony from crucial witnesses; and (9) assertions which are diametrically opposite to the logical inferences to be drawn from the relevant testimony or evidence.

In this constellation, as in the case of the "mistaken" witnesses, there is one constant: the effect of each inaccuracy, omission, or misrepresentation is to fortify the fragmentary and dubious evidence for the lone-assassin thesis and to minimize or suppress the contrary evidence. To that constant must be linked the Commission's unashamed refusal to permit Oswald a defense, as formally requested by his mother, in contravention of the most elementary concept of fairness and judicial procedure. The excuse that Marina Oswald, chief witness for the prosecution, did not desire a defender to represent the man whose guilt she proclaimed and reiterated hardly merits discussion. If that position had any moral or legal merit, it was vitiated completely when the Commission appointed the President of the American Bar Association, Walter Craig, "to participate in the investigation and to advise the Commission whether in his opinion the proceedings conformed to the basic principles of American justice."[3] This compromise was worse than meaningless. The Commission should not have required a reminder from the head of the ABA to recall that an accused person has a fundamental right to self-defense and the benefit of reasonable doubt—even posthumously—and in any case no such reminder issued from Mr. Craig or his appointed observers. Craig and his representatives participated in the examination of witnesses from February 27 to March 12, 1964 (after Marina, Marguerite, and Robert Oswald had completed their 468 pages of testimony), the most memorable of their infrequent interventions being a question hostile to Oswald's interests. Thereafter, by agreement with the Commission's chief counsel, the ABA representatives "made suggestions" to counsel instead of participating directly in the proceedings. Therefore, it became impossible to isolate any contribution on their part, much less to infer that there was any safeguard of the interests of the accused or the propriety of the proceedings. Moreover, the ABA observers took no part whatever in the examination of 395 witnesses who did not appear before the Commission but were deposed by counsel. The whole sorry

---

[3] WR xiv.

arrangement was a mockery that further compromised the Commission's claim to impartiality.

Although the Commission excluded the use of the adversary procedure, it did not hesitate to take advantage of its prerogatives—for example, engaging in the preparation of witnesses. The records show repeated instances of "dry runs" in which counsel questioned the witness in advance of his formal testimony. Such prior rehearsal is essential in a trial where the witness's story will be challenged in cross-examination, but in a fact-finding investigation resort to dry runs in advance of testimony can only feed suspicion that there was no search for truth but only for testimony which would buttress a preconceived and fixed conclusion.

A reading of the full testimony also leads to the irresistible conclusion that the witnesses fall into two general categories—the "friendly" and the "unfriendly"—which again is alien to the impartial fact-finding process. In the case of some "unfriendly" witnesses the Commission went beyond a show of antipathy and set out to discredit character. As Paul L. Freese wrote in the *New York University Law Review*, "The technique of character impeachment used by the Commission has disturbing implications."[1] While Freese ascribes the Commission's publication of defamatory comments on certain witnesses to its "zeal to publish the full truth,"[5] it is susceptible to other interpretations. It is striking that the Commission regarded as unimpeachable a number of witnesses whose testimony is inherently disordered and strongly suggestive of falsification or mental incompetence, or both. When Jack Ruby, a convicted murderer, gave testimony in conflict with the testimony of Seth Kantor, a responsible and respected member of the White House press corps, the Commission chose to believe Ruby and decided that Kantor was mistaken. As already mentioned, it relied on Marina Oswald and Helen Markham, both of whom became flagrantly ensnarled in self-contradiction if not outright falsification. By contrast, the Commission set out to impeach the character of a number of witnesses who were disinterested and whose testimony was corroborated by others, apparently for the sole reason that their testimony came into conflict with a theory which was not subject to change regardless of the evidence.

Moreover, it is arresting that off-the-record discussion took place well over two hundred times during the examination of witnesses, on occasion at crucial points in the testimony and as frequently as seven or eight times per witness. Some of those off-the-record passages undoubtedly were innocuous; in many instances, this discussion was placed on the record immediately afterward. However, one witness who was deposed by counsel subsequently appeared before the Commission at his

[1] Paul L. Freese, *New York University Law Review*, Vol. XL, No. 3, May 1965, pp. 424–465.
[5] Ibid., p. 449.

own request to report that during an off-the-record interruption, counsel had accused him of perjury and had threatened him with the loss of his job. If the witness had not placed those facts on the record himself, they would have remained completely concealed from public knowledge. We are therefore entitled to regard the constant resort to off-the-record discussion as an unsatisfactory if not a suspicious practice.

Of the 489 witnesses who gave testimony, less than one-fourth appeared before the Commission itself. Even in those cases, the seven members of the full Commission were never present as a body or throughout an entire session. The Chairman was in attendance at least part of the time for all 94 witnesses who came before the Commission, but his colleagues heard only the following estimated numbers of witnesses:

Representative Ford 70	Mr. McCloy 35
Mr. Dulles 60	Representative Boggs 20
Senator Cooper 50	Senator Russell 6

Some of the difficulties encountered by the members in finding time to spare from other duties for the Commission's needs were almost comical, as may be seen in the following colloquy.

> *Chairman:* Senator Cooper, at this time I am obliged to leave for our all-day conference on Friday at the Supreme Court, and I may be back later in the day, but if I don't, you continue, of course.
> *Cooper:* I will this morning. If I can't be here this afternoon whom do you want to preside?
> *Chairman:* Congressman Ford, would you be here this afternoon at all?
> *Ford:* Unfortunately, Mr. McCloy and I have to go to a conference out of town.
> *Chairman:* You are both going out of town, aren't you?
> *Cooper:* I can go and come back if it is necessary.
> *Chairman:* I will try to be here myself. Will Mr. Dulles be here?
> *McCloy:* He is out of town.

But if attendance was irregular, at least some members of the Commission heard some of the testimony of some of the 94 witnesses who came before the panel. None of the members heard any of the witnesses (well over 350) who testified by deposition; they included such important witnesses as Forrest V. Sorrels, Billy Lovelady, Seymour Weitzman, Earlene Roberts, Sheriff Bill Decker, Abraham Zapruder, Harry Holmes, Domingo Benavides, Nelson Delgado, George De Mohrenschildt, George Bouhe, Jean Lollis Hill, James Tague, Albert Guy Bogard, Dial Ryder, Sylvia Odio, Carlos Bringuier, Gertrude Hunter, Edith Whitworth, George Senator, Harry Olsen, Karen Carlin, and Curtis (Larry) Crafard. A number of witnesses who should have been examined with particular care are represented in the Hearings only by an affidavit. Most appalling of all are the numbers of persons whose names are found nowhere in the list of the Commission's witnesses, from whom no testimony in any form was taken despite indications that they possessed important or crucial information. The failure to examine or, in some instances, to locate such witnesses—including those who gave an account of the Tippit shooting wholly different from the official one—is one of the most serious defects in the Commission's work, and suggests, at the very least, a high degree of negligence.

The Commission's housekeeping is another area in which its performance was inept and undeserving of public confidence. Because of the Commission's inability to maintain control over its internal records, disclosures flowed steadily to the press, including the complete transcript of the examination of Jack Ruby. The Chairman and other spokesmen made a series of ill-advised public statements; the former made an unwarranted attack on the character of a witness and never retracted it, even when the witness exonerated himself from suspicion and requested a retraction. The Chairman also made the shocking statement, still unexplained, that the whole truth might never be known in our lifetime. At least one Commission member capitalized commercially on his experience by publishing an article[6] and later a book[7] purporting to provide a "portrait of the assassin." Apparently the same Commission member is unwilling or unable to explain ambiguities in the Report, including those revealed in his own book, to the taxpayer.

The Commission's failures manifest a contempt for the citizens whom this body pretended to serve—a contempt not for their rights alone but for their intelligence. It must be said, without apology to the authors and advocates of the Warren Report, that it resembles a tale told for fools, full of sophistry and deceit, signifying capitulation to compromise and the degradation of justice by its most eminent guardians.

In June 1966, publication of Edward Jay Epstein's book, *Inquest*,[8] sparked a long overdue national debate on the Warren Report. *Inquest* was followed almost immediately by the private editions *Whitewash* by Harold Weisberg (issued later by Dell as a paperback)[9] and *Forgive My Grief* by Penn Jones, Jr.;[10] and by *Rush to Judgment* by Mark Lane,[11] *The Oswald Affair* by Léo Sauvage,[12] and *The Second Oswald* by Rich-

---

[6] Representative Gerald R. Ford, "Piecing Together the Evidence," *Life*, October 2, 1964, pp. 42–50B.

[7] Representative Gerald R. Ford, *Portrait of the Assassin* (New York: Simon and Schuster and Ballantine Books, 1965).

[8] *Inquest* (New York: Viking Press, 1966).

[9] *Whitewash* (Hyattsville, Maryland: Weisberg, 1966); and *Whitewash: The Report on the Warren Report* (New York: Dell Publishing Co., Inc., 1966).

[10] *Forgive My Grief* (The Midlothian [Tex.] Mirror, 1966).

[11] *Rush to Judgment* (New York: Holt, Rinehart, and Winston, 1966).

[12] *The Oswald Affair* (New York: World Publishing Co., 1966).

ard Popkin.[13] *The Oswald Affair* had appeared in the original French edition (Éditions Minuit, Paris) early in 1965, the first full-length book to assess the official findings on the basis of both the Warren Report and the 26 volumes of Hearings and Exhibits. Unfortunately, it did not become available to American readers until a year and a half after publication in France.

The writers of these books began to be heard on radio and television; news stories and editorials began to appear in respected newspapers, reflecting serious concern about the validity of the Warren Report and suggesting—or demanding, in some cases—that the Commission answer the charges against its Report or that a new investigation be carried out. As this is written, a long list of prominent names are on record as favoring one or another form of new inquiry. Representative Theodore R. Kupferman (R., N.Y.) has presented a joint resolution in the Congress calling for a reappraisal of the Warren Report and, if need be, a new investigation. Former Assistant Counsel Wesley J. Liebeler, embarrassed by his acknowledged contributions to *Inquest*—the book without which no public controversy might now be raging—has launched an attempt to rehabilitate himself. He has organized a new investigation with the stated purpose of reinstating the discredited findings of the Warren Commission, perhaps by re-interpreting the evidence or finding new information. Liebeler is conducting this new investigation with the assistance of 20 law students at the University of California. (*New York Times*, October 23, 1966, p. 66; News broadcast, WINS (N.Y.C.) radio, Oct. 22, 1966.) That a spokesman for the Commission cannot defend the Report as it stands but is seeking a means by which to restore its respectability is in itself a total default to the opposition. Liebeler seems unaware of that.

The critical books and articles that began to appear in June 1966 (and those published earlier that had been ignored before the new wave of skepticism) served as catalytic agents for several major events. One was the sudden announcement early in November 1966 that the notorious autopsy photographs and X-rays had been deposited in the National Archives by the Kennedy family, at the request of the Justice Department (admittedly made as a result of the mounting criticism and questions about the Warren Report). But the terms of the transfer of this evidence to the Archives were such that the photographs and X-rays will not be made available to any individual or organization except a new governmental investigatory body, if one is appointed to further investigate the assassination.[14]

---

[13] *The Second Oswald* (New York: Avon Books/The New York Review of Books, 1966).

[14] *The Reporter*, December 15, 1966, p. 46.

On the third anniversary of President Kennedy's death, *Life*,[15] *Ramparts*,[16] and other influential publications called editorially for further investigation and openly questioned the evidence and the findings of the Warren Commission. The silent principals suddenly spoke up; Governor Connally, Senator Russell, Commander Boswell, and J. Edgar Hoover, among others, tripped over each other in their haste to issue public statements, which, deliberately or inadvertently—and in some instances, unintentionally contravening the purpose of the statement—created new doubt and mystery. The gambit of "producing" the missing autopsy photographs and X-rays, if it was a gambit, in no way stilled the controversy.

We now have a climate in which the news media and public opinion acknowledge what was formerly unthinkable: that the Warren Commission may have erred, or worse. This healthier climate perhaps signifies recovery of the skepticism, independence of mind, and sense of justice to which Americans as a people lay claim as national attributes. Too often, and especially in the Oswald case, the public has been apathetic, ready to accept government "truth," callously indifferent to injustice.

If closed minds continue to open, to receive and evaluate objectively the facts which are on the record, we may yet proceed to pursue the truth to its ultimate reaches—regardless of attendant dangers and doubts —so that history will know with certainty what happened in Dallas, and why.

To that end, investigation into the assassination and the related murders should be reopened, entrusted to an uncompromisingly independent, competent, and impartial body—a body committed to the use of adversary procedure, the rules of evidence, and total respect for justice, in both the letter and the spirit. In other words, a body different from the Warren Commission.

Whether or not that comes to pass in the immediate future, the country owes profound gratitude to the critics and researchers whose work, published or unpublished, has helped to destroy the myth of the Warren Report. Because of their courage, intelligence, and integrity, "it is the majestic Warren Commission itself that is in the dock today, rather than the lonely Oswald," as Anthony Howard wrote in the *London Observer* on August 7, 1966.[17] The Commission must receive justice—that justice which was denied to Oswald in death as in life—but nothing less than justice.

---

[15] *Life*, November 25, 1966, pp. 38–48.
[16] *Ramparts*, November 1966, p. 3.
[17] "The Clamour Rises for Kennedy X-Rays," *The London Observer*, August 7, 1966, p. 10.

For Discussion

1. Evaluate Meagher's summary of the events beginning with the day of the assassination and terminating with the death of Ruby. What are the advantages and limitations of this summary?
2. Why does Meagher attempt to characterize the mood of Dallas and of the nation at the time of the assassination? What can you add from your own personal experience and reading?
3. What basic contradiction does Meagher see between the Warren Report and the Hearings and Exhibits?
4. Compare the position of the advocates of the Report with that of its critics. What does each consider important? What do you?
5. What basic concept of justice does Meagher find abused in regard to Oswald? What other irregularities does she find in the conduct of the Commission? Consider the differences between an investigation and a trial.
6. What does the fact that Meagher independently produced the only index to the Commission's Hearings and Exhibits tell you about her? About the Warren Report?
7. What is the current status of the Warren Report?
8. What examples of ironic humor can you find?
9. To what extent does Meagher allow her feelings to be shown? What is the effect?

AMERICAN FRIENDS SERVICE COMMITTEE

Struggle for Justice

Crime, justice, and punishment have become major public issues today. They have always been among the best-known concerns of the Society of Friends (Quakers), whose basic belief in the dignity of the human personality has long found expression in opposition to war, capital punishment, and the oppression of minorities. Its American Friends Service Committee, formed in 1917 to aid the innocent victims of World War I, works not only to alleviate physical hardship but also to protect civil rights and to effect social change. The following selection, taken from a report on crime and punishment in America, was prepared for the Service Committee by men and women who were familiar with the criminal justice system through their work, visitation, or life inside.

A criminal justice system reflects the values of those who hold power in society. In colonial Massachusetts, for example, the most serious crimes were blasphemy, not attending church, and other activities that would appear harmless to us but were heinous to the ruling theocracy. As we examine the contemporary criminal justice system we can expect to find reflected the values and fears of those who hold power in our society. By their control of the legislative, policing, and criminal labeling processes they define what acts are criminal and set the penalties. Thus criminal law, in both content and administration, often becomes a political instrument, formulated and enforced by those with status and power against those who, predominantly, are status-poor and powerless.

The Founding Fathers were aware of these problems. With the Constitution, the Bill of Rights, and the Fourteenth Amendment they constructed a legal system to protect the exercise of political freedoms unmatched anywhere in the history of representative government. These procedural safeguards include prohibition of ex post facto laws, guarantees of due process and equal protection under the law, and the outlawing of cruel and unusual punishment. They attempted to create an independent judiciary, protecting judges from political reprisals and temptations by means of high salaries and long (or lifelong) terms. Our federal system, a "government of laws not men," was developed to act as a brake on transitory majority opinion and the growth of governmental power.

Yet we see gross inequities in American criminal justice.

. . .

By and large our prisons are reserved for those with dark skins, little money, or unconventional life-styles. In our view crimes committed by all those now in prison are far less damaging to our society than acts against life and health perpetrated by the powerful. We refer to those who develop and manufacture genocidal weapons, those who perpetuate the arms race or prolong the Indochina war for their own commercial advantage, those who pollute or destroy this country's natural resources for financial profit, those who manufacture unsafe automobiles and other dangerous products, price fixers, slum landlords, and others.

Not only do the powerful manage, by and large, to escape the sanctions of the criminal justice system, they also manipulate the system for their own political ends. These are the functions of the criminal justice system we will examine here.

ECONOMIC DOMINANCE

Manipulation of the criminal justice system by the powerful is perhaps most evident in the economic sphere. The struggle by labor for the right to organize is one of the bloodiest chapters in American history. Throughout the nineteenth century and into the twentieth, the courts and police repeatedly took the side of industrialists in blocking attempts to form labor unions and in preventing workers from striking. Violence marked many labor struggles, including the 1877 railroad strike, the 1910 Chicago clothing-industry strike, the 1919 strike against U.S. Steel, and the CIO's attempt to organize Little Steel in 1937, when eighteen were killed.

Judicial intervention was also used in labor disputes. When owners were unable to find excuses for court action in the law itself, they obtained court injunctions against strikers. As late as 1921, the United

States Supreme Court upheld the position that peaceful picketing could be enjoined on the grounds that it was inherently intimidating and coercive in a strike controversy. Court injunctions against picketing in labor disputes are not uncommon even today.

The prosecution of labor leaders under the Sherman Antitrust Act, originally intended to curb business monopolies, indicates the extent to which the Justice Department and the courts identified themselves with business interests. Although the act is a criminal law, the government is given the option of administrative or criminal proceedings. In the 438 actions initiated by the government between 1890 and 1929 with decisions favorable to the government prosecution, 27 percent of the actions against businesses and business associations were criminal, compared with 71 percent of the actions against labor unions.

The use of the courts and police to hamper the organization of labor continues today. The United Farm Workers are a prime example. Their struggle to gain collective strength has been a bitter one, hampered by court injunctions granted the owners of large grape and lettuce farms. Cesar Chavez and other organizers have been jailed for defying such injunctions. Their organizing successes probably would have been impossible without the support of nationwide consumer boycotts.

In New Jersey and other states where migrant laborers have not yet been able to initiate collective efforts, the local institutions of justice are still used to protect the exploitative economic relationship, subordinating the well-being of the pickers to the profits of the growers. Predictable abuses occur within the courts and local jails, especially for Spanish-speaking people. Migrants are arrested without real cause or are given a phony reason. A man arrested on a minor charge who does not have a driver's license or other acceptable identification can be held in jail until the court in that municipality meets—and in some places the court meets only once a month! Bail is set beyond the capacity to pay. Loosely worded trespass laws are enforced in an intimidating manner. As one migrant worker complained to a reporter, "It's very bad. If you don't do what the farmer says, if you cause any trouble, he call the police and get you arrested. Don't tell me about justice here. There is no justice for Puerto Ricans here."[1] Legal Services lawyers attempting to remedy this situation have won a series of legal victories. If these decisions are implemented, the migrant worker will have a little more freedom in Cumberland County, New Jersey.

Tax laws are another means whereby the powerful increase their economic dominance. Efforts to plug scandalous tax loopholes have been unsuccessful for years. Today there are dozens of millionaires who pay no income tax at all. Taxes are extracted from salaried workers every

[1] *The New York Times*, August 17, 1970.

payday by means of withholding; those in the upper brackets have considerably more opportunity to avoid taxes, legally, semilegally, or illegally. When violations are detected, the government rarely invokes the criminal process. The tax cheater can usually get off by paying a fine.

War tax resisters are particularly aware of the selective enforcement of tax laws. These citizens are convinced of the illegality and the immorality of the war in Vietnam and of the genocidal weapons being developed and manufactured. On grounds of conscience they refuse to pay taxes for these activities. They find that they are sometimes hounded by IRS agents for insignificant sums. Refusers have had automobiles seized and auctioned for tax liabilities of less than $5. Refusers acting publicly have been convicted of income-tax fraud. Rather than securing compliance with the tax laws, government efforts to penalize principaled tax refusers may serve, rather, to build a resistance movement.

The government has been extremely reluctant to prosecute business leaders for such widespread and socially harmful crimes as deceptive advertising, pollution, selling dangerous merchandise, and violating antitrust laws. Real-estate agents are almost never prosecuted for blockbusting or for practicing racial discrimination in renting and selling, even though these practices are illegal. Election laws limiting political campaign contributions are violated every two and four years but enforcement policies are lax to the point of not existing. The campaign chests of politicians are regularly enriched by contributions from unions and corporations, even though the Corrupt Practices Act prohibits such institutions from giving money to federal candidates. In its massive *Federal Civil Rights Enforcement Efforts*, the United States Civil Rights Commission recently documented widespread governmental refusal to enforce civil-rights statutes, particularly in the fields of employment, housing, education, agricultural services, labor programs, public accommodations, and public facilities.

When the government acts at all in such cases, it again usually prefers administrative rather than criminal proceedings. Enforcement statutes for economic regulations regularly provide for a variety of mechanisms for enforcement, with criminal procedure clearly regarded as a last resort. Dealing with violations by written warnings was the course the government took in the vast majority of the 980 white-collar crimes E. H. Sutherland found the top seventy corporations to have committed.[2] Only in 159 of the cases was an adverse decision reached in criminal court; the other 821 adverse decisions were all reached either by an administrative commission or by courts under civil or equity jurisdiction. In those rare instances when criminal procedures are used, penalties are relatively mild, usually including a fine and a short term in a minimum-security

[2] *White Collar Crime* (New York: Holt, Rinehart and Winston, 1949).

prison farm. We do not mean to imply that civil procedures are in themselves unjustified; what must be faulted is the class nature of the law enforcement process. Price-fixing General Electric executives receive a penalty of one month, while a thief who may steal only one item receives a penalty of several years.

Studies indicate that white-collar criminals such as the General Electric executives are far from rare. A 1947 study,[3] for example, revealed that 91 percent of a group of almost seventeen hundred New York City residents, chosen for their resemblance to the general population's socioeconomic characteristics but weighted accidentally toward upper income brackets, had committed at least one felony or serious misdemeanor. Among the forty-nine offenses listed on the questionnaire were robbery, bribery, disorderly conduct, malicious mischief, criminal libel, falsification and fraud, perjury, indecency, and health code violations. Thirteen percent of the males had committed grand larceny, 26 percent auto theft, 17 percent burglary. The mean number of offenses per person was eighteen. Roughly half had committed at least one felony for which he had not been caught. Other studies have also documented the universality of undetected or unreported crime.

These results are confirmed by everyday experience. Many Americans at some time have removed items from a motel room, failed to report income tax accurately, smoked pot, or cashed a check without sufficient funds. Most of these offenses are trivial and injure no one, which explains why we can commit them occasionally or even frequently without regarding ourselves as criminals. But then again, people have been sentenced to long prison terms for offenses equally trivial. The boundary line between harmless middle-class offenses and someone else's harmful violations of the law is a fuzzy one. This prejudice in favor of "our own kind" can be seen at its most blatant in the suggestion made in standard reference works on criminal procedure that prosecutors wisely refrain from prosecuting in cases of law violation where the offender comes from a "respectable" background. It never occurs to those who write lawbooks, apparently, that people other than professors and white businessmen might be hurt by a trial or a conviction.

SLAVERY AND RACISM

The justice system functions to maintain a racist relationship between the white majority and the black, brown, red and yellow minorities in America. The command-obedience structure of racism has existed in the

[3] James Wallerstein and C. J. Wyle, "Our Law-abiding Law-breakers," *Probation*, 1947, pp. 107–112.

criminal justice system since the settlement of the country. Possessing the status of real estate or livestock under the cruel system of chattel slavery, black slaves were legal nullities in the eyes of the courts. They were systematically excluded from jury service, holding judgeships, acting in their own defense, and every other provision of criminal law procedure that protected white propertied males. Rendered "three-fifths of a man" by the Constitution, the slave came to know the legal system only as an extension of the rule of the slave system.

Before the Civil War the legal status of the freed Negro paralleled the slave's utter legal powerlessness. Criminal sentences often included the provision that freedmen could be sold into slavery as punishment for a criminal offense or in lieu of payment of taxes, fines, or civil judgments. Vaguely worded vagrancy statutes were ideal weapons for intimidating supposedly free black people. Vagrancy and other laws commonly provided for immediate punishment—usually whipping—without trial, empowering slave patrols and private citizens to be at one time complainant, judge, jury, and enforcement officer.

States outside the South also passed freed Negro laws which, though often less severe than the South's, served the same purpose. The testimony of persons with "one-eighth Negro blood" was declared incompetent by Illinois and Delaware statutes. In Iowa free black persons could not be witnesses in cases involving whites. In Ohio blacks had to post bond as a condition of good behavior to secure residence. In 1853 Illinois made it a misdemeanor for a black to enter the state with the intention of residing. Throughout the country, by law and tradition, blacks were nonpersons in the eyes of the justice system, a status that mirrored their lack of rights of any political, economic, or social consequence in any other area of life.

After the Civil War emancipated black people saw the master-slave relationship replaced by a master-servant relationship. Many of the restrictive provisions originally applied to freed Negroes were included in the infamous Black Codes. Several states created separate systems of criminal courts for blacks, who could not testify in white courts, nor could they serve as judges or jurors in either court system. Although such punishments had been abolished for whites, blacks could be confined in public stocks or whipped.

As blatantly discriminatory laws were repealed during the era of Radical Reconstruction, more subtly restrictive statutes replaced them. Blacks were allowed to serve as witnesses, but a widely enacted statute provided that "whenever a person of color shall be examined as a witness, the court shall warn the witness to declare the truth." Whites were not similarly warned. Although the Black Code of Texas provided that "there shall be no discrimination against such persons [blacks] in the administration of the criminal laws of this state," it included the qualifications that the law did not permit blacks to intermarry with whites, serve on juries, vote, or testify in cases involving whites.

The socially subordinate position of blacks within the criminal justice system has remained practically unchanged. Police brutality and summary violence still characterize the police presence in the black community. Jury service remains a restricted white privilege, making a mockery of the concept of investigation and judgment by one's peers. With token exceptions, the personnel of the justice system are white, forcing members of minority groups to face police, district attorneys, wardens, judges, and parole-board members who represent historically the oppressor's caste. Other forms of racism are more hidden. A judge or jury may weigh the credibility of a black witness's testimony differently from a white's. Cultural differences in dress, hairstyle, and speech may work to the disadvantage of minority men and women. Residual racial practices surviving from the era of slavery show that discrimination is not simply a matter of intentional policy; it also emerges from deeply ingrained attitudes and institutional prejudices that still survive.

In prisons racism is manifested in unequal job assignments, with blacks assigned to the most menial tasks. Black nationalist and Black Muslim literature is often banned. Individual guards who are racists or sadists or both have ample opportunity to abuse prisoners. Blacks who are affirming their cultural and racial identity are particularly likely targets. Those who show signs of becoming inmate leaders or who challenge institutional practices through lawsuits commonly suffer administrative punishments (the hole, strip cells, restricted diet, loss of privileges), or are transferred punitively, often to prisons with notorious reputations for brutal racist environments.

Racism is often consciously encouraged by prison officials who hope to keep black, brown, and white inmates occupied with fighting each other and hence more easily managed. Their strategy is to divide the races and control the convicts. A letter smuggled out by a black prisoner in Soledad Prison gives a picture of the depths of racial oppression and degradation that can occur behind walls:

> Never more than 6 blacks were allowed on max. row, which houses 24 inmates. Thus the remaining 18 cells were occupied by anti-black Caucasian and Mexican inmates who race talk us in shifts so that it's done 24 hours a day. On their exercise periods they spit, throw urine and feces in our cells while the officials stand by in indifference and approval. They, the officials call us HAMMERS and NIGGERS too. (Both expressions mean the same thing.) The prison officials here stopped serving the meals and deliberately selected the Caucasian and Mexican inmates (described throughout this letter) to serve the meals and they immediately proceeded to poison our meals

by filling food to be issued to us with cleanser powder, crushed up glass, spit, urine and feces while the officials stood by and laughed.[4]

Another example of officially inspired racism is given by a prisoner at the Federal Youth Center in Ashland, Kentucky, who described an incident in which a black inmate beat up a white guard.

Notice that this "race trouble" was initiated by a fight between an inmate and a guard, and that the inmate got the better of the guard. Recognizing that the event could readily inspire similar attacks on them, the dormitory guards played up their racist solidarity with white southerners by interpreting the fray as a conflict between black and white instead of as a conflict between guard and prisoner. If they could sell their interpretation, they would at least gain a few white inmate protectors and possibly create enough tension between black and white inmates that the threat to themselves would be removed. The crew bosses' lectures the next day performed the same function of convincing prisoners to fight each other rather than the staff. The racial attack that was successfully instigated in this way set the whole compound on edge and effectively took the heat off the Man.[5]

The experiences of other oppressed minorities within the justice system parallel the treatment of blacks. An an instrument of Anglo domination, the justice apparatus serves to oppress Mexican-Americans in the Southwest. The United States Civil Rights Commission has reported widespread patterns of excessive police violence, discriminatory treatment of Chicano juveniles, biased enforcement of motor vehicle regulations, discourtesies to local Chicano citizens, and excessive use of stop-and-frisk laws to harass and intimidate local communities.[6] The commission found an almost total absence of Mexican-Americans on juries and noted that the "wide disparities" between jury service and population proportion could not be accounted for by language difficulties, educational levels, or other commonly offered excuses. Officials "abused their discretion" in setting excessive bail. In noting an almost total absence of Mexican-Americans among justice system employees, the commission found an almost systematic avoidance of the Spanish language by law enforcement personnel, which meant that routine contacts with police could easily escalate into major conflicts and that Chicanos in criminal courts "cannot plead intelligently, advise their lawyers with respect to the facts, fully understand the testimony of witnesses against them, or otherwise adequately prepare or assist in their

[4] "Black Caucus Report: Treatment of Prisoners at California Training Facility at Soledad Central," Black Caucus in the California State Legislature, July 1970.
[5] Jim Wessner, "Racism in Federal Prison," *The Peacemaker*, May 2, 1970, pp. 1–2.
[6] "Mexican-Americans and the Administration of Justice in the Southwest," March 1970.

own defense." The same pattern extends to probation and parole boards.

The brutality of racism and the indignities of second-class citizenship still characterize much of the administration of criminal justice. The racist ideologies of chattel slavery and of "separate but equal" have been declared legally dead, but the funeral continues and the ugly corpse has not yet been buried. The justice system remains an instrument of white Anglo domination and a barrier to the development of full power within communities of oppressed peoples.

JUVENILES

Blacks and Chicanos are not the only groups in our society upon whom cultural assimilation has been forced. The American majority has found all minority races and cultures threatening and has treated many of them ruthlessly. Consider the wholesale slaughter of the American Indian.

In the nineteenth century the waves of European immigrants came in for their share of forced assimilation. Being less different from the majority than Indians and blacks, they were treated less barbarically, but they were still treated as second-class citizens. The criminal justice apparatus was part of the social structure used to repress them. One method of accomplishing this was through the creation of a new category of criminals: juvenile delinquents.

Under the guise of saving children from a debauching environment, juvenile delinquency laws made into crimes types of youthful behavior that in the past had been handled informally—sexual promiscuity, staying out late at night, drinking, smoking, reading comic books, truancy, running away, and disobedience to parents and teachers.

Of course the child-saving movement was bathed in a sea of self-righteousness.[7] Heavy emphasis was placed on "rescuing" victims of unhealthy environments—usually city slums—and "elevating" them to a middle-class style of life. An 1855 report from a New York City agency makes reference to

> large numbers of poor Italian children engaged in street occupations, following the heart and the hand-organ, selling newspapers, blackening boots, and the like, who were growing up utterly without education or moral discipline . . . The greatest difficulties were the greed of the parents to get all possible earnings from their children without regard to their education, the bigotry of some of their advisers and the existence amongst them of a species of serfdom.

[7] We have drawn on Anthony Platt, *The Child-Savers: The Invention of Delinquency* (Chicago: University of Chicago Press, 1969).

This kind of theme runs with monotonous regularity through report after report: Get the Italian children (in Boston it would have been the Irish) away from their "bigoted" advisers (who else but the Catholic priest?) so that they can receive moral and religious treatment from instructors whose denominational neutrality, so the report tells us, runs the gamut from Episcopalian to Unitarian. Save these children from greedy parents and the labor of blackening boots by placing them in child-labor manufacturing establishments or, if female, in domestic service in respectable homes.

To accomplish these ends, new judicial and correctional institutions were created. Since criminal court procedures were thought to be unsuitable to cases involving juveniles—who were, after all, being "helped," not "punished"—procedural guarantees were abolished in favor of an informal approach. Almost every conceivable abuse occurs—the use of unsubstantiated rumor as evidence, coercive, imposition of psychiatric or social welfare treatment on the basis of presumed need, confusing procedures that leave parents and child unable to present evidence without the assistance of a lawyer, confusion of child-neglect cases with delinquency, arbitrary sentences, and unnecessary stigmatization through failure to keep records confidential.

Although the juvenile may expect to be rewarded in return for the waiver of so many rights, the rewards are often scanty. The juvenile court system of "Metropolitan City," studied by Abraham Blumberg,[8] convicted juveniles more frequently than adults. Sentences are indeterminate and may be longer than for adults. Perhaps the worst feature of the juvenile court system is that no specific law-violating act has to be committed by a juvenile for him or her to be brought under the "parental" care of the courts. Thus, "growing up in idleness," exhibiting "vicious or immoral behavior," "incorrigibility," or "living with any vicious or disreputable person" can justify judicial intervention.

In addition, the shortcomings of the criminal justice system already described are inflicted upon juvenile offenders as well. Often, because of their youth, the consequences are worse. In reformatories there is probably more brutality, intimidation, and homosexual coercion than in adult prisons. Educational and vocational programs are probably more outmoded. The juvenile offender probably has less chance than his adult counterpart of breaking away from a life of repeated return to imprisonment.

WOMEN

The law is both the mirror of a biased society and the source of prejudice. Just as the black man was described originally in the Constitution as three-fifths of a man, so under common law "a woman has no legal

[8] *Criminal Justice* (Chicago: Quadrangle, 1967).

existence separate from her husband, who was regarded as her head and representative in the social state," according to a United States Supreme Court decision in 1872. Some years later, in 1898, a Virginia court decided that under law a "woman" is not a "person." In 1966 the Supreme Court upheld a Texas law providing that a married woman does not have the capacity to enter into a binding contract. Justice Hugo Black dissented, deploring the fact that the Court "should exalt this archaic remnant of a primitive caste system . . . This rule has worked out in reality to mean that though the husband and wife are one, the one is the husband."[9]

A woman under the common-law tradition loses her legal personality when she marries. Issues are raised of "right to a separate domicile; capacity to sue and be sued; change in citizenship upon marriage to an alien."[10] One contemporary example of hardship resulting from a denial of the right to separate domicile is the case of a young woman who tried to enter law school in a Pennsylvania state-supported university. Because her husband, from whom she was separated but not divorced, had his legal residence in another state, the fee would have been doubled and, consequently, she was unable to enroll. In another instance, the woman on welfare has been subjected in recent years to the searching of her home to see if she is having a sexual relationship and if so, cutting off her welfare. Known as the "man in the house" rule, it was not balanced by a "woman in the house" rule.

Gunnar Myrdal, in his classic *An American Dilemma*, comments that the myth of the "contented woman," who does not want suffrage or other civil rights and equal opportunities, has the same social function as the myth of the "contented Negro." Women, black and white, remained unenfranchised until 1920—sixty-five years after the vote had technically at least been granted to males of any race.

Almost one-fourth of the complaints received since passage of Title VII of the 1964 Civil Rights Act, which forbids discrimination, including discrimination on the basis of sex, in employment, have been from women.[11] Approximately half of the women surveyed in a recent study covering all women law-school graduates of the years 1956–1965 stated that they have been discriminated against by employers and that their average income differed sharply, based on sex.[12]

In 1968 the United States Supreme Court considered the case of a girl who was imprisoned for "lascivious carriage" under a Connecticut law authorizing imprisonment of young women if they are "in manifest danger of falling into habits of vice." Laws may provide for different lengths of jail sentences for the same crime, depending on whether the

[9] Quoted by Diane B. Schulder, "Does the Law Oppress Women?" in *Sisterhood Is Powerful*, Robin Morgan, ed. (New York: Vintage, 1970), p. 149. This excellent article also contains complete citations of the court decisions mentioned.
[10] Ibid.
[11] "Report of the U.S. Commission on Civil Rights," 1970.
[12] Schulder, op. cit., p. 146.

perpetrator is male or female (1968). In many states, dispensing birth-control information is a crime and the struggle of women for legalized and safe abortion is far from won. Thus in the areas of sex and repro-duction the law has more direct control over women than men.

One of the most discriminatory areas of criminal law relates to prosti-tution. "In New York City policemen actively entrap women and then charge them with prostitution . . . This despite the fact that New York law states that prostitutes and their customers are guilty of equal viola-tions . . . The New York District Attorney's office has also chosen not to prosecute the men customers [lest] big business conventions . . . cancel out of New York City and go elsewhere."[13] This practice is not confined to New York City.

Little has been written about women in prison. The definitive report of the President's Commission on Law Enforcement and the Administra-tion of Justice devotes not even a paragraph to the female "offender." Although only a very small percentage of the crimes committed by women involve violence, alternatives to incarceration are almost non-existent. "The only advantage women have over men [in America's] penal system is that fewer of them are in it. . . . But those who are hand-cuffed and ushered into cells [throughout the nation] face some of the worst conditions available."[14] A special torment for women is separation from their children and the fear that the state may take them away. Often women who are arrested and prohibited from making a phone call have left young children at home and become frantic about their safety. One of the grievances of the inmates of the Tombs was the lack of respect shown by the guards to their wives, mothers, and sisters who came to visit. The wives of prisoners must shoulder responsibility for both parents, often face the scorn and hostility of the community, and are often subjected to insulting treatment from the administrators of prisons.

Jails for women include one federal reformatory, at Alderson, Vir-ginia, which also has the only woman superintendent in the Federal Bureau of Prisons. Some inmates feel that because a woman is its chief officer it is perhaps the "best of the worst" of all the places that incar-cerate women. The superintendent has said:

> I don't like jails and I'm not going to defend them. There's no jail in the world that's any good. They're bad places and you're in them against your will. If you're black, poor or a woman in twentieth-century America the dice have been loaded against you.[15]

[13] Ibid., pp. 155–156.
[14] Kitsi Burkhart in a prizewinning series on prisons in the Philadelphia *Evening Bulletin*, January 1971.
[15] Kitsi Burkhart, "Women in Prison," *Ramparts*, June 1971.

CULTURAL ASSIMILATION TODAY

As part of treatment and rehabilitation, cultural assimilation is forced upon wayward, threatening, or unconventional groups. Every day criminal justice personnel make hundreds of low-level discretionary decisions that glorify their middle-class life-style. This can be seen in a batch of probation and parole reports involving neglect proceedings against mothers of very young children.

The reports constantly reiterate such factors as the "subject's" "slovenly housekeeping," "sexual promiscuity," "failure to keep her appointments," "frequenting taverns," "allowing older children to loiter on street corners," and "her apparent willingness to let welfare continue supporting her." We will look at the implications of some of these phrases.

The designation of the mother-defendant as a "subject" demeans her, emphasizing her inequality. It also reflects the cold impersonality of a bureaucracy too dehumanized to call her by name.

References to "slovenly housekeeping" reveal a Puritanical dust phobia. References to "promiscuity," "taverns," and "loitering" reflect the pervasive middle-class inability to understand why the poor do not unwind in the privacy and quiet of their living rooms instead of in public establishments of dubious propriety. Why don't they take the air on golf courses instead of loitering on street corners? Why don't they conduct their love affairs secretly? Why do they shoot craps in back alleys instead of playing bingo at a neighborhood church? Or why don't they fly to Las Vegas for more elaborate entertainment? References to "welfare" reveal the increasingly outmoded Protestant work ethic.

Complaints about not keeping appointments are frequent in welfare and correctional literature. Woe betide the parolee who misses an appointment! Here we have in microcosm the clash between a life-style where time is relatively unimportant and an establishment whose agencies have long waiting lists, whose courts are smothered by their dockets, whose social workers are bowed down by their case loads, and whose officials exaggerate their own importance. One can imagine Thoreau, who believed in wide margins and had little use for those who voluntarily spent their lives under the crushing weight of a barn and forty acres, siding with the "subjects" and joining in an amused contemplation of the uptight caseworker.

For the prisoner time has a different perspective. It is something to be marked off, endured. He has already learned all too painfully in most contacts with officials that what he really wants or feels or thinks will be ignored. By the time the case worker gets to him, the "subject" will already have experienced an appointed counsel or public defender who gave him the once over lightly; a judge who disposed of his life alternatives in a moment or two of judicial time as part of an assembly-line process; and a whole series of unthinking, unfeeling functionaries within institutions. No wonder the "subjects" keep failing to keep their appointments with those who are trying to "help" them.

One could search the criminal code in vain to find laws prohibiting lateness to appointments or unconventionality of dress and social habits. Yet these are the standards being enforced. Many prison treatment programs carry this degradation to an extreme. Heavy emphasis is placed on unquestioned obedience to authority, the sanctity of the employer-employee relationship, acquiescence to perform drudgery work or service occupations, and the centrality of money and materialistic goals.

POLITICAL REPRESSION

A fundamental though unacknowledged function of the criminal justice system is political repression. This was the motive for passage of the federal Antiriot and Conspiracy Act of 1968 and for its use in the Chicago and Seattle trials. These trials are in every substantial respect today's counterpart of the prosecution of Communists during the Smith Act trials of the 1950s, the aim in each case being to discredit political opponents. In both instances there were already ample statutes on the books to punish violent disruption and to safeguard society.

The prosecutions of H. Rap Brown, Lee Otis Johnson, John Sinclair, and the Harrisburg 6 are similarly political in motivation. Likewise, a strong element of vindictiveness and persecution for political reasons pervades the treatment of those whose conscience has led them to break the law. We refer, for example, to the Catonsville 9 and the Washington May Day demonstrators. Whatever one may think about the necessity of pressing criminal charges in such cases, the government has responded with overkill tactics in the press and in the courtroom.

The same response to "political" crimes may also be observed on the local level. The authorities find some offenses more offensive than others. The Philadelphia Police Department swiftly removes and arrests peace demonstrators blocking the Induction Center but has yet to arrest housewives conducting sit-ins in busy intersections to protest the absence of a traffic light.

At times the police have acted as political executioners, as seems to be the case in the alleged murder of Black Panther leaders Mark Clark and Fred Hampton by sheriff's deputies while they slept.

The use of the courts and police against radicals is nothing new in American history. Abolitionists and labor organizers came up against these sorts of repression time and time again. In the first decades of this century the Wobblies—Industrial Workers of the World—were persecuted from coast to coast. They were convicted of such crimes as "criminal syndicalism" and their movement was eventually smashed. During the 1960s the full range of repression was used against civil-rights workers in the South.

This country now appears to be entering a new phase of repression against activist forces struggling for change. In addition to the overt political repression already mentioned, there is an ominous expansion of police power that has scarcely been noticed. Police forces, built up after the civil and campus disorders of the late 1960s, have become paramilitary. They have received training from the Department of Defense and are adapting to domestic use weapons developed for Vietnam.

This trend within police departments has led to the emergence of a police/industrial/educational complex spawned by the Pentagon. The Law Enforcement Assistance Administration (LEAA), a federal agency created in 1968, is budgeted for $1,750,000,000 in 1973 and is slated to continue to expand.[16] LEAA funds police training programs in 880 colleges and universities. It also includes work on counterinsurgency techniques and the development of new weapons and equipment.

Secret police have sprung up like mushrooms in recent years. Not only the FBI, the CIA, and the Intelligence branches of the various armed forces, but dozens of other agencies, national and local, are spying on hundreds of thousands of us. They have at their disposal sophisticated electronic surveillance equipment and computerized storage and retrieval of information. Spying has snowballed and is now out of control. Implications for the future are frightening.

In the face of this strong thrust toward highly centralized, strongly armed, computerized, and professionalized police departments, plus secret police, the traditional concept of the police function in a free society is breaking down. The police are no longer peacekeepers under the control of civilian governments and responsive to the needs and wishes of the people. What can be done to bring the police back under the control of the communities they are supposed to serve? The prospect is not bright.

In a totalitarian society the repressive functions we have enumerated . . . dominate the criminal justice system. In a free society such functions should be minimized or eliminated. We hope that an awareness of the pervasiveness of these functions in the American system can lead to change. We will not be able to do away with these repressive functions until social prejudice and inequality are uprooted and eradicated from society as a whole.

---

[16] Lee Webb, "Back Home: Campus Beat," in *Police on the Homefront* (Philadelphia: National Action/Research on the Military-Industrial Complex, 1971), p. 8.

For Discussion

1. What basic assertions about the criminal justice system are presented in the opening paragraphs of this selection?
2. How does the criminal justice system discriminate against laborers? Salaried workers? War tax resisters?
3. What examples are given to show that the criminal justice system remains "an instrument of white Anglo domination"? What additional examples can you provide to support or modify this claim?
4. What was the moral justification for the creation of juvenile delinquency laws? How well have they served their declared purpose?
5. What assumptions about women are implicit in the discriminatory practices of the legal system?
6. In what ways do criminal justice personnel impose their middle-class standards on the public they serve?
7. In what ways has the criminal justice system made political activities a crime?
8. Give examples of the expansion of police powers in recent years at both the local and national levels.
9. What current developments support or modify the assertions made about the criminal justice system in this selection?
10. Identify the ways in which the authors support their assertions. Comment upon the nature and/or authority of their sources.

THOMAS S. SZASZ

The Ethics
of Addiction

Born in Hungary in 1920, Thomas S. Szasz came to this country
when he was eighteen. A year later he entered the University
of Cincinnati, earning an A.B. degree in physics in two years,
and then went on to earn his M.D., graduating first in his class.
After an internship at Harvard, he trained as a psychiatrist at the
University of Chicago and a psychoanalyst at the Chicago
Institute for Psychoanalysis. In 1956 he moved to Syracuse,
where he became professor of psychiatry at the State University
of New York Upstate Medical Center, a position he still holds.
Szasz has written many books on psychiatry and psychology,
including *The Myth of Mental Illness* and *The Manufacture of
Madness.*

To avoid clichés about "drug abuse," let us analyze its official definition. According to the World Health Organization, "Drug addiction is a
state of periodic or chronic intoxication detrimental to the individual and
to society, produced by the repeated consumption of a drug (natural or
synthetic). Its characteristics include: 1) an overpowering desire or need
(compulsion) to continue taking the drug and to obtain it by any means,
2) a tendency to increase the dosage, and 3) a psychic (psychological)
and sometimes physical dependence on the effects of the drug."

Since this definition hinges on the harm done to both the individual
and society, it is clearly an ethical one. Moreover, by not specifying what
is "detrimental," it consigns the problem of addiction to psychiatrists
who define the patient's "dangerousness to himself and others."

Next, we come to the effort to obtain the addictive substance "by any
means." This suggests that the substance must be prohibited, or is very

expensive, and is hence difficult for the ordinary person to obtain (rather than that the person who wants it has an inordinate craving for it). If there were an abundant and inexpensive supply of what the "addict" wants, there would be no reason for him to go to "any means" to obtain it. Thus by the WHO's definition, one can be addicted only to a substance that is illegal or otherwise difficult to obtain. This surely removes the problem of addiction from the realm of medicine and psychiatry, and puts it squarely into that of morals and law.

In short, drug addiction or drug abuse cannot be defined without specifying the proper and improper uses of certain pharmacologically active agents. The regular administration of morphine by a physician to a patient dying of cancer is the paradigm of the proper use of a narcotic; whereas even its occasional self-administration by a physically healthy person for the purpose of "pharmacological pleasure" is the paradigm of drug abuse.

I submit that these judgments have nothing whatever to do with medicine, pharmacology, or psychiatry. They are moral judgments. Indeed, our present views on addiction are astonishingly similar to some of our former views on sex. Until recently, masturbation—or self-abuse, as it was called—was professionally declared, and popularly accepted, as both the cause and the symptom of a variety of illnesses. Even today, homosexuality—called a "sexual perversion"—is regarded as a disease by medical and psychiatric experts as well as by "well-informed" laymen.

To be sure, it is now virtually impossible to cite a contemporary medical authority to support the concept of self-abuse. Medical opinion holds that whether a person masturbates or not is medically irrelevant; and that engaging in the practice or refraining from it is a matter of personal morals or life-style. On the other hand, it is virtually impossible to cite a contemporary medical authority to oppose the concept of drug abuse. Medical opinion holds that drug abuse is a major medical, psychiatric, and public health problem; that drug addiction is a disease similar to diabetes, requiring prolonged (or lifelong) and careful, medically supervised treatment; and that taking or not taking drugs is primarily, if not solely, a matter of medical responsibility.

Thus the man on the street can only believe what he hears from all sides—that drug addiction is a disease, "like any other," which has now reached "epidemic" proportions," and whose "medical" containment justifies the limitless expenditure of tax monies and the corresponding aggrandizement and enrichment of noble medical warriors against this "plague."

PROPAGANDA TO JUSTIFY PROHIBITION

Like any social policy, our drug laws may be examined from two entirely different points of view: technical and moral. Our present inclination is either to ignore the moral perspective or to mistake the technical for the moral.

Since most of the propagandists against drug abuse seek to justify certain repressive policies because of the alleged dangerousness of various drugs, they often falsify the facts about the true pharmacological properties of the drugs they seek to prohibit. They do so for two reasons: first, because many substances in daily use are just as harmful as the substances they want to prohibit; second, because they realize that dangerousness alone is never a sufficiently persuasive argument to justify the prohibition of any drug, substance, or artifact. Accordingly, the more they ignore the moral dimensions of the problem, the more they must escalate their fraudulent claims about the dangers of drugs.

To be sure, some drugs are more dangerous than others. It is easier to kill oneself with heroin than with aspirin. But it is also easier to kill oneself by jumping off a high building than a low one. In the case of drugs, we regard their potentiality for self-injury as justification for their prohibition; in the case of buildings, we do not.

Furthermore, we systematically blur and confuse the two quite different ways in which narcotics may cause death: by a deliberate act of suicide or by accidental overdosage.

Every individual is capable of injuring or killing himself. This potentiality is a fundamental expression of human freedom. Self-destructive behavior may be regarded as sinful and penalized by means of informal sanctions. But it should not be regarded as a crime or (mental) disease, justifying or warranting the use of the police powers of the state for its control.

Therefore, it is absurd to deprive an adult of a drug (or of anything else) because he might use it to kill himself. To do so is to treat everyone the way institutional psychiatrists treat the so-called suicidal mental patient: they not only imprison such a person but take everything away from him—shoelaces, belts, razor blades, eating utensils, and so forth—until the "patient" lies naked on a mattress in a padded cell—lest he kill himself. The result is degrading tyrannization.

Death by accidental overdose is an altogether different matter. But can anyone doubt that this danger now looms so large precisely because the sale of narcotics and many other drugs is illegal? Those who buy illicit drugs cannot be sure what drug they are getting or how much of it. Free trade in drugs, with governmental action limited to safeguarding the purity of the product and the veracity of the labeling, would reduce the risk of accidental overdose with "dangerous drugs" to the same levels that prevail, and that we find acceptable, with respect to other chemical agents and physical artifacts that abound in our complex technological society.

This essay is not intended as an exposition on the pharmacological properties of narcotics and other mind-affecting drugs. However, I want to make it clear that in my view, *regardless* of their danger, all drugs should be "legalized" (a misleading term I employ reluctantly as a concession to common usage). Although I recognize that some drugs—notably heroin, the amphetamines, and LSD, among those now in vogue—may have undesirable or dangerous consequences, I favor free trade in drugs for the same reason the Founding Fathers favored free trade in ideas. In an open society, it is none of the government's business what idea a man puts into his mind; likewise, it should be none of the government's business what drug he puts into his body.

WITHDRAWAL PAINS FROM TRADITION

It is a fundamental characteristic of human beings that they get used to things: one becomes habituated, or "addicted," not only to narcotics, but to cigarettes, cocktails before dinner, orange juice for breakfast, comic strips, and so forth. It is similarly a fundamental characteristic of living organisms that they acquire increasing tolerance to various chemical agents and physical stimuli: the first cigarette may cause nothing but nausea and headache; a year later, smoking three packs a day may be pure joy. Both alcohol and opiates are "addictive" in the sense that the more regularly they are used, the more the user craves them and the greater his tolerance for them becomes. Yet none of this involves any mysterious process of "getting hooked." It is simply an aspect of the universal biological propensity for *learning*, which is especially well developed in man. The opiate habit, like the cigarette habit or food habit, can be broken—and without any medical assistance—provided the person wants to break it. Often he doesn't. And why, indeed, should he, if he has nothing better to do with his life? Or, as happens to be the case with morphine, if he can live an essentially normal life while under its influence?

Actually, opium is much less toxic than alcohol. Just as it is possible to be an "alcoholic" and work and be productive, so it is (or, rather, it used to be) possible to be an opium addict and work and be productive. According to a definitive study published by the American Medical Association in 1929, ". . . morphine addiction is not characterized by physical deterioration or impairment of physical fitness . . . There is no evidence of change in the circulatory, hepatic, renal, or endocrine functions. When it is considered that these subjects had been addicted for at least five years, some of them for as long as twenty years, these negative observations are highly significant." In a 1928 study, Lawrence Kolb, an Assistant Surgeon General of the United States Public Health Service, found that of 119 persons addicted to opiates through medical practice, "90 had good industrial records and only 29 had poor ones . . . Judged by the output of labor and their own statements, none of the normal persons had [his] efficiency reduced by opium. Twenty-two of them worked regularly while taking opium for twenty-five years or more; one of them, a woman aged 81 and still alert mentally, had taken 3 grains of morphine daily for 65 years. [The usual therapeutic dose is one-quarter grain, three to four grains being fatal for the nonaddict.] She gave birth to and raised six children, and managed her household affairs with more than average efficiency. A widow, aged 66, had taken 17 grains of morphine daily for most of 37 years. She is alert mentally . . . does physical labor every day, and makes her own living."

I am not citing this evidence to recommend the opium habit. The point is that we must, in plain honesty, distinguish between pharmacological effects and personal inclinations. Some people take drugs to help them function and conform to social expectations; others take them for the very opposite reason, to ritualize their refusal to function and conform to social expectations. Much of the "drug abuse" we now witness—perhaps nearly all of it—is of the second type. But instead of acknowledging that "addicts" are unfit or unwilling to work and be "normal," we prefer to believe that they act as they do because certain drugs—especially heroin, LSD, and the amphetamines—make them "sick." If only we could get them "well," so runs this comforting view, they would become "productive" and "useful" citizens. To believe this is like believing that if an illiterate cigarette smoker would only stop smoking, he would become an Einstein. With a falsehood like this, one can go far. No wonder that politicians and psychiatrists love it.

The concept of free trade in drugs runs counter to our cherished notion that everyone must work and idleness is acceptable only under special conditions. In general, the obligation to work is greatest for healthy, adult, white men. We tolerate idleness on the part of children, women, Negroes, the aged, and the sick, and even accept the responsibility to support them. But the new wave of drug abuse affects mainly young adults, often white males, who are, in principle at least, capable of working and supporting themselves. But they refuse: they "drop out"; and in doing so, they challenge the most basic values of our society.

The fear that free trade in narcotics would result in vast masses of our population spending their days and nights smoking opium or mainlining heroin, rather than working and taking care of their responsibilities, is a bugaboo that does not deserve to be taken seriously. Habits of work and idleness are deep-seated cultural patterns. Free trade in abortions has not made an industrious people like the Japanese give up work for fornication. Nor would free trade in drugs convert such a people from hustlers to hippies. Indeed, I think the opposite might be the case: it is questionable whether, or for how long, a responsible people can tolerate being treated as totally irresponsible with respect to drugs and drug-taking. In other words, how long can we live with the inconsistency of being expected to be responsible for operating cars and computers, but not for operating our own bodies?

Although my argument about drug-taking is moral and political, and does not depend upon showing that free trade in drugs would also have fiscal advantages over our present policies, let me indicate briefly some of its economic implications.

The war on addiction is not only astronomically expensive; it is also counterproductive. On April 1, 1967, New York State's narcotics addiction control program, hailed as "the most massive ever tried in the nation," went into effect. "The program, which may cost up to $400 million in three years," reported the *New York Times*, "was hailed by Governor Rockefeller as 'the start of an unending war.'" Three years later, it was conservatively estimated that the number of addicts in the state had tripled or quadrupled. New York State Senator John Hughes reports that the cost of caring for each addict during this time was $12,000 per year (as against $4,000 per year for patients in state mental hospitals). It's been a great time, though, for some of the ex-addicts. In New York City's Addiction Services Agency, one ex-addict started at $6,500 a year in 1967, and was making $16,000 seven months later. Another started at $6,500 and soon rose to $18,100. The salaries of the medical bureaucrats in charge of these programs are similarly attractive. In short, the detection and rehabilitation of addicts is good business. We now know that the spread of witchcraft in the late Middle Ages was due more to the work of witchmongers than to the lure of witchcraft. Is it not possible that the spread of addiction in our day is due more to the work of addictmongers than to the lure of narcotics?

Let us see how far some of the monies spent on the war on addiction could go in supporting people who prefer to drop out of society and drug themselves. Their "habit" itself would cost next to nothing; free trade would bring the price of narcotics down to a negligible amount. During the 1969–70 fiscal year, the New York State Narcotics Addiction Control Commission had a budget of nearly $50 million, excluding capital construction. Using these figures as a tentative base for calculation, here is what we come to: $100 million will support 30,000 drug addicts at $3,300 per year. Since the population of New York State is roughly one-tenth that of the nation, if we multiply its operating budget for addiction control by ten, we arrive at a figure of $500 million, enough to support 150,000 addicts.

I am not advocating that we spend our hard-earned money in this way. I am only trying to show that free trade in narcotics would be more economical for those of us who work, even if we had to support legions of addicts, than is our present program of trying to "cure" them. Moreover, I have not even made use, in my economic estimates, of the incalculable sums we would have by reducing crimes now engendered by the illegal traffic in drugs.

THE RIGHT OF SELF-MEDICATION

Clearly, the argument that marijuana—or heroin, methadone, or morphine—is prohibited because it is addictive or dangerous cannot be supported by facts. For one thing, there are many drugs, from insulin to penicillin, that are neither addictive nor dangerous but are nevertheless also prohibited; they can be obtained only through a physician's prescription. For another, there are many things, from dynamite to guns, that are much more dangerous than narcotics (especially to others) but are not prohibited. As everyone knows, it is still possible in the United States to walk into a store and walk out with a shotgun. We enjoy this right not because we believe that guns are safe but because we believe even more strongly that civil liberties are precious. At the same time, it is not possible in the United States to walk into a store and walk out with a bottle of barbiturates, codeine, or other drugs.

I believe that just as we regard freedom of speech and religion as fundamental rights, so we should also regard freedom of self-medication as a fundamental right. Like most rights, the right of self-medication should apply only to adults; and it should not be an unqualified right. Since these are important qualifications, it is necessary to specify their precise range.

John Stuart Mill said (approximately) that a person's right to swing his arm ends where his neighbor's nose begins. And Oliver Wendell Holmes said that no one has a right to shout "Fire!" in a crowded theater. Similarly, the limiting condition with respect to self-medication should be the inflicting of actual (as against symbolic) harm on others.

Our present practices with respect to alcohol embody and reflect this individualistic ethic. We have the right to buy, possess, and consume alcoholic beverages. Regardless of how offensive drunkenness might be to a person, he cannot interfere with another person's "right" to become inebriated so long as that person drinks in the privacy of his own home or at some other appropriate location, and so long as he conducts himself in an otherwise law-abiding manner. In short, we have a right to be intoxicated—in private. Public intoxication is considered an offense to others and is therefore a violation of the criminal law. It makes sense that what is a "right" in one place may become, by virtue of its disruptive or disturbing effect on others, an offense somewhere else.

The right to self-medication should be hedged in by similar limits. Public intoxication, not only with alcohol but with any drug, should be an offense punishable by the criminal law. Furthermore, acts that may injure others—such as driving a car—should, when carried out in a drug-intoxicated state, be punished especially strictly and severely. The right to self-medication must thus entail unqualified responsibility for the effects of one's drug-intoxicated behavior on others. For unless we are willing to hold ourselves responsible for our own behavior, and hold others responsible for theirs, the liberty to use drugs (or to engage in other acts) degenerates into a license to hurt others.

Such, then, would be the situation of adults, if we regarded the freedom to take drugs as a fundamental right similar to the freedom to read and worship. What would be the situation of children? Since many people who are now said to be drug addicts or drug abusers are minors, it is especially important that we think clearly about this aspect of the problem.

I do not believe, and I do not advocate, that children should have a right to ingest, inject, or otherwise use any drug or substance they want. Children do not have the right to drive, drink, vote, marry, or make binding contracts. They acquire these rights at various ages, coming into their full possession at maturity, usually between the ages of eighteen and twenty-one. The right to self-medication should similarly be withheld until maturity.

In short, I suggest that "dangerous" drugs be treated, more or less, as alcohol is treated now. Neither the use of narcotics, nor their possession, should be prohibited, but only their sale to minors. Of course, this would result in the ready availability of all kinds of drugs among minors—though perhaps their availability would be no greater than it is now, but would only be more visible and hence more easily subject to proper controls. This arrangement would place responsibility for the use of all drugs by children where it belongs: on parents and their children. This is where the major responsibility rests for the use of alcohol. It is a tragic symptom of our refusal to take personal liberty and responsibility seriously that there appears to be no public desire to assume a similar stance toward other "dangerous" drugs.

Consider what would happen should a child bring a bottle of gin to school and get drunk there. Would the school authorities blame the local liquor stores as pushers? Or would they blame the parents and the child himself? There is liquor in practically every home in America and yet chlidren rarely bring liquor to school. Whereas marijuana, Dexedrine, and heroin—substances children usually do not find at home and whose very possession is a criminal offense—frequently find their way into the school.

Our attitude toward sexual activity provides another model for our attitude toward drugs. Although we generally discourage children below a certain age from engaging in sexual activities with others, we do not prohibit such activities by law. What we do prohibit by law is the sexual seduction of children by adults. The "pharmacological seduction" of children by adults should be similarly punishable. In other words, adults who give or sell drugs to children should be regarded as offenders. Such a specific and limited prohibition—as against the kinds of generalized prohibitions that we had under the Volstead Act or have now with respect to countless drugs—would be relatively easy to enforce. Moreover, it would probably be rarely violated, for there would be little psychological interest and no economic profit in doing so.

THE TRUE FAITH: SCIENTIFIC MEDICINE

What I am suggesting is that while addiction is ostensibly a medical and pharmacological problem, actually it is a moral and political problem. We ought to know that there is no necessary connection between facts and values, between what is and what ought to be. Thus, objectively quite harmful acts, objects, or persons may be accepted and tolerated—by minimizing their dangerousness. Conversely, objectively quite harmless acts, objects, or persons may be prohibited and persecuted—by exaggerating their dangerousness. It is always necessary to distinguish—and especially so when dealing with social policy—between description and prescription, fact and rhetoric, truth and falsehood.

In our society, there are two principal methods of legitimizing policy: social tradition and scientific judgment. More than anything else, time is the supreme ethical arbiter. Whatever a social practice might be, if people engage in it, generation after generation, that practice becomes acceptable.

Many opponents of illegal drugs admit that nicotine may be more harmful to health than marijuana; nevertheless, they urge that smoking cigarettes should be legal but smoking marijuana should not be, because the former habit is socially accepted while the latter is not. This is a perfectly reasonable argument. But let us understand it for what it is—a plea for legitimizing old and accepted practices, and for illegitimizing novel and unaccepted ones. It is a justification that rests on precedent, not evidence.

The other method of legitimizing policy, ever more important in the modern world, is through the authority of science. In matters of health, a vast and increasingly elastic category, physicians play important roles as legitimizers and illegitimizers. This, in short, is why we regard being medicated by a doctor as drug use, and self-medication (especially with certain classes of drugs) as drug abuse.

This, too, is a perfectly reasonable arrangement. But we must understand that it is a plea for legitimizing what doctors do, because they do it with "good therapeutic" intent; and for illegitimizing what laymen do, because they do it with bad self-abusive ("masturbatory" or mind-altering) intent. This justification rests on the principles of professionalism, not of pharmacology. Hence we applaud the systematic medical use of methadone and call it "treatment for heroin addiction," but decry the occasional nonmedical use of marijuana and call it "dangerous drug abuse."

Our present concept of drug abuse articulates and symbolizes a fundamental policy of scientific medicine—namely, that a layman should not medicate his own body but should place its medical care under the supervision of a duly accredited physician. Before the Reformation, the practice of True Christianity rested on a similar policy—namely, that a layman should not himself commune with God but should place his spiritual care under the supervision of a duly accredited priest. The self-interests of the church and of medicine in such policies are obvious enough. What might be less obvious is the interest of the laity: by delegating responsibility for the spiritual and medical welfare of the people to a class of authoritatively accredited specialists, these policies—and the practices they ensure—relieve individuals from assuming the burdens of responsibility for themselves. As I see it, our present problems with drug use and drug abuse are just one of the consequences of our pervasive ambivalence about personal autonomy and responsibility.

I propose a medical reformation analogous to the Protestant Reformation: specifically, a "protest" against the systematic mystification of man's relationship to his body and his professionalized separation from it. The immediate aim of this reform would be to remove the physician as intermediary between man and his body and to give the layman direct access to the language and contents of the pharmacopoeia. If man had unencumbered access to his own body and the means of chemically altering it, it would spell the end of medicine, at least as we now know it. This is why, with faith in scientific medicine so strong, there is little interest in this kind of medical reform. Physicians fear the loss of their privileges; laymen, the loss of their protections.

Finally, since luckily we still do not live in the utopian perfection of "one world," our technical approach to the "drug problem" has led, and will undoubtedly continue to lead, to some curious attempts to combat it.

Here is one such attempt: the American government is now pressuring Turkey to restrict its farmers from growing poppies (the source of morphine and heroin). If turnabout is fair play, perhaps we should expect the Turkish government to pressure the United States to restrict its farmers from growing corn and wheat. Or should we assume that Muslims have enough self-control to leave alcohol alone, but Christians need all the controls that politicians, policemen, and physicians can bring to bear on them to enable them to leave opiates alone?

LIFE, LIBERTY, AND THE PURSUIT OF HIGHS

Sooner or later we shall have to confront the basic moral dilemma underlying this problem: does a person have the right to take a drug, any drug—not because he needs it to cure an illness, but because he wants to take it?

The Declaration of Independence speaks of our inalienable right to "life, liberty, and the pursuit of happiness." How are we to interpret this? By asserting that we ought to be free to pursue happiness by playing golf or watching television, but not by drinking alcohol, or smoking marijuana, or ingesting pep pills?

The Constitution and the Bill of Rights are silent on the subject of drugs. This would seem to imply that the adult citizen has, or ought to have, the right to medicate his own body as he sees fit. Were this not the case, why should there have been a need for a Constitutional Amendment to outlaw drinking? But if ingesting alcohol was, and is now again, a Constitutional right, is ingesting opium, or heroin, or barbiturates, or anything else, not also such a right? If it is, then the Harrison Narcotic Act is not only a bad law but is unconstitutional as well, because it prescribes in a legislative act what ought to be promulgated in a Constitutional Amendment.

The questions remain: as American citizens, should we have the right to take narcotics or other drugs? If we take drugs and conduct ourselves as responsible and law-abiding citizens, should we have a right to remain unmolested by the government? Lastly, if we take drugs and break the law, should we have a right to be treated as persons accused of crime, rather than as patients accused of mental illness?

These are fundamental questions that are conspicuous by their absence from all contemporary discussions of problems of drug addiction and drug abuse. The result is that instead of debating the use of drugs in moral and political terms, we define our task as the ostensibly narrow technical problem of protecting people from poisoning themselves with substances for whose use they cannot possibly assume responsibility. This, I think, best explains the frightening national consensus against personal responsibility for taking drugs and for one's conduct while under their influence. In 1965, for example, when President Johnson sought a bill imposing tight federal controls over pep pills and goof balls, the bill cleared the House by a unanimous vote, 402 to 0.

The failure of such measures to curb the "drug menace" has only served to inflame our legislators' enthusiasm for them. In October 1970 the Senate passed, again by a unanimous vote (54 to 0) "a major narcotics crackdown bill."

To me, unanimity on an issue as basic and complex as this means a complete evasion of the actual problem and an attempt to master it by attacking and overpowering a scapegoat—"dangerous drugs" and "drug abusers." There is an ominous resemblance between the unanimity with which all "reasonable" men—and especially politicians, physicians, and priests—formerly supported the protective measures of society against witches and Jews, and that with which they now support them against drug addicts and drug abusers.

After all is said and done, the issue comes down to whether we accept or reject the ethical principle John Stuart Mill so clearly enunciated:

> The only purpose [he wrote in *On Liberty*] for which power can be rightfully exercised over any member of a civilized community, against his will, is to prevent harm to others. His own good, either physical or moral, is not a sufficient warrant. He cannot rightfully be compelled to do or forbear because it will make him happier, because in the opinions of others, to do so would be wise, or even right . . . In the part [of his conduct] which merely concerns himself, his independence is, of right, absolute. Over himself, over his own body and mind, the individual is sovereign.

By recognizing the problem of drug abuse for what it is—a moral and political question rather than a medical or therapeutic one—we can choose to maximize the sphere of action of the state at the expense of the individual, or of the individual at the expense of the state. In other words, we could commit ourselves to the view that the state, the representative of many, is more important than the individual; that it therefore has right, indeed the duty, to regulate the life of the individual in the best interests of the group. Or we could commit ourselves to the view that individual dignity and liberty are the supreme values of life, and that the foremost duty of the state is to protect and promote these values.

In short, we must choose between the ethic of collectivism and individualism, and pay the price of either—or of both.

For Discussion

1. If you delete the phrases to which Szasz objects in WHO's definition of drug addiction, to what else can this definition apply?
2. How valid is the analogy between drugs and buildings as vehicles of suicide?
3. Upon what principle does Szasz base his argument that all drugs be legalized?
4. What two reasons does Szasz give for people's taking drugs? Which one does he feel is more prevalent today? In what ways are the reasons he gives limited or underdeveloped?

5. What economic arguments does Szasz offer for the legalization of all drugs? How convincing are these arguments?
6. What limits would Szasz place upon the right of self-medication? How valid are the comparisons he makes with alcohol?
7. In what ways is Szasz's proposal akin to the Protestant Reformation?
8. What flaws, if any, can you find in Szasz's arguments?
9. What authority does Szasz's position lend to his argument?
10. What attitude does Szasz display toward his subject? Toward his audience?

GARRETT HARDIN

The Economics of Wilderness

A Texan by birth and a graduate of Stanford University, Garrett Hardin is currently professor of biology at the University of California at Santa Barbara. One of the most articulate writers in the field of science, he has written widely in the past twenty-five years, focusing his attention upon the social implications of biology. Among the many books he has published are *Nature and Man's Fate, 39 Steps to Biology,* and, most recently, *Stalking the Wild Taboo.* The following essay is based upon a talk given at the Sierra Club's Wilderness Conference in San Francisco on March 15, 1969.

To some it may seem anathema to mention wilderness and economics in the same breath. Certainly, in the past, some of the most dangerous enemies of wilderness have been men who spoke the economic lingo. Despite this historic war I think the brush of economics is a proper one for painting a picture of wilderness as a problem in human choice.

Economics may be defined as the study of choice necessitated by scarcity. There is something odd, and even improper, in speaking of the "economics of abundance" as Stuart Chase once did. With true abundance all economics ceases, except for the ultimately inescapable economics of time. Of the economics of time there is no general theory, and perhaps cannot be. But for the *things* of the world there is an economics, something that can be said.

Although there really is no such thing as an economics of abundance, the belief that there is, is one of the suppurating myths of our time. This belief had its origin partly in a genuine economic phenomenon, "the economy of scale." For complex artifacts in general the unit cost goes down as the scale of manufacture increases. In general, the more complex the artifact, the more striking the economy of scale: the cost per unit to build a million automobiles per year is far, far less than the cost per unit when only one is manufactured. Because artifacts are so pervasive in modern life, most of us unconsciously assume "the bigger the better," and "the more the cheaper." It takes a positive effort of imagination to realize that there are things the supply of which cannot be multiplied indefinitely. Natural resources in general, and wilderness in particular, fall in this group.

This is obvious enough to Sierra Club members. It should be obvious to everyone, but it is not. Not long ago, for example, discussing some proposed improvements in a national park, the *Toronto Financial Post* said: "During 1968 and early 1969, campsites will be expanded and roads paved to enable the visitor to enjoy the wilderness atmosphere that was nearly inaccessible only a few years ago." This is an astonishing sentence, but I will bet that one would have to argue with the writer of it for quite a while before he could be made to see the paradox involved in speaking of building a road into the wilderness.

Wilderness cannot be multiplied, and it can be subdivided only a little. It is not increasing; we have to struggle to keep it from decreasing as population increases. Were we to divide up the wilderness among even a small fraction of the total population, there would be no real wilderness available to anyone. So what should we do?

The first thing to do is to see where we stand, to make a list of possibilities without (initially) making any judgment of their desirability. On the first level of analysis there are just three possibilities.

1. The wilderness can be opened to everyone. The end result of this is completely predictable: absolute destruction. Only a nation with a small population, perhaps no greater than one percent of our present population, a nation that does not have at its disposal our present means of transportation could maintain a wilderness that was open to all.

2. We can close the wilderness to everyone. In a limited sense, this action would preserve the wilderness. But it would be a wilderness like Bishop Berkeley's "tree in the quad" when no one is there: does wilderness really exist if no one experiences it? Such an action would save wilderness for the future, but it would do no one any good now.

3. We can allow only limited access to the wilderness. This is the only course of action that can be rationally defended. Only a small percentage of a large population can ever enjoy wilderness. By suitably defining our standards, and by studying the variables in the situation, we can (in principle) work out a theory for maximizing the enjoyment of wilderness under a system of limited access. Whatever our theory, we

shall have to wrestle with the problem of choice, the problem of determining what small number among a vast population of people shall have the opportunity to enjoy this scarce good, wilderness. It is this problem of choice that I wish to explore here.

What I have to say applies not only to wilderness in the sense in which that term is understood by all good outdoorsmen, but also to all other kinds of outdoor recreational areas—to national parks, to ski areas, and the like. All of these can be destroyed by localized overpopulation. They differ in their "carrying capacity." The carrying capacity of a Coney Island (for those who like it, and there are such people) is very high; the carrying capacity of wilderness, in the sense defined by Howard Zahniser, is very low. In the Wilderness Bill of 1964 Zahniser's felicitous definition stands for all to admire:

> A wilderness, in contrast with those areas where man and his own works dominate the landscape is hereby recognized as an area where the earth and its community of life are untrammeled by man, where man himself is a visitor who does not remain.

The carrying capacity of Coney Island is, I suppose, something like 100 people per acre; the carrying capacity of a wilderness is perhaps one person per square mile. But whatever the carrying capacity as population inexorably increases, each type of recreational area sooner or later comes up against the problem of allocation of this scarce resource among the more than sufficient number of claimants to it. It is at this point that the problem of limited access must be faced.

How shall we limit access? How shall we choose from among the too-abundant petitioners those few who shall be allowed in? Let's run over the various possibilities.

First: By the marketplace. We can auction off the natural resource, letting those who are richest among the sufficiently motivated buy. In our part of the world and in our time most of us unhesitatingly label this method of allotment "unfair." Perhaps it is. But don't forget that many an area of natural beauty available to us today has survived unspoiled precisely because it was preserved in an estate of the wealthy in past times. This method of allotment has at least the virtue that it preserves natural treasures until a better, or perhaps we should merely say a more acceptable, method of distribution can be devised. The privilege of wealth has in the past carried many of the beauties of nature through the first, destructive eras of nascent democracy to the more mature, later stages that were capable of appreciating and preserving them.

Second: By queues. Wilderness could be made available on a first-come, first-served basis, up to the extent of the carrying capacity. People would simply line up each day in a long queue and a few would be allowed in. It would be a fatiguing and wasteful system, but while it would be "fair," it might not be stable.

Third: By lottery. This would be eminently "fair," and it would not be terribly fatiguing or wasteful. In earlier days, the decision of a lottery was regarded as the choice of God. We cannot recapture the consoling belief (now that "God is dead"), but we are still inclined to accept the results of a lottery. Lotteries serve well for the allocation of hunting rights in some of our states where big game abounds.

Fourth: By merit. Whether one regards this as "unfair" or "fair" depends on the complexion of one's political beliefs. Whether it is fair or not, I will argue that it is the best system of allocation. Anyone who argues for a merit system of determining rights immediately raises an *argumentum ad hominem.* He immediately raises the suspicion that he is about to define merit in such a way as to include himself in the meritorious group.

The suspicion is justified, and because it is justified it must be met. To carry conviction, he who proposes standards must show that his argument is not self-serving. What I hereby propose as a criterion for admission to the wilderness is great physical vigor. I explicitly call your attention to this significant fact: I myself cannot pass the test I propose. I had polio at the age of four, and got around moderately well for more than 40 years, but now I require crutches. Until today, I have not traded on my infirmity. But today I must, for it is an essential part of my argument.

I am not fit for the wilderness I praise. I cannot pass the test I propose. I cannot enter the area I would restrict. Therefore I claim that I speak with objectivity. The standard I propose is not an example of special pleading in my own interest. I can speak loudly where abler men would have to be hesitant.

To restrict the wilderness to physically vigorous people is inherently sensible. What is the experience of wilderness? Surely it has two major components. The first is the experience of being there, of (in Thoreau's words) being refreshed "by the sight of inexhaustible vigor, vast and titanic features," of seeing "that nature is so rife with life that myriads can afford to be sacrificed and suffered to prey on one another; that tender organizations can be so serenely squashed out of existence like pulp. . . ."

The experience of being there is part of the experience of wilderness, but only a part. If we were dropped down from a line by helicopter into the middle of this experience we would miss an important part of the total experience, namely the experience of getting there. The exquisite sight, sound and smell of wilderness is many times more powerful if it is earned through physical achievement, if it comes at the end of a long and fatiguing trip for which vigorous good health is a necessity.

Practically speaking, this means that no one should be able to enter a wilderness by mechanical means. He should have to walk many miles on his own two feet, carrying all his provisions with him. In some cases, entrance might be on horse or mule back, or in a canoe, or by snowshoes, but there should be no automobiles, no campers, no motorcycles, no totegoats, no outboard motors, no airplanes. Just unmechanized man and nature—this is a necessary ingredient of the prescription for the wilderness experience.

That mechanical aids threaten wilderness is already recognized by managers of our wildernesses. Emergency roads, it is said, should be used sparingly. I submit that this cautious policy is not cautious enough. I submit that there should be *no* emergency roads, that the people who go into the wilderness should go in without radio transmitters, that they should know for certain that if an emergency arises they can get no help from the outside. If injured, they must either somehow struggle to the outside under their own power or (if lucky) catch the attention of another rare wanderer in the wilderness and get him to help. For people who are physically prepared for it, the wilderness is not terribly dangerous—but such danger as there is, is a precious part of the total experience. The knowledge that one is really on one's own is a powerful tonic. It would be cruelly sentimental to take this away from the wilderness adventurer.

There is not even a public interest in making the wilderness safe. Making great and spectacular efforts to save the life of an individual makes sense only when there is a shortage of people. I have not lately heard that there is a shortage of people.

There is, however, a public interest in making the wilderness as difficult and dangerous as it legitimately can be. There is, I think, a well-founded suspicion that our life has become, if anything, too safe for the best psychological health, particularly among the young. The ever greater extension of the boundaries of legal liability has produced a controlled and fenced-in environment in which it is almost impossible to hurt oneself—unless one tries. The behavior of the young clearly indicates that they really try. Drag races, road races, "rumbles," student sit-ins, marches, and tauntings of the police—all these activities look like the behavior of people looking for danger. I do not wish to deny that some of the activities may arise from other motivations, also, e.g., idealistic political beliefs. I am only saying that it looks like deliberate seeking of danger is part of the motivation of our obstreperous young. I think it is an important part. I think we would do well to tear down some of the fences that now deprive people of the possibility of danger. A wilderness without rescue services would contribute to the stability of society.

There is a second way in which the interest of society is furthered by a rigorous wilderness. From time to time a president of the United States endeavors to improve the physical condition of the average citizen by resorting to a rhetorical bombardment. The verbal ammunition consists principally of the words "responsibility," "duty," and "patriotism." These rhetorical duds no longer move the young. The negative motivation of shame is, in general, not as effective as the positive motivation of prestige. A wilderness that can be entered only by a few of the most physically fit of the population will act as an incentive to myriads more to improve their physical condition. The motivation will be more effective if we have (as I think we should) a graded series of wilderness and park areas. Areas in which the carrying capacity is reckoned at one person per thousand acres should be the most difficult to enter; those with a capacity of one per hundred acres should be easier; those with one per ten, still easier, and so on. Yosemite Valley should, I suggest, be assigned a carrying capacity of about one per acre which might mean that it could be opened to anyone who could walk ten miles. At first, of course, the ten-mile walkers would be a very small class, but once the prestige factor took effect more and more people would be willing to walk such a distance. Then the standard should be made more rigorous.

I am sure other details of such a system would eventually have to be faced and worked out. It might be necessary to combine it with a lottery. Or some independent, easily administered test of physical fitness might be instituted. These are details, and in principle can be solved, so I will not spend time on them. But whatever the details, it is clear that many of our present national parks and national forests and other recreation areas should be forever closed to people on crutches, to small children, to fat people, to people with heart condition, and to old people in the usual state of physical disrepair. On the basis of their lack of merit, such people (and remember, I am a member of this deprived group) should give up all claim of right to the wilderness experience.

The poet Goethe once said, "We must earn again for ourselves what we have inherited," recognizing that only those things that are earned can be precious. To be precious the heritage of wilderness must be open only to those who can earn it again for themselves. The rest, since they cannot gain the genuine treasure by their own efforts, must relinquish the shadow of it.

We need not be so righteous as to deny the excluded ones all experience of the out-of-doors. There is no reason in the world why we cannot expand our present practice of setting up small outdoor areas where we permit a high density of people to get a tiny whiff of nature. Camping cheek by jowl with thousands of others in an outdoor slum does not appeal to me personally—have not visited Yosemite Valley in thirty years—but there are people who simply love this slummy togetherness, a fact that Sierra Clubbers sometimes forget or find hard to believe. By all means, let us create some *al fresco* slums for the people, but not in the likes of Yosemite Valley, which is too good for this purpose. But there will be little loss if some of the less attractive forest areas are turned into outdoor slums to relieve the pressure on the really good areas. We must have lakes that fairly pullulate with water skiers in order that we may be able to set aside other lakes for quiet canoeing. We must have easily reached beaches that fairly writhe with oily bodies and vibrate to a steady cacophony of transistor radios, in order to keep up other beaches, difficult of access, on which we can forbid all noise makers.

The idea of wilderness is a difficult one, but it is precisely because it is difficult that clarifying it is valuable. In discovering how to justify a restricted good to a nation of 200 million people that is still growing, we find a formula that extends beyond wilderness to a whole spectrum of recreational activities in the national commons. The solution of the difficult case erects a framework into which other cases can be easily fitted.

For Discussion

1. Explain the title of this essay.
2. What basic difference is there between the wilderness and the products with which economics usually deals?
3. What is paradoxical about opening the wilderness to everyone?
4. What does Hardin mean by "carrying capacity"? How is it determined? What local illustrations can you give?
5. The basic object of Hardin's proposals for access to the wilderness is to get people and wilderness together. What other considerations enter in as he eliminates the first three plans? What value determines his final choice?
6. Discuss the appeal of a rigorous wilderness to those seeking danger.
7. What language is particularly effective in conveying Hardin's feeling about the alternate out-of-doors experiences for those denied access to the wilderness?
8. What difficulties, if any, do you envision in carrying out Hardin's plan?
9. Identify the tone of the essay. How would a more impassioned tone influence its effectiveness?

ERNEST CALLENBACH

Getting Free

Ernest Callenbach, author of *Living Poor with Style,* in which this essay is the opening chapter, has "lived poor" for much of his life. Raised in a poor area in central Pennsylvania, he moved to Chicago, where he lived in the slums while attending the University of Chicago. In the 1950s Callenbach moved to Berkeley, where he currently lives and edits *Film Quarterly.* His book, he says, is a compendium of all the tricks he and his friends learned while living as poor students in a prosperous society.

> Sometimes history is changed in great sweeps but more often it is changed by the sum total of apparently ineffectual and almost meaningless existential actions out of which a new culture is built and from which new values arise. . . . You want a society that is loving, decent, and has integrity? Then pay the dues.
>
> —DAVID MC REYNOLDS

> Everything that gets done within a society is done by individuals.
>
> —ALDOUS HUXLEY

An unexpected crisis has come upon America. We have finally realized that the rosy picture of life given us in the fifties and sixties by magazines and newspapers and politicians is false. Our draft-weary armies are bogged down in an endless land war in Asia which has produced a crushing burden of inflation. Our money is steadily worth less; our cities rot while billions are spent on armaments. Our citizens are at each other's throats over race, war, corruption. The image of "affluent" America has vanished and been replaced by one of a nation with miserable standards of health care, education, and public welfare; malnutrition, infant mortality and desperate poverty are still widespread in America.

This failure of the old American way is naturally generating a new life-style, arising to challenge the old. Millions of young people who grew up in the rank atmosphere of warfare-state "affluence" have seen the consequences of that way—and found it wanting. They are not sure what they want instead, but they know what they don't want.

They don't want to be the unwilling backers of troops in costly and immoral foreign wars. They don't want to be obedient consumers, salivating like Pavlov's dogs before an advertisement. They don't want to work at meaningless jobs—producing junk or shuffling a corporation's bureaucratic papers—in order to buy more stuff from which neither they nor their families nor their friends get any real joy. They want to be free men and women. And to be that, they are willing to be poor: to drop out of the corporations and universities and official culture and instead try building up a life-style that will suit them. This can mean scrounging, scavenging, welfare, do-it-yourself, subsistence farming, communes, odd jobs, part-time jobs. It's not an easy life. But it can be a real and personal and satisfying life—fit for a man to live. . . .

The Ten Commandments tell us that we are not to covet our neighbor's wife, or his goods. If we took this seriously, modern business would collapse in a day. The very foundation of contemporary society is covetousness. We are trained to covet practically from the day of birth.

If we get into situations where there is nothing around to covet, we get nervous—like first-time campers, or tourists in East European countries who wonder why there aren't more downtown shop windows. We are, in fact, conditioned exactly like trained rats in a maze. Galvanized into action by a paycheck, we nose around, hunting for the ultimate purchase which will satisfy our hunger. Since most of us never have enough money for more than a few of the available toys, we are spared the dreadful realization that comes to the rich: there really isn't that much worth coveting. We go on busily and endlessly sniffing after the bait, and finally we drop dead in the maze, without ever stopping to consider whose game we have been playing.

In order to stop coveting, it may be necessary to be able to enjoy a lot of goods for a while. At any rate, this seems to be why the majority of hippies are from middle-class backgrounds: they've seen all their parents' toys and had a lot of their own, and they know by experience (which is how we learn almost everything we ever learn) that coveting is a bum trip. To people who all their lives have been deprived of the goodies enjoyed by the middle classes and the rich, the suggestion of doing without sounds like the old recommendation from rich people that the poor should enjoy being poor and honest.

But if coveting is your trip, you should at least try to get through it as quickly as possible. Work your ass off, put your money into all the goodies you can manage, spend your time in stores, read *Consumer Reports*, talk to experts: really sink yourself into it for a while.

Then kick it, and get back to figuring out what you really want to do with your life.

Every culture, like every person's life, has both a material and a spiritual side. In the development of an American counter-culture, much of the ground clearing has already been done: we have rejected the decadent national values of militarism, unbridled polluting technology, and the obnoxious pursuit of individual profit at the expense of the people at large.

We are not yet so certain about how we *do* wish to live. However, many new philosophical and political ideas are busily threading their way through our society. Some people who reject the anti-sex and anti-nature bias of Western "civilization" turn to Zen or other kinds of Buddhism which emphasize man's existence as part of nature, and encourage simplicity and directness in living. Some people who reject the authoritarian relationships inherent in modern business and even in electoral democracy turn to anarchism—which is not a doctrine of chaos, but an elaborate political theory based on the assumption that man is just as capable of living in relative peace without a coercive social structure as other animals are. People who are disgusted at the rape of the landscape caused by industrial society sometimes turn back to the American Indians for inspiration about how to live on the land without wrecking it— gathering wild foods, living in portable houses. Some people study other so-called "primitive" cultures for ideas about how man can achieve a better ecological balance with his environment. And some people, by experimenting with drugs that affect perception or produce visions, attempt to get in touch with the underlying realities of their own minds —or a least to escape the dead routines of the conventional thinking they have been taught.

Living has to do with how you eat and sleep and where you live and with whom; with how you relate to jobs and money; with machinery, furniture, and other objects; with how you dress; with how you deal with the law, the government, the police, the army. To every habit and convention of the old American culture, we are developing counter-patterns and counter-habits—anti-habits, sometimes, or the rejection of any habits at all, in favor of a fluidity from which new things may come.

So far the new ways have only begun to challenge the old. But already they have aroused the fears and resistances commonly stirred up by revolutionary thinking. The new ways have a powerful attraction, and they are spreading out from our tumultuous cities throughout the land. Their outward signs have begun to appear even in small cities and towns: brighter clothes, longer hair, funky old cars, rock music, drugs, organic and unsprayed foods, freer sexual relationships. Like a vast tribe of wandering Gypsies, people freed from the old conventions are spreading out.

Some preach the gospel to willing (and sometimes unwilling) ears. Some prefer to live quietly, letting the force of their example serve. Some are political, ready to argue how the miserable, desperate psychological condition of middle-class life is the result of the needs of the giant corporations and the military-industrial elite which controls them—and how American foreign policy is an extension abroad of these oppressive policies. Some are mystical, believing that only by putting your own soul in order, through meditation or drugs or religion, can you hope to live a contented life. But through all these variations of emphasis there runs a common disdain for the traditional American way—the life of work-work-work, buy-buy-buy.

And slowly, even among the squarest of citizens, the suspicion is growing that it is the very nature of our vastly developed industrial system to produce an environment which is poisonous to our bodies and toxic to our minds. Perhaps the making and buying of goods is *not* the main goal of a sane society. Perhaps a bigger Gross National Product is not a god worth sacrificing our lives to. Perhaps we must question the whole orientation of American values. The early labor-union leader Sam Gompers once summed up the aims of the labor movement as "More!" But maybe now we need less—and better?

Paradoxically, this question is being asked just when millions of black Americans are making a strong push to get what has been denied them since slavery. Black revolutionaries see this trend toward acquisitiveness as evil because it obscures the fact that the black population as a whole is still getting poorer relative to the white population. It seems clear, at any rate, that poor people of all races must stand together and organize politically to bring about a new life of real freedom and equality.

We must recognize that politicians' manifestoes about "ending poverty" are just middle-class guilt talking. Fine-sounding new programs are often put forward by presidents knowing they have no chance of approval by Congress. Fine-sounding bills are scuffled over in the back rooms of Congress, and sometimes even get passed—but later, when it comes time to back them up with money, little is appropriated, and much of that is wasted.

What is different about the present moment is that modern education and mass communications have made practically everybody realize that we now have the resources and the technology to provide a decent living for all. And for the first time in history, sizable masses of people are deciding that a decent modest living is all they want: they are leaving the middle-class money chase and *deciding* to be poor—not miserably poor, of course, but poorer in money so they can be richer in time, in enjoyments, in living a life that makes sense to human beings instead of to machines and accountants.

Changing your life in this way means questioning many of the old ideals Americans have thought they had to live by.

Take *labor saving*, for example. Saving the labor of walking or bicycling by riding around in cars all the time has put Americans into probably the worst physical shape of any nation on earth. Saving labor by buying precooked or prefabricated foods not only makes your diet less interesting, but it may actually make you work *harder*: you have to work about ten extra minutes at your job to earn the difference between a cake made from a mix and a scratch cake. And the scratch cake will contain no preservatives or other suspect chemicals; besides, it will taste better, and will give you the pleasure of having done something satisfying for yourself, in just the way you want it.

Take *technological progress*. For years we have been told about the wonders of modern science. But it is now clear that much of our proud progress is illusory—and that many of our supposed advances do at least as much harm as good. Thus, for instance, chemical insecticides like DDT were welcomed as miracles of chemistry that would save crops from every kind of bug. It has taken us twenty years to realize that DDT kills some bugs but gives free rein to others, so that an orchard may be saved from peach borers but is then overrun with tiny mites. Worse still, DDT accumulates in water, in vegetables, in animals and fish. In 1969 it was discovered that Lake Michigan salmon were so full of DDT they were dangerous to eat. Human breast milk contains so much DDT that if it were bottled it would be illegal to ship it across state lines. (It is still better than cow's milk, however.) DDT has even led to the virtual extermination of several bird species whose eggshells are becoming too fragile to hatch.

The heavy industries we rely on to produce our steel, oil, electricity, and plastics belch forth into the air enormous quantities of heat, gases, particles of dusty ash, and corroding chemicals. Our precious cars fart out vast amounts of lethal carbon monoxide, and also other gases which are more or less poisonous. The mixture of gases at street level in a place like Manhattan on a quiet summer day sometimes approaches the concentration where people will just keel over and die. Worse still, our pollutants are so extensive that we are degrading the stable, highly complex natural plant and animal world into simpler, degenerate forms with far less evolutionary (or even just useful) potential. We might even be able to wreck the atmosphere's careful balance of oxygen and carbon dioxide and turn the earth into a lifeless, barren rock like the moon.

Much of the new technology, then, seems to be bad for the human race, and we should subject all innovations to careful, personal, human, and ecological checks. If a new device contributes to the ugliness, impersonality, dirt, heat, noise, garbage, and air pollution of the world, we ought to reject it. Certainly we should keep it out of our houses.

Take *respectability*, that great dead weight upon tens of millions of Americans who might otherwise live far more exciting and contented lives. It is the dread of seeming unconventional that drives perfectly pleasant-looking women to frizz or pouf their hair, to lather themselves with cosmetics, to dress in hideous clothes because they are fashionable. The same kind of fear drives men to think they need shiny, superpowered cars, to drink too much, to pretend they are lady-killers. People fear others' opinions only if they have none of their own. It is the mind of a slave which allows others to control its opinions. Americans call themselves a free people—yet they obediently follow the dictates of a way of life which constantly controls and impoverishes their choices, deadens the possibilities for real freedom in their lives, stagnates their emotions and feelings, and puts them incessantly at the mercy of a ruthlessly exploitative economic system.

This is a kind of insanity, and it has been recognized as such, especially by young people, because in the postwar era they have been subjected to two special kinds of experience: the draft, and the college system. Both of these (which together involve about half our youth at any given time) are huge, impersonal institutions which confine and exploit the natural energies and talents of young people in ways everyone can easily see as base and evil: in the army young men are taught to kill, to brutalize, to obey orders blindly, while in the colleges youth are processed into the technical and managerial robots needed by the military-industrial state. (Both institutions also serve temporarily to keep them out of the labor market.) Like the blacks, young people have learned from bitter experience that they cannot get what they want from the white middle-class way.

Take *cleanliness*. Americans have a fetish for washing. They buy staggering quantities of soaps and detergents and are constantly washing themselves, their children, their cars, their clothes. They tend to feel that unless a thing shines there must be something wicked about it. But biologically man does not take well to all this shininess. Soaps and detergents wreck his skin and hair and give him rashes. Shiny cars hurt his eyes on the highways; his cities are so glaring he has to wear sunglasses. Having varnished or lacquered or polished everything, he is deprived of the variations in texture and pattern which occur in the natural world for which evolution prepared him.

Even natural smells are suppressed. Does anyone really want to smell another person who is "soapy-clean"? Our sense of smell happens to be a highly personal and immensely powerful emotional force; whether we like it or not, we are extremely sensitive to the smells of our families, our lovers, our households, our own bodies. Americans are willing to admit that babies smell nice, but that's about all. Basically, the American tradition is anti-biological.

Since the notion of funkiness recurs in this book, let me say here what I mean by it. The term comes from black street and jazz speech, like many slang terms, and was applied to art works by Bruce Conner, a San Francisco sculptor, painter, and moviemaker. Conner began to make assemblages that were hairy, greasy, covered with cobwebs, filled with old salvaged bits of this or that. They were the opposite of the charmingly beautiful, and yet they were fascinating. Other artists took up the term, and funk became a movement. In time the term gained an opposite in "plastic," which connotes all the superficial, shiny, ugly, mass-manufactured qualities of contemporary American decadence. Funk was personal, oozy, disorganized, variable, mammalian; it bore the mark of man rather than the machine.

Nonetheless, it is possible to love funkiness and also to appreciate the kind of neatness, lightness, and excellence of function that we associate with boats, Dutch cities, well-made knives and other artifacts which have been refined over the years. There is a lovable disorder that comes from humanness; there is also an admirable order that comes from humanness. We can, I think, prize and practice both. A person who does everything funkily is a slob; a person who does everything neatly is an anal-compulsive neurotic. The free person can be funky when he feels like it, and precise when he feels like it.

Take the idea of *"new."* The American mania for newness is drummed into us to convince us that our old things can't be any good, and we'd better hurry up and earn some money to replace them. But the new ones probably won't be as much fun to use as the old. They'll break down quicker, they are almost sure to be uglier, and they cost a hell of a lot more. A handy rule for a saner life is this: If you are lucky enough to possess something you like that's lasted for more than a couple of years, hang on to it. You'll probably never find a new one half as good.

Take the concept of the *nuclear family*. Earlier Americans lived in "extended-family" groups—a dwelling contained not only a father, mother, and children, but probably an aunt or uncle or so, probably a grandfather or grandmother, and possibly nephews, cousins, or other relatives. Houses were, on the whole, larger in those days, though many city people lived in slum tenements as they do now.

Today a family is supposed to consist of only two parents and their children. Grandparents are shoved off into rest homes or left to live by themselves. Everybody who is single is expected to provide for himself or herself. The present way has its advantages, as anybody with a senile parent will quickly point out. But it is on the whole a colder, more impersonal way. Like many other aspects of the American traditional pattern, it puts people into closer touch with machines, but removes them from human contact.

Modern young people are less and less convinced that the nuclear family pattern is habitable, and they are therefore experimenting with communal living, both in the cities and countryside. These experiments are usually attempted by people who are not related to each other except through common experience: drugs, disillusionment with the university, political or religious consciousness. Some communes share vegetarian food practices. Some who have rejected the whole idea of city living turn to American Indian ways. There are many disagreements in and between communes, for once you cast off the old ideas, many new ones spring up, and it takes time to test them. Like the two-person family or any other human arrangement where people are in extended contact and intimacy with each other, communes are not havens of peace and tranquility. (As is well known, the best way to be perfectly tranquil is to be dead.)

The old extended-family pattern was based on two things: blood relationship and economic necessity. The big family enabled the individual to spend less money, have more pleasures, and be better protected against the dangers of life. Today, we like to ignore the dangers and imagine that science or the police have conquered them. However, as Americans become more realistic, they are becoming aware of their own vulnerability: they know that they will need help against disease, accident, crime, poverty, death, and their own families are often far away—at the other end of the country, or off at war. Commune dwellers, thus, are trying to see whether the bonds of common ideas and common needs are strong enough to sustain new kinds of groupings, where say ten to thirty people, often including permanent or married couples and children, live together and share housing, food, child raising, and so on.

The economic advantages are impressive. Let's take a group of only ten persons—three couples, two children, and two single persons. (This is roughly the minimum size of another stable social grouping—the wolf pack.) Under the conventional way of life they would have to rent five separate apartments or houses; as a commune they rent one large house or very large apartment. Each day, under the old system, fifteen separate meals would have to be prepared—and at a far greater cost than if all the cooking were done in one place. Costs for laundry, heating, lights, and so on will be far less per person than if separate dwellings are maintained. Even if each couple or person has individual radio/TVs, typewriters, irons, and other small items of personal property, it is possible on the average to live in a commune for less than half of what the old way requires. For many people existing on welfare, unemployment, disability, or retirement incomes, this can mean the difference between pleasant survival and utter poverty.

Communes usually try to operate democratically, with each person having one vote. However, disagreements sometimes become bitter, and people leave or the group splits up.

The commitment a commune requires should not be underestimated. People who really aren't ready to settle down into any regular way of living should not kid themselves that they are going to fit into a commune. One may for a time live as the *guest* of a commune (which is what would-be freeloaders have in mind when they offer themselves as members). But the only way to be "free of commitments" is to live by yourself, or on the road. This has many satisfactions, but intense mutual reliance on other people is not one of them.

Dedicated communards sometimes think that since life is to be shared, people should also share each other sexually, without any bourgeois hang-ups or jealousies. This is a lovely ideal, and can be great while it lasts, but I have not been able to discover any groups where it has been successfully put into practice for very long. Whether this is due to carry-overs of the old morality, or whether it is something about the sexual biology of man, we do not yet know. (If geese are naturally monogamous, it is possible men are too.) Perhaps continued ingenious experimentation will yield new knowledge. It is my own hunch that sexual morality, most of which can be reduced to the rule of one mate at a time, is fundamentally a territorial or defensive phenomenon, perhaps like the need to eat and sleep in safety.

Many communes, especially in rural areas, have been started on ambitious scales. Often rural groups plan to be self-sufficient concerning food, shelter, and clothing—though the land to live on generally comes from a family inheritance, a gift, or some other outside source. Some communes are positively puritanical, with rigid work duties, obligatory ceremonies, and careful planning of every aspect of life—totally opposite from the middle-class view of communes as permanent round-the-clock orgies. However, a former country dweller like myself knows that subsistence farming is extremely difficult to survive on in this country no matter how hard-working the communards may be. City kids who don't know a ewe from a moo will obviously have a very hard time, but so will handy, skilled, and reasonably lucky people who take advantage of every agricultural advance and work doggedly. The fact is that to produce all your food and even part of your clothing through individual farming takes such large amounts of energy that very few Americans are up to it. Every commune that hopes to endure, therefore, needs some steady, though perhaps not very large source of outside income—occasional or part-time jobs, welfare, or whatever. This will make it possible to divert some energies to the production of things which are unavailable commercially in the desired quality, or things which are overpriced commercially, things which can be produced with little money risked.

There is as yet no solid, effective, comfortable style of living poor in this country. Instead of working out ways of living that are suitable for human beings who are free, we tend to straggle along in the foul exhausts of the advertisers.

In America—the richest of all countries—it is especially hard to be poor. Public transit, except in central New York, San Francisco, and Boston, is so pitiful that the expense of a car is practically forced on you. (All other advanced industrial countries have elaborate systems of city and inter-city transit by subway, train, bus, etc., with moderate fares, and their cities have been built for people to get around in without cars.) We lack the family allowances—payments which help poor and lower-middle-class families during the difficult years when their children are small—which are found in all other industrialized countries. Though our tax system is theoretically supposed to make rich people pay more, in fact it lets them off through loopholes and deductions, while poor people's taxes are taken out in withholding. Our welfare systems are punitive and operate to discourage people's initiative. Public housing is so scarce that it might as well not exist at all. Our public-health programs and health-care facilities are weak, underfinanced, disorganized; we take criminally bad care of our mentally ill, our old, and our chronically sick. . . . Small wonder, then, that poor people sometimes just feel like giving up; our government has the worst social services of any advanced nation.

The misery caused by these problems affects tens of millions of people, poor and not so poor. And added to the physical misery that you suffer if you don't have enough to eat or can't get proper medical care for your children, you are taught to suffer mental anguish if you can't eat meat every day, or have a new car or a washing machine or the latest kind of hair spray plugged on TV—psychological misery that would never exist unless the system called it into being through advertising and similar pressures. There are plenty of people around who won't eat meat when it is offered to them, who would just sell a new car if you gave it to them, who don't want to worry about a washer, and who would sooner cut off their hair than put chemical glop on it. We must learn from them how to avoid the psychological miseries generated by the advertisers.

. . . [T]he real point is to *stop being a consumer*—that is to say, a creature whose social role is to buy stuff. A "consumer" is a kind of servant of the industrial society. It produces tons of lettuce; he eats lettuce, perhaps selecting one type over another. It produces hair dryers; he buys hair dryers, studiously comparing brand names. In short, he is playing the corporations' game.

You only really save money, and time, and your freedom, by *not* buying—ultimately, by "paying" attention not to what they are trying to get you to pay attention to, but to things that personally matter to you.

It is not easy to discover what personally matters to you. By the time a kid is six or eight, he has been exposed to thousands of hours of television commercials. And by the time he has finished high school, he has been thoroughly brainwashed into thinking about (and wanting) all the stuff that has been presented on TV, in magazines, and in the households of fellow brainwashed ciitzens.

We must stop being consumers and become *producers*: producers of ideas, of friendships, of beautiful objects, of better relationships among all people, of a more humane and decent society.

. . . The central question is *how to organize your life.* If you decide to organize it by your own standards and desires and needs, you will find that buying takes on an entirely different aspect.

For one thing, you will come to know what your necessities really are. Obviously these will include food and shelter and clothes—possibly on a more modest scale than you tended to think. But they may also include music, or flowers or a southern-exposure window; privacy or an open-door policy; lots of heat or lots of fresh air; bright lights or dim.

Furthermore, you will discover that buying is not the only and often not a desirable way to obtain things. St. Francis is said to have remarked that to beg is best, to steal is next, and to buy is worst of all. This doctrine tends to appeal most to those who crave the excitement of stealing. But I would think that the saintly bird lover did not sufficiently study his birds: to a bird, begging, stealing, and buying are all irrelevant terms; and in this and other respects we can learn by watching our fellow animals who have not been corrupted by speech or ideas.

American Indians too once lived upon the land like birds—taking what they needed, but without destroying the fabric of plant and animal life which produced it. The "taking" was hard—as anyone knows who has tried to subsist even a short time by hunting and gathering food, or who has tried to construct a shelter and implements without machine-made tools. And it is an aristocratic illusion, usually held by people with unearned income from parents or inheritances, that men can live in any numbers without a good deal of hard work. Occasional saints (or sinners) bring it off, but they are isolated persons for whom the essentials of life—some bread, a roof at night, some wine—can indeed be begged, or borrowed, or shoplifted. The real problem in modern industrial society, capitalist or socialist, is that we must work *for others*, not for ourselves. When we seek money by offering our time and energy in the labor market we are putting ourselves at the disposal of others, and the purposes of the work we are assigned are often so remote they have no meaning.

We do need money to buy food and shelter. Still, by redirecting our energies, we may find that we need to *buy* far less and can *make* far more.

This also saves money: instead of paying $75 for a bed in a furniture store, you can make one for $25. But that is only a fringe benefit. What counts most is that instead of working for someone else over the hours needed to produce that extra $50, you were working for yourself, in your own place, with your own companions, at your own pace, with your own ideas and designs and materials and tools. The resulting bed is *your* bed—in a way no Simmons bed could ever be.

Calling themselves consumers, modern Americans are literally consumed by the industrial system—and on two fronts: they must sacrifice to it their alienated labor, to get money; and to get food, shelter, and other needs they are confined in the maw of the marketplace, which offers many choices but only with the exchange of money. Thus money becomes the measure of all things, including your life: all goods and all people become cost-rated commodities. While the U.S. government rates a Vietnamese civilian killed "by accident" at a few thousand dollars (if anything), a good wage-earner run down by a truck at home may be worth a hundred thousand—as defined by his potential earning power, or perhaps his insurance policies. When such standards become widespread, the value of human life *in itself* is forgotten. All life is consumed by "the cash nexus," as Marx called it—the bargaining act by which every thing and person is weighed at somebody's cash register.

We can escape the cash nexus only to the extent we escape dealing with cash.

.   .   .

In the full-blown industrial state such as we inhabit, the "duties" of the citizen are to work steadily and obediently, pay taxes and union dues, vote when called upon, consume enough goods to keep the economy going, and occasionally trot off to the other side of the world to fight for some dictatorial regime and save the national face. We must struggle politically to defend ourselves from such a well-organized fate—let them build robots! But in order to struggle we must also and at the same time develop a different way of living: of eating and sleeping, of loving, of traveling about, of educating ourselves and our children, of amusing ourselves, of securing medical care and political redress. The old-style American way of life has been gobbled up by the industrial age, and shat out upon the ruined landscape. What we must do now is build a counter-culture, a new Way.

The problems we face, in trying to make modern America habitable for human beings again, are not to any serious degree technical. They are problems of *holiness*: we are searching for ways of restoring dignity and importance to daily events. It is, in a sense, a religious quest. We have to relearn how to pay true attention to what we are doing, because there is little solid pleasure in things done thoughtlessly or mechanically.

We must learn to eat holy, dress holy, smoke holy, wash holy, and so on.

Since organized religion has abandoned the people, people must create their own religion. The beginning seems to lie in something rather like the American Indian's concept of "medicine." The things we use and wear, if we make them with care and use them with respect, take on "good medicine"; they become holy because of the sincerity of our regard for them and the extent of our commitment to them. It is hard for disposable goods to be holy. When we buy manufactured goods, even of honest quality (which is hard to find), it is always doubtful whether our spirit can enter into them. Best of all are those things which are old, have been well loved, and have become holy through association with people we love and respect: ancestors, old friends, great men or women.

It is very hard to find the right way, and no person should lightly despise another's way. Out of the welter of present industrial society, it will probably take us several generations to sort out those few things which are essential to mankind—and to reject the others, of which no truly human or holy use can be made. We should be patient with each other's experiments, but cleave to our task, now that we know what it is; it leaves little room for cant or credulity.

For Discussion

1. Agree or disagree with Callenbach's statement that "we are conditioned to covetousness."
2. What examples of new ways of living do you observe among your contemporaries?
3. Which of the "old ideals of American life" that Callenbach questions are still important to you? Why? Suggest other "old ideals" which might need questioning.
4. Do you consider the nuclear family realistic or unrealistic today? Why or why not?
5. Why is it especially hard to "live poor" comfortably in the United States?
6. Consider and discuss the implications of Callenbach's advice to us to stop being consumers.
7. How does organizing one's life determine what one buys?
8. What "duties" are citizens expected to perform in the United States, according to Callenbach? How important do you consider these "duties"? Explain.
9. What evidence can you cite that, as Callenbach says, ". . . we are searching for ways of restoring dignity and importance to daily events"?
10. What qualities of good discursive style are evident in this essay? (See introduction to "The Discursive NO.")

LARRY CASALINO

This Land Is Their Land

The problems of land reform discussed in this essay have profound implications beyond the economics of the subject: the whole quality of American life is threatened. Casalino, who worked with the Food, Land, and Power Project in California during the writing of this essay, was aided by the research of Stuart Burns and Leah Honea.

The wheat field is ten miles long. There's a machine—one colossal machine—harvesting the wheat, rumbling toward the setting sun on tracks which keep it from compacting the soil. A helicopter sprays pesticide on the adjacent soybeam field. Another helicopter circles, scanning crop conditions, transmitting data to a computer. Two men sit in a bubble-topped control tower, watching the instrument panels which surround them. The lengthening shadows of three giant skyscrapers—skyscrapers filled with cattle—fall on the men. In these nearly fully-automated structures they (the cattle) are fed various chemicals, fattened, killed, processed, and packed into cylinders for shipment by monorail to the Cities, which are, presumably, where all the people are.

This is a picture of the American farm in the year 2015, as sketched by U.S. Department of Agriculture (USDA) specialists. To them it is irresistibly appealing: ten whole miles filled with great amber waves of grain. Yet the implications of their vision are chilling: environmental ruin, nutritional famine, wrenching social dislocation. Who will own this futuristic farm? What will be its economic and environmental costs, and who will pay them? The government's crystal-gazing agronomists cannot be relied upon for answers. But already, at every link in America's economic food chain, vast transformations are at work which provide

Reprinted by permission of *Ramparts* Magazine from the July, 1972, issue.

some exceedingly disturbing clues. We can begin with an implausible assertion and a surprising fact.

(1) When we think of land reform, Asia and Latin America immediately come to mind. Things like the breakup of enormous "latifundistas" in steaming banana republics. Most of us think that such land reform is generally a good idea. But what most people would find pretty hard to believe is that the indispensable condition of sound agricultural development in America is land reform—right here in the fields of California, Mississippi, Maine. But consider this: (2) if you are the "average American," you eat a *less* nutritious diet today than you did ten years ago. (The Department of Agriculture admits this.) Only one-half of American families have "good" diets by USDA standards. How many more years of this kind of progress can we afford? The fact is our thinking about large-scale concentration in the economy of food has been dominated by the wrong agricultural cliche: it is not reaping the benefits of efficiency; it is sowing the seeds of disaster.

The general trend towards control of our food and land by a number of large "agri-business" corporations has received a certain amount of attention. But considering that the "food and fiber" industry is America's biggest business—accounting for almost a third of all private employment and nearly a fifth of the entire GNP—agri-business has managed to arouse very little interest and debate, much less serious opposition. Indeed the process of concentration has been so swift that there is remarkably little awareness of just how far it has already gone.

By 1958, the U.S. Food Marketing Commission classified 80 percent of the food industry as being under "oligopoly" control. Some samples: 95 percent of all prepared soups are sold by Campbell Soup, four corporations make 85 percent of American breakfast cereals.

On the farming end, in 1969 just 2 percent of U.S. farms made 30 percent of all farm sales, and 5 percent made more than half. One percent of U.S. feedlots now handle 52 percent of our beef, and 90 percent of all broiler chickens are bought up by five companies.

Food corporations continue to swallow up direct competitors, extending their "horizontal" expansion (as when one retail store is taken over by another, or a canner by a canner). But, even more significant, they are striving for "vertical integration," "total food systems" which encompass every step from farming through processing, distribution and retailing. And in recent years, huge conglomerates (like Greyhound, ITT and Tenneco) have been heavily diversifying into the food industry—particularly into farming.

Tenneco, roughly the 30th biggest U.S. industrial corporation, although a fairly new entry into agri-business, could be considered the vertically integrated food corporation *par excellence*, with its stated aim of controlling food production "from seedling to supermarket." In 1967 Tenneco acquired Kern County Land Company, California's third largest landowner. Three years later it took control of Heggblade-Marguleas, the nation's largest marketer of fresh fruits and vegetables. Tenneco also owns J. I. Case Co., which manufactures, among other things, farm machinery, and the Packaging Corporation of America, which manufactures food containers.

So Tenneco plows its own land, fertilized and sprayed with chemicals from its own chemical division, using its own tractors fueled with gas and oil from its own oil wells and refineries. The food is processed, packaged, and distributed by Tenneco subsidiaries. Tenneco is presently attempting to develop its own national brandname (Sun Giant) for produce, which it intends to sell at "premium prices." Tenneco doesn't have its own supermarket chain yet. Unlike traditional farmers, when Tenneco needs capital it can look to its other operations for help: Tenneco is also busy searching out oil off the coast of Southeast Asia and is the world's largest transporter of natural gas, building two nuclear-powered aircraft carriers.

Most Americans are not farmers, and probably never get much closer to the source of the food they eat than the deep freeze department at the supermarket. So for them, if agriculture has been replaced by agri-business, what real harm is done?

To begin with, there is the habit agri-business has of slipping poison into one's dinner. As we now know, much of the food these corporations supply has had much of the taste and nutritional value processed out, and has become a witches' brew of potentially harmful chemicals which have been processed in. So that many people find shopping in the supermarket a queasy balancing act, selecting the least deleterious diet they can from alternatives that range from U.S. meat, already banned as unsafe in twenty-one more scrupulous countries, to "fresh" fruits and vegetables which are picked before ripe, then waxed, gassed and injected with implausibly vivid dyes.

Highly processed foods are the hard-sell specialties of the agri-corporations. The use of chemical food additives, part and parcel of the rise of agri-business, has risen from a minor phenomenon thirty years ago to become a $500 million a year business in its own right. It is hardly a secret that, as one marketing spokesman enthused, "The profit margin on food additives is fantastically good—much better than the profit margin on basic traditional foods." Every reader of Sylvia Porter or Consumer Reports knows that the more intensively processed, synthesized and "convenienced" a food, the more exorbitant its price. But processed foods are not only a source of profit to their parent companies; today's giant food corporations simply could not exist without them.

Wonder Bread may not be the best for you—although you can store it forever, mail it to a friend, squeeze it 'til you can hold a loaf in your fist—but it sure is convenient for IT&T, which owns Continental Baking. It is the heavy doses of chemical additives that opened the way for a handful of powerful corporations to centralize control of food markets in the United States. Chemicals make it possible to stabilize color, texture and other illusions of freshness during the extended storage and transport involved in wide regional and national distribution. Previously food markets had been localized and fragmented by the very nature of the simpler farm-to-table foods. Besides being perishable, they were undistinctive, unpatentable, effectively unbrandable. They provided no basis for the packaging, distribution and promotion involved in national market exploitation.

Along with additives, agri-business has brought an upsurge in pesticide use, which has more than doubled since Rachel Carson's *The Silent Spring* was published in 1962. Large agricultural corporations (which often have their own holdings in the farm chemical business) are totally geared to large-scale farming methods that depend on disproportionately larger amounts of pesticides and inorganic fertilizers. They are firmly locked into the familiar vicious circle: extensive use of monoculture (using a field to grow a single crop without rotation), pesticides, and inorganic fertilizers, which together have increased the variety and resistance of pests and impaired the quality of the soil, so that ever greater amounts of even more toxic and costly chemicals are soaked into the land. Agri-business corporations decidedly are uninterested in alternatives like organic fertilizer and biological control of pests. And they are in a position to make their lack of interest count. As a National Agricultural Chemicals Association spokesman candidly points out: "There really is not much biological control in industry research; they would research themselves right out of the market."

Among the many social costs of agri-business concentration is its effect on the prices people pay for food. In areas such as breakfast cereals where concentration is far advanced, its inflationary effect is already very clear. And continued growth of agri-business concentrations sets the stage for inflated prices throughout the industry in the future, when the market will be dominated by sufficiently few "competitors" to make possible what is euphemistically called "administered pricing"—in other words the kind of price fixing, both tacit and conspiratorial, that has long prevailed in other highly concentrated industries.

But the question of food prices is problematic in other ways. For instance, when people switch to high-priced processed foods which are often made from cheap imitation ingredients (soy protein for meat or milk), are they paying more for their food or getting more for their money? A large part of what we pay for food goes for such things as advertising, which is neither edible nor convenient. In fact, the food industry spends more on advertising and less on research than any other industry in America. Betsy Wood, of the Consumers Cooperative of Berkeley, estimates that consumers pay 15–25 percent more for national brand names—an average family would save $200 a year buying local labels. Are the taxes we pay that go to finance agri-business (in the form of subsidies, credits and special allowances) part of the price we pay for food? And when you consider the poisoning of our bodies and our environment, or the brutal exploitation of farm workers, it's even more difficult to count the cost.

The most direct cost of agri-business power is that it prospers at the ruinous expense of the great mass of American farmers. For them the situation is desperate. Half the farms in America had gone out of business by World War II, and shutdowns continue at a rate of 2000 farms a week. The Department of Agriculture admits that the number of American farms remaining by 1980 may be reduced to less than a tenth of what it is today.

It might seem reasonable to conclude that the ability of agri-business to overwhelm the smaller traditional farmer demonstrates the superior efficiency of its large-scale, integrated mode of operation, and that we are seeing an outmoded economic unit, no longer able to compete, replaced by a more advanced form of organization. Thus, we might sympathize with those who are displaced and perhaps attempt to soften the blow, but to try to turn back the clock would be merely sentimental and quixotic.

At any rate this is what agri-business would like us to believe. In reality the big corporations have not prevailed by their farming competence which is dubious at best. What has happened is that agri-business, being more efficient at farming the American people than at farming the soil, has been able to draw upon a fascinating array of lucrative subsidies, which the smaller traditional farmer did not enjoy, and against which he has been unable to compete.

At least five major subsidies have combined over the years to give its economic edge:

THE CROP SUBSIDY

In January this year Senator Adlai Stevenson III's Senate Subcommittee on Migratory Labor conducted three days of hearings in San Francisco and Fresno. Over and over the Senator heard the same basic complaint: "My government taxes me to the extent of confiscation to subsidize and create favorable conditions for vertically integrated corporations," said Gus Stamenson, for 26 years a grower of almonds and walnuts on 40 California acres. "Give me a $4 million dollar subsidy and I'll be the most efficient farmer west of the Mississippi."

Ronald Reagan, Richard Nixon, and other politicians throughout the country have been very successful in persuading people that welfare is a major problem. They never mention the fact that federal crop subsidy programs cost the taxpayers more than all federal, state, and local welfare programs combined. In 1970 Tenneco received crop subsidies of over a million dollars. California's J. G. Boswell, one of the world's largest cotton growers, received $5 million.

Welfare *is* a problem for taxpayers—welfare for the rich. In a recent year 500 large growers in California's Imperial Valley received $12 million in farm subsidies—or $24,000 each. Meanwhile 10,000 poor, landless residents of the Valley received less than $8 million in welfare payments —or $800 each. George Thayer, a California almond grower, told Stevenson's committee: "I believe we have created the worst welfare system of all times—the welfare system for the corporate farm."

THE WATER SUBSIDY

Last summer the Ralph Nader-originated Center for the Study of Responsive Law published a massive, thousand-page study titled *Power and Land in California*. The study blasted the California State Water Project as "possibly the largest special interest boondoggle in history." It claims that, when finished, the project will have cost roughly ten *billion* dollars—$500 for every man, woman, and child in California. Yet economists estimate that the project will return only 50 cents of benefit for every dollar it costs!

Why build such an economically irrational project? Well, some folks do benefit from it a great deal—large landowners, large water-using industries, and developers. A 1959 study by the California Labor Federation reported that eleven landowners including Southern Pacific, Tenneco, and Standard Oil owned 33 percent of the land to be irrigated by the project. Southern Pacific and Tejon Ranch were the biggest donors to the successful 1960 campaign to persuade California voters to approve a bond issue to finance the project. And Bank of America is the biggest holder of the bonds.

The water is a speculator's dream. It raises land values by at least $300 an acre. So, if you own 20,000 acres, your land is suddenly worth $6 million more than it was before California citizens built a water project for you. And the taxpayers pay about half the cost of the water, so you can irrigate your crops much more cheaply.

Agri-business could have tried getting irrigation water even cheaper by pressing for a comparable federal water plan. They were deterred from that route because there's a catch—the federal 160-acre limitation.

This law would go far toward breaking up the large corporate landholdings. But the law has, from the beginning, been flagrantly violated.

Jack Henning of the California AFL-CIO estimates, on the basis of his organization's research, that 900,000 California acres held by owners who own over 160 acres are receiving water from the federal Bureau of Reclamation. Among these owners are the old familiar names—Tenneco, Southern Pacific, Standard Oil.

THE RESEARCH SUBSIDY

The University of California's Agricultural Extension Service was originally founded to provide easily available local technical assistance to small farmers. Late in 1971 David Talamante of the Tri-County Economic Development Association approached his local Extension "Service" for assistance for a Chicano cooperative which grows strawberries in greenhouses. Talamante was laughed at and told: "If you want to do that kind of farming, why don't you go to Guam?"

This attitude is typical. Nearly all of the more than $20 million a year of state and federal tax dollars spent by the University of California on agricultural research are aimed at aiding the biggest farms. Some of the University's most brilliant inventions have been machine, like the tomato harvester, which allow corporate farms to dispense with troublesome farm workers. In the bitter grape strike of the late sixties, the University came to the growers' assistance during pruning season and allowed them to use a pneumatic pruning machine it had under development.

The situation is simple: we pay the University of California for technological development deliberately skewed in favor of large corporate farms. Then we are told that it is technology that makes corporate takeover of agriculture inevitable.

THE LABOR SUBSIDY

American Indians were the first to toil as farmworkers in the fields of California. They were followed by Chinese (who were 90 percent of farmworkers in the 1870s), Japanese, Filipinos, and, today, Chicanos. Jack Hanna, one of the developers of the tomato harvester, observed: "I'd seen nationality after nationality in the fields, and I felt that someday we might run out of nationalities to do our hard work."

Farmworkers, who have fed us for many years, are the least protected of all workers by federal and state labor laws. They have no protected organizing rights, and cannot insist on union representation elections or collective bargaining. The government has actively intervened to obstruct the United Farmworkers Organizing Committee's attempts to organize farmworkers. For instance, the Defense Department more than tripled its purchases of lettuce from Dow Chemical subsidiary Bud Antle during the UFWOC lettuce boycott.

Thus the government helps to provide big farmers with a cheap, easily exploitable labor force. Seven percent of California farms hire 75 percent of the state's farm labor. The larger the farm, the more labor the farmer can exploit, thus cutting costs of production and raising profits. The small farmer has no one to exploit but himself, in competition with $1.50 an hour wages paid to many farm laborers. And taxpayers pay the welfare costs of keeping farm laborers alive between seasons of peak work.

THE TAX SUBSIDY

There are numerous tax breaks in the IRS cookie jar that may be of benefit to any knowledgeable farmer. The important edge obtained by diversified corporate farmers comes from a number of special tax breaks that enable money expended in farming operations to cancel out substantial amounts of otherwise taxable profits from an owner's *non-farming* operations. Since the old-fashioned farmer doesn't have any significant non-farming profits, this is of no use to him. But to agribusiness companies, which operate in many non-farming industries, this kind of tax shelter has proved extremely lucrative.

In the past couple of years reform moves have been made to curtail the special tax breaks (as well as the inequities) in the crop subsidy program. But corporate ingenuity has found ample loopholes remaining in both these areas through which to make its way. There is little evidence that they have suffered much more from these reforms than the inconvenience of devious legal maneuvers.

The fact is, giant farms are *not* more efficient than small farms, even in a strictly economic sense. The government's own studies conclude that all of the economics of size can be achieved by modern, fully mechanized, one- or two-person farms ranging from 100 to 600 or sometimes to 1000 acres, depending on the crop (see Ag. E. Report No. 107, Economic Research Service, U.S. Department of Agriculture). It's worth remembering that "inefficient" family farms have been producing national food surpluses for decades.

Concern for small farms is not nostalgia for the past—it makes economic, political, social, and ecological sense. We have been taught to assume without thinking that big and powerful equals efficient and good. The demise of small farms has profound effects on both urban and rural America. As 2000 farm families a week leave their land, local businesses, schools, and community groups shut down. More people crowd into the cities (75 percent of Americans now live on 2 percent of the land), where they will be dependent on big agri-business corporations for their food (and possibly for their jobs, housing, etc.). As large landholdings, replace family farms, and the cities become even more crowded, rural communities turn into company towns. A 1944 study by anthropologist Walter Goldschmidt compared two farm communities in California's San Joaquin Valley, Arvin and Dinuba. Arvin was characterized by large landholdings, Dinuba by family farms. The differences are striking: The majority of workers in Dinuba were self-employed, while two-thirds of the workers in Arvin were agricultural wage laborers. Dinuba supported twice as many independent businesses and did 61 percent more retail business. Dinuba had many more parks, schools, and community groups, as well as more institutions for local political decision-making.

Goldschmidt originally planned to extend his research to include all farm communities in the San Joaquin Valley, but a vigorous campaign, spearheaded by the powerful Associated Farmers, forced him to discontinue his work. To this day, no follow-up study has been done—it's difficult to get research funds to look into the American power structure. But it seems likely that comparable study today would yield even more striking results.

In California, by far the nation's leading agricultural state, less than one tenth of one percent of the farms own roughly 40 percent of the cropland. Tenneco and Standard Oil each own over 300,000 acres of California land—much of it agricultural. Tenneco also has vast landholdings in Arizona—altogether it controls a land area more than twice the size of Rhode Island (it actually *advertises* this in its annual report).

Southern Pacific is California's biggest landowner with 2.4 million acres, about 150,000 agricultural (originally given to it free by the government to build a railroad). Other big California "farmers" include the 348,000-acre Tejon Ranch (with a big interest held by the *L.A. Times-Mirror*) and Kaiser with 111,000 acres. In the early 1940s California's largest agricultural landholder with over 600,000 acres was the Bank of America, which had foreclosed on a farm a day during the preceding depression years. Today the Bank of America, the world's largest agricultural lender, works closely with big corporate farmers while frequently refusing loans to small farms, thus giving another non-agricultural impetus to corporate control of the land.

California is only the most important example of the need for land reform in the United States. The situation varies somewhat from region to region—in the deep South landholdings are highly concentrated, in Maine 12 corporations own 52 percent of the land, in the Midwest things are not yet quite as bad. But everywhere the pattern is the same: land, whether agricultural, timber, urban, is increasingly controlled by big corporate interests.

The kind of concentrated control of such basic resources as food and land vastly increases the power of a few corporations over the lives of millions of people. Most of us are alienated from the land—unlike most people who have ever lived, we've pretty much forgotten about it. But there is no more basic resource, none that on as many levels—physical, social, and spiritual—so critically determines the dimensions of human life. And the corporations own it.

Land reform does not just mean a return to small farms. It means a radical restructuring of society. Corporate control of land helps force people into the cities and keep them there. Think for a moment about the vast changes in U.S. society if 75 percent of the people did *not* live on 2 percent of the land—you begin to get an idea of the profound implications of land reform. A certain tradition might suggest that the alternative to the USDA farm of 2015 is for "the people" to "take control" of the same ten-mile wheat field and the skyscraper cattle factories. But the people can never control such things, which inherently centralize power and which point to a world of Super Cities worse than we have today. Ultimately, land reform should not just mean opening the land up for people who want to farm, but opening it up for everyone, for communities of farmers *and* carpenters, poets, printers, teachers, tailors, plumbers, jacks-of-all-trades. It should mean a decentralized society, in which the countryside is an attractive, healthy place where people live and work, where people are able to obtain and make use of simple, durable tools and machines, and build regionally a substantial self-sufficiency and independence. If we are really serious about having a direct say in decisions which affect our lives, we will first have to take the basic organization of our society out of the skyscrapers and bring it down to earth.

For Discussion

1. How does large-scale concentration in the production and distribution of food affect our diets?
2. Discuss the advantages and disadvantages of processed foods.
3. What is "welfare for the rich"?
4. How are the rich aided by the crop subsidy? By the water subsidy? By the research subsidy? By the tax subsidy?
5. In what ways are farm workers deprived of their rights according to Casalino?
6. How do giant farms work against the community?
7. What benefits does land reform offer to all Americans? What benefits would you add to those stated by Casalino?

ALEXANDER WALKER

The Case of the Vanishing Bloodstains

Violence has become almost commonplace in American films. In the following essay, Alexander Walker, a British film critic, examines the growth of this phenomenon in recent years. Using six Hollywood movies produced after the liberalization of the Production Code in 1965–1966 as the basis of his discussion, he examines the nature and extent of film violence and speculates about its moral implications. Born in Ireland and educated in Europe, Walker also attended the University of Michigan, where he did postgraduate studies and lectured in comparative government. He then turned to journalism and has been feature writer and film critic for the *London Evening Standard* since 1959. In 1970 he was named Critic of the Year in the International Press awards. He is author of many articles and four books about the cinema: *Sex in the Movies, Stardom, Stanley Kubrick Directs*, and *Hollywood U.K.*

> Holmes bent over this grotesque frieze for some minutes and then suddenly sprang to his feet with an exclamation of surprise and dismay. His face was haggard with anxiety.
> "We have let this affair go far enough," said he.
> —*The Dancing Men*

About five years ago a change came over the character of death on the cinema screen. What came into being has been called "medical materialism," a phrase I owe to Dr. Jonathan Miller. By this he meant that death, which had hitherto been a fairly ritual affair, was turning into an anatomy lesson, or, rather, an autopsy.

Reprinted by permission of the author from *Encounter* Magazine, March 1973.

Previously the gun barked, the victim jackknifed, a token bloodstain welled up on his shirt front, another public enemy lay down and died. The damage was more sartorial than arterial; and the censor's work was correspondingly simplified, since deserving justice had been seen to be done and there was really no mess to speak of. It is curious considering the high place that *ciné-verité* techniques occupy in the screen's approach to life that the film which probably did more than any other to change this approach to death has been overlooked, in spite of being seen by more people in the world than any other American movie.

Let me momentarily conceal the event it recorded, as well as the names of the parties at the center of it, and quote instead from a synopsis written some time afterward but very like the "continuity" script that's put together from the completely edited film:

> The [car] continues to slow down. The interior is a place of horror. The last bullet has torn through [his] cerebellum, the lower part of his brain. Leaning towards her husband [she] has seen a piece of his skull detach itself. At first there is no blood. And then, in the very next instant, there is nothing but blood spattering him. . . . Gobs of blood as thick as a man's hand are soaking the floor of the back seat, [his] clothes are steeped in it, the roses are drenched, [his] body is lurching soundlessly towards his wife, and Motor Cycle Police Officer Hargis, two feet from her, is doused in the face by a red sheet. To Kellerman it appears that the air is full of moist sawdust.[1]

Those who have read William Manchester's landmark piece of investigative reporting, *The Death of a President*, will hardly need to be told by now that what this describes is the assassination of President Kennedy in Dallas in November 1963.

But what makes it relevant to this enquiry into the contemporary cinema's approach to death is the way that Manchester duplicates the effect of a camera's eye seeing in slow motion, and thereby giving itself the *time* to see, the bloody havoc accompanying the onset of sudden and extremely public death. As well as the eye-witnesses he names, Manchester had indeed the supplementary evidence of a camera's eye—the one with the famous Zoomar lens being wielded by Abe Zapruder, the garment manufacturer and amateur cinematographer who happened to be filming the Presidential motorcade at the precise moment of the assassination. In the 8.3 seconds which it took the color film to register it on 152 frames the most notorious piece of "medical materialism" was recorded to be later relayed throughout the world during one of the most deeply shared periods of grief in history.

It is odd how this reproduction of an event dramatically heightens it.

[1] William Manchester, *The Death of a President* (1967), p. 196.

As the narrator in Stanley Kubrick's *A Clockwork Orange* says, "The colors of the real world only seem really real when you viddy them on the screen. . . ." Not that the Zapruder film recorded the anatomical detail of the Manchester "scenario," although once the posthumous event is treated to an "action replay"—as it was, countless times in the course of the subsequent enquiries, lay and official—one seems to be seeing it broken down into the factions of time in a slow motion version. Over the years it has assumed an iconographic vividness irresistible to any film-maker disposed to draw his inspiration from an historical and moral shock of its magnitude.

So one is not at all surprised to find this confirmed in an Arthur Penn interview in *Les Cahiers du Cinéma*, four years after Kennedy's assassination, in which the director of *Bonnie and Clyde* explicitly refers to the earlier event when speaking of the fusillade of 87 bullets fired at the end of his film into the eponymous hero and heroine. "We put on the bullet holes," says Penn, "and there's even a piece of Warren's [Beatty's] head that comes off, like that famous photograph of Kennedy."[2] In fact if one turns to the screenplay of *Bonnie and Clyde*, written by David Newman and Robert Benton, what one finds is an eerie echo of the precise, present-tense tone of the Manchester "scenario" which came out in the same year as the film, 1967:

> We see alternately the bodies of Clyde and Bonnie twisting, shaking, horribly distorted; much of the action is in slow motion. Clyde is on the ground, his body arching and rolling from the impact of the bullets. Bonnie is still in her seat; her body jerking and swaying as the bullets thud relentlessly into her and the framework of the car.
>
> EXTERIOR: THE CAR ON THE VERGE.
>
> Bonnie's body slews out sideways, head first. A final burst and her head and shoulders drop down on to the running board. Clyde's body rolls over and over on the ground and then lies still. The firing stops.[3]

The reason Penn used a slow-motion technique at this point in the film was to get what he called "the spasm of death," and a most sophisticated technique it was. It involved no fewer than four cameras shooting at 24, 48, 72 and 96 frames a second "so that I could cut to get the shock and at the same time the ballet of death. There's a moment in death when the body no longer functions, when it becomes an object and has a certain kind of detached ugly beauty. . . ."

[2] *Les Cahiers du Cinéma* (December 1967), Arthur Penn interviewed by André Labarthe and Jean-Louis Comolli.
[3] *The Bonnie and Clyde Book*, compiled and edited by Sandra Wake and Nicola Hayden. New York: Simon & Schuster; London: Lorrimer, pp. 162–4.

Now anyone who talks of the "beauty" of death is treading in a grey area of aesthetics; yet can anyone doubt that Penn acquitted himself responsibly in *Bonnie and Clyde*? Freely admitting to the fascination he found in rendering the kinetic effects of violence, which is what makes it so dangerously appealing where most spectators of events real or imaginary are concerned, he nevertheless saves himself from the charge of mortuary gloating by what one can only call an act of charity toward his victims. While slow motion gives us the time to see them die by protracting the moment of death into an eternity, it nevertheless withholds the full destructive force of the medical materialism which 87 bullets ripping into two people would have conveyed to us. They would have literally been torn apart. What really horrifies us is the "overkill" nature of the lawmen, almost believing that their victims had charmed lives and must be filled with their own weight of lead. All the same their outlines are intact as they lie there, like effigies. What Penn has done is extinguish the life but preserve the legend.

When we next saw slow-motion used to record the violent rhythms of death it was in a far more materialistic cause. Sam Peckinpah's film *The Wild Bunch* also derived from the Kennedy assassination, more precisely from the debate on the role of the gun in American life which in the aftermath of this event and the deaths of Robert Kennedy and Martin Luther King, looked like ushering in far tighter curbs on the sale and ownership of firearms in a society traditionally based on a man's right to bear and use them.

Peckinpah's film celebrated the power of the gun by showing it in action, which meant showing the bloody destruction contained in one split second. Blood spurts like a drinking fountain from a burst artery in the opening massacre, a body bumps up off the ground like a rubber toy, dust rises in slow motion, a limb trails out at a ghastly angle as if in a state of weightlessness and the corpse settles down with a spasm that has the effect in slow motion of a small avalanche. *The Wild Bunch* always keeps returning to the gun. It is the hero if anything is, far more so than the human beings, a bunch of aging cowboys feeling their obsolescence, whereas their guns will go marching on into the new century, coming out in ever-improving models. The brand-new machine-gun that goes off like a fractious baby in the arms of the ignorant peon cuddling it is a quantum leap into totalitarian destructiveness.

But what is the film saying to us? This is more difficult to answer and even after a prudent second viewing I am driven to conclude that it *says* nothing for the very reason that it *shows* everything. The end doesn't simply justify the means, as it always does in a Peckinpah film; the end is the means in the way (remember?) that the medium is the message.

Now this should have put us on our guard. I know that some people were; but to me, reviewing the film at the time, its bloody excesses seemed justified as a response to the contemporary wave of revulsion against violence. I am far less certain of this now, especially after Peckinpah's *Straw Dogs*—which I shall return to.

. . .

I don't think it was accidental that the curve of violence in films began its steep rise just about the time one would expect the new Hollywood films, which had profited from the 1965–66 revision of the Production Code to deal with sex more and more candidly, began to face the problem of their subsequent sale to television. Sex undressed is patently sex; violence on the other hand can be dressed up as many things. Moreover, the motion-picture code, reflecting the taboos of the early Legion of Decency and the Roman Catholic Church as well as the truisms at the center of the American historical experience, was basically more tolerant to the depiction of violence than sex. One has also to reckon with a number of film-makers, all men whose forte lay in the harsh-grained action film, now finding that the dangerous but exhilarating tide of fashion was running with them and even propelling their ingrained aggressiveness along almost faster than they could keep up with it.

The world's escalating violence finds its most vivid metaphor in the movies; which is not to say that the movies predispose us to add to the violence. But as the power of certain films proves so strong that we tend to conceptualize real events in their terms I think that it may predispose us to tolerate violence, or at least its latest form when it is succeeded by some new and awful escalation. The imitative pressures of the industry drive its film-makers to let themselves rip on a spiraling ascent into new levels of death and destruction until it "peaks" in some explosive display of psychopathy.

For film censors, this creates increasingly difficult problems. One of the recent crises, according to many commentators, came near to dislodging the new British incumbent, Mr. Stephen Murphy, who learned in his first few painful months in office that he was caught between two irreconcilable duties—protecting the public from the excesses of the film-makers and at the same time shielding the film-makers from the intolerance of the public. Central to this crisis was the new character of death on the screen.

I am not going to allude in any detail to the two films over which the debate raged, *Straw Dogs* and *A Clockwork Orange*.

. . .

In brief Mr. Murphy had viewed the film [*Straw Dogs*] which Sam Peckinpah had shot in Britain when it was in its final rough-cut, an unofficial procedure sometimes resorted to by his predecessor, Mr. John Trevelyan, when it was a question of "tricky" material requiring a helpful indication of attitude on the censor's part before he or his examiners were asked to pass it officially. Mr. Murphy advised the producer and distributor that he did not feel able to pass it in its present form. When it was officially submitted some weeks later he was gratified to find his advice had been heeded. The shot of a man's guts being blown out of him by a double-barreled gun had gone; the protracted rape scene in which two youths assaulted the hero's wife had been broken up by cuts to the absent husband on his duck shoot; and the double rape had been shortened although the unintentional effect of this was to make it appear as if the unfortunate girl, caught the wrong side up after the "conventional" assault on her, was now being buggered as well!

Even in its surviving form the rape was one of the most protracted and calculated acts of sexual violence I and others had seen on the screen up to then, the girl being beaten into submission and then having her scanty clothing ripped slowly off her to the accompaniment of the noise of tearing material which showed how Peckinpah knew the emotive value of the sound as well as the sight of violence.

But it was the climacteric of violence when Dustin Hoffman is forced to abandon his pacifist stance against the wild bunch of assailants and turn into a somewhat unlikely vest-pocket Hercules, which revealed the ferocious extent of the film's anti-humanism. Bodies were filled with buckshot, beaten insensible with iron bars; one man accidentally blew off his own foot and was left gawking at a close-up of the shattered stump; and the *specialité* of this particular *maison* came when the last assailant alive, or conscious, choked to death with his head caught in the toothed jaws of a game-keeper's mantrap.

There was a difference, though, compared to *The Wild Bunch* whose slow-motion techniques also found their way into the mayhem. This film said something as well as showed it—namely that a man needed to be put in touch with his primal instincts before he could call himself a Man. Peckinpah had come out of hiding with this one. Instead of bidding an elegaic valedictory to *The Wild Bunch* and giving a helpless shrug at the continuing rule of the gun, he appeared as the champion of the Superman and gave his blessing to the machismo ethic which equates violence with virility, and suffering with manliness. *"The knock at the door meant the birth of a man and the death of seven others,"* was the film's publicity slogan in Britain.

. . .

A Clockwork Orange is a useful reminder that in this enquiry we must pay more regard to intention than content measured in quantitative terms. Though Kubrick's film has its violent sequences (not so many of them as the outcry might lead us to expect), it is a film that's really about choice, not violence. While Peckinpah asserts that a man only becomes a man when he kills, Kubrick is saying that a man ceases to be a man if he cannot choose. Better that he should have the right to choose, even if it is the right to sin, than that his moral functioning should be replaced by the programmed mechanism of the State. What violence there is is not of the medically materialist nature. Very little physical injury is depicted, though much is suggested, and what there is gets "distanced" from the audience by the "ballet" of the gang fight and the "vaudeville" of the assault-and-rape to the melody of "Singin' in the Rain."

I happened to be present while Kubrick shot the death of the Cat Woman, brained by the sculptured phallus, and it was a matter of lengthy deliberation by him not to let any physical injury be seen. This was to preserve the scene's nightmare dimension. For it's well known that in dreaming the mind's censor tends to exclude this kind of anatomical gruesomeness which would otherwise jerk the dreamer awake by his own too horrible imaginings. Kubrick's regard for the quality of the story as a "controlled dream" made him take the same precautions.

. . .

Now the feast of death that *The Godfather* provides is so well known that I may be spared running through the obits. I only observe that the garrotings, assassinations and serial slayings have their appeal deftly enhanced by the care taken never to repeat the slaughter in quite the same way twice. It is the principle of pornography, too. In contrast, what the censor advised should be cut out of *Trash*, in order to give it an "*X*" Certificate, was almost entirely sexual and included a fellatio scene (shortened) and a moment when a beer bottle was put to an unusual use to obtain an orgasm (though as the self-pleasurer was a male-in-drag it remains a mystery what arcane technique the censor ascribed to him/her). The interpretation is irresistible—that the film censor deplores violence, but what he cuts is sex.

For anyone operating on this double standard *The Godfather* is a gift. For in spite of being one of the most continuously violent films ever made, it contain absolutely no sex—none at all. This has escaped general notice, perhaps by its very obviousness. It was brought home to me by the satisfaction with which a rather staid friend, who had frequently deplored the growing permissiveness of the movies, expressed his pleasure to me that here at last was a film to which he could take his wife without embarrassment. No distressing full frontals, you see, at least not where sex was concerned. I think he might have been more appalled, or maybe his wife would have been, if one of the early victims whose gun hand is skewered to the bar with a knife while his throat is garroted had been in a state of nudity at the time.

A film cannot be estimated to earn 150 million dollars world-wide without this layman's opinion of what is decent for him and his wife to see being shared by the majority of those who will go to *The Godfather*. Indeed the audience reaction is interesting. I saw the film several times, having had to take along friends from backward countries, lands where *The Godfather* hadn't been opened, and on each occasion the audience sat dumbly through the plethora of Mafia killings. When they did react audibly it was only once, a low collective whistle of shock at the end when the "godson" deliberately lies to his wife. Seeing death at its most anatomically violent on the screen had apparently lost its power to repel: lying to your wife, on the other hand, is still something that goes home to the heart of the petit bourgeoisie. Nothing else has so sharply indicated to me how the tolerance-level of violence is rising.

I don't ascribe the fact that the film fails to shock or outrage to the nice-safe feeling its paradoxically generates—keeping death inside the family, so to speak. Of course these Mafia bosses are "golden oldies"— the slaughter of '46 out of the summer of '42. But distance lending security to the viewer doesn't satisfactorily explain its appeal. As I see it, we are witnessing a far more frightening phenomenon than the deaths on the screen; we are witnessing nothing less than the death of people's humanity. We have been so raped by violence that we are like the daughter heeding her mother's injunction as she leaves on a dubious date: that if you can't resist it, lie back and enjoy it. And even this residual pleasure is losing its savor. It is drying up the way the emotions are on the screen. Death no longer has any humanity, so it can offer no purgative satisfaction. Not even our pity is solicited. Man-made monsters once had hearts, which broke even as they crushed their makers. Now all they exhibit is the coolness of successful psychopaths—no emotions whatsoever. There is scarcely a gangster film out of the 1930s which hadn't some particle of humanity embedded in it, besides the slugs of rivals for the South Side, even if it was only misguided mother-love for Jimmy Cagney.

In the second half of *The Godfather* an extraordinary change comes over Al Pacino which is relevant to this. At the start of the film it is almost as if Paramount were making him into a 1940s *Love Story* figure, with his air of diminished cuddliness as he nibbles his courtship on the fringe of the family. When he takes over power (and the story) he reverts to a much earlier decade than the 1940s: he affects the glossy, brushed-back hair-style and close-fitting wardrobe of the 1930s. He appears a stereotype companion to Humphrey Bogart and George Raft except in one vital respect. The movie still assigns to him the arid, passionless, mechanistic ethos which is its own attitude to all human life in the 1970s. Its nostalgia only goes back so far: when it comes to the killing, it is bang up-to-date.

The Mechanic may look like a freelance Godfather, operating exogamously against any target he is paid to eliminate. In Michael Winner's film, as in The Godfather, one is overwhelmed by the same emotionally drained attitude to death. But whereas the "godson" reminds his doubting girl-friend that "everybody kills today, the Army, the Government, Big Business," the professional assassin in The Mechanic takes this acceptance of the world as it is to its logical conclusion and propagandizes that anybody has the right to kill anybody. The same refrain was heard from the acolytes of Charles Manson. It is language being used as an instrument of murder. The Mechanic in fact takes it a stage beyond Manson. Charles Bronson's assassin doesn't kill for the thrill of it all; to him, it is simply "the Job," carried out dispassionately upon receipt of a registered envelope of instructions. Whom he kills, much less why, we are never told. What does it matter, since the act of killing is all that counts? We have come a long way in the few years from the pathetic dimension of the massacre in which Bonnie and Clyde died and made us care to the almost bloodless killings of The Mechanic in which we don't know who dies and couldn't care less.

There are literally "clean" killings. The only scene in which I can recall blood actually flowing and lingered over is the one in which the jilted girl-friend of the mechanic's young male apprentice deliberately severs her wrists with a razor blade as the two men sit looking on.

Her pitiful gesture is an attempt to move at least one of them into emotional involvement with her; they simply regard her suicide as the test of how "cool" they can remain. Such men are smooth operators; but their essence is their refusal to sympathize, to become involved. It is the black side of Kennedy's avowal of "grace under pressure"—"coolness under stress." The essay on The White Negro which Norman Mailer wrote in 1957 praising the "psychopathic brilliance" of the hip style that models itself on the Black experience has been brought to life in The Mechanic—if "life" is the word for a mode of existence dedicated to keeping on top by extinguishing all human feelings and maintaining one's mechanistic responses in trim for taking human life.

In an earlier script, I am told, the liaison in The Mechanic between both men was homosexual as well as homicidal. Even that has been siphoned out of them, leaving only their mutual boast that in a society which is actually no better than they are, the psychopath is king.

Even this is not the film's most ominous feature. The way it has been accepted is highly unsettling. Far from being given a British "X" Certificate, putting it on the same shelf beside The Godfather, it has drawn a straight "AA" Certificate, a much milder rating allowing 14-year-old children to see it. This view is presumably based on the belief that in its externals it differs little from a standard gangster drama of the 1930s. There could scarcely be a more dangerous misreading of its essential significance. In it as in other films we are being asked to accept the ascendancy of the Psychopath, the man who has no doubts, knows no fears, experiences no guilt, feels no humanity, but simply acts in the only way he believes gives meaning to a society in which the rejection of restraints has become epidemic. He kills.

From the addition of medical materialism to its repertoire, the cinema has passed on to the celebration of moral anarchy. And it has us staring at the panorama as ambiguously as the Mechanic himself stares at the reproduction of the Bosch painting known alternatively as *Earthly Pleasures* or as *Lust*, depicting a carnival of hideous fantasies, which hangs on his living-room wall. Is it a foretaste of Hell that he draws from it? Or is it fresh inspiration? And is there any difference?

The bloodstains we've been following have given out: in the moral void in which much of the contemporary screen exists and flourishes, the only guide is our own fears.

For Discussion

1. What are the characteristics of "medical materialism"?
2. Make a case for or against the slow-motion camera as a valid treatment of the "ballet of death."
3. Discuss Walker's judgment of *The Wild Bunch* that "it *says* nothing for the very reason that it *shows* everything."
4. Why, according to Walker, did the 1965–1966 revision of the Production Code lead to more violence rather than more sex?
5. Discuss exactly what Walker objects to in each of the films he discusses. What mitigating factors, if any, does he present?
6. Walker suggests that the lack of sex in *The Godfather* has contributed to its financial success. Do you agree that it contains no sex? That sex is less popular than violence?
7. What recent films have you seen which support or contradict Walker's view of screen violence?
8. How does Walker attempt to compensate for the fact that he discusses films which many of his readers may not have seen? How successful do you think he is?
9. What principles have guided Walker in organizing and presenting the material in this essay?

THE
REFLECTIVE
NO

I always as I admit seem to be talking but talking can be a way of listening that is if one has the profound need of hearing and seeing what every one is telling.

GERTRUDE STEIN
"The Gradual Making of
The Making of Americans"

Of the four "voices" in *The Rhetoric of NO*, the reflective is the most personal, and for this reason the most difficult to define. However, if we compare it to the impassioned and discursive voices, we see that it has its own distinctive and identifiable qualities—qualities found in some of the most effective writing.

An essential difference is in the author's relationship to his reader. The impassioned writer reaches out to the reader principally with his feeling; the discursive writer reaches out to the reader with his subject, trusting him to perceive its validity. But unlike both of these, the reflective writer reaches out to his reader only incidentally. His primary interest is in *what his subject means to him*. As Gertrude Stein suggests, his talking is "a way of listening" to himself, a way of exploring his own opinions and feelings. Thus the reader becomes an extension of the writer, a kind of alter-ego listening in to what is being thought.

This is not to say that the reflective writer is unconscious of his reader but rather that his writing stems more from a need to formulate, for himself, the substance of his subject than from a desire to condemn, judge, or convert others. He is impelled to express himself even when he feels that what he is saying will cause no change in the world. He may explain himself (as in King's "Letter from Birmingham Jail") or advise others (as in Tolstoy's "Advice to a Draftee"), but his real purpose is to give outward expression to his inner thoughts and feelings.

When an author expresses himself reflectively, therefore, he is writing about a subject which deeply and personally involves him. His tone reveals a feeling of intimacy with his subject—a quiet, familiar concern instead of either an impassioned or impersonal one. His attitude toward his subject remains relatively calm; he doesn't shout or demand, accuse or command. He doesn't necessarily try to arrange his argument in a formally logical way to be analyzed or evaluated. Even when he is writing to a particular person (in a letter, for example), his main interest is in *sharing*, rather than *presenting*, his argument. If the reader listens, fine; but if not, no matter. The author has accomplished his purpose by articulating his subject for its own sake.

"The Reflective NO" contains a variety of writers who express their dissent in various styles and forms—letters, journals, essays, articles. They all speak in a similar voice, inviting us to share with them the working out of their ideas.

HENRY DAVID THOREAU

On the Duty of Civil Disobedience

Born in 1817 in Concord, Massachusetts, and educated at Harvard College, Henry David Thoreau spent most of his life in and around Concord, teaching for a brief time but preferring the freedom of manual labor to the academic life while he continued to write. Pre-eminent as a nature writer (notably *Walden*), Thoreau has gained increasing prestige with the years. His emphasis on simplicity, his nonconformity, and his dedication to a life of high principle have influenced countless thinkers and writers as diverse as Hemingway and Gandhi, Henry Miller and Martin Luther King, Jr. His friend and mentor, Emerson, delivering his obituary address in 1862 said, "His soul was made for the noblest society." The essay which follows, first published in 1849, has become a world classic.

I heartily accept the motto,—"That government is best which governs least"; and I should like to see it acted up to more rapidly and systematically. Carried out, it finally amounts to this, which also I believe,—"That government is best which governs not at all"; and when men are prepared for it, that will be the kind of government which they will have. Government is at best but an expedient; but most governments are usually, and all governments are sometimes, inexpedient. The objections which have been brought against a standing army, and they are many and weighty, and deserve to prevail, may also at last be brought against a standing government. The standing army is only an arm of the standing government. The government itself, which is only the mode which the people have chosen to execute their will, is equally liable to be abused and perverted before the people can act through it. Witness the present Mexican war, the work of comparatively a few individuals using the standing government as their tool; for, in the outset, the people would not have consented to this measure.

This American government—what is it but a tradition, though a recent one, endeavoring to transmit itself unimpaired to posterity, but each instant losing some of its integrity? It has not the vitality and force of a single living man; for a single man can bend it to his will. It is a sort of wooden gun to the people themselves. But it is not the less necessary for this; for the people must have some complicated machinery or other, and hear its din, to satisfy that idea of government which they have. Governments show thus how successfully men can be imposed on, even impose on themselves, for their own advantage. It is excellent, we must all allow. Yet this government never of itself furthered any enterprise, but by the alacrity with which it got out of its way. *It* does not keep the country free. *It* does not settle the West. *It* does not educate. The character inherent in the American people has done all that has been accomplished; and it would have done somewhat more, if the government had not sometimes got in its way. For government is an expedient by which men would fain succeed in letting one another alone; and, as has been said, when it is most expedient, the governed are most let alone by it. Trade and commerce, if they were not made of India-rubber, would never manage to bounce over the obstacles which legislators are continually putting in their way; and, if one were to judge these men wholly by the effects of their actions and not partly by their intentions, they would deserve to be classed and punished with those mischievous persons who put obstructions on the railroads.

But, to speak practically and as a citizen, unlike those who call themselves no-government men, I ask for, not at once no government, but *at once* a better government. Let every man make known what kind of government would command his respect, and that will be one step toward obtaining it.

After all, the practical reason why, when the power is once in the hands of the people, a majority are permitted, and for a long period continue, to rule is not because they are most likely to be in the right, nor because this seems fairest to the minority, but because they are physically the strongest. But a government in which the majority rule in all cases cannot be based on justice, even as far as men understand it. Can there not be a government in which majorities do not virtually decide right and wrong, but conscience?—in which majorities decide only those questions to which the rule of expediency is applicable? Must the citizen ever for a moment, or in the least degree, resign his conscience to the legislator? Why has every man a conscience, then? I think that we should be men first, and subjects afterward. It is not desirable to cultivate a respect for the law, so much as for the right. The only obligation which I have a right to assume is to do at any time what I think right. It is truly enough said, that a corporation has no conscience; but a corporation of conscientious men is a corporation *with* a conscience. Law never made men a whit more just; and, by means of their respect for it, even the well-disposed are daily made the agents of injustice. A common and natural result of an undue respect for law is, that you may see a file of soldiers, colonel, captain, corporal, privates, powder-monkeys, and all, marching in admirable order over hill and dale to the wars, against their wills, ay, against their common sense and consciences, which makes it very steep marching indeed, and produces a palpitation of the heart. They have no doubt that it is damnable business in which they are concerned; they are all peaceably inclined. Now, what are they? Men at all? or small movable forts and magazines, at the service of some unscrupulous man in power? Visit the Navy-Yard, and behold a marine, such a man as an American government can make, or such as it can make a man with its black arts,—a mere shadow and reminiscence of humanity, a man laid out alive and standing, and already, as one may say, buried under arms with funeral accompaniments, though it may be,—

> Not a drum was heard, not a funeral note,
> As his corse to the rampart we hurried;
> Not a soldier discharged his farewell shot
> O'er the grave where our hero we buried.

The mass of men serve the state thus, not as men mainly, but as machines, with their bodies. They are the standing army, and the militia, jailers, constables, posse comitatus, etc. In most cases there is no free exercise whatever of the judgment or of the moral sense; but they put themselves on a level with wood and earth and stones; and wooden men can perhaps be manufactured that will serve the purpose as well. Such commend no more respect than men of straw or a lump of dirt. They have the same sort of worth only as horses and dogs. Yet such as these even are commonly esteemed good citizens. Others—as most legislators, politicians, lawyers, ministers, and officeholders—serve the state chiefly with their heads; and, as they rarely make any moral distinctions, they are as likely to serve the Devil, without *intending* it, as God. A very few, as heroes, patriots, martyrs, reformers in the great sense, and *men*, serve the state with their consciences also, and so necessarily resist it for the most part; and they are commonly treated as enemies by it. A wise man will only be useful as a man, and will not submit to be "clay," and "stop a hole to keep the wind away," but leave that office to his dust at least:—

> I am too high-born to be propertied,
> To be a secondary at control,
> Or useful serving-man and instrument
> To any sovereign state throughout the world.

He who gives himself entirely to his fellow-men appears to them useless and selfish; but he who gives himself partially to them is pronounced a benefactor and philanthropist.

How does it become a man to behave toward this American government to-day? I answer, that he cannot without disgrace be associated with it. I cannot for an instant recognize that political organization as *my* government which is the *slave's* government also.

All men recognize the right of revolution; that is, the right to refuse allegiance to, and to resist, the government, when its tyranny or its inefficiency are great and unendurable. But almost all say that such is not the case now. But such was the case, they think, in the Revolution of '75. If one were to tell me that this was a bad government because it taxed certain foreign commodities brought to its ports, it is most probable that I should not make an ado about it, for I can do without them. All machines have their friction; and possibly this does enough good to counterbalance the evil. At any rate, it is a great evil to make a stir about it. But when the friction comes to have its machine, and oppression and robbery are organized, I say, let us not have such a machine any longer. In other words, when a sixth of the population of a nation which has undertaken to be the refuge of liberty are slaves, and a whole country is unjustly overrun and conquered by a foreign army, and subjected to military law, I think that it is not too soon for honest men to rebel and revolutionize. What makes this duty the more urgent is the fact that the country so overrun is not our own, but ours is the invading army.

Paley, a common authority with many on moral questions, in his chapter on the "Duty of Submission to Civil Government," resolves all civil obligation into expediency; and he proceeds to say, "that so long as the interest of the whole society requires it, that is, so long as the established government cannot be resisted or changed without public inconveniency, it is the will of God that the established government be obeyed, and no longer. . . . This principle being admitted, the justice of every particular case of resistance is reduced to a computation of the quantity of the danger and grievance on the one side, and of the probability and expense of redressing it on the other." Of this, he says, every man shall judge for himself. But Paley appears never to have contemplated those cases to which the rule of expediency does not apply, in which a people, as well as an individual, must do justice, cost what it may. If I have unjustly wrested a plank from a drowning man, I must restore it to him though I drown myself. This, according to Paley, would be inconvenient. But he that would save his life, in such a case, shall lose it. This people must cease to hold slaves, and to make war on Mexico, though it cost them their existence as a people.

In their practice, nations agree with Paley; but does any one think that Massachusetts does exactly what is right at the present crisis?

> A drab of state, a cloth-o'-silver slut,
> To have her train borne up, and her soul trail in the dirt.

Practically speaking, the opponents to a reform in Massachusetts are not a hundred thousand politicians at the South, but a hundred thousand merchants and farmers here, who are more interested in commerce and agriculture than they are in humanity, and are not prepared to do justice to the slave and to Mexico, *cost what it may*. I quarrel not with far-off foes, but with those who, near at home, coöperate with, and do the bidding of, those far away, and without whom the latter would be harmless. We are accustomed to say, that the mass of men are unprepared; but improvement is slow, because the few are not materially wiser or better than the many. It is not so important that many should be as good as you, as that there be some absolute goodness somewhere; for that will leaven the whole lump. There are thousands who are *in opinion* opposed to slavery and to the war, who yet in effect do nothing to put an end to them; who, esteeming themselves children of Washington and Franklin, sit down with their hands in their pockets, and say that they know not what to do, and do nothing; who even postpone the question of freedom to the question of free-trade, and quietly read the prices-current along with the latest advices from Mexico, after dinner, and, it may be, fall asleep over them both. What is the price-current of an honest man and patriot to-day? They hesitate, and they regret, and sometimes they petition; but they do nothing in earnest and with effect. They will wait, well disposed, for others to remedy the evil, that they may no longer have it to regret. At most, they give only a cheap vote, and a feeble countenance and Godspeed, to the right, as it goes by them. There are nine hundred and ninety-nine patrons of virtue to one virtuous man. But it is easier to deal with the real possessor of a thing than with the temporary guardian of it.

All voting is a sort of gaming, like checkers or backgammon, with a slight moral tinge to it, a playing with right and wrong, with moral questions; and betting naturally accompanies it. The character of the voters is not staked. I cast my vote, perchance, as I think right; but I am not vitally concerned that that right should prevail. I am willing to leave it to the majority. Its obligation, therefore, never exceeds that of expediency. Even voting *for the right* is *doing* nothing for it. It is only expressing to men feebly your desire that it should prevail. A wise man will not leave the right to the mercy of chance, nor wish it to prevail through the power of the majority. There is but little virtue in the action of masses of men. When the majority shall at length vote for the abolition of slavery, it will be because they are indifferent to slavery, or because there is but little slavery left to be abolished by their vote. *They* will then be the only slaves. Only *his* vote can hasten the abolition of slavery who asserts his own freedom by his vote.

I hear of a convention to be held at Baltimore, or elsewhere, for the selection of a candidate for the Presidency, made up chiefly of editors, and men who are politicians by profession; but I think, what is it to any independent, intelligent, and respectable man what decision they may come to? Shall we not have the advantage of his wisdom and honesty, nevertheless? Can we not count upon some independent votes? Are there not many individuals in the country who do not attend conventions? But no: I find that the respectable man, so called, has immediately drifted from his position, and despairs of his country, when his country has more reason to despair of him. He forthwith adopts one of the candidates thus selected as the only *available* one, thus proving that he is himself *available* for any purposes of the demagogue. His vote is of no more worth than that of any unprincipled foreigner or hireling native, who may have been bought. O for a man who is a *man*, and, as my neighbor says, has a bone in his back which you cannot pass your hand through! Our statistics are at fault: the population has been returned too large. How many *men* are there to a square thousand miles in this country? Hardly one. Does not America offer any inducement for men to settle here? The American has dwindled into an Odd Fellow,—one who may be known by the development of his organ of gregariousness, and a manifest lack of intellect and cheerful self-reliance; whose first and chief concern, on coming into the world, is to see that the Almshouses are in good repair; and, before yet he has lawfully donned the virile garb, to collect a fund for the support of the widows and orphans that may be; who, in short, ventures to live only by the aid of the Mutual Insurance Company, which has promised to bury him decently.

It is not a man's duty, as a matter of course, to devote himself to the eradication of any, even the most enormous wrong; he may still properly have other concerns to engage him; but it is his duty, at least, to wash his hands of it, and if he gives it no thought longer, not to give it practically his support. If I devote myself to other pursuits and contemplations, I must first see, at least, that I do not pursue them sitting upon another man's shoulders. I must get off him first, that he may pursue his contemplations too. See what gross inconsistency is tolerated. I have heard some of my townsmen say, "I should like to have them order me out to help put down an insurrection of the slaves, or to march to Mexico;—see if I would go;" and yet these very men have each, directly by their allegiance, and so indirectly, at least, by their money, furnished a substitute. The soldier is applauded who refuses to serve in an unjust war by those who do not refuse to sustain the unjust government which makes the war; is applauded by those whose own act and authority he disregards and sets at naught; as if the state were penitent to that degree that it hired one to scourge it while it sinned, but not to that degree that it left off sinning for a moment. Thus, under the name of Order and Civil Government, we are all made at last to pay homage to and support our own meanness. After the first blush of sin comes its indifference; and from immoral it becomes, as it were, *un*moral, and not quite unnecessary to that life which we have made.

The broadest and most prevalent error requires the most disinterested virtue to sustain it. The slight reproach to which the virtue of patriotism is commonly liable, the noble are most likely to incur. Those who, while they disapprove of the character and measures of a government, yield to it their allegiance and support are undoubtedly its most conscientious supporters, and so frequently the most serious obstacles to reform. Some are petitioning the state to dissolve the Union, to disregard the requisitions of the President. Why do they not dissolve it themselves,—the union between themselves and the state,—and refuse to pay their quota into its treasury? Do not they stand in the same relation to the state that the state does to the Union? And have not the same reasons prevented the state from resisting the Union which have prevented them from resisting the state?

How can a man be satisfied to entertain an opinion merely, and enjoy *it*? Is there any enjoyment in it, if his opinion is that he is aggrieved? If you are cheated out of a single dollar by your neighbor, you do not rest satisfied with knowing that you are cheated, or with saying that you are cheated, or even with petitioning him to pay you your due; but you take effectual steps at once to obtain the full amount, and see that you are never cheated again. Action from principle, the perception and the performance of right, changes things and relations; it is essentially revolutionary, and does not consist wholly with anything which was. It not only divides states and churches, it divides families; ay, it divides the *individual*, separating the diabolical in him from the divine.

Unjust laws exist: shall we be content to obey them, or shall we endeavor to amend them, and obey them until we have succeeded, or shall we transgress them at once? Men generally, under such a government as this, think that they ought to wait until they have persuaded the majority to alter them. They think that, if they should resist, the remedy would be worse than the evil. But it is the fault of the government itself that the remedy *is* worse than the evil. *It* makes it worse. Why is it not more apt to anticipate and provide for reform? Why does it not cherish its wise minority? Why does it cry and resist before it is hurt? Why does it not encourage its citizens to be on the alert to point out its faults, and *do* better than it would have them? Why does it always crucify Christ, and excommunicate Copernicus and Luther, and pronounce Washington and Franklin rebels?

One would think, that a deliberate and practical denial of its authority was the only offense never contemplated by government; else, why has it not assigned its definite, its suitable and proportionate penalty? If a man who has no property refuses but once to earn nine shillings for the state, he is put in prison for a period unlimited by any law that I know, and determined only by the discretion of those who placed him there; but if he should steal ninety times nine shillings from the state, he is soon permitted to go at large again.

If the injustice is part of the necessary friction of the machine of government, let it go, let it go: perchance it will wear smooth,—certainly the machine will wear out. If the injustice has a spring, or a pulley, or a rope, or a crank, exclusively for itself, then perhaps you may consider whether the remedy will not be worse than the evil; but if it is of such a nature that it requires you to be the agent of injustice to another, then, I say, break the law. Let your life be a counter friction to stop the machine. What I have to do is to see, at any rate, that I do not lend myself to the wrong which I condemn.

As for adopting the ways which the state has provided for remedying the evil, I know not of such ways. They take too much time, and a man's life will be gone. I have other affairs to attend to. I came into this world, not chiefly to make this a good place to live in, but to live in it, be it good or bad. A man has not everything to do, but something; and because he cannot do *everything*, it is not necessary that he should do *something* wrong. It is not my business to be petitioning the Governor or the Legislature any more than it is theirs to petition me; and if they should not hear my petition, what should I do then? But in this case the state has provided no way: its very Constitution is the evil. This may seem to be harsh and stubborn and unconciliatory; but it is to treat with the utmost kindness and consideration the only spirit that can appreciate or deserves it. So is all change for the better, like birth and death, which convulse the body.

I do not hesitate to say, that those who call themselves Abolitionists should at once effectually withdraw their support, both in person and property, from the government of Massachusetts, and not wait till they constitute a majority of one, before they suffer the right to prevail through them. I think that it is enough if they have God on their side, without waiting for that other one. Moreover, any man more right than his neighbors constitutes a majority of one already.

I meet this American government, or its representative, the state government, directly, and face to face, once a year—no more—in the person of its tax-gatherer; this is the only mode in which a man situated as I am necessarily meets it; and it then says distinctly, Recognize me; and the simplest, the most effectual, and, in the present posture of affairs, the indispensablest mode of treating with it on this head, of expressing your little satisfaction with and love for it, is to deny it then. My civil neighbor, the tax-gatherer, is the very man I have to deal with,—for it is, after all, with men and not with parchment that I quarrel,—and he has voluntarily chosen to be an agent of the government. How shall he ever know well what he is and does as an officer of the government, or as a man, until he is obliged to consider whether he shall treat me, his neighbor, for whom he has respect, as a neighbor and well-disposed man, or as a maniac and disturber of the peace, and see if he can get over this obstruction to his neighborliness without a ruder and more impetuous thought or speech corresponding with his action. I know this well, that if one thousand, if one hundred, if ten men whom I could name,—if ten *honest* men only,—ay, if *one* HONEST man, in this State of Massachusetts, *ceasing to hold slaves*, were actually to withdraw from this copartnership, and be locked up in the county jail therefor, it would be the abolition of slavery in America. For it matters not how small the beginning may seem to be: what is once well done is done forever. But we love better to talk about it: that we say is our mission. Reform keeps many scores of newspapers in its service, but not one man. If my esteemed neighbor, the State's ambassador, who will devote his days to the settlement of the question of human rights in the Council Chamber, instead of being threatened with the prisons of Carolina, were to sit down the prisoner of Massachusetts, that State which is so anxious to foist the sin of slavery upon her sister,—though at present she can discover only an act of inhospitality to be the ground of a quarrel with her,—the Legislature would not wholly waive the subject the following winter.

Under a government which imprisons any unjustly, the true place for a just man is also a prison. The proper place to-day, the only place which Massachusetts has provided for her freer and less desponding spirits, is in her prisons, to be put out and locked out of the State by her own act, as they have already put themselves out by their principles. It is there that the fugitive slave, and the Mexican prisoner on parole, and the Indian come to plead the wrongs of his race should find them; on that separate, but more free and honorable ground, where the State places those who are not *with* her, but *against* her,—the only house in a slave State in which a free man can abide with honor. If any think that their influence would be lost there, and their voices no longer afflict the ear of the State, that they would not be as an enemy within its walls, they do not know by how much truth is stronger than error, nor how much more eloquently and effectively he can combat injustice who has experienced a little in his own person. Cast your whole vote, not a strip of paper merely, but your whole influence. A minority is powerless while it conforms to the majority; it is not even a minority then; but it is irresistible when it clogs by its whole weight. If the alternative is to keep all just men in prison, or give up war and slavery, the State will not hesitate which to choose. If a thousand men were not to pay their tax-bills this year, that would not be a violent and bloody measure, as it would be to pay them, and enable the State to commit violence and shed innocent blood. This is, in fact, the definition of a peaceable revolution, if any such is possible. If the tax-gatherer, or any other public officer, asks me, as one has done, "But what shall I do?" my answer is, "If you really wish to do anything, resign your office." When the subject has refused allegiance, and the officer has resigned his office, then the revolution is accomplished. But even suppose blood should flow. Is there not a sort of blood shed when the conscience is wounded? Through this wound a man's real manhood and immortality flow out, and he bleeds to an everlasting death. I see this blood flowing now.

. . .

Some years ago, the State met me in behalf of the Church, and commanded me to pay a certain sum toward the support of a clergyman whose preaching my father attended, but never I myself. "Pay," it said, "or be locked up in the jail." I declined to pay. But, unfortunately, another man saw fit to pay it. I did not see why the schoolmaster should be taxed to support the priest, and not the priest the schoolmaster; for I was not the State's schoolmaster, but I supported myself by voluntary subscription. I did not see why the lyceum should not present its tax-bill, and have the State to back its demand, as well as the Church. However, at the request of the selectmen, I condescended to make some such statement as this in writing:—"Know all men by these presents, that I, Henry Thoreau, do not wish to be regarded as a member of any incorporated society which I have not joined." This I gave to the town clerk; and he has it. The State, having thus learned that I did not wish to be regarded as a member of that church, has never made a like demand on me since; though it said that it must adhere to its original presumption that time. If I had known how to name them, I should then have signed off in detail from all the societies which I never signed on to; but I did not know where to find a complete list.

I have paid no poll-tax for six years. I was put into a jail once on this account, for one night; and, as I stood considering the walls of solid stone, two or three feet thick, the door of wood and iron, a foot thick, and the iron grating which strained the light, I could not help being struck with the foolishness of that institution which treated me as if I were mere flesh and blood and bones, to be locked up. I wondered that it should have concluded at length that this was the best use it could put me to, and had never thought to avail itself of my services in some way. I saw that, if there was a wall of stone between me and my towns-men, there was a still more difficult one to climb or break through before they could get to be as free as I was. I did not for a moment feel con-fined, and the walls seemed a great waste of stone and mortar. I felt as if I alone of all my townsmen had paid my tax. They plainly did not know how to treat me, but behaved like persons who are underbred. In every threat and in every compliment there was a blunder; for they thought that my chief desire was to stand the other side of that stone wall. I could not but smile to see how industriously they locked the door on my meditations, which followed them out again without let or hind-rance, and *they* were really all that was dangerous. As they could not reach me, they had resolved to punish my body; just as boys, if they can-not come at some person against whom they have a spite, will abuse his dog. I saw that the State was half-witted, that it was timid as a lone woman with her silver spoons, and that it did not know its friends from its foes, and I lost all my remaining respect for it, and pitied it.

Thus the State never intentionally confronts a man's sense, intellectual or moral, but only his body, his senses. It is not armed with superior wit or honesty, but with superior physical strength. I was not born to be forced. I will breathe after my own fashion. Let us see who is the strong-est. What force has a multitude? They only can force me who obey a higher law than I. They force me to become like themselves. I do not hear of *men* being *forced* to live this way or that by masses of men. What sort of life were that to live? When I meet a government which says to me, "Your money or your life," why should I be in haste to give it my money? It may be in a great strait, and not know what to do: I cannot help that. It must help itself; do as I do. It is not worth the while to snivel about it. I am not responsible for the successful working of the machinery of society. I am not the son of the engineer. I perceive that, when an acorn and a chestnut fall side by side, the one does not remain inert to make way for the other, but both obey their own laws, and spring and grow and flourish as best they can, till one, perchance, over-shadows and destroys the other. If a plant cannot live according to its nature, it dies; and so a man.

. . .

When I came out of prison,—for some interfered, and paid that tax—I did not perceive that great changes had taken place on the common, such as he observed who went in a youth and emerged a tottering and gray-headed man; and yet a change had to my eyes come over the scene,—the town, and State, and country,—greater than any that mere time could effect. I saw yet more distinctly the State in which I lived. I saw to what extent the people among whom I lived could be trusted as good neighbors and friends; that their friendship was for summer weather only; that they did not greatly propose to do right; that they were a distinct race from me by their prejudices and superstitions, as the Chinamen and Malays are; that in their sacrifices to humanity they ran no risks, not even to their property; that after all they were not so noble but they treated the thief as he had treated them, and hoped, by a certain outward observance and a few prayers, and by walking in a particular straight though useless path from time to time, to save their souls. This may be to judge my neighbors harshly; for I believe that many of them are not aware that they have such an institution as the jail in their village.

It was formerly the custom in our village, when a poor debtor came out of jail, for his acquaintances to salute him, looking through their fingers, which were crossed to represent the grating of a jail window, "How do ye do?" My neighbors did not thus salute me, but first looked at me, and then at one another, as if I had returned from a long journey. I was put into jail as I was going to the shoemaker's to get a shoe which was mended. When I was let out the next morning, I proceeded to finish my errand, and having put on my mended shoe, joined a huckleberry party, who were impatient to put themselves under my conduct; and in half an hour,—for the horse was soon tackled,—was in the midst of a huckleberry field, on one of our highest hills, two miles off, and then the State was nowhere to be seen.

· · ·

I have never declined paying the highway tax, because I am as desirous of being a good neighbor as I am of being a bad subject; and as for supporting schools, I am doing my part to educate my fellow-countrymen now. It is for no particular item in the tax-bill that I refuse to pay it. I simply wish to refuse allegiance to the State, to withdraw and stand aloof from it effectually. I do not care to trace the course of my dollar, if I could, till it buys a man or a musket to shoot one with,—the dollar is innocent—but I am concerned to trace the effects of my allegiance. In fact, I quietly declare war with the State, after my fashion, though I will still make what use and get what advantage of her I can, as is usual in such cases.

· · ·

I do not wish to quarrel with any man or nation. I do not wish to split hairs, to make fine distinctions, or set myself up as better than my neighbors. I seek rather, I may say, even an excuse for conforming to the laws of the land. I am but too ready to conform to them. Indeed, I have reason to suspect myself on this head; and each year, as the tax-gatherer comes round, I found myself disposed to review the acts and position of the general and State governments, and the spirit of the people, to discover a pretext for conformity.

> We must affect our country as our parents,
> And if at any time we alienate
> Our love or industry from doing it honor,
> We must respect effects and teach the soul
> Matter of conscience and religion,
> And not desire of rule or benefit.

I believe that the State will soon be able to take all my work of this sort out of my hands, and then I shall be not better a patriot than my fellow-countrymen. Seen from a lower point of view, the Constitution, with all its faults, is very good; the law and the courts are very respectable; even this State and this American government are, in many respects, very admirable, and rare things, to be thankful for, such as a great many have described them; but seen from a point of view a little higher, they are what I have described them; seen from a higher still, and the highest, who shall say what they are, or that they are worth looking at or thinking of at all?

However, the government does not concern me much, and I shall bestow the fewest possible thoughts on it. It is not many moments that I live under a government, even in this world. If a man is thought-free, fancy-free, imagination-free, that which *is not* never for a long time appearing *to be* to him, unwise rulers or reformers cannot fatally interrupt him.

· · ·

The authority of government, even such as I am willing to submit to, —for I will cheerfully obey those who know and can do better than I, and in many things even those who neither know nor can do so well,— is still an impure one: to be strictly just, it must have the sanction and consent of the governed. It can have no pure right over my person and property but what I concede to it. The progress from an absolute to a limited monarchy, from a limited monarchy to a democracy, is a progress toward a true respect for the individual. Even the Chinese philosopher was wise enough to regard the individual as the basis of the empire. Is a democracy, such as we know it, the last improvement possible in government? Is it not possible to take a step further towards recognizing and organizing the rights of man? There will never be a really free and enlightened State until the State comes to recognize the individual as a higher and independent power, from which all its own power and authority are derived, and treats him accordingly. I please myself with imagining a State at last which can afford to be just to all men, and to treat the individual with respect as a neighbor; which even would not think it inconsistent with its own repose if a few were to live aloof from it, not meddling with it, nor embraced by it, who fulfilled all the duties of neighbors and fellow-men. A State which bore this kind of fruit, and suffered it to drop off as fast as it ripened, would prepare the way for a still more perfect and glorious State, which also I have imagined, but not yet anywhere seen.

For Discussion

1. What situations prompted Thoreau to declare that a man could not without disgrace be associated with the American government?
2. Does Thoreau's idea of the function of government make him an anarchist? (Also see Goldman in "The Impassioned NO.")
3. What is Thoreau's objection to working through government to remedy unjust laws?
4. Are Thoreau's objections to rule by majority valid today? How can a "wise minority" make its power felt? (Also see Tocqueville in "The Discursive NO.")
5. What is the difference between Thoreau's "The only obligation which I have a right to assume is to do at any time what I think right" and ". . . to do my own thing"? (Also see Camus in this section on rebellion and the educated man.)
6. Discuss the "patron of virtue" and the "Oddfellow" today.
7. How do the following quotations apply today?
   a. "All voting is a sort of gaming, like checkers or backgammon, with a slight moral tinge to it, a playing with right and wrong, with moral questions; and betting naturally accompanies it."
   b. "If I devote myself to other pursuits and contemplations, I must first see, at least, that I do not pursue them sitting upon another man's shoulders."
   c. "Let your life be a counter friction to stop the machine."
   d. "So is all change for the better, like birth and death, which convulse the body."
   e. "Under a government which imprisons any unjustly, the true place for a just man is also a prison."
   f. "Absolutely speaking, the more money, the less virtue; . . ."
   g. "I am as desirous of being a good neighbor as I am of being a bad subject; . . ."
8. What is the basic concept of man underlying Thoreau's social and political ideas?
9. Discuss Thoreau's metaphorical use of the term "machine."
10. What in this essay makes Thoreau's voice primarily reflective? Where is he also impassioned, discursive, and ironic?

LEO TOLSTOY

Advice to a Draftee

Leo Tolstoy, a Russian nobleman born in 1828, began to write fiction while serving as an artillery officer in the Crimean War. He became one of Russia's greatest novelists *(Anna Karenina* and *War and Peace)* as well as an important religious thinker. His religious beliefs caused him to renounce his material possessions and to live a life of a Christian ascetic until his death in 1910. The following letter was written to a young Hessian named Ernst Schramm in 1899, when the Hessian army was a peacetime army and the penalty for evading conscription was death. The letter was forwarded from Darmstadt to Bavaria, a fact which suggests that Schramm left the country rather than be conscripted.

In my last letter I answered your question as well as I could. It is not only Christians but all just people who must refuse to become soldiers— that is, to be ready on another's command (for this is what a soldier's duty actually consists of) to kill all those one is ordered to kill. The question as you state it—which is more useful, to become a good teacher or to suffer for rejecting conscription—is falsely stated. The question is falsely stated because it is wrong for us to determine our actions according to their results, to view actions merely as useful or destructive. In the choice of our actions we can be led by their advantages or disadvantages only when the actions themselves are not opposed to the demands of morality.

We can stay home, go abroad, or concern ourselves with farming or science according to what we find useful for ourselves or others; for neither in domestic life, foreign travel, farming, nor science is there anything immoral. But under no circumstance can we inflict violence on people, torture or kill them because we think such acts could be of use to us or to others. We cannot and may not do such things, especially because we can never be sure of the results of our actions. Often actions which seem the most advantageous of all turn out in fact to be destructive; and the reverse is also true.

The question should not be stated: which is more useful, to be a good teacher or to go to jail for refusing conscription? but rather: what should a man do who has been called upon for military service—that is, called upon to kill or to prepare himself to kill?

And to this question, for a person who understands the true meaning of military service and who wants to be moral, there is only one clear and incontrovertible answer: such a person must refuse to take part in military service no matter what consequences this refusal may have. It may seem to us that this refusal could be futile or even harmful, and that it would be a far more useful thing, after serving one's time, to become a good village teacher. But in the same way, Christ could have judged it more useful for himself to be a good carpenter and submit to all the principles of the Pharisees than to die in obscurity as he did, repudiated and forgotten by everyone.

Moral acts are distinguished from all other acts by the fact that they operate independently of any predictable advantage to ourselves or to others. No matter how dangerous the situation may be of a man who finds himself in the power of robbers who demand that he take part in plundering, murder, and rape, a moral person cannot take part. Is not military service the same thing? Is one not required to agree to the deaths of all those one is commanded to kill?

But how can one refuse to do what everyone does, what everyone finds unavoidable and necessary? Or, must one do what no one does and what everyone considers unnecessary or even stupid and bad? No matter how strange it sounds, this strange argument is the main one offered against those moral acts which in our times face you and every other person called up for military service. But this argument is even more incorrect than the one which would make a moral action dependent upon considerations of advantage.

If I, finding myself in a crowd of running people, run with the crowd without knowing where, it is obvious that I have given myself up to mass hysteria; but if by chance I should push my way to the front, or be gifted with sharper sight than the others, or receive information that this crowd was racing to attack human beings and toward its own corruption, would I really not stop and tell the people what might rescue them? Would I go on running and do these things which I knew to be bad and corrupt? This is the situation of every individual called up for military service, if he knows what military service means.

I can well understand that you, a young man full of life, loving and loved by your mother, friends, perhaps a young woman, think with a natural terror about what awaits you if you refuse conscription; and perhaps you will not feel strong enough to bear the consequences of refusal, and knowing your weakness, will submit and become a soldier. I understand completely, and I do not for a moment allow myself to blame you, knowing very well that in your place I might perhaps do the same thing. Only do not say that you did it because it was useful or because everyone does it. If you did it, know that you did wrong.

In every person's life there are moments in which he can know himself, tell himself who he is, whether he is a man who values his human dignity above his life or a weak creature who does not know his dignity and is concerned merely with being useful (chiefly to himself). This is the situation of a man who goes out to defend his honor in a duel or a soldier who goes into battle (although here the concepts of life are wrong). It is the situation of a doctor or a priest called to someone sick with plague, of a man in a burning house or a sinking ship who must decide whether to let the weaker go first or shove them aside and save himself. It is the situation of a man in poverty who accepts or rejects a bribe. And in our times, it is the situation of a man called to military service. For a man who knows its significance, the call to the army is perhaps the only opportunity for him to behave as a morally free creature and fulfill the highest requirement of his life—or else merely to keep his advantage in sight like an animal and thus remain slavishly submissive and servile until humanity becomes degraded and stupid.

For these reasons I answered your question whether one has to refuse to do military service with a categorical "yes"—if you understand the meaning of military service (and if you did not understand it then, you do now) and if you want to behave as a moral person living in our times must.

Please excuse me if these words are harsh. The subject is so important that one cannot be careful enough in expressing oneself so as to avoid false interpretation.

April 7, 1899   LEO TOLSTOY

For Discussion

1. Why does Tolstoy see the draftee's question as "falsely stated"? Put his objection into your own words.
2. Tolstoy takes an absolutist position regarding practical action. How does he relate it to violence?
3. What point does Tolstoy make in using Jesus as an illustration? What do you think of the argument?

4. Examine the "strange argument" in terms of today's draftee.
5. What is the meaning of military service as Tolstoy sees it?
6. What is the actual *advice* which Tolstoy gives the draftee?
7. Tolstoy apologizes for his harsh words. Do you agree that they are harsh? Why, or why not?
8. What is Tolstoy's attitude toward the draftee, and how is it revealed?

MOHANDAS K. GANDHI

Passive Resistance

The life of the Mahatma, Mohandas K. Gandhi (1869–1948), is the history of Indian independence, for he devoted his life to the cause of *Swaraj* (home rule) for India. When it was granted, Gandhi sought to unite Hindus and Moslems to form a single country; but he was unsuccessful, and in 1947 India was partitioned into Pakistan and India. He continued to work for religious and social harmony until he was assassinated by a Hindu extremist in 1948. Revered as a saint throughout the world, Gandhi exemplified the virtues he championed—peace, humility, charity, and love. Among his writings, many of which were written in prison, is the following dialogue from a pamphlet printed in 1909. Gandhi addresses his audience as Reader.

READER: Is there any historical evidence as to the success of what you have called soul-force or truth-force? No instance seems to have happened of any nation having risen through soul-force. I still think that the evil-doers will not cease doing evil without physical punishment.

EDITOR: The poet Tulsidas has said: "Of religion, pity (or love) is the root, as egotism of the body. Therefore, we should not abandon pity so long as we are alive." This appears to me to be a scientific truth. I believe in it as much as I believe in two and two being four. The force of love is the same as the force of the soul or truth. We have evidence of its working at every step. The universe would disappear without the existence of that force. But you ask for historical evidence. It is, therefore, necessary to know what history means. The Gujarati equivalent means: "It so happened." If that is the meaning of history, it is possible to give copious evidence. But, if it means the doings of kings and emperors, there can be no evidence of soul-force or passive resistance in such history. You cannot expect silver ore in a tin mine. History, as we know it, is a record of the wars of the world, and so there is a proverb among Englishmen that a nation which has no history, that is, no wars, is a happy nation. How kings played, how they became enemies of one another, how they murdered one another, is found accurately recorded in history, and if this were all that had happened in the world, it would have been ended long ago. If the story of the universe had commenced with wars, not a man would have been found alive today. Those people who have been warred against have disappeared as, for instance, the natives of Australia of whom hardly a man was left alive by the intruders. Mark, please, that these natives did not use soul-force in self-defense, and it does not require much foresight to know that the Australians will share the same fate as their victims. "Those that take the sword shall perish by the sword." With us the proverb is that professional swimmers will find a watery grave.

The fact that there are so many men still alive in the world shows that it is based not on the force of arms but on the force of truth or love. Therefore, the greatest and most unimpeachable evidence of the success of this force is to be found in the fact that, in spite of the wars of the world, it still lives on.

Thousands, indeed tens of thousands, depend for their existence on a very active working of this force. Little quarrels of millions of families in their daily lives disappear before the exercise of this force. Hundreds of nations live in peace. History does not and cannot take note of this fact. History is really a record of every interruption of the even working of the force of love or of the soul. Two brothers quarrel; one of them repents and re-awakens the love that was lying dormant in him; the two again begin to live in peace; nobody takes note of this. But if the two brothers, through the intervention of solicitors or some other reason, take up arms or go to law—which is another form of the exhibition of brute force—their doings would be immediately noticed in the press, they would be the talk of their neighbors and would probably go down to history. And what is true of families and communities is true of nations. There is no reason to believe that there is one law for families and another for nations. History, then, is a record of an interruption of the course of nature. Soul-force, being natural, is not noted in history.

READER: According to what you say, it is plain that instances of this kind of passive resistance are not to be found in history. It is necessary to understand this resistance more fully. It will be better, therefore, if you enlarge upon it.

EDITOR: Passive resistance is a method of securing rights by personal suffering; it is the reverse of resistance by arms. When I refuse to do a thing that is repugnant to my conscience, I use soul-force. For instance, the Government of the day has passed a law which is applicable to me. I do not like it. If by using violence I force the Government to repeal the law, I am employing what may be termed body-force. If I do not obey the law and accept the penalty for its breach, I use soul-force. It involves sacrifice of self.

Everybody admits that sacrifice of self is infinitely superior to sacrifice of others. Moreover, if this kind of force is used in a cause that is unjust, only the person using it suffers. He does not make others suffer for his mistakes. Men have before now done many things which were subsequently found to have been wrong. No man can claim that he is absolutely in the right or that a particular thing is wrong because he thinks so, but it is wrong for him so long as that is his deliberate judgment. It is therefore meet that he should not do that which he knows to be wrong, and suffer the consequence whatever it may be. This is the key to the use of soul-force.

READER: You would then disregard laws—this is rank disloyalty. We have always been considered a law-abiding nation. You seem to be going even beyond the extremists. They say that we must obey the laws that have been passed, but that if the laws be bad, we must drive out the law-givers even by force.

EDITOR: Whether I go beyond them or whether I do not is a matter of no consequence to either of us. We simply want to find out what is right and to act accordingly. The real meaning of the statement that we are a law-abiding nation is that we are passive resisters. When we do not like certain laws, we do not break the heads of law-givers but we suffer and do not submit to the laws. That we should obey laws whether good or bad is a new-fangled notion. There was no such thing in former days. The people disregarded those laws they did not like and suffered the penalties for their breach. It is contrary to our manhood if we obey laws repugnant to our conscience. Such teaching is opposed to religion and means slavery. If the Government were to ask us to go about without any clothing, should we do so? If I were a passive resister, I would say to them that I would have nothing to do with their law. But we have so forgotten ourselves and become so compliant that we do not mind any degrading law.

A man who has realized his manhood, who fears only God, will fear no one else. Man-made laws are not necessarily binding on him. Even the Government does not expect any such thing from us. They do not say: "You must do such a thing," but they say: "If you do not do it, we will punish you." We are sunk so low that we fancy that it is our duty and our religion to do what the law lays down. If man will only realize that it is unmanly to obey laws that are unjust, no man's tyranny will enslave him. This is the key to self-rule or home-rule.

It is a superstition and ungodly thing to believe that an act of a majority binds a minority. Many examples can be given in which acts of majorities will be found to have been wrong and those of minorities to have been right. All reforms owe their origin to the initiation of minorities in opposition to majorities. If among a band of robbers a knowledge of robbing is obligatory, is a pious man to accept the obligation? So long as the superstition that men should obey unjust laws exists, so long will their slavery exist. And a passive resister alone can remove such a superstition.

To use brute force, to use gunpowder, is contrary to passive resistance, for it means that we want our opponent to do by force that which we desire but he does not. And if such a use of force is justifiable, surely he is entitled to do likewise by us. And so we should never come to an agreement. We may simply fancy, like the blind horse moving in a circle round a mill, that we are making progress. Those who believe that they are not bound to obey laws which are repugnant to their conscience have only the remedy of passive resistance open to them. Any other must lead to disaster.

READER: From what you say I deduce that passive resistance is a splendid weapon of the weak, but that when they are strong they may take up arms.

EDITOR: This is a gross ignorance. Passive resistance, that is, soul-force, is matchless. It is superior to the force of arms. How, then, can it be considered only a weapon of the weak? Physical-force men are strangers to the courage that is requisite in a passive resister. Do you believe that a coward can ever disobey a law that he dislikes? Extremists are considered to be advocates of brute force. Why do they, then, talk about obeying laws? I do not blame them. They can say nothing else. When they succeed in driving out the English and they themselves become governors, they will want you and me to obey their laws. And that is a fitting thing for their constitution. But a passive resister will say he will not obey a law that is against his conscience, even though he may be blown to pieces at the mouth of a cannon.

What do you think? Wherein is courage required—in blowing others to pieces from behind a cannon, or with a smiling face to approach a cannon and be blown to pieces? Who is the true warrior—he who keeps death always as a bosom-friend, or he who controls the death of others? Believe me that a man devoid of courage and manhood can never be a passive resister.

This, however, I will admit: that even a man weak in body is capable of offering this resistance. One man can offer it just as well as millions. Both men and women can indulge in it. It does not require the training of an army; it needs no jiu-jitsu. Control over the mind is alone necessary, and when that is attained, man is free like the king of the forest and his very glance withers the enemy.

Passive resistance is an all-sided sword, it can be used anyhow; it blesses him who uses it and him against whom it is used. Without drawing a drop of blood it produces far-reaching results. It never rusts and cannot be stolen. Competition between passive resisters does not exhaust. The sword of passive resistance does not require a scabbard. It is strange indeed that you should consider such a weapon to be a weapon merely of the weak. . . .

READER: From what you say, then, it would appear that it is not a small thing to become a passive resister, and, if that is so, I should like you to explain how a man may become one.

EDITOR: To become a passive resister is easy enough but it is also equally difficult. I have known a lad of fourteen years become a passive resister; I have known also sick people do likewise; and I have also known physically strong and otherwise happy people unable to take up passive resistance. After a great deal of experience it seems to me that those who want to become passive resisters for the service of the country have to observe perfect chastity, adopt poverty, follow truth, and cultivate fearlessness.

* * *

Just as there is necessity for chastity, so is there for poverty. Pecuniary ambition and passive resistance cannot go well together. Those who have money are not expected to throw it away, but they are expected to be indifferent about it. They must be prepared to lose every penny rather than give up passive resistance.

Passive resistance has been described in the course of our discussion as truth-force. Truth, therefore, has necessarily to be followed and that at any cost. In this connection, academic questions such as whether a man may not lie in order to save a life, etc., arise, but these questions occur only to those who wish to justify lying. Those who want to follow truth every time are not placed in such a quandary; and if they are, they are still saved from a false position.

Passive resistance cannot proceed a step without fearlessness. Those alone can follow the path of passive resistance who are free from fear, whether as to their possessions, false honor, their relatives, the government, bodily injuries or death.

These observances are not to be abandoned in the belief that they are difficult. Nature has implanted in the human breast ability to cope with any difficulty or suffering that may come to man unprovoked. These qualities are worth having, even for those who do not wish to serve the country. Let there be no mistake, as those who want to train themselves in the use of arms are also obliged to have these qualities more or less. Everybody does not become a warrior for the wish. A would-be warrior will have to observe chastity and to be satisfied with poverty as his lot. A warrior without fearlessness cannot be conceived of. It may be thought that he would not need to be exactly truthful, but that quality follows real fearlessness. When a man abandons truth, he does so owing to fear in some shape or form. The above four attributes, then, need not frighten anyone. It may be as well here to note that a physical-force man has to have many other useless qualities which a passive resister never needs. And you will find that whatever extra effort a swordsman needs is due to lack of fearlessness. If he is an embodiment of the latter, the sword will drop from his hand that very moment. He does not need its support. One who is free from hatred requires no sword. A man with a stick suddenly came face to face with a lion and instinctively raised his weapon in self-defense. The man saw that he had only prated about fearlessness when there was none in him. That moment he dropped the stick and found himself free from all fear.

For Discussion

1. What is "soul-force" or "truth-force"? How does the life of man support it? The history of man ignore it?
2. Discuss Gandhi's explanation of passive resistance. How does it relate to soul-force?
3. How does Gandhi's concept of civil disobedience function within the framework of government? (Also see Thoreau and Brown in "The Impassioned NO.")
4. Contrast passive resistance and brute force as methods of protest. Cite examples of each in current situations.
5. Discuss the implications of the following statements as applied to contemporary society:
   a. "All reforms owe their origin to the initiation of minorities in opposition to majorities."
   b. "When a man abandons truth he does so owing to fear in some shape or form."
   c. "One who is free from hatred requires no sword."
6. Examine Gandhi's rationale for the four qualities needed by the person who resists passively. Do you agree? Explain.
7. How appropriate is the metaphor of the sword? How effective?
8. In what sense is this essay reflective?

D. H. LAWRENCE

Sex Versus Loveliness

David Herbert Lawrence, born in England in 1885, completed an enormous body of work—novels, short stories, poetry, travel writings, and literary criticism—before his death from tuberculosis in 1930. Always a nonconformist, Lawrence was highly criticized for his unconventional private life as well as for his frank treatment of love and sex in his novels, particularly *Sons and Lovers, The Rainbow, Women in Love,* and *Lady Chatterley's Lover.* Because his books were banned on charges of obscenity, Lawrence experienced financial difficulties which, along with his hatred of English industrialism and his poor health, prompted him to live abroad. He lived in various exotic places throughout the world, at one time settling in Taos, New Mexico, where his interest in primitive cultures found stimulus and where a shrine commemorates him.

It is a pity that *sex* is such an ugly little word. An ugly little word, and really almost incomprehensible. What *is* sex, after all? The more we think about it the less we know.

Science says it is an instinct; but what is an instinct? Apparently an instinct is an old, old habit that has become ingrained. But a habit, however old, has to have a beginning. And there is really no beginning to sex. Where life is, there it is. So sex is no "habit" that has been formed.

Again, they talk of sex as an appetite, like hunger. An appetite; but for what? An appetite for propagation? It is rather absurd. They say a peacock puts on all his fine feathers to dazzle the peahen into letting him satisfy his appetite for propagation. But why should the peahen not put on fine feathers, to dazzle the peacock, and satisfy *her* desire for propagation? She has surely quite as great a desire for eggs and chickens as he has. We cannot believe that her sex-urge is so weak that she needs all that blue splendor of feathers to rouse her. Not at all.

As for me, I never even saw a peahen so much as look at her lord's bronze and blue glory. I don't believe she ever sees it. I don't believe for a moment that she knows the difference between bronze, blue, brown or green.

If I had ever seen a peahen gazing with rapt attention on her lord's flamboyancy, I might believe that he had put on all those feathers just to "attract" her. But she never looks at him. Only she seems to get a little perky when he shudders all his quills at her, like a storm in the trees. Then she does seem to notice, just casually, his presence.

These theories of sex are amazing. A peacock puts on his glory for the sake of a wall-eyed peahen who never looks at him. Imagine a scientist being so naïve as to credit the peahen with a profound, dynamic appreciation of a peacock's color and pattern. Oh, highly aesthetic peahen!

And a nightingale sings to attract his female. Which is mighty curious, seeing he sings his best when courtship and honeymoon are over and the female is no longer concerned with him at all, but with the young. Well, then, if he doesn't sing to attract her, he must sing to distract her and amuse her while she's sitting.

How delightful, how naïve theories are! But there is a hidden will behind them all. There is a hidden will behind all theories of sex, implacable. And that is the will to deny, to wipe out the mystery of beauty.

Because beauty is a mystery. You can neither eat it nor make flannel out of it. Well, then, says science, it is just a trick to catch the female and induce her to propagate. How naïve! As if the female needed inducing. She will propagate in the dark, even—so where, then, is the beauty trick?

Science has a mysterious hatred of beauty, because it doesn't fit in the cause-and-effect chain. And society has a mysterious hatred of sex, because it perpetually interferes with the nice money-making schemes of social man. So the two hatreds made a combine, and sex and beauty are mere propagation appetite.

Now sex and beauty are one thing, like flame and fire. If you hate sex you hate beauty. If you love *living* beauty, you have a reverence for sex. Of course you can love old, dead beauty and hate sex. But to love living beauty you must have a reverence for sex.

Sex and beauty are inseparable, like life and consciousness. And the intelligence which goes with sex and beauty, and arises out of sex and beauty, is intuition. The great disaster of our civilization is the morbid hatred of sex. What, for example, could show a more poisoned hatred of sex than Freudian psycho-analysis?—which carries with it a morbid fear of beauty, "alive" beauty, and which causes the atrophy of our intuitive faculty and our intuitive self.

The deep psychic disease of modern men and women is the diseased, atrophied condition of the intuitive faculties. There is a whole world of life that we might know and enjoy by intuition, and by intuition alone. This is denied us, because we deny sex and beauty, the source of the intuitive life and of the insouciance which is so lovely in free animals and in plants.

Sex is the root of which intuition is the foliage and beauty the flower. Why is a woman lovely, if ever, in her twenties? It is the time when sex rises softly to her face, as a rose to the top of a rose bush.

And the appeal is the appeal of beauty. We deny it wherever we can. We try to make the beauty as shallow and trashy as possible. But, first and foremost, sex appeal is the appeal of beauty.

Now beauty is a thing about which we are so uneducated we can hardly speak of it. We try to pretend it is a fixed arrangement: straight nose, large eyes, etc. We think a lovely woman must look like Lillian Gish, a handsome man must look like Rudolph Valentino. So we *think*.

In actual life we behave quite differently. We say: "She's quite beautiful, but I don't care for her." Which shows we are using the word *beautiful* all wrong. We should say: "She has the stereotyped attributes of beauty, but she is not beautiful to me."

Beauty is an *experience*, nothing else. It is not a fixed pattern or an arrangement of features. It is something *felt*, a glow or a communicated sense of fineness. What ails us is that our sense of beauty is so bruised and blunted, we miss all the best.

But to stick to the films—there is a greater essential beauty in Charlie Chaplin's odd face than ever there was in Valentino's. There is a bit of true beauty in Chaplin's brows and eyes, a gleam of something pure.

But our sense of beauty is so bruised and clumsy, we don't see it, and don't know it when we do see it. We can only see the blatantly obvious, like the so-called beauty of Rudolph Valentino, which only pleases because it satisfies some ready-made notion of handsomeness.

But the plainest person can look beautiful, can *be* beautiful. It only needs the fire of sex to rise delicately to change an ugly face to a lovely one. That is really sex appeal: the communicating of a sense of beauty.

And in the reverse way, no one can be quite so repellent as a really pretty woman. That is, since beauty is a question of experience, not of concrete form, no one can be as acutely ugly as a really pretty woman. When the sex-glow is missing, and she moves in ugly coldness, how hideous she seems, and all the worse for her externals of prettiness.

What sex is, we don't know, but it must be some sort of fire. For it always communicates a sense of warmth, of glow. And when the glow becomes a pure shine, then we feel the sense of beauty.

But the communicating of the warmth, the glow of sex, is true sex appeal. We all have the fire of sex slumbering or burning inside us. If we live to be ninety, it is still there. Or, if it dies, we become one of those ghastly living corpses which are unfortunately becoming more numerous in the world.

Nothing is more ugly than a human being in whom the fire of sex has gone out. You get a nasty clayey creature whom everybody wants to avoid.

But while we are fully alive, the fire of sex smoulders or burns in us. In youth it flickers and shines; in age it glows softer and stiller, but there it is. We have some control over it; but only partial control. That is why society hates it.

While ever it lives, the fire of sex, which is the source of beauty and anger, burns in us beyond our understanding. Like actual fire, while it lives it will burn our fingers if we touch it carelessly. And so social man, who only wants to be "safe," hates the fire of sex.

Luckily, not many men succeed in being merely social men. The fire of the old Adam smoulders. And one of the qualities of fire is that it calls to fire. Sex-fire here kindles sex-fire there. It may only rouse the smoulder into a soft glow. It may call up a sharp flicker. Or rouse a flame; and then flame leans to flame, and starts a blaze.

Whenever the sex-fire glows through, it will kindle an answer somewhere or other. It may only kindle a sense of warmth and optimism. Then you say: "I like that girl; she's a real good sort." It may kindle a glow that makes the world look kindlier, and life feel better. Then you say: "She's an attractive woman. I like her."

Or she may rouse a flame that lights up her own face first, before it lights up the universe. Then you say: "She's a lovely woman. She looks lovely to me."

It takes a rare woman to rouse a real sense of loveliness. It is not that a woman is born beautiful. We say that to escape our own poor, bruised, clumsy understanding of beauty. There have been thousands and thousands of women quite as good-looking as Diane de Poitiers, or Mrs. Langtry, or any of the famous ones. There are today thousands and thousands of superbly good-looking women. But oh, how few lovely women!

And why? Because of the failure of their sex appeal. A good-looking woman becomes lovely when the fire of sex rouses pure and fine in her and flickers through her face and touches the fire in me.

Then she becomes a lovely woman to me, then she is in the living flesh a lovely woman: not a mere photograph of one. And how lovely a lovely woman! But, alas! how rare! How bitterly rare in a world full of unusually handsome girls and women!

Handsome, good-looking, but not lovely, not beautiful. Handsome and good-looking women are the women with good features and the right hair. But a lovely woman is an experience. It is a question of communicated fire. It is a question of sex appeal in our poor, dilapidated modern phraseology. Sex appeal applied to Diane de Poiters, or even, in the lovely hours, to one's wife—why, it is a libel and a slander in itself. Nowadays, however, instead of the fire of loveliness, it is sex appeal. The two are the same thing, I suppose, but on vastly different levels.

The business man's pretty and devoted secretary is still chiefly valuable because of her sex appeal. Which does not imply "immoral relations" in the slightest.

Even today a girl with a bit of generosity likes to feel she is helping a man if the man will take her help. And this desire that he shall take her help is her sex appeal. It is the genuine fire, if of a very mediocre heat.

Still, it serves to keep the world of "business" alive. Probably, but for the introduction of the lady secretary into the business man's office, the business man would have collapsed entirely by now. She calls up the sacred fire in her and she communicates it to her boss. He feels an added flow of energy and optimism, and—business flourishes.

There is, of course, the other side of sex appeal. It can be the destruction of the one appealed to. When a woman starts using her sex appeal to her own advantage it is usually a bad moment for some poor devil. But this side of sex appeal has been overworked lately, so it is not nearly as dangerous as it was.

The sex-appealing courtesans who ruined so many men in Balzac no longer find it smooth running. Men have grown canny. They fight shy even of the emotional vamp. In fact, men are inclined to think they smell a rat the moment they feel the touch of feminine sex appeal today.

Which is a pity, for sex appeal is only a dirty name for a bit of life-flame. No man works so well and so successfully as when some woman has kindled a little fire in his veins. No woman does her housework with real joy unless she is in love—and a woman may go on being quietly in love for fifty years almost without knowing it.

If only our civilization had taught us how to let sex appeal flow properly and subtly, how to keep the fire of sex clear and alive, flickering or glowing or blazing in all its varying degrees of strength and communication, we might, all of us, have lived all our lives in love, which means we should be kindled and full of zest in all kinds of ways and for all kinds of things. . . .

Whereas, what a lot of dead ash there is in life now.

For Discussion

1. What theories regarding sex does Lawrence reject? What are his arguments?
2. Explain what Lawrence means by the word "mystery."
3. What is the relationship among sex, beauty, and intuition?
4. Discuss Lawrence's concept of beauty. Who determines what is beautiful?
5. Suggest modern counterparts to Valentino, Gish, and Chaplin.
6. What is the current connotation of sex appeal? What is Lawrence's definition?
7. According to Lawrence, why does society hate sex?
8. How accurate is Lawrence's idea that our sense of beauty is "bruised and blunted"?
9. What recurring metaphor dominates this essay?
10. Examine the tone of the last two paragraphs. What attitude does it reveal toward sex? Toward people? Toward life?

ALBERT CAMUS

The Rebel

An Algerian by birth and education, Albert Camus began his career as an actor and theatrical manager, then worked as a journalist in Algeria and Paris during the late 1930s. He joined the French Resistance movement in World War II and wrote for the underground newspaper *Combat*. Between the years 1942–1947, Camus' novels, *The Stranger* and *The Plague;* his plays, *Caligula* and *The Misunderstanding;* and his philosophical treatise, "The Myth of Sisyphus," created for him an extraordinary following, both in France and throughout the world. Publication of *The Rebel* in 1951, of which the following essay is the opening chapter, and *The Exile and the Kingdom* in 1957 enhanced his position as a leading existential and political philosopher. In 1957 he was awarded the Nobel Prize for Literature. Camus was only forty-six, at the height of his creative power, when he was killed in an automobile accident in 1960.

What is a rebel? A man who says no, but whose refusal does not imply a renunciation. He is also a man who says yes, from the moment he makes his first gesture of rebellion. A slave who has taken orders all his life suddenly decides that he cannot obey some new command. What does he mean by saying "no"?

He means, for example, that "this has been going on too long," "up to this point yes, beyond it no," "you are going too far," or, again, "there is a limit beyond which you shall not go." In other words, his no affirms the existence of a borderline. The same concept is to be found in the rebel's feeling that the other person "is exaggerating," that he is exerting his authority beyond a limit where he begins to infringe on the rights of others. Thus the movement of rebellion is founded simultaneously on the categorical rejection of an intrusion that is considered intol-

From *The Rebel* by Albert Camus, trans. by Anthony Bower. Copyright © 1956 by Alfred A. Knopf, Inc. Reprinted by permission of the publisher.

erable and on the confused conviction of an absolute right which, in the rebel's mind, is more precisely the impression that he "has the right to. . . ." Rebellion cannot exist without the feeling that, somewhere and somehow, one is right. It is in this way that the rebel slave says yes and no simultaneously. He affirms that there are limits and also that he suspects—and wishes to preserve—the existence of certain things on this side of the borderline. He demonstrates, with obstinancy, that there is something in him which "is worth while . . ." and which must be taken into consideration. In a certain way, he confronts an order of things which oppresses him with the insistence on a kind of right not to be oppressed beyond the limit that he can tolerate.

In every act of rebellion, the rebel simultaneously experiences a feeling of revulsion at the infringement of his rights and a complete and spontaneous loyalty to certain aspects of himself. Thus he implicitly brings into play a standard of values so far from being gratuitous that he is prepared to support it no matter what the risks. Up to this point he has at least remained silent and has abandoned himself to the form of despair in which a condition is accepted even though it is considered unjust. To remain silent is to give the impression that one has no opinions, that one wants nothing, and in certain cases it really amounts to wanting nothing. Despair, like the absurd, has opinions and desires about everything in general and nothing in particular. Silence expresses this attitude very well. But from the moment that the rebel finds his voice—even though he says nothing but "no"—he begins to desire and to judge. The rebel, in the etymological sense, does a complete turnabout. He acted under the lash of his master's whip. Suddenly he turns and faces him. He opposes what is preferable to what is not. Not every value entails rebellion, but every act of rebellion tacitly invokes a value. Or is it really a question of values?

Awareness, no matter how confused it may be, develops from every act of rebellion: the sudden, dazzling perception that there is something in man with which he can identify himself, even if only for a moment. Up to now this identification was never really experienced. Before he rebelled, the slave accepted all the demands made upon him. Very often he even took orders, without reacting against them, which were far more conducive to insurrection than the one at which he balks. He accepted them patiently, though he may have protested inwardly, but in that he remained silent he was more concerned with his own immediate interests than as yet aware of his own rights. But with loss of patience—with impatience—a reaction begins which can extend to everything that he previously accepted, and which is almost always retroactive. The very moment the slave refuses to obey the humiliating orders of his master, he simultaneously rejects the condition of slavery. The act of rebellion carries him far beyond the point he had reached by simply refusing. He exceeds the bounds that he fixed for his antagonists, and now demands to be treated as an equal. What was at first the man's obstinate resistance now becomes the whole man, who is identified with and summed up in his resistance. The part of himself that he wanted to be respected he proceeds to place above everything else and proclaims it preferable to everything, even to life itself. It becomes for him the supreme good. Having up to now been willing to compromise, the slave suddenly adopts ("because this is how it must be . . .") an attitude of All or Nothing. With rebellion, awareness is born.

But we can see that the knowledge gained is, at the same time, of an "all" that is still rather obscure and of a "nothing" that proclaims the possibility of sacrificing the rebel to this "All." The rebel himself wants to be "all"—to identify himself completely with this good of which he has suddenly become aware and by which he wants to be personally recognized and acknowledged—or "nothing"; in other words, to be completely destroyed by the force that dominates him. As a last resort, he is willing to accept the final defeat, which is death, rather than be deprived of the personal sacrament that he would call, for example, freedom. Better to die on one's feet than to live on one's knees.

Values, according to good authorities, "most often represent a transition from facts to rights, from what is desired to what is desirable (usually through the intermediary of what is generally considered desirable)."[1] The transition from facts to rights is manifest, as we have seen, in rebellion. So is the transition from "this must be" to "this is how I should like things to be," and even more so, perhaps, the idea of the sublimation of the individual in a henceforth universal good. The sudden appearance of the concept of "All or Nothing" demonstrates that rebellion, contrary to current opinion, and though it springs from everything that is most strictly individualistic in man, questions the very idea of the individual. If the individual, in fact, accepts death and happens to die as a consequence of his act of rebellion, he demonstrates by doing so that he is willing to sacrifice himself for the sake of a common good which he considers more important than his own destiny. If he prefers the risk of death to the negation of the rights that he defends, it is because he considers these rights more important than himself. Therefore he is acting in the name of certain values which are still indeterminate but which he feels are common to himself and to all men. We see that the affirmation implicit in every act of rebellion is extended to something that transcends the individual in so far as it withdraws him from his supposed solitude and provides him with a reason to act. But it is already worth noting that this concept of values as pre-existent to any kind of action contradicts the purely historical philosophies, in which values are

[1] Lalande: *Vocabulaire philosophique.*

acquired (if they are ever acquired) after the action has been completed. Analysis of rebellion leads at least to the suspicion that, contrary to the postulates of contemporary thought, a human nature does exist, as the Greeks believed. Why rebel if there is nothing permanent in oneself worth preserving? It is for the sake of everyone in the world that the slave asserts himself when he comes to the conclusion that a command has infringed on something in him which does not belong to him alone, but which is common ground where all men—even the man who insults and oppresses him—have a natural community.[2]

Two observations will support this argument. First, we can see that an act of rebellion is not, essentially, an egoistic act. Of course, it can have egoistic motives. But one can rebel equally well against lies as against oppression. Moreover, the rebel—once he has accepted the motives and at the moment of his greatest impetus—preserves nothing in that he risks everything. He demands respect for himself, of course, but only in so far as he identifies himself with a natural community.

Then we note that rebellion does not arise only, and necessarily, among the oppressed, but that it can also be caused by the mere spectacle of oppression of which someone else is the victim. In such cases there is a feeling of identification with another individual. And it must be pointed out that this is not a question of psychological identification—a mere subterfuge by which the individual imagines that it is he himself who has been offended. On the contrary, it can often happen that we cannot bear to see offenses done to others which we ourselves have accepted without rebelling. The suicides of the Russian terrorists in Siberia as a protest against their comrades' being whipped is a case in point. Nor is it a question of the feeling of a community of interests. Injustices done to men whom we consider enemies can, actually, be profoundly repugnant to us. There is only identification of one's destiny with that of others and a choice of sides. Therefore the individual is not, in himself alone, the embodiment of the values he wishes to defend. It needs all humanity, at least, to compromise them. When he rebels, a man identifies himself and other men and so surpasses himself, and from this point of view human solidarity is metaphysical. But for the moment we are only talking of the kind of solidarity that is born in chains.

It would be possible for us to define the positive aspect of the values implicit in every act of rebellion by comparing them with a completely negative concept like that of resentment as defined by Scheler. Rebellion is, in fact, much more than pursuit of a claim, in the strongest sense of

---

[2] The community of victims is the same as that which unites victim and executioner. But the executioner does not know this.

the word. Resentment is very well defined by Scheler as an autointoxication—the evil secretion, in a sealed vessel, of prolonged impotence. Rebellion, on the contrary, breaks the seal and allows the whole being to come into play. It liberates stagnant waters and turns them into a raging torrent. Scheler himself emphasizes the passive aspect of resentment and remarks on the prominent place it occupies in the psychology of women who are dedicated to desire and possession. The fountainhead of rebellion, on the contrary, is the principle of superabundant activity and energy. Scheler is also right in saying that resentment is always highly colored by envy. But one envies what one does not have, while the rebel's aim is to defend what he is. He does not merely claim some good that he does not possess or of which he was deprived. His aim is to claim recognition for something which he has and which has already been recognized by him, in almost every case, as more important than anything of which he could be envious. Rebellion is not realistic. According to Scheler, resentment always turns into either unscrupulous ambition or bitterness, depending on whether it is implanted in a strong person or a weak one. But in both cases it is a question of wanting to be something other than what one is. Resentment is always resentment against oneself. The rebel, on the contrary, from his very first step, refuses to allow anyone to touch what he is. He is fighting for the integrity of one part of his being. He does not try, primarily, to conquer, but simply to impose.

Finally, it would seem that resentment takes delight, in advance, in the pain that it would like the object of its envy to feel. Nietzsche and Scheler are right in seeing an excellent example of this in the passage where Tertullian informs his readers that one of the greatest sources of happiness among the blessed will be the spectacle of the Roman emperors consumed in the fires of hell. This kind of happiness is also experienced by the decent people who go to watch executions. The rebel, on the contrary, limits himself, as a matter of principle, to refusing to be humiliated without asking that others should be. He will even accept pain provided his integrity is respected.

It is therefore hard to understand why Scheler completely identifies the spirit of rebellion with resentment. His criticism of the resentment to be found in humanitarianism (which he treats as the non-Christian form of love for mankind) could perhaps be applied to certain indeterminate forms of humanitarian idealism, or to the techniques of terror. But it rings false in relation to man's rebellion against his condition—the movement that enlists the individual in the defense of a dignity common to all men. Scheler wants to demonstrate that humanitarian feelings are always accompanied by a hatred of the world. Humanity is loved in general in order to avoid having to love anybody in particular. This is correct, in some cases, and it is easier to understand Scheler when we realize that for him humanitarianism is represented by Bentham and Rousseau. But man's love for man can be born of other things than a mathematical calculation of the resultant rewards of a theoretical confidence in human nature. In face of the utilitarians, and of Emile's preceptor, there is, for example, the kind of logic, embodied by Dostoievsky in Ivan Karamazov, which progresses from an act of rebellion to metaphysical insurrection. Scheler is aware of this and sums up the concept in the following manner: "There is not enough love in the world to squander it on anything but human beings." Even if this proposition were true, the appalling despair that it implies would merit anything but contempt. In fact, it misunderstands the tortured character of Karamazov's rebellion. Ivan's drama, on the contrary, arises from the fact that there is too much love without an object. This love finding no outlet and God being denied, it is then decided to lavish it on human beings as a generous act of complicity.

Nevertheless, in the act of rebellion as we have envisaged it up to now, an abstract ideal is not chosen through lack of feeling and in pursuit of a sterile demand. We insist that the part of man which cannot be reduced to mere ideas should be taken into consideration—the passionate side of his nature that serves no other purpose than to be part of the act of living. Does this imply that no rebellion is motivated by resentment? No, and we know it only too well in this age of malice. But we must consider the idea of rebellion in its widest sense on pain of betraying it; and in its widest sense rebellion goes far beyond resentment. When Heathcliff, in *Wuthering Heights*, says that he puts his love above God and would willingly go to hell in order to be reunited with the woman he loves, he is prompted not only by youth and humiliation but by the consuming experience of a whole lifetime. The same emotion causes Eckart, in a surprising fit of heresy, to say that he prefers hell with Jesus to heaven without Him. This is the very essence of love. Contrary to Scheler, it would therefore be impossible to overemphasize the passionate affirmation that underlies the act of rebellion and distinguishes it from resentment. Rebellion, though apparently negative, since it creates nothing, is profoundly positive in that it reveals the part of man which must always be defended.

But, to sum up, are not rebellion and the values that it implies relative? Reasons for rebellion do seem to change, in fact, with periods and civilizations. It is obvious that a Hindu pariah, an Inca warrior, a primitive native of central Africa, and a member of one of the first Christian communities had not at all the same ideas about rebellion. We could even assert, with considerable assurance, that the idea of rebellion has no meaning in these particular cases. However, a Greek slave, a serf, a *condottiere* of the Renaissance, a Parisian bourgeois during the Regency, a Russian intellectual at the beginning of the twentieth century, and a contemporary worker would undoubtedly agree that rebellion is legitimate, even if they differed about the reasons for it. In other words, the problem of rebellion seems to assume a precise meaning only within the confines of Western thought. It is possible to be even more explicit by remarking, like Scheler, that the spirit of rebellion finds few means of expression in societies where inequalities are very great (the Hindu caste system) or, again, in those where there is absolute equality (certain primitive societies). The spirit of rebellion can exist only in a society where a theoretical equality conceals great factual inequalities. The problem of rebellion, therefore, has no meaning except within our own Western society. One might be tempted to affirm that it is relative to the development of individualism if the preceding remarks had not put us on our guard against this conclusion.

On the basis of the evidence, the only conclusion that can be drawn from Scheler's remark is that, thanks to the theory of political freedom, there is, in the very heart of our society, an increasing awareness in man of the idea of man and, thanks to the application of this theory of freedom, a corresponding dissatisfaction. Actual freedom has not increased in proportion to man's awareness of it. We can only deduce from this observation that rebellion is the act of an educated man who is aware of his own rights. But there is nothing which justifies us in saying that it is only a question of individual rights. Because of the sense of solidarity we have already pointed out, it would rather seem that what is at stake is humanity's gradually increasing self-awareness as it pursues its course. In fact, for the Inca and the pariah the problem never arises, because for them it had been solved by a tradition, even before they had had time to raise it—the answer being that the tradition is sacred. If in a world where things are held sacred the problem of rebellion does not arise, it is because no real problems are to be found in such a world, all the answers having been given simultaneously. Metaphysic is replaced by myth. There are no more questions, only eternal answers and commentaries, which may be metaphysical. But before man accepts the sacred world and in order that he should be able to accept it—or before he escapes from it and in order that he should be able to escape from it—there is always a period of soul-searching and rebellion. The rebel is a man who is on the point of accepting or rejecting the sacred and determined on laying claim to a human situation in which all the answers are human— in other words, formulated in reasonable terms. From this moment every question, every word, is an act of rebellion while in the sacred world every word is an act of grace. It would be possible to demonstrate in this manner that only two possible worlds can exist for the human mind: the sacred (or, to speak in Christian terms, the world of grace)[3] and the world of rebellion. The disappearance of one is equivalent to the appearance of the other, despite the fact that this appearance can take place in disconcerting forms. There again we rediscover the *All or Nothing*. The present interest of the problem of rebellion only springs from the fact that nowadays whole societies have wanted to discard the sacred. We live in an unsacrosanct moment in history. Insurrection is certainly not the sum total of human experience. But history today, with all its storm and strife, compels us to say that rebellion is one of the essential dimensions of man. It is our historic reality. Unless we choose to ignore reality, we must find our values in it. Is it possible to find a rule of conduct outside the realm of religion and its absolute values? That is the question raised by rebellion.

We have already noted the confused values that are called into play by incipient rebellion. Now we must inquire if these values are to be found again in contemporary forms of rebellious thought and action, and if they are, we must specify their content. But, before going any farther, let us note that the basis of these values is rebellion itself. Man's solidarity is founded upon rebellion, and rebellion, in its turn, can only find its justification in this solidarity. We have, then, the right to say that any rebellion which claims the right to deny or destroy this solidarity loses simultaneously its right to be called rebellion and becomes in reality an acquiescence in murder. In the same way, this solidarity, except in so far as religion is concerned, comes to life only on the level of rebellion. And so the real drama of revolutionary thought is announced. In order to exist, man must rebel, but rebellion must respect the limit it discovers in itself—a limit where minds meet and, in meeting, begin to exist. Rebellious thought, therefore, cannot dispense with memory: it is a perpetual state of tension. In studying its actions and its results, we shall have to say, each time, whether it remains faithful to its noble promise or if, through indolence or folly, it forgets its original purpose and plunges into a mire of tyranny or servitude.

Meanwhile, we can sum up the initial progress that the spirit of rebellion provokes in a mind that is originally imbued with the absurdity and apparent sterility of the world. In absurdist experience, suffering is individual. But from the moment when a movement of rebellion begins, suffering is seen as a collective experience. Therefore the first progressive step for a mind overwhelmed by the strangeness of things is to realize that this feeling of strangeness is shared with all men and that human reality, in its entirety, suffers from the distance which separates

[3] There is, of course, an act of metaphysical rebellion at the beginning of Christianity, but the resurrection of Christ and the annunciation of the kingdom of heaven interpreted as a promise of eternal life are the answers that render it futile.

it from the rest of the universe. The malady experienced by a single man becomes a mass plague. In our daily trials rebellion plays the same role as does the *"cogito"* in the realm of thought: it is the first piece of evidence. But this evidence lures the individual from his solitude. It founds its first value on the whole human race. I rebel—therefore we exist.

For Discussion

1. How does Camus relate "despair" and "silence"? "Rebellion" and "awareness"?
2. According to Camus, how do "resentment" and "rebellion" differ?
3. How does Camus argue that rebellion is affirmative?
4. Why does Camus say that the "spirit of rebellion" applies only to Western society? Do you agree?
5. How does Camus respond to the common belief that one should rebel against an injustice only when one has a solution? In this regard discuss current rebellion on the part of students, blacks, and other groups.
6. By what reasoning does Camus reach the conclusion that "every act of rebellion tacitly invokes a value"?
7. Camus is very abstract in describing the proper limits of rebellion. In your opinion, what should these limits be?
8. Camus, like Sartre and other existentialists, is involved with "the absurd." After reading this essay, what is your understanding of the term?
9. "I rebel—therefore we exist" is a modern descendant of Descartes' "I think; therefore I am" and Rousseau's "I feel; therefore I am." Discuss the implications of each of these statements.

SIMONE de BEAUVOIR

Old Age

The life and writings of Simone de Beauvoir, French author and philosopher, eloquently testify to her existential belief that "man, and man alone, is responsible for the direction of his life" and must accept the responsibility for the consequences of his freedom. The details of her life are recounted in a series of autobiographical volumes, beginning with *The Memoirs of a Dutiful Daughter,* which opens with her birth in Paris in 1908 and includes her introduction to Jean-Paul Sartre, with whom she formed an intimate and lifelong association. After being awarded a degree and diploma to teach philosophy by the University of Paris, Beauvoir began a teaching career which lasted until 1943, when she decided to spend more of her time writing. The past thirty years have seen the publication of a score of her works, including the explosive *The Second Sex* (1949), which documented the inferior position of women in Western culture; *The Mandarins* (1954), a Prix Goncourt-winning novel which chronicled the influential role of existential leaders in post-World War II France; and, most recently, *The Coming of Age* (1970), which indicted modern civilization for its cruel neglect of the elderly. The selection which follows is the concluding chapter of this latest book.

Old age is not a necessary end to human life. It does not even represent what Sartre has called the "necessity of our contingency," as the body does. A great many creatures—the may-flies, for example—die after having reproduced their kind, without going through any phase of degeneration. However, it is an empiric and universal truth that after a certain number of years the human organism undergoes a decline. The

Reprinted by permission of G. P. Putnam's Sons from *The Coming of Age* by Simone de Beauvoir. Copyright © 1972 by André Deutsch, Weidenfeld & Nicolson, and G. P. Putnam's Sons.

process is inescapable. At the end of a certain time it results in a reduction in the individual's activities: very often it also brings about a diminution in his mental faculties and an alteration in his attitude toward the world.

A particular value has sometimes been given to old age for social or political reasons. For some individuals—women in ancient China, for instance—it has been a refuge against the harshness of life in the adult years. Others, from a pessimistic general outlook on life, settle comfortably into it: for if the will to live is regarded as a source of unhappiness, then it is reasonable to prefer a semi-death to life. But the vast majority of mankind look upon the coming of old age with sorrow or rebellion. It fills them with more aversion than death itself.

And indeed, it is old age, rather than death, that is to be contrasted with life. Old age is life's parody, whereas death transforms life into a destiny: in a way it preserves it by giving it the absolute dimension—"As into himself eternity changes him at last." Death does away with time. Let us take a man who has just been buried: his last days had no greater truth than the rest; his life has become a whole, all of whose parts are equally present in so far as they have all been engulfed by the void. Victor Hugo is at the same time both thirty and eighty; and he is both thirty and eighty for ever. But when he *was* eighty, the present he was living through overlaid the past. This dominance of the present is saddening when it is a degradation or even a denial of what has been; and almost always this is so. Former happenings and acquired knowledge retain their place, but in a life whose fire has died: they *have been*. When memory decays, they sink and vanish in a mocking darkness; life unravels stitch by stitch like a frayed piece of knitting, leaving nothing but meaningless strands of wool in the old person's hands. . . . Not all old people give up the struggle: far from it—many are remarkable for their stubborn perseverance. But in this case they often become caricatures of themselves. Their will goes on, by its own impetus, with no reason or even against all reason. They began by forming their desire, their will, with a given end in view. Now they desire because they have desired. Broadly speaking habit, automatic reactions and hardened, set ways take the place of invention among the old. There is some truth in Faguet's[1] observation: "Old age is a perpetual play that a man acts in order to deceive others and himself, and whose chief drollery lies in the fact that he acts badly."

Morality teaches a serene acceptance of those ills which science and technology are powerless to abolish—pain, disease, old age. It claims that the courageous endurance of that very condition which lessens us

[1] He wrote a furious little essay against old age called *Les dix commandements de la vieillesse.*

is a way of increasing our stature. If he lacks other projects, the elderly man may commit himself to this. But here we are playing with words. Projects have to do only with our activities. Undergoing age is not an activity. Growing, ripening, aging, dying—the passing of time is predestined, inevitable.

There is only one solution if old age is not to be an absurd parody of our former life, and that is to go on pursuing ends that give our existence a meaning—devotion to individuals, to groups or to causes, social, political, intellectual or creative work. In spite of the moralists' opinion to the contrary, in old age we should wish still to have passions strong enough to prevent us turning in upon ourselves. One's life has value so long as one attributes value to the life of others, by means of love, friendship, indignation, compassion. When this is so, then there are still valid reasons for activity or speech. People are often advised to "prepare" for old age. But if this merely applies to setting aside money, choosing the place for retirement and laying on hobbies, we shall not be much the better for it when the day comes. It is far better not to think about it too much, but to live a fairly committed, fairly justified life so that one may go on in the same path even when all illusions have vanished and one's zeal for life has died away.

But these possibilities are granted only to a handful of privileged people: it is in the last years of life that the gap between them and the vast majority of mankind becomes deepest and most obvious. When we set these two old ages side by side we can answer the question we asked at the beginning of this book: what are the inescapable factors in the individual's decline? And to what degree is society responsible for them?

As we have seen, the age at which this decline begins has always depended upon the class to which a man belongs. Today a miner is finished, done for, at the age of fifty, whereas many of the privileged carry their eighty years lightly. The worker's decline begins earlier; its course is also far more rapid. During his years of "survival" his shattered body is the victim of disease and infirmity; whereas an elderly man who has had the good fortune of being able to look after his health may keep it more or less undamaged until his death.

When they are old the exploited classes are condemned if not to utter destitution then at least to extreme poverty, to uncomfortable, inconvenient dwellings, and to loneliness, all of which results in a feeling of failure and a generalized anxiety. They sink into a torpid bewilderment that has physical repercussions: even the mental diseases from which they suffer are to a great extent the product of the system. Even if he keeps his health and his clarity of mind, the retired man is nevertheless the victim of that terrible curse, boredom. Deprived of his hold upon the world, he is incapable of finding another because apart from his work his free time was alienated, rendered sterile. The manual worker does not even manage to kill time. His gloomy idleness leads to an apathy that endangers what physical and intellectual balance he may still possess.

The injury he has suffered during the course of his life is still more radical. The reason that the retired man is rendered hopeless by the want of meaning in his present life is that the meaning of his existence has been stolen from him from the very beginning. A law, as merciless as Lassalle's "brazen law" of wages, allows him no more than the right to reproduce his life: it refuses him the possibility of discovering any justification for it. When he escapes from the fetters of his trade or calling, all he sees around him is an arid waste: he has not been granted the possibility of committing himself to projects that might have peopled the world with goals, values and reasons for existence.

That is the crime of our society. Its "old-age policy" is scandalous. But even more scandalous still is the treatment that it inflicts upon the majority of men during their youth and their maturity. It prefabricates the maimed and wretched state that is theirs when they are old. It is the fault of society that the decline of old age begins too early, that it is rapid, physically painful and, because they enter in upon it with empty hands, morally atrocious. Some exploited, alienated individuals inevitably become "throw-outs," "rejects," once their strength has failed them.

That is why all the remedies that have been put forward to lessen the distress of the aged are such a mockery: not one of them can possibly repair the systematic destruction that has been inflicted upon some men throughout their lives. Even if they are treated and taken care of, their health cannot be given back. Even if decent houses are built for them, they cannot be provided with the culture, the interests and the responsibilities that would give their life a meaning. I do not say that it would be entirely pointless to improve their condition here and now; but doing so would provide no solution whatsover to the real problem of old age. What should a society be, so that in his last years a man might still be a man?

The answer is simple: he would always have to have been treated as a man. By the fate it allots to its members who can no longer work, society gives itself away—it has always looked upon them as so much material. Society confesses that as far as it is concerned, profit is the only thing that counts, and that its "humanism" is mere window-dressing. In the nineteenth century the ruling classes explicitly equated the proletariat with barbarism. The struggles of the workers succeeded in making the proletariat part of mankind once more. But only in so far as it is productive. Society turns away from the aged worker as though he belonged to another species.

That is why the whole question is buried in a conspiracy of silence. Old age exposes the failure of our entire civilization. It is the whole man that must be re-made, it is the whole relationship between man and man that must be recast if we wish the old person's state to be acceptable. A man should not start his last years alone and empty-handed. If culture were not a mere inactive mass of information, acquired once and for all and then forgotten, if it were effectual and living, and if it meant that the individual had a grasp upon his environment that would fulfill and renew itself as the years go by, then he would be an active, useful citizen at every age. If he were not atomized from his childhood, shut away and isolated among other atoms, and if he shared in a collective life, as necessary and as much a matter of course as his own, then he would never experience banishment. Nowhere, and in no century, have these conditions obtained. Although the socialist countries may have come a little closer to them than the capitalist, they still have a very long way to go.

We may dream that in the ideal society that I have just spoken of old age would be virtually non-existent. As it does happen in certain privileged cases, the individual, though privately weakened by age but not obviously lessened by it, would one day be attacked by some disease from which he would not recover: he would die without having suffered any degradation. The last age would really comply with the definition given by certain bourgeois ideologists—a period of life different from youth and maturity, but possessing its own balance and leaving a wide range of possibilities open to the individual.

We are far from this state of affairs. Society cares about the individual only in so far as he is profitable. The young know this. Their anxiety as they enter in upon social life matches the anguish of the old as they are excluded from it. Between these two ages, the problem is hidden by routine. The young man dreads this machine that is about to seize hold of him, and sometimes he tries to defend himself by throwing half-bricks; the old man, rejected by it, exhausted and naked, has nothing left but his eyes to weep with. Between youth and age there turns the machine, the crusher of men—of men who let themselves be crushed because it never even occurs to them that they can escape it. Once we have understood what the state of the aged really is, we cannot satisfy ourselves with calling for a more generous "old-age policy," higher pensions, decent housing and organized leisure. It is the whole system that is at issue, and our claim cannot be otherwise than radical—change life itself.

For Discussion

1. What are some common attitudes people have toward growing old?
2. In what way does Beauvoir see death as more positive than old age?
3. In what ways, according to Beauvoir, does one give life value? To what extent do these parallel your own convictions?
4. What effect does a person's class or work have upon the onset and character of his/her old age?
5. Why is society ultimately responsible for the crime of old age?

6. How satisfactory would Beauvoir find Medicare, Medicaid, government housing for the aged, and retirement communities as solutions for the problems of the aged?

7. To what extent does your experience with an aged person reflect the conditions Beauvoir describes in her essay?

8. Examine the image of the raveling stitch in the third paragraph and that of the machine in the last paragraph, and comment upon their effectiveness.

9. Does this essay seem more philosophical than sociological? How is its position reflected in the tone?

RACHEL CARSON

A Fable for Tomorrow

Rachel L. Carson (1907–1964) did her graduate work in biology at Johns Hopkins and the Marine Biological Laboratory at Woods Hole, Massachusetts, and taught biology at Johns Hopkins and the University of Maryland. Author of *The Sea Around Us* and *The Edge of the Sea*, she reveals a skill with language that equals her professional standing in science. Underlying all her work is a basic interest in the relation of life to its environment, an interest which caused her to spend four and one-half years gathering data from all over America, and other parts of the world, on the effects of pesticides now in general use. The result was *Silent Spring*, from which the following selection is taken.

There was once a town in the heart of America where all life seemed to live in harmony with its surroundings. The town lay in the midst of a checkerboard of prosperous farms, with fields of grain and hillsides of orchards where, in spring, white clouds of bloom drifted above the green fields. In autumn, oak and maple and birch set up a blaze of color that flamed and flickered across a backdrop of pines. Then foxes barked in the hills and deer silently crossed the fields, half hidden in the mists of the fall mornings.

Along the roads, laurel, viburnum and alder, great ferns and wild-flowers delighted the traveler's eye through much of the year. Even in winter the roadsides were places of beauty, where countless birds came to feed on the berries and on the seed heads of the dried weeds rising above the snow. The countryside was, in fact, famous for the abundance and variety of its bird life, and when the flood of migrants was pouring through in spring and fall people traveled from great distances to observe them. Others came to fish the streams, which flowed clear and cold out of the hills and contained shady pools where trout lay. So it had been from the days many years ago when the first settlers raised their houses, sank their wells, and built their barns.

Then a strange blight crept over the area and everything began to change. Some evil spell had settled on the community: mysterious maladies swept the flocks of chickens; the cattle and sheep sickened and died. Everywhere was a shadow of death. The farmers spoke of much illness among their families. In the town the doctors had become more and more puzzled by new kinds of sickness appearing among their patients. There had been several sudden and unexplained deaths, not only among adults but even among children, who would be stricken suddenly while at play and die within a few hours.

There was a strange stillness. The birds, for example—where had they gone? Many people spoke of them, puzzled and disturbed. The feeding stations in the backyards were deserted. The few birds seen anywhere were moribund; they trembled violently and could not fly. It was a spring without voices. On the mornings that had once throbbed with the dawn chorus of robins, catbirds, doves, jays, wrens, and scores of other bird voices there was now no sound; only silence lay over the fields and woods and marsh.

On the farms the hens brooded, but no chicks hatched. The farmers complained that they were unable to raise any pigs—the litters were small and the young survived only a few days. The apple trees were coming into bloom but no bees droned among the blossoms, so there was no pollination and there would be no fruit.

The roadsides, once so attractive, were now lined with browned and withered vegetation as though swept by fire. These, too, were silent, deserted by all living things. Even the streams were now lifeless. Anglers no longer visited them, for all the fish had died.

In the gutters under the eaves and between the shingles of the roofs, a white granular powder still showed a few patches; some weeks before it had fallen like snow upon the roofs and the lawns, the fields and streams.

No witchcraft, no enemy action had silenced the rebirth of new life in this stricken world. The people had done it themselves.

This town does not actually exist, but it might easily have a thousand counterparts in America or elsewhere in the world. I know of no community that has experienced all the misfortunes I describe. Yet every one of these disasters has actually happened somewhere, and many real communities have already suffered a substantial number of them. A grim specter has crept upon us almost unnoticed, and this imagined tragedy may easily become a stark reality we all shall know.

For Discussion

1. What quality of life does Carson stress in describing the town before the blight? After the blight?
2. What recent ecological misfortunes can you cite which fulfill the prophecy of the fable?
3. Identify and discuss those images of sight and sound that you think especially effective.
4. Carson chooses to express her ideas in the form of a fable. Discuss the appropriateness of this form to her purpose.

JAMES BALDWIN

My Dungeon Shook

Letter to My Nephew on the One Hundredth Anniversary of the Emancipation

Author-essayist-playwright James Baldwin, born in Harlem in 1924, grew up in the ghetto and lived and worked in Greenwich Village until a Rosenwald Fellowship enabled him to go to Paris to write. He remained abroad until 1957, writing his first two novels, *Go Tell It on the Mountain* (1952) and *Giovanni's Room* (1956), as well as the essays published as *Notes of a Native Son* (1955), wherein he introduced his theme of the Negro as "the conscience of the country." *Nobody Knows My Name* followed in 1961. Upon publication of *Another Country* (1962), the racial situation in the United States had created the need for a black artist-spokesman, a position in which Baldwin found himself. His collection, *The Fire Next Time* (1962), contains the following essay.

DEAR JAMES:

I have begun this letter five times and torn it up five times. I keep seeing your face, which is also the face of your father and my brother. Like him, you are tough, dark, vulnerable, moody—with a very definite tendency to sound truculent because you want no one to think you are soft. You may be like your grandfather in this, I don't know, but certainly both you and your father resemble him very much physically. Well, he is dead, he never saw you, and he had a terrible life; he was defeated long before he died because, at the bottom of his heart, he really believed what white people said about him. This is one of the reasons that he became so holy. I am sure that your father has told you something about all that. Neither you nor your father exhibit any tendency towards holiness: you really *are* of another era, part of what happened when the Negro left the land and came into what the late E. Franklin Frazier called "the cities of destruction." You can only be destroyed by believing that you really are what the white world calls a *nigger*. I tell you this because I love you, and please don't you ever forget it.

I have known both of you all your lives, have carried your Daddy in my arms and on my shoulders, kissed and spanked him and watched him learn to walk. I don't know if you've known anybody from that far back; if you've loved anybody that long, first as an infant, then as a child, then as a man, you gain a strange perspective on time and human pain and effort. Other people cannot see what I see whenever I look into your father's face, for behind your father's face as it is today are all those other faces which were his. Let him laugh and I see a cellar your father does not remember and a house he does not remember and I hear in his present laughter his laughter as a child. Let him curse and I remember him falling down the cellar steps, and howling, and I remember, with pain, his tears, which my hand or your grandmother's so easily wiped away. But no one's hand can wipe away those tears he sheds invisibly today, which one hears in his laughter and in his speech and in his songs. I know what the world has done to my brother and how narrowly he has survived it. And I know, which is much worse, and this is the crime of which I accuse my country and my countrymen, and for which neither I nor time nor history will ever forgive them, that they have destroyed and are destroying hundreds of thousands of lives and do not know it and do not want to know it. One can be, indeed one must strive to become, tough and philosophical concerning destruction and death, for this is what most of mankind has been best at since we have heard of man. (But remember: *most* of mankind is not *all* of mankind.) But it is not permissible that the authors of devastation should also be innocent. It is the innocence which constitutes the crime.

Now, my dear namesake, these innocent and well-meaning people, your countrymen, have caused you to be born under conditions not very far removed from those described for us by Charles Dickens in the London of more than a hundred years ago (I hear the chorus of the innocents screaming, "No! This is not true! How *bitter* you are!"—but I am writing this letter to *you*, to try to tell you something about how to handle *them*, for most of them do not yet really know that you exist. I *know* the conditions under which you were born, for I was there. Your countrymen were *not* there, and haven't made it yet. Your grandmother was also there, and no one has ever accused her of being bitter. I suggest that the innocents check with her. She isn't hard to find. Your countrymen don't know that *she* exists, either, though she has been working for them all their lives.)

Well, you were born, here you came, something like fifteen years ago; and though your father and mother and grandmother, looking about the streets through which they were carrying you, staring at the walls into which they brought you, had every reason to be heavyhearted, yet they were not. For here you were, Big James, named for me—you were a big baby, I was not—here you were: to be loved. To be loved, baby, hard, at once, and forever, to strengthen you against the loveless world. Remember that: I know how black it looks today, for you. It looked bad that day, too, yes, we were trembling. We have not stopped trembling yet, but if we had not loved each other none of us would have survived. And now you must survive because we love you, and for the sake of your children and your children's children.

This innocent country set you down in a ghetto in which, in fact, it intended that you should perish. Let me spell out precisely what I mean by that, for the heart of the matter is here, and the root of my dispute with my country. You were born where you were born and faced the future that you faced because you were black and *for no other reason*. The limits of your ambition were, thus, expected to be set forever. You were born into a society which spelled out with brutal clarity, and in as many ways as possible, that you were a worthless human being. You were not expected to aspire to excellence: you were expected to make peace with mediocrity. Wherever you have turned, James, in your short time on this earth, you have been told where you could go and what you could do (and *how* you could do it) and where you could live and whom you could marry. I know your countrymen do not agree with me about this, and I hear them saying, "You exaggerate." They do not know Harlem, and I do. So do you. Take no one's word for anything, including mine—but trust your experience. Know whence you came. If you know whence you came, there is really no limit to where you can go. The details and symbols of your life have been deliberately constructed to make you believe what white people say about you. Please try to remember that what they believe, as well as what they do and cause you to endure, does not testify to your inferiority but to their inhumanity and fear. Please try to be clear, dear James, through the storm which rages about your youthful head today, about the reality which lies behind the words *acceptance* and *integration*. There is no reason for you to try to become like white people and there is no basis whatever for their impertinent assumption that *they* must accept *you*. The really terrible thing, old buddy, is that *you* must accept *them*. And I mean that very seriously. You must accept them and accept them with love. For these innocent people have no other hope. They are, in effect, still trapped in a history which they do not understand; and until they understand it, they cannot be released from it. They have had to believe for many years, and for innumerable reasons, that black men are inferior to white men. Many of them, indeed, know better, but, as you will discover, people find it very difficult to act on what they know. To act is to be committed, and to be committed is to be in danger. In this case, the danger, in the minds of most white Americans, is the loss of their identity. Try to imagine how you would feel if you woke up one morning to find the sun shining and all the stars aflame. You would be frightened because it is out of the order of nature. Any upheaval in the universe is terrifying because it so profoundly attacks one's sense of one's own reality. Well, the black man has functioned in the white man's world as a fixed star, as an immovable pillar: and as he moves out of his place, heaven and earth are shaken to their foundations. You, don't be afraid. I said that it was intended that you should perish in the ghetto, perish by never being allowed to go behind the white man's definitions, by never being allowed to spell your proper name. You have, and many of us have, defeated this intention; and, by a terrible law, a terrible paradox, those innocents who believed that your imprisonment made them safe are losing their grasp of reality. But these men are your brothers—your lost, younger brothers. And if the word *integration* means anything, this is what it means: that we, with love, shall force our brothers to see themselves as they are, to cease fleeing from reality and begin to change it. For this is your home, my friend, do not be driven from it; great men have done great things here, and will again, and we can make America what America must become. It will be hard, James, but you come from sturdy, peasant stock, men who picked cotton and dammed rivers and built railroads, and, in the teeth of the most terrifying odds, achieved an unassailable and monumental dignity. You come from a long line of great poets, some of the greatest poets since Homer. One of them said, *The very time I thought I was lost, My dungeon shook and my chains fell off.*

You know, and I know, that the country is celebrating one hundred years of freedom one hundred years too soon. We cannot be free until they are free. God bless you, James, and Godspeed.

Your uncle,
JAMES

For Discussion

1. This essay is included in Baldwin's *The Fire Next Time*, the title of which is taken from a slave song containing the lines "God gave Noah the rainbow sign/No more water, the fire next time." How does this relate to Baldwin's message?

2. What are Baldwin's feelings toward his father's holiness?
3. What does Baldwin say about the innocence of Americans?
4. Discuss Baldwin's definition of integration.
5. How does each member of Baldwin's family (with the exception of his nephew) represent a typical response to being a black American? Why does Baldwin make the nephew an exception?
6. It has been pointed out that much of Baldwin's style comes from his youthful experience as a preacher. What evidence of this influence can you find? In this regard, read aloud the paragraph beginning "I have known both of you all your lives. . . ."
7. Reread selected paragraphs aloud, trying to convey, as closely as possible, what you feel to be Baldwin's tone: his attitude toward his subject and his audience.

MARTIN LUTHER KING, JR.

Letter from Birmingham Jail

A Baptist minister and president of the Southern Christian Leadership Conference, Martin Luther King, Jr., was the acknowledged leader of the civil rights movement in America until his assassination in 1968. An eloquent speaker, Dr. King united blacks and whites by the force of his love and by his dedication to his people. He was honored in his lifetime, receiving the Nobel Prize for Peace in 1964, and in his death became the symbol of black martyrdom. In the months preceding his assassination, Dr. King had moved to a more militant position in regard to racial issues and a highly critical position on United States foreign policy.

April 16, 1963

MY DEAR FELLOW CLERGYMEN:

While confined here in the Birmingham city jail, I came across your recent statement calling my present activities "unwise and untimely."

This response to a published statement by eight fellow clergymen from Alabama (Bishop C. C. J. Carpenter, Bishop Joseph A. Durick, Rabbi Hilton L. Grafman, Bishop Paul Hardin, Bishop Holan B. Harmon, the Reverend George M. Murray, the Reverend Edward V. Ramage and the Reverend Earl Stallings) was composed under somewhat constricting circumstances. Begun on the margins of the newspaper in which the statement appeared while I was in jail, the letter was continued on scraps of writing paper supplied by a friendly Negro trusty, and concluded on a pad my attorneys were eventually permitted to leave me. Although the text remains in substance unaltered, I have indulged in the author's prerogative of polishing it for publication.—MARTIN LUTHER KING, JR.

Seldom do I pause to answer criticism of my work and ideas. If I sought to answer all the criticisms that cross my desk, my secretaries would have little time for anything other than such correspondence in the course of the day, and I would have no time for constructive work. But since I feel that you are men of genuine good will and that your criticisms are sincerely set forth, I want to try to answer your statement in what I hope will be patient and reasonable terms.

I think I should indicate why I am here in Birmingham, since you have been influenced by the view which argues against "outsiders coming in." I have the honor of serving as president of the Southern Christian Leadership Conference, an organization operating in every southern state, with headquarters in Atlanta, Georgia. We have some eighty-five affiliated organizations across the South, and one of them is the Alabama Christian Movement for Human Rights. Frequently we share staff, educational and financial resources with our affiliates. Several months ago the affiliate here in Birmingham asked us to be on call to engage in a nonviolent direct-action program if such were deemed necessary. We readily consented, and when the hour came we lived up to our promise. So I, along with several members of my staff, am here because I was invited here. I am here because I have organizational ties here.

But more basically, I am in Birmingham because injustice is here. Just as the prophets of the eighth century B.C. left their villages and carried their "thus saith the Lord" far beyond the boundaries of their home towns, and just as the Apostle Paul left his village of Tarsus and carried the gospel of Jesus Christ to the far corners of the Greco-Roman world, so am I compelled to carry the gospel of freedom beyond my own home town. Like Paul, I must constantly respond to the Macedonian call for aid.

Moreover, I am cognizant of the interrelatedness of all communities and states. I cannot sit idly by in Atlanta and not be concerned about what happens in Birmingham. Injustice anywhere is a threat to justice everywhere. We are caught in an inescapable network of mutuality, tied in a single garment of destiny. Whatever affects one directly, affects all indirectly. Never again can we afford to live with the narrow, provincial "outside agitator" idea. Anyone who lives inside the United States can never be considered an outsider anywhere within its bounds.

You deplore the demonstrations taking place in Birmingham. But your statement, I am sorry to say, fails to express a similar concern for the conditions that brought about the demonstrations. I am sure that none of you would want to rest content with the superficial kind of social analysis that deals merely with effects and does not grapple with underlying causes. It is unfortunate that demonstrations are taking place in Birmingham, but it is even more unfortunate that the city's white power structure left the Negro community with no alternative.

In any nonviolent campaign there are four basic steps: collection of the facts to determine whether injustices exist; negotiation; self-purification; and direct action. We have gone through all these steps in Birmingham. There can be no gainsaying the fact that racial injustice engulfs this community. Birmingham is probably the most thoroughly segregated city in the United States. Its ugly record of brutality is widely known. Negroes have experienced grossly unjust treatment in the courts. There have been more unsolved bombings of Negro homes and churches in Birmingham than in any other city in the nation. These are the hard, brutal facts of the case. On the basis of these conditions, Negro leaders sought to negotiate with the city fathers. But the latter consistently refused to engage in good-faith negotiation.

Then, last September, came the opportunity to talk with leaders of Birmingham's economic community. In the course of the negotiations, certain promises were made by the merchants—for example, to remove the stores' humiliating racial signs. On the basis of these promises, the Reverend Fred Shuttlesworth and the leaders of the Alabama Christian Movement for Human Rights agreed to a moratorium on all demonstrations. As the weeks and months went by, we realized that we were the victims of a broken promise. A few signs, briefly removed, returned; the others remained.

As in so many past experiences, our hopes had been blasted, and the shadow of deep disappointment settled upon us. We had no alternative except to prepare for direct action, whereby we would present our very bodies as a means of laying our case before the conscience of the local and the national community. Mindful of the difficulties involved, we decided to undertake a process of self-purification. We began a series of workshops on nonviolence, and we repeatedly asked ourselves: "Are you able to accept blows without retaliating?" "Are you able to endure the ordeal of jail?" We decided to schedule our direct-action program for the Easter season, realizing that except for Christmas, this is the main shopping period of the year. Knowing that a strong economic-withdrawal program would be the by-product of direct action, we felt that this would be the best time to bring pressure to bear on the merchants for the needed change.

Then it occurred to us that Birmingham's mayoral election was coming up in March, and we speedily decided to postpone action until after election day. When we discovered that the Commissioner of Public Safety, Eugene "Bull" Connor, had piled up enough votes to be in the run-off, we decided again to postpone action until the day after the run-off so that the demonstrations could not be used to cloud the issues. Like many others, we waited to see Mr. Connor defeated, and to this end we endured postponement after postponement. Having aided in this community need, we felt that our direct-action program could be delayed no longer.

You may well ask: "Why direct action? Why sit-ins, marches and so forth? Isn't negotiation a better path?" You are quite right in calling for negotiation. Indeed, this is the very purpose of direct action. Nonviolent direct action seeks to create such a crisis and foster such a tension that a community which has constantly refused to negotiate is forced to confront the issue. It seeks so to dramatize the issue that it can no longer be ignored. My citing the creation of tension as part of the work of the nonviolent-resister may sound rather shocking. But I must confess that I am not afraid of the word "tension." I have earnestly opposed violent tension, but there is a type of constructive, nonviolent tension which is necessary for growth. Just as Socrates felt that it was necessary to create a tension in the mind so that individuals could rise from the bondage of myths and half-truths to the unfettered realm of creative analysis and objective appraisal, so must we see the need for nonviolent gadflies to create the kind of tension in society that will help men rise from the dark depths of prejudice and racism to the majestic heights of understanding and brotherhood.

The purpose of our direct-action program is to create a situation so crisis-packed that it will inevitably open the door to negotiation. I therefore concur with you in your call for negotiation. Too long has our beloved Southland been bogged down in a tragic effort to live in monologue rather than dialogue.

One of the basic points in your statement is that the action that I and my associates have taken in Birmingham is untimely. Some have asked: "Why didn't you give the new city administration time to act?" The only answer that I can give to this query is that the new Birmingham administration must be prodded about as much as the outgoing one, before it will act. We are sadly mistaken if we feel that the election of Albert Boutwell as mayor will bring the millennium to Birmingham. While Mr. Boutwell is a much more gentle person than Mr. Connor, they are both segregationists, dedicated to maintenance of the status quo. I have hope that Mr. Boutwell will be reasonable enough to see the futility of massive resistance to desegregation. But he will not see this without pressure from devotees of civil rights. My friends, I must say to you that we have not made a single gain in civil rights without determined legal and nonviolent pressure. Lamentably, it is an historical fact that privileged groups seldom give up their privileges voluntarily. Individuals may see the moral light and voluntarily give up their unjust posture; but, as Reinhold Niebuhr has reminded us, groups tend to be more immoral than individuals.

We know through painful experience that freedom is never voluntarily given by the oppressor; it must be demanded by the oppressed. Frankly, I have yet to engage in a direct-action campaign that was "well timed" in the view of those who have not suffered unduly from the disease of segregation. For years now I have heard the word "Wait!" It rings in the ear of every Negro with piercing familiarity. This "Wait" has almost always meant "Never." We must come to see, with one of our distinguished jurists, that "justice too long delayed is justice denied."

We have waited for more than 340 years for our constitutional and God-given rights. The nations of Asia and Africa are moving with jetlike speed toward gaining political independence, but we still creep at horse-and-buggy pace toward gaining a cup of coffee at a lunch counter. Perhaps it is easy for those who have never felt the stinging darts of segregation to say, "Wait." But when you have seen vicious mobs lynch your mothers and fathers at will and drown your sisters and brothers at whim; when you have seen hate-filled policemen curse, kick and even kill your black brothers and sisters; when you see the vast majority of your twenty million Negro brothers smothering in an airtight cage of poverty in the midst of an affluent society; when you suddenly find your tongue twisted and your speech stammering as you seek to explain to your six-year-old daughter why she can't go to the public amusement park that has just been advertised on television, and see tears welling up in her eyes when she is told that Funtown is closed to colored children, and see ominous clouds of inferiority beginning to form in her little mental sky, and see her beginning to distort her personality by developing an unconscious bitterness toward white people; when you have to concoct an answer for a five-year-old son who is asking: "Daddy, why do white people treat colored people so mean?"; when you take a cross-country drive and find it necessary to sleep night after night in the uncomfortable corners of your automobile because no motel will accept you; when you are humiliated day in and day out by nagging signs reading "white" and "colored"; when your first name becomes "nigger," your middle name becomes "boy" (however old you are) and your last becomes "John," and your wife and mother are never given the respected title "Mrs."; when you are harried by day and haunted by night by the fact that you are a Negro, living constantly at tiptoe stance, never quite knowing what to expect next, and are plagued with inner fears and outer resentments; when you are forever fighting a degenerating sense of "nobodiness"—then you will understand why we find it difficult to wait. There comes a time when the cup of endurance runs over, and men are no longer willing to be plunged into the abyss of despair. I hope, sirs, you can understand our legitimate and unavoidable impatience.

You express a great deal of anxiety over our willingness to break laws. This is certainly a legitimate concern. Since we so diligently urge people to obey the Supreme Court's decision of 1954 outlawing segregation in the public schools, at first glance it may seem rather paradoxical for us consciously to break laws. One may well ask: "How can you advocate breaking some laws and obeying others?" The answer lies in the fact that there are two types of laws: just and unjust. I would be the first to advocate obeying just laws. One has not only a legal but a moral responsibility to obey just laws. Conversely, one has a moral responsibility to disobey unjust laws. I would agree with St. Augustine that "an unjust law is no law at all."

Now, what is the difference between the two? How does one determine whether a law is just or unjust? A just law is a man-made code that squares with the moral law or the law of God. An unjust law is a code that is out of harmony with the moral law. To put it in the terms of St. Thomas Aquinas: An unjust law is a human law that is not rooted in eternal law and natural law. Any law that uplifts human personality is just. Any law that degrades human personality is unjust. All segregation statutes are unjust because segregation distorts the soul and damages the personality. It gives the segregator a false sense of superiority and the segregated a false sense of inferiority. Segregation, to use the terminology of the Jewish philosopher Martin Buber, substitutes an "I—it" relationship for an "I—thou" relationship and ends up relegating persons to the status of things. Hence segregation is not only politically, economically and sociologically unsound, it is morally wrong and sinful. Paul Tillich has said that sin is separation. Is not segregation an existential expression of man's tragic separation, his awful estrangement, his terrible sinfulness? Thus it is that I can urge men to obey the 1954 decision of the Supreme Court, for it is morally right; and I can urge them to disobey segregation ordinances, for they are morally wrong.

Let us consider a more concrete example of just and unjust laws. An unjust law is a code that a numerical or power majority group compels a minority group to obey but does not make binding on itself. This is *difference* made legal. By the same token, a just law is a code that a majority compels a minority to follow and that it is willing to follow itself. This is *sameness* made legal.

Let me give another explanation. A law is unjust if it is inflicted on a minority that, as a result of being denied the right to vote, had no part in enacting or devising the law. Who can say that the legislature of Alabama which set up the state's segregation laws was democratically elected? Throughout Alabama all sorts of devious methods are used to prevent Negroes from becoming registered voters, and there are some counties in which, even though Negroes constitute a majority of the population, not a single Negro is registered. Can any law enacted under such circumstances be considered democratically structured?

Sometimes a law is just on its face and unjust in its application. For instance, I have been arrested on a charge of parading without a permit. Now, there is nothing wrong in having an ordinance which requires a permit for a parade. But such an ordinance becomes unjust when it is used to maintain segregation and to deny citizens the First-Amendment privilege of peaceful assembly and protest.

I hope you are able to see the distinction I am trying to point out. In no sense do I advocate evading or defying the law, as would the rabid segregationist. That would lead to anarchy. One who breaks an unjust law must do so openly, lovingly, and with a willingness to accept the penalty. I submit that an individual who breaks a law that conscience tells him is unjust, and who willingly accepts the penalty of imprisonment in order to arouse the conscience of the community over its injustice, is in reality expressing the highest respect for law.

Of course, there is nothing new about this kind of civil disobedience. It was evidenced sublimely in the refusal of Shadrach, Meshach and Abednego to obey the laws of Nebuchadnezzar, on the ground that a higher moral law was at stake. It was practiced superbly by the early Christians, who were willing to face hungry lions and the excruciating pain of chopping blocks rather than submit to certain unjust laws of the Roman Empire. To a degree, academic freedom is a reality today because Socrates practiced civil disobedience. In our own nation, the Boston Tea Party represented a massive act of civil disobedience.

We should never forget that everything Adolf Hitler did in Germany was "legal" and everything the Hungarian freedom fighters did in Hungary was "illegal." It was "illegal" to aid and comfort a Jew in Hitler's Germany. Even so, I am sure that, had I lived in Germany at the time, I would have aided and comforted my Jewish brothers. If today I lived in a Communist country where certain principles dear to the Christian faith are suppressed, I would openly advocate disobeying that country's antireligious laws.

I must make two honest confessions to you, my Christian and Jewish brothers. First, I must confess that over the past few years I have been gravely disappointed with the white moderate. I have almost reached the regrettable conclusion that the Negro's great stumbling block in his stride toward freedom is not the White Citizens' Counciler or the Ku Klux Klanner, but the white moderate, who is more devoted to "order" than to justice; who prefers a negative peace which is the absence of tension to a positive peace which is the presence of justice; who constantly says: "I agree with you in the goal you seek, but I cannot agree with your methods of direct action"; who paternalistically believes he can set the timetable for another man's freedom; who lives by a mythical concept of time and who constantly advises the Negro to wait for a "more convenient season." Shallow understanding from people of good will is more frustrating than absolute misunderstanding from people of ill will. Lukewarm acceptance is much more bewildering than outright rejection.

I had hoped that the white moderate would understand that law and order exist for the purpose of establishing justice and that when they fail in this purpose they become the dangerously structured dams that block the flow of social progress. I had hoped that the white moderate would understand that the present tension in the South is a necessary phase of the transition from an obnoxious negative peace, in which the Negro passively accepted his unjust plight, to a substantive and positive peace, in which all men will respect the dignity and worth of human personality. Actually, we who engage in nonviolent direct action are not the creators of tension. We merely bring to the surface the hidden tension that is already alive. We bring it out in the open, where it can be seen and dealt with. Like a boil that can never be cured so long as it is covered up must be opened with all its ugliness to the natural medicines of air and light, injustice must be exposed, with all the tension its exposure creates, to the light of human conscience and the air of national opinion before it can be cured.

In your statement you assert that our actions, even though peaceful, must be condemned because they precipitate violence. But is this a logical assertion? Isn't this like condemning a robbed man because his possession of money precipitated the evil act of robbery? Isn't this like condemning Socrates because his unswerving commitment to truth and his philosophical inquiries precipitated the act by the misguided populace in which they made him drink hemlock? Isn't this like condemning Jesus because his unique God-consciousness and never-ceasing devotion to God's will precipitated the evil act of crucifixion? We must come to see that, as the federal courts have consistently affirmed, it is wrong to urge an individual to cease his efforts to gain his basic constitutional rights because the quest may precipitate violence. Society must protect the robbed and punish the robber.

I had also hoped that the white moderate would reject the myth concerning time in relation to the struggle for freedom. I have just received a letter from a white brother in Texas. He writes: "All Christians know that the colored people will receive equal rights eventually, but it is possible that you are in too great a religious hurry. It has taken Christianity almost two thousand years to accomplish what it has. The teachings of Christ take time to come to earth." Such an attitude stems from a tragic misconception of time, from the strangely irrational notion that there is something in the very flow of time that will inevitably cure all ills. Actually, time itself is neutral; it can be used either destructively or constructively. More and more I feel that the people of ill will have used time much more effectively than have the people of good will. We will have to repent in this generation not merely for the hateful words and actions of the bad people but for the appalling silence of the good people. Human progress never rolls in on wheels of inevitability; it comes through the tireless efforts of men willing to be co-workers with God, and without this hard work, time itself becomes an ally of the forces of social stagnation. We must use time creatively, in the knowledge that the time is always ripe to do right. Now is the time to make real the promise of democracy and transform our pending national elegy into a creative psalm of brotherhood. Now is the time to lift our national policy from the quicksand of racial injustice to the solid rock of human dignity.

You speak of our activity in Birmingham as extreme. At first I was rather disappointed that fellow clergymen would see my nonviolent efforts as those of an extremist. I began thinking about the fact that I stand in the middle of two opposing forces in the Negro community. One is a force of complacency, made up in part of Negroes who, as a result of long years of oppression, are so drained of self-respect and a sense of "somebodiness" that they have adjusted to segregation; and in part of a few middle-class Negroes who, because of a degree of academic and economic security and because in some ways they profit by segregation, have become insensitive to the problems of the masses. The other force is one of bitterness and hatred, and it comes perilously close to advocating violence. It is expressed in the various black nationalist groups that are springing up across the nation, the largest and best-known being Elijah Muhammad's Muslim movement. Nourished by the Negro's frustration over the continued existence of racial discrimination, this movement is made up of people who have lost faith in America, who have absolutely repudiated Christianity, and who have concluded that the white man is an incorrigible "devil."

I have tried to stand between these two forces, saying that we need emulate neither the "do-nothingism" of the complacent nor the hatred and despair of the black nationalist. For there is the more excellent way of love and nonviolent protest. I am grateful to God that, through the influence of the Negro church, the way of nonviolence became an integral part of our struggle.

If this philosophy had not emerged, by now many streets of the South would, I am convinced, be flowing with blood. And I am further convinced that if our white brothers dismiss as "rabble-rousers" and "outside agitators" those of us who employ nonviolent direct action, and if they refuse to support our nonviolent efforts, millions of Negroes will, out of frustration and despair, seek solace and security in black-nationalist ideologies—a development that would inevitably lead to a frightening racial nightmare.

Oppressed people cannot remain oppressed forever. The yearning for freedom eventually manifests itself, and that is what has happened to the American Negro. Something within has reminded him of his birth-right of freedom, and something without has reminded him that it can be gained. Consciously or unconsciously, he has been caught up by the

Zeitgeist, and with his black brothers of Africa and his brown and yellow brothers of Asia, South America and the Caribbean, the United States Negro is moving with a sense of great urgency toward the promised land of racial justice. If one recognizes this vital urge that has engulfed the Negro community, one should readily understand why public demonstrations are taking place. The Negro has many pent-up resentments and latent frustrations, and he must release them. So let him march; let him make prayer pilgrimages to the city hall; let him go on freedom rides—and try to understand why he must do so. If his repressed emotions are not released in nonviolent ways, they will seek expression through violence; this is not a threat but a fact of history. So I have not said to my people: "Get rid of your discontent." Rather, I have tried to say that this normal and healthy discontent can be channeled into the creative outlet of nonviolent direct action. And now this approach is being termed extremist.

But though I was initially disappointed at being categorized as an extremist, as I continued to think about the matter I gradually gained a measure of satisfaction from the label. Was not Jesus an extremist for love: "Love your enemies, bless them that curse you, do good to them that hate you, and pray for them which despitefully use you, and persecute you." Was not Amos an extremist for justice: "Let justice roll down like waters and righteousness like an ever-flowing stream." Was not Paul an extremist for the Christian gospel: "I bear in my body the marks of the Lord Jesus." Was not Martin Luther an extremist: "Here I stand; I cannot do otherwise, so help me God." And John Bunyan: "I will stay in jail to the end of my days before I make a butchery of my conscience." And Abraham Lincoln: "This nation cannot survive half slave and half free." And Thomas Jefferson: "We hold these truths to be self-evident, that all men are created equal. . . ." So the question is not whether we will be extremists, but what kind of extremists we will be. Will we be extremists for hate or for love? Will we be extremists for the preservation of injustice or for the extension of justice? In that dramatic scene on Calvary's hill three men were crucified. We must never forget that all three were crucified for the same crime—the crime of extremism. Two were extremists for immorality, and thus fell below their environment. The other, Jesus Christ, was an extremist for love, truth and goodness, and thereby rose above his environment. Perhaps the South, the nation and the world are in dire need of creative extremists.

I had hoped that the white moderate would see this need. Perhaps I was too optimistic; perhaps I expected too much. I suppose I should have realized that few members of the oppressor race can understand the deep groans and passionate yearnings of the oppressed race, and still fewer have the vision to see that injustice must be rooted out by strong, persistent and determined action. I am thankful, however, that some of our white brothers in the South have grasped the meaning of this social revolution and committed themselves to it. They are still all too few in quantity, but they are big in quality. Some—such as Ralph McGill, Lillian Smith, Harry Golden, James McBride Dabbs, Ann Braden and Sarah Patton Boyle—have written about our struggle in eloquent and prophetic terms. Others have marched with us down nameless streets of the South. They have languished in filthy, roach-infested jails, suffering the abuse and brutality of policemen who view them as "dirty nigger-lovers." Unlike so many of their moderate brothers and sisters, they have recognized the urgency of the moment and sensed the need for powerful "action" antidotes to combat the disease of segregation.

Let me take note of my other major disappointment. I have been so greatly disappointed with the white church and its leadership. Of course, there are some notable exceptions. I am not unmindful of the fact that each of you has taken some significant stands on this issue. I commend you, Reverend Stallings, for your Christian stand on this past Sunday, in welcoming Negroes to your worship service on a nonsegregated basis. I commend the Catholic leaders of this state for integrating Spring Hill College several years ago.

But despite these notable exceptions, I must honestly reiterate that I have been disappointed with the church. I do not say this as one of those negative critics who can always find something wrong with the church. I say this as a minister of the gospel, who loves the church; who was nurtured in its bosom; who has been sustained by its spiritual blessings and who will remain true to it as long as the cord of life shall lengthen.

When I was suddenly catapulted into the leadership of the bus protest in Montgomery, Alabama, a few years ago, I felt we would be supported by the white church. I felt that the white ministers, priests and rabbis of the South would be among our strongest allies. Instead, some have been outright opponents, refusing to understand the freedom movement and misrepresenting its leaders; all too many others have been more cautious than courageous and have remained silent behind the anesthetizing security of stained-glass windows.

In spite of my shattered dreams, I came to Birmingham with the hope that the white religious leadership of this community would see the justice of our cause and, with deep moral concern, would serve as the channel through which our just grievances could reach the power structure. I had hoped that each of you would understand. But again I have been disappointed.

I have heard numerous southern religious leaders admonish their worshipers to comply with a desegregation decision because it is the law, but I have longed to hear white ministers declare: "Follow this decree because integration is morally right and because the Negro is your brother." In the midst of blatant injustices inflicted upon the Negro, I have watched white churchmen stand on the sideline and mouth pious irrelevancies and sanctimonious trivialities. In the midst of a mighty struggle to rid our nation of racial and economic injustice, I have heard many ministers say: "Those are social issues, with which the gospel has no real concern." And I have watched many churches commit themselves to a completely otherworldly religion which makes a strange, un-Biblical distinction between body and soul, between the sacred and the secular.

I have traveled the length and breadth of Alabama, Mississippi and all the other southern states. On sweltering summer days and crisp autumn mornings I have looked at the South's beautiful churches with their lofty spires pointing heavenward. I have beheld the impressive outlines of her massive religious-education buildings. Over and over I have found myself asking: "What kind of people worship here? Who is their God? Where were their voices when the lips of Governor Barnett dripped with words of interposition and nullification? Where were they when Governor Wallace gave a clarion call for defiance and hatred? Where were their voices of support when bruised and weary Negro men and women decided to rise from the dark dungeons of complacency to the bright hills of creative protest?"

Yes, these questions are still in my mind. In deep disappointment I have wept over the laxity of the church. But be assured that my tears have been tears of love. There can be no deep disappointment where there is not deep love. Yes, I love the church. How could I do otherwise? I am in the rather unique position of being the son, the grandson and the great-grandson of preachers. Yes, I see the church as the body of Christ. But, oh! How we have blemished and scarred that body through social neglect and through fear of being nonconformists.

There was a time when the church was very powerful—in the time when the early Christians rejoiced at being deemed worthy to suffer for what they believed. In those days the church was not merely a thermometer that recorded the ideas and principles of popular opinion; it was a thermostat that transformed the mores of society. Whenever the early Christians entered a town, the people in power became disturbed and immediately sought to convict the Christians for being "disturbers of the peace" and "outside agitators." But the Christians pressed on, in the conviction that they were "a colony of heaven," called to obey God rather than man. Small in number, they were big in commitment. They were too God-intoxicated to be "astronomically intimidated." By their effort and example they brought an end to such ancient evils as infanticide and gladitorial contests.

Things are different now. So often the contemporary church is a weak, ineffectual voice with an uncertain sound. So often it is an archdefender of the status quo. Far from being disturbed by the presence of the church, the power structure of the average community is consoled by the church's silent—and often even vocal—sanction of things as they are.

But the judgment of God is upon the church as never before. If today's church does not recapture the sacrificial spirit of the early church, it will lose its authenticity, forfeit the loyalty of millions, and be dismissed as an irrelevant social club with no meaning for the twentieth century. Every day I meet young people whose disappointment with the church has turned into outright disgust.

Perhaps I have once again been too optimistic. Is organized religion too inextricably bound to the status quo to save our nation and the world? Perhaps I must turn my faith to the inner spiritual church, the church within the church, as the true *ekklesia* and the hope of the world. But again I am thankful to God that some noble souls from the ranks of organized religion have broken loose from the paralyzing chains of conformity and joined us as active partners in the struggle for freedom. They have left their secure congregations and walked the streets of Albany, Georgia, with us. They have gone down the highways of the South on tortuous rides for freedom. Yes, they have gone to jail with us. Some have been dismissed from their churches, have lost the support of their bishops and fellow ministers. But they have acted in the faith that right defeated is stronger than evil triumphant. Their witness has been the spiritual salt that has preserved the true meaning of the gospel in these troubled times. They have carved a tunnel of hope through the dark mountain of disappointment.

I hope the church as a whole will meet the challenge of this decisive hour. But even if the church does not come to the aid of justice, I have no despair about the future. I have no fear about the outcome of our struggle in Birmingham, even if our motives are at present misunderstood. We will reach the goal of freedom in Birmingham and all over the nation, because the goal of America is freedom. Abused and scorned though we may be, our destiny is tied up with America's destiny. Before the pilgrims landed at Plymouth, we were here. Before the pen of Jefferson etched the majestic words of the Declaration of Independence across the pages of history, we were here. For more than two centuries our forebears labored in this country without wages; they made cotton king; they built the homes of their masters while suffering gross injustice and shameful humiliation—and yet out of a bottomless vitality they continued to thrive and develop. If the inexpressible cruelties of slavery could not stop us, the opposition we now face will surely fail. We will win our freedom because the sacred heritage of our nation and the eternal will of God are embodied in our echoing demands.

Before closing I feel impelled to mention one other point in your statement that has troubled me profoundly. You warmly commended the Birmingham police force for keeping "order" and "preventing violence."

I doubt that you would have so warmly commended the police force if you had seen its dogs sinking their teeth into unarmed, nonviolent Negroes. I doubt that you would so quickly commend the policemen if you were to observe their ugly and inhumane treatment of Negroes here in the city jail; if you were to watch them push and curse old Negro women and young Negro girls; if you were to see them slap and kick old Negro men and young boys; if you were to observe them, as they did on two occasions, refuse to give us food because we wanted to sing our grace together. I cannot join you in your praise of the Birmingham police department.

It is true that the police have exercised a degree of discipline in handling the demonstrators. In this sense they have conducted themselves rather "nonviolently" in public. But for what purpose? To preserve the evil system of segregation. Over the past few years I have consistently preached that nonviolence demands that the means we use must be as pure as the ends we seek. I have tried to make clear that it is wrong to use immoral means to attain moral ends. But now I must affirm that it is just as wrong, or perhaps even more so, to use moral means to preserve immoral ends. Perhaps Mr. Connor and his policemen have been rather nonviolent in public, as was Chief Pritchett in Albany, Georgia, but they have used the moral means of nonviolence to maintain the immoral end of racial injustice. As T. S. Eliot has said: "The last temptation is the greatest treason: To do the right deed for the wrong reason."

I wish you had commended the Negro sit-inners and demonstrators of Birmingham for their sublime courage, their willingness to suffer and their amazing discipline in the midst of great provocation. One day the South will recognize its real heroes. They will be the James Merediths, with the noble sense of purpose that enables them to face jeering and hostile mobs, and with the agonizing loneliness that characterizes the life of the pioneer. They will be old, oppressed, battered Negro women, symbolized in a seventy-two-year-old woman in Montgomery, Alabama, who rose up with a sense of dignity and with her people decided not to ride segregated buses, and who responded with ungrammatical profundity to one who inquired about her weariness: "My feets is tired, but my soul is at rest." They will be the young high school and college students, the young ministers of the gospel and a host of their elders, courageously and nonviolently sitting in at lunch counters and willingly going to jail for conscience' sake. One day the South will know that when these disinherited children of God sat down at lunch counters, they were in reality standing up for what is best in the American dream and for the most sacred values in our Judaeo-Christian heritage, thereby bringing our nation back to those great wells of democracy which were dug deep by the founding fathers in their formulation of the Constitution and the Declaration of Independence.

Never before have I written so long a letter. I'm afraid it is much too long to take your precious time. I can assure you that it would have been much shorter if I had been writing from a comfortable desk, but what else can one do when he is alone in a narrow jail cell, other than write long letters, think long thoughts and pray long prayers?

If I have said anything in this letter that overstates the truth and indicates an unreasonable impatience, I beg you to forgive me. If I have said anything that understates the truth and indicates my having a patience that allows me to settle for anything less than brotherhood, I beg God to forgive me.

I hope this letter finds you strong in the faith. I also hope that circumstances will soon make it possible for me to meet each of you, not as an integrationist or a civil-rights leader but as a fellow clergyman and a Christian brother. Let us all hope that the dark clouds of racial prejudice will soon pass away and the deep fog of misunderstanding will be lifted from our fear-drenched communities, and in some not too distant tomorrow the radiant stars of love and brotherhood will shine over our great nation with all their scintillating beauty.

Yours for the cause of Peace and Brotherhood,
MARTIN LUTHER KING, JR.

For Discussion

1. According to King, when is a law unjust?
2. What is King's implicit definition of anarchy?
3. To what extent does King's letter reflect the spirit of the black people today? Which specific examples of discrimination are still valid?
4. How is King's letter similar to the Declaration of Independence? Consider both the assumptions about the nature of man and the development of the argument.
5. Explain the difference between an "I-it" and an "I-thou" relationship. Suggest other examples of "I-it" relationships in current society.
6. What is King's purpose in comparing the civil rights movement to early Christian agitation?
7. How does King universalize the Negro struggle?
8. What does King say about the moral relationship between means and ends?
9. In what important respects does King agree with Gandhi? With Thoreau?
10. What qualities that made Martin Luther King, Jr., a leader of his people are reflected in this letter?
11. Compare the style of the final paragraph to that of Baldwin's final paragraph in "My Dungeon Shook."
12. King's voice is reflective because he is personally involved in exploring his own thoughts. However, one might argue that he is also discursive. **Why?**

HUNTER S. THOMPSON

Conclusion to Hell's Angels

Hunter Thompson's first popular success, *Hell's Angels*, from which this selection is the concluding chapter, was the result of more than a year of close association with the outlaw motorcycle gangs of California. Thompson has since written exposés: *Fear and Loathing in Las Vegas* and *Fear and Loathing on the Campaign Trail.* He is currently Washington correspondent for *Rolling Stone*, a counterculture magazine.

> He who makes a beast of himself gets rid of the pain of being a man. —DR. JOHNSON

> The neighborhood suddenly exploded with excited, morbid crowds. Hysterical women surged forward in a frenzy, screeching in almost sexual ecstasy, scratching and fighting the agents and police in their attempt to reach the body. One fat-breasted woman with stringy red hair broke through the cordon and dipped her handkerchief in the blood, clutched it to her sweaty dress and waddled off down the street . . .
> —From an account of the death of John Dillinger

Toward Christmas the action slowed down and the Angels dropped out of the headlines. Tiny lost his job, Sonny got involved in a long jury trial on the attempted-murder charge,[1] and the El Adobe was demolished by the wrecker's ball. The Angels drifted from one bar to another, but they found it harder to establish a hangout than to maintain one. In San

---

[1] Which ended with a hung jury and eventual reduction of the charge to "assault with a deadly weapon"—to which Barger pleaded guilty and served six months in jail.

Francisco it was just as slow. Frenchy spent three months in General Hospital when a can of gasoline blew up on him, and Puff went to jail after a fracas with two cops who raided an Angel birthday party. Winter is always slow for the outlaws. Many have to go to work to stay eligible for next summer's unemployment insurance, it is too cold for big outdoor parties, and the constant rain makes riding an uncomfortable hazard.

It seemed like a good time to get some work done, so I dropped off the circuit. Terry came by now and then to keep me posted. One day he showed up with a broken arm, saying he'd wrecked his bike, his old lady had left him and the niggers had blown up his house. I'd heard about the house from Barger's wife, Elsie, who was handling the communications post at their home in Oakland. During one of the sporadic flare-ups between the Hell's Angels and the Oakland Negroes somebody had thrown a home-made bomb through the window of the house that Terry was renting in East Oakland. The fire destroyed the house and all of Marilyn's paintings. She was a pretty little girl about nineteen, with long blond hair and a respectable family in one of the valley towns. She'd been living with Terry for nearly six months, covering the walls with her artwork, but she had no stomach for bombs. The divorce was effected soon after they moved to another dwelling. "I came back one night and she was gone," said Terry. "All she left was a note: 'Dear Terry, Fuck it.'" And that was that.

Nothing else happened until January, when Mother Miles got snuffed. He was riding his bike through Berkeley when a truck came out of a side street and hit him head on, breaking both legs and fracturing his skull. He hung in a coma for six days, then died on a Sunday morning, less than twenty-four hours before his thirtieth birthday—leaving a wife, two children and his righteous girl friend, Ann.

Miles had been president of the Sacramento chapter. His influence was so great that in 1965 he moved the whole club down to Oakland, claiming the police had made life intolerable for them by constant harassment. The outlaws simply picked up and moved, not questioning Miles' wisdom. His real name was James, but the Angels called him Mother.

"I guess it was because he was kind of motherly," said Gut. "Miles was great, great people. He took care of everybody. He worried. You could always depend on him."

I knew Miles in a distant kind of way. He didn't trust writers, but there was nothing mean about him, and once he decided I wasn't going to get him locked up somehow, he was friendly. He had the build of a pot-bellied stevedore, with a round face and a wide, flaring beard. I never thought of him as a hoodlum. He had the usual Hell's Angel police record: drunk, disorderly, fighting, vagrancy, loitering, petty larceny and a handful of ominous "suspicion of" charges that had never gone to trial.

But he wasn't plagued by the same demons that motivate some of the others. He wasn't happy with the world, but he didn't brood about it, and his appetite for revenge didn't extend beyond specific wrongs done to the Angels or to him personally. You could drink with Miles without wondering when he was going to swing on somebody or lift your money off the bar. He wasn't that way. Booze seemed to make him more genial. Like most of the Angels' leaders, he had a quick mind and a quality of self-control which the others relied on.

When I heard he'd been killed I called Sonny to ask about the funeral, but by the time I finally got hold of him the details were already on the radio and in the newspapers. Miles' mother was arranging for the funeral in Sacramento. The outlaw caravan would form at Barger's house at eleven on Thursday morning. The Angels have gone to plenty of funerals for their own people, but until this one they had never tried to run the procession for ninety miles along a major highway. There was also a chance that the Sacramento police would try to keep them out of town.

The word went out on Monday and Tuesday by telephone. This was not going to be any Jay Gatsby funeral; the Angels wanted a full-dress rally. Miles' status was not the point; the death of any Angel requires a show of strength by the others. It is a form of affirmation—not for the dead, but the living. There are no set penalties for not showing up, because none are necessary. In the cheap loneliness that is the overriding fact of every outlaw's life, a funeral is a bleak reminder that the tribe is smaller by one. The circle is one link shorter, the enemy jacks up the odds just a little bit more, and defenders of the faith need something to take off the chill. A funeral is a time for counting the loyal, for seeing how many are left. There is no question about skipping work, going without sleep or riding for hours in a cold wind to be there on time.

Early Thursday morning the bikes began arriving in Oakland. Most of the outlaws were already in the Bay Area, or at least within fifty or sixty miles, but a handful of Satan's Slaves rode all of Wednesday night, five hundred miles from Los Angeles, to join the main caravan. Others came from Fresno and San Jose and Santa Rosa. There were Hangmen, Misfits, Presidents, Nightriders, Crossmen and some with no colors at all. A hard-faced little man whom nobody spoke to wore an olive-drab bombardier's jacket with just the word "Loner" on the back, written in small, blue-inked letters that looked like a signature.

I was crossing the Bay Bridge when a dozen Gypsy Jokers came roaring past, ignoring the speed limit as they split up to go around me on both sides of the car. Seconds later they disappeared up ahead in the fog. The morning was cold and bridge traffic was slow except for motorcycles. Down in the Bay there were freighters lined up, waiting for open piers.

The procession rolled at exactly eleven—a hundred and fifty bikes and about twenty cars. A few miles north of Oakland, at the Carquinez Bridge, the outlaws picked up a police escort assigned to keep them under control. A Highway Patrol car led the caravan all the way to Sacramento. The lead Angels rode two abreast in the right lane, holding a steady sixty-five miles an hour. At the head, with Barger, was the scruffy Praetorian Guard: Magoo, Tommy, Jimmy, Skip, Tiny, Zorro, Terry and Charger Charley the Child Molester. The spectacle disrupted traffic all along the way. It looked like something from another world. Here was the "scum of the earth," the "lowest form of animals," an army of unwashed gang rapists . . . being escorted toward the state capital by a Highway Patrol car with a flashing yellow light. The steady pace of the procession made it unnaturally solemn. Not even Senator Murphy could have mistaken it for a dangerous run. There were the same bearded faces; the same earrings, emblems, swastikas and grinning death's-heads flapping in the wind—but this time there were no party clothes, no hamming it up for the squares. They were still playing the role, but all the humor was missing. The only trouble en route came when the procession was halted after a filling-station owner complained that somebody had stolen fourteen quarts of oil at the last gas stop. Barger quickly took up a collection to pay the man off, muttering that whoever stole the oil was due for a chainwhipping later on. The Angels assured each other that it must have been a punk in one of the cars at the rear of the caravan, some shithead without any class.

In Sacramento there was no sign of harassment. Hundreds of curious spectators lined the route between the funeral home and the cemetery. Inside the chapel a handful of Jim Miles' childhood friends and relatives waited with his body, a hired minister and three nervous attendants. They knew what was coming—Mother Miles' "people," hundreds of thugs, wild brawlers and bizarre-looking girls in tight Levis, scarves and waist-length platinum-colored wigs. Miles' mother, a heavy middle-aged woman in a black suit, wept quietly in a front pew, facing the open casket.

At one-thirty the outlaw caravan arrived. The slow rumble of motorcycle engines rattled glass in the mortuary windows. Police tried to keep traffic moving as TV cameras followed Barger and perhaps a hundred others toward the door of the chapel. Many outlaws waited outside during the service. They stood in quiet groups, leaning against the bikes and killing time with lazy conversation. There was hardly any talk about Miles. In one group a pint of whiskey made the rounds. Some of the outlaws talked to bystanders, trying to explain what was happening. "Yeah, the guy was one of our leaders," said an Angel to an elderly man in a baseball cap. "He was good people. Some punk ran a stop sign and snuffed him. We came to bury him with the colors."

Inside the pine-paneled chapel the minister was telling his weird congregation that "the wages of sin is death." He looked like a Norman Rockwell druggist and was obviously repelled by the whole scene. Not all the pews were full, but standing room in the rear was crowded all the way back to the door. The minister talked about "sin" and "justification," pausing now and then as if he expected a rebuttal from the crowd. "It's not my business to pass judgment on anybody," he continued. "Nor is it my business to eulogize anybody. But it *is* my business to speak out a warning that *it will happen to you!* I don't know what philosophy some of you have about death, but I know the Scriptures tell us that God takes no pleasure in the death of the wicked . . . Jesus didn't die for an animal, he died for a man . . . What I say about Jim won't change anything, but I can preach the gospel to you and I have a responsibility to warn you that you will all have to *answer to God!*"

The crowd was shifting and sweating. The chapel was so hot that it seemed like the Devil was waiting in one of the anterooms, ready to claim the wicked just as soon as the sermon was over.

"How many of you—" asked the minster, "how many of you asked yourselves on the way up here, *'Who is next?'* "

At this point several Angels in the pews rose and walked out, cursing quietly at a way of life they had long ago left behind. The minister ignored these mutinous signs and launched into a story about a Philippian jailer. "Holy shit!" mumbled Tiny. He'd been standing quietly in the rear for about thirty minutes, pouring sweat and eying the minister as if he meant to hunt him down later in the day and extract all his teeth. Tiny's departure caused five or six others to leave. The minister sensed he was losing his audience, so he brought the Philippian story to a quick end.

There was no music as the crowd filed out. I passed by the casket and was shocked to see Mother Miles clean-shaven, lying peacefully on his back in a blue suit, white shirt and a wide maroon tie. His Hell's Angels jacket, covered with exotic emblems, was mounted on a stand at the foot of the casket. Behind it were thirteen wreaths, some bearing names of other outlaw clubs.

I barely recognized Miles. He looked younger than twenty-nine and very ordinary. But his face was calm, as though he were not at all surprised to find himself there in a box. He wouldn't have liked the clothes he was wearing, but since the Angels weren't paying for the funeral, the best they could do was make sure the colors went into the casket before it was sealed. Barger stayed behind with the pallbearers to make sure the thing was done right.

After the funeral more than two hundred motorcycles followed the hearse to the cemetery. Behind the Angels rode all the other clubs, including a half dozen East Bay Dragons—and, according to a radio commentator, "dozens of teen-age riders who looked so solemn that you'd think Robin Hood had just died."

The Hell's Angels knew better. Not all of them had read about Robin Hood, but they understood that the parallel was complimentary. Perhaps the younger outlaws believed it, but there is room in their margin for one or two friendly illusions. Those who are almost thirty, or more than that, have been living too long with their own scurvy image to think of themselves as heroes. They understand that heroes are always "good guys," and they have seen enough cowboy movies to know that good guys win in the end. The myth didn't seem to include Miles, who was "one of the best." But all he got in the end was two broken legs, a smashed head and a tongue-lashing from the preacher. Only his Hell's Angels identity kept him from going to the grave as anonymously as any ribbon clerk. As it was, his funeral got nationwide press coverage: *Life* had a picture of the procession entering the cemetery, TV newscasts gave the funeral a solemn priority, and the *Chronicle* headline said: HELL'S ANGELS BURY THEIR OWN—BLACK JACKETS AND AN ODD DIGNITY. Mother Miles would have been pleased.

Moments after the burial the caravan was escorted out of town by a phalanx of police cars, with sirens howling. The brief truce was ended. At the city limits the Angels screwed it on and roared back to Richmond, across the Bay from San Francisco, where they held an all-night wake that kept police on edge until long after dawn. On Sunday night there was a meeting in Oakland to confirm Miles' successor, Big Al. It was a quiet affair, but without the grimness of the funeral. The banshee's wail that had seemed so loud on Thursday was already fading away. After the meeting there was a beer party at the Sinners Club, and by the time the place closed they had already set the date for the next run. The Angels would gather in Bakersfield, on the first day of spring.

All my life my heart has sought a thing I cannot name.
—Remembered line from a long-forgotten poem

Months later, when I rarely saw the Angels, I still had the legacy of the big machine—four hundred pounds of chrome and deep red noise to take out on the Coast Highway and cut loose at three in the morning, when all the cops were lurking over on 101. My first crash had wrecked the bike completely and it took several months to have it rebuilt. After that I decided to ride it differently: I would stop pushing my luck on curves, always wear a helmet and try to keep within range of the nearest speed limit . . . my insurance had already been canceled and my driver's license was hanging by a thread.

So it was always at night, like a werewolf, that I would take the thing out for an honest run down the coast. I would start in Golden Gate Park, thinking only to run a few long curves to clear my head . . . but in a matter of minutes I'd be out at the beach with the sound of the engine in my ears, the surf booming up on the sea wall and a fine empty road stretching all the way down to Santa Cruz . . . not even a gas station in the whole seventy miles; the only public light along the way is an all-night diner down around Rockaway Beach.

There was no helmet on those nights, no speed limit, and no cooling it down on the curves. The momentary freedom of the park was like the one unlucky drink that shoves a wavering alcoholic off the wagon. I would come out of the park near the soccer field and pause for a moment at the stop sign, wondering if I knew anyone parked out there on the midnight humping strip.

Then into first gear, forgetting the cars and letting the beast wind out . . . thirty-five, forty-five . . . then into second and wailing through the light at Lincoln Way, not worried about green or red signals, but only some other werewolf loony who might be pulling out, too slowly, to start his own run. Not many of these . . . and with three lanes on a wide curve, a bike coming hard has plenty of room to get around almost any-thing . . . then into third, the boomer gear, pushing seventy-five and the beginning of a windscream in the ears, a pressure on the eyeballs like diving into water off a high board.

Bent forward, far back on the seat, and a rigid grip on the handlebars as the bike starts jumping and wavering in the wind. Taillights far up ahead coming closer, faster, and suddenly—zaaapppp—going past and leaning down for a curve near the zoo, where the road swings out to sea.

The dunes are flatter here, and on windy days sand blows across the highway, piling up in thick drifts as deadly as any oil-slick . . . instant loss of control, a crashing, cartwheeling slide and maybe one of those two-inch notices in the paper the next day: "An unidentified motorcyclist was killed last night when he failed to negotiate a turn on Highway I."

Indeed . . . but no sand this time, so the lever goes up into fourth, and now there's no sound except wind. Screw it all the way over, reach through the handlebars to raise the headlight beam, the needle leans down on a hundred, and wind-burned eyeballs strain to see down the centerline, trying to provide a margin for the reflexes.

But with the throttle screwed on there is only the barest margin, and no room at all for mistakes. It has to be done right . . . and that's when the strange music starts, when you stretch your luck so far that fear becomes exhilaration and vibrates along your arms. You can barely see at a hundred; the tears blow back so fast that they vaporize before they get to your ears. The only sounds are wind and a dull roar floating back from the mufflers. You watch the white line and try to lean with it . . . howling through a turn to the right, then to the left and down the long hill to Pacifica . . . letting off now, watching for cops, but only until the next dark stretch and another few seconds on the edge . . . The Edge . . . There is no honest way to explain it because the only people who really know where it is are the ones who have gone over. The others—the living —are those who pushed their control as far as they felt they could handle it, and then pulled back, or slowed down, or did whatever they had to when it came time to choose between Now and Later.

But the edge is still Out there. Or maybe it's In. The association of motorcycles with LSD is no accident of publicity. They are both a means to an end, to the place of definitions.

For Discussion

1. Characterize the mode of life portrayed in the first two-thirds of this selection.
2. What qualities of Miles are typical of the Angels? Why are they admired?
3. How does the funeral dramatize the Angels as dissenters?
4. How does the image of the Angels which Thompson projects differ from that usually presented by the news media?
5. What makes the description of the ride to Sacramento vivid?
6. Discuss the relevance of the three epigraphs.
7. What is Thompson's feeling in the final episode? How does it relate to what has gone before?
8. What is "the edge"? What does it say about Hell's Angels?
9. In what way does this selection express dissent? How does it differ from others in the book?

LAWRENCE FERLINGHETTI

Prison Diary

Lawrence Ferlinghetti, born in Paris in 1920, is best known as a poet. He is also a painter, translator, publisher, and founder of the City Lights Bookstore in San Francisco, the first all-paperback bookstore in the United States. He currently heads City Lights Publications, an avant garde press. The following piece, originally titled "Santa Rita Journal," was written after his arrest for taking part in an antiwar protest at the Oakland Induction Center in 1967.

Santa Rita Rehabilitation Center, January 4, 1968—What are we doing here in this dank tank? Probing the limits of legitimate political dissent in this unenlightened country? Nonviolent gesture of blocking the entrance to war at Oakland Army Induction Center hereby judged beyond that limit. Rehabilitate us, please. . . . First rough impressions of anybody's first time in jail: suddenly realizing what "incarcerated" really means. Paranoid fear of the unknown, fear of not knowing what's going to happen to your body, fear of getting thrown in The Hole. . . . Routine of being booked, fingerprinted, mugged, shunted from bullpen to bullpen itself a shock for any "first offender." . . . Naive vestigial illusions about the inherent goodness of man fly out the barred window. . . . From Oakland jail, shunted through a series of sealed boxes, the first on wheels—long gray bus, windows blinded, 50 inmates behind locked grate, the freeway where yesterday we rode free now visible only through holes in grate. . . . Prison sighted half hour later on a forlorn plain at Pleasanton. . . . Barbed wire fences and watchtowers. Poor man's concentration camp? . . . Shunted through another series of holding cells, several more hours of not knowing one's immediate fate, just as likely you'll be put in "Graystone" maximum security pen as in General Compound. . . . I take the easier way out: I don't refuse to shave or work. Reforming the prison system is another issue. Rather have a pen than a beard (and so keep this journal). Pen mightier than beard. Opportunity to infiltrate general prison population with nonviolent ideas? Another naive liberal illusion!

The prison is about two-thirds black, and the other third is Mexican, Pachuco and white North American. They've got their own problems and their own enemies, and they've no use for "nonviolence." The jungle is full of felons and, as for the war, most of them have the attitudes of their jailers and think what we're doing in Vietnam is great, violence being one way of life they fully understand. This sure deflates the myth promoted by Our President equating anti-war demonstrations with "crime in the streets" and with ghetto wars. If there were any blacks busted this time at the Oakland Induction Center, I didn't see them. (And if I were black, in Oakland, I'd stay away too.) . . .

January 5—There's not a political prisoner in my barracks. The most "uncooperative" of the demonstrators are in Graystone, two in a cell or in The Hole on bread and skimmed milk. A larger group is in Compound 8 with no privileges and a meal-and-a-half a day. A little incident happened today when they were marching back from the mess hall. The last in the line suddenly went limp and sat down in the middle of the Compound street. He was a kid of about 20 with medium-long hair he'd refused to cut. One officer ran up to him and tried to make him get up. He would not. The officer made a signal and four other officers wearing black leather gloves came at the double up the center of the street from the gate. They had no guns or night sticks. Each took an arm or a leg of the boy and started dragging him. He was a big kid, and they couldn't get his tail off the ground. They got him out of sight in a hurry. When I got back to barracks, someone had an Oakland Tribune with a photo of four Marines carrying a dead Marine buddy away from a Vietnam battle-field in the same style. . . .

January 6—I told them I had printing experience, and they put me stencilling pants! "Santa Rita" in pure white on every pair. "Gives us something to aim at!" the deputy told me, laughing, sighting his fingers at the stencil marks. Very funny. Holy prison, named for a Spanish saint. . . . Goya should have seen a place like this. He did, he did. Goya faces in the morning chowline, a thousand of them sticking out of blue denims, out of Goya's "Disasters of War." These are the disasters of peace. Down rows and rows of long wooden tables, half of skid row mixed with Oakland ghettos and the backwash of various nearby penitentiaries, long-term cons now here hung up on short-term crimes—petty boosters, bad check artists, child molesters, freeway drag-racers, car thieves, armed robbers, mail frauds, sex-freaks, winos, hypes, pushers, you name it. And political prisoners. . . . Sit swine-like at the trough, gobbling the chow from metal trays. Great place to keep from getting too refined; dig these myriad beat faces. . . . Here comes "Orfeo"—very handsome young Negro dude with a fine great black beard. Walked out of a Genet prison novel. Just stood there smiling like a black angel without wings when they told him to shave or get thrown in The Hole. They came back later and took him away. Now he shows up again in the mess hall, looking as wild and gentle as ever. I believe he is truly mad and they know it. I don't believe he understood anything they told him. They let him keep his beard. He'll fly away over the rooftops one day, to a shack on a hillside above Rio and live with a beautiful mulatto and tend goats, blowing a wreathed horn. And the horn full of grass. . . .

Another face in the gallery across the table from me: enormous ragged gray head, with hogshead snout, on a 200-pound body in ragged jeans. Great hams of white hands. But the face, the face: white stubble from shaggy hair to throat, rum-pot eyes. Small pig-eyes, but not mean looking. Just dumb and staring. This is what has become of "The Man with the Hoe." Long, heavy jaw with great, protruding rows of white teeth. Grunted and snuffled as he slurped his pancakes. When he called for the coffee pitcher, his voice came out in a thin squeal. Man, what have you done to this man? Man, who made you like that? Man, has Mother ever seen you, seen what has become of you? Man, you still alive inside? (I hear your stentor breath.) Man, are you to be born again? Live again, love again? Man. Who is there to redeem you. Fidel Castro? The true revolutionary, Fidel said, is one whose first concern is the *redemption* of mankind. . . . Faces fallen out of wombs somewhere, long ago. Now rolled down streets and come to rest among writhing bodies in a painting by Bosch, Garden of Paradise. . . . Feed and shuffle out, doubles of models Goya used in a Toledo madhouse. "By Graystone's foetid walls." . . . One doesn't eat here to consume food; one eats to consume time. And time is life. . . .

January 7—Sunday in the Compound, and "religious services": let them explain away the existence of evil here. The older one gets, the more one learns to believe in the very real existence of evil. This place proves it. The making of criminals. The redemption of mankind? The rehabilitation of man? They put 19-year-old Judith Bloomberg and Joan Baez on bread and milk for three days. (On the men's side, Gary Lisman fasted for 12 days.) These kids are the greatest. They are busted for disturbing the "peace" and are hauled away. They plead *nolo contendere.* They do not wish to contend. They are telling their elders they can have it. They are telling the Establishment that they want nothing to do with its power structure and refuse even to dispute the legal terms of that evil. . . . As long as there are guns, they will shoot, telescopically. . . . At the weekly movie tonight, the inmates spy Joan Baez through a crack in the curtain hiding the balcony where the women prisoners sit. A hundred felons turn and raise their hands in the Peace Sign and shout, "We love you, Joan!"

January 8—The Enormous Room of my barracks: a black inmate is reading "Synanon" (the place is full of junkies). He doesn't realize what an elite place Synanon may be. Diedrich, the founder, must have read Hermann Hesse's *Magister Ludi* (the Bead Game) and seized upon the conception of an elite world-within-a-world depicted by Hesse in Germany—Castallia being the name of the German intellectual elite created to govern society, with its own special *esprit de corps*, its own hierarchy, its own pecking order—a self-contained world of its own—Synanon also having developed its own cadre of first leaders framed on the wall, approval and status in its society dependent on length of residence, etc., the drug user rejected by the outside straight world here able to reject that society himself in favor of Synanon's own hierarchy: the Bead Game on its own level. And the prison system with its own Bead Game. . . . Shigeyoshi Murao comes to see me during visiting hours and tells me it looks just like the prisoner of war camps they kept Nisei in during World War Two.

January 9—Obscenity: violation of the Penal Code: today in the Commissary line when I tried to exchange a word with Dr. Lee Rather (a political prisoner), Officer Dykes hollered at me: "Get your fucking ass out of here, you motherfucker!"

January 10—Back in the barracks, the sealed life goes on. We are on some blind ship, all portholes sealed. Siren sounds and loudspeaker barks. Up for the count. Then down again, felon shipmates stretched in their bunks, staring at the overhead. . . . You spend a lot of time staring at nothing in a place like this. Great place to develop the Tragic Sense of Life. "Lucy in the Sky with Diamonds" comes over the barracks radio, and I picture myself in a boat on a river, where newspaper taxis await on the shore, waiting to take me away. . . .

January 11—Awakened at exactly three A.M. by a guard with a flashlight and told to get up and stand by my bunk. "You're going to court today." From three to eight A.M. I wait in a bullpen with over 50 other inmates going to court. The cell is 20' by 15', and over half the inmates have to stand up all the time. I talk to one black felon who has been gotten up like this three days in a row, and if he wants to fight his case this is the way he can do it. . . . Life goes on at Santa Rita. Or death. . . . I got the Santa Rita blues. . . .

Afterthoughts and vituperations: Really realize how a hole like this literally makes criminals: 18-year-old first-offender thrown in for disturbing society's deep sleep now making his first hard connection with hard drugs (they are shooting it up in the john!) and enforced homo-sexuality (bend over, buddy!). . . .

Guards with hard-edge voices careful not to show any human feelings for inmates, on the watch for the slightest lack of obsequiousness on the part of prisoners, now and then goading them a bit with a choice obscenity . . . a slip of the tongue in return, and you're in The Hole with your tongue hanging out. . . .

Plus mail officers with German names withholding mail and books at will, first class letters opened and censored. . . . Working in the mailroom I note two books (sent directly to an inmate from City Lights Bookstore) withheld: Debray's *Revolution in the Revolution?* and *Black Power*. . . . Burn, baby, burn—but in here, baby, it's you who'll be burning. . . . Later, when I am loose, I send *Gandhi on Non-Violence* to an inmate felon, and it comes back stamped "Unacceptable."

Unhappy Dehabilitation Center, man-made excrescence befouling the once-beautiful landscape in the shadow of distant Mount Diablo: Devil's mount!

If only revolution can blot out such scenes, let there be revolution; but not a revolution of hate leading in the end to just another super-state. . . .

For Discussion

1. Much of the power of this writing derives from personal observations of prison life. What images does Ferlinghetti present of buildings, food, other prisoners, guards? Describe the cumulative effect of these details.
2. The irony depends in part on a familiarity with some of Ferlinghetti's literary and artistic allusions. Which can you identify? Why are they ironic?
3. What other examples of irony can you find?
4. What do you know about Synanon? The Nisei in World War II?
5. Comment on the paragraph dealing with "the disasters of peace." How might this idea compare to Darrow's thesis (see "The Discursive NO")?
6. Ferlinghetti obliquely refers to himself as a "political prisoner." To what extent do you agree?
7. What unifying principle guided Ferlinghetti in his selection of details?
8. How does the fact that this is a journal influence Ferlinghetti's style and voice?

STEPHEN H. WILDSTROM

Mugged by Sheriffs: An Anecdote

Stephen H. Wildstrom, the 1968–1969 managing editor of the *Michigan Daily*, is now doing research in the field of police-community relations. In writing of his personal experience with the police, he focuses on a subject which drew national attention during the 1968 Democratic convention in Chicago and which has been of increasing public concern.

When I was growing up in a pleasant, tree-shaded part of near-suburban Detroit, I was taught that policemen are our friends. Once a year, friendly Sergeant somebody or another from the Youth Bureau would come to a school assembly with his trained dog to teach us how to cross streets safely and show us how friendly cops were. Like most middle-class kids, I believed the line.

It was in high school that I began to doubt. I saw Bull Connor's cops do their stuff in Birmingham, but that was only on television and anyway the cops up North weren't like that. Then in the summer of 1967, I was a wire service reporter during the Detroit riot and I got a first-hand look at cops unleashed. I began to think maybe the talk I'd heard about police brutality was more than just rhetoric. My negative view of police was reinforced when I saw the Detroit police mount a cavalry charge into a group of unarmed, peaceful members of the Poor People's March last spring.

But it took the Washtenaw County (Michigan) sheriff's department to bring it all home.

In September 1968 a group of welfare mothers staged a series of

Reprinted by permission of *Dissent* Magazine and the author.

demonstrations at the County Building to protest Aid to Dependent Children payments which were insufficient to buy their children school clothes. The demonstrations culminated in the arrest of more than 200 mothers and University of Michigan students. As managing editor of the *Michigan Daily*, I went over to the County Building on the second day of the protest to complain to the sheriff about the continued harassment of our reporters by his deputies.

I walked up to the door and found it guarded by a group of helmeted deputies, the same cops who had given me a hard time the day before. When I attempted to open the door, I was told I couldn't go in. I explained who I was and what I wanted and asked why a person could not enter a public building during normal business hours. "You can't go in," they repeated. When I tried to argue the point further, I was jumped from behind by one of the deputies, pushed face down against the concrete pavement, and generally beaten.

When they felt I had been adequately pummeled, I was handcuffed and dragged over to the jail. After a couple of hours, I was set free on bond of $25, waiting arraignment that will probably never come, on a charge of assault and battery that would be funny if someone else were the defendant.

Though I've never been a victim of a mugging—crime in the streets variety—I imagine it is a terrifying experience. But to receive the equivalent of a mugging at the hands of a duly deputized law officer is probably the most terrifying experience in modern American society.

There is no situation in which a citizen can feel more helpless than when a man with a badge lands a solid blow to his stomach, and another pushes his face into a concrete curbstone. At least when attacked by a civilian mugger, you can make an effort to fight back. To do so against a cop is to invite a charge of resisting arrest or, in most states, of assaulting an officer, which is a felony.

The incident at the County Building cost me two nights of sleep and a couple of weeks of soreness. Slowly, the terror gave way to anger—anger which turned to rage as I discovered that I had virtually no legal recourse. I decided to throw the book at the cops who beat me, but that book turned out to be exceedingly thin.

I was lucky to know the name of the ringleader of the group of deputies and to have had a good enough look at the others to identify one or two on sight. It seemed the first thing to do was to file criminal assault charges against the deputies. Naively, I filed such a complaint with the city police; it disappeared into a bureaucratic morass. Relations between the city police and the sheriff's department are none too good in Ann Arbor, but a cop is a cop and they don't like stepping on one another's jurisdictions. A citizen can't bring a complaint against another unless a State's attorney issues a warrant. So much for that angle.

Next, I was going to file a civil suit for false arrest and damages. But I was informed that no one in recent memory had won a false arrest suit in this county, and that even if I won the case legal fees would far exceed anything I could hope to collect in damages.

Finally, there is a state statute which makes it a felony to commit a legal act in an illegal manner and an obscure 19th-century federal civil rights law which makes it a misdemeanor to conspire to deprive a citizen of civil rights under color of law without due process. But conspiracy was well-nigh impossible to establish in this case, and going through the Justice Department on the federal charge seemed of very limited utility.

So here I am, still raging and still without redress. About the best I can hope for at this point is to get the still pending criminal charge against me dropped and my arrest records destroyed, thus clearing my record.

A current theory has it that urban blacks have suffered so much for so long at the hands of city cops because they are ignorant of their rights. The truth is much simpler: the citizen doesn't have any viable rights in such cases. As a white middle-class student with some background in the law, I was no better able to obtain redress than a 16-year-old black kid roughed up by cops in the ghetto.

American society will never be peaceful so long as significant portions of that society are systematically terrorized by the police. There will be no peace because, as blacks have learned and students are learning, the cops are above the law, and the only satisfying way to respond to their violence is with violence of one's own. And no matter what kind of pronouncements come down from the police brass, the terror will continue as long as individual cops are immune from attempts by citizens to make them responsible for their acts. Despite the assertions of commissioners, chiefs and mayors, police departments have proved themselves to be at best unable, and at worst unwilling, to discipline their own.

The only hope is true civilian community control of the police. Not just a police review board but a community control board which would hire and fire officers and which would have full disciplinary powers. Considering the powerful vested interests of the cops and the widespread belief in the white community that the cops are always right, that day will be a long time coming.

For Discussion

1. Characterize the speaker. Why is his identity important?
2. Enumerate the legal courses of action open to Wildstrom after the mugging and evaluate his decisions concerning them.
3. What conditions does Wildstrom stipulate for a peaceful society? What evidence can you offer that some of these conditions are being met?
4. Comment on Wildstrom's recommendation for a "community control board."
5. What do you think has caused such widespread publicity of police brutality?
6. Wildstrom tells his story in order to argue inductively. How valid is his conclusion?
7. Discuss the effect of Wildstrom's use of narrative to argue his point.

GLORIA EMERSON

Getting Back

A *New York Times* correspondent in Vietnam for twenty-five months, Gloria Emerson was awarded the 1970 George Polk Memorial Award for Achievement in Foreign Reporting. In highly charged and frequently moving accounts, she had personalized the war, making the American reading public aware of its horrors and its poignancy. Upon her return she wrote the following essay, which focuses on the responses of Americans at home to the Indochina war. A Fellow of the Institute of Politics, John F. Kennedy School of Government at Harvard, she is a contributor to such magazines as *Harper's* and *Esquire.*

New York: So far I have seen no one here weeping, or crying out for help. Not a single person has crept up to me in the streets, holding out his hands for money. There are no children playing on the pavements. The city appears exhausted and more gentle. It is quieter than Saigon and there is no barbed wire at all. New York is very vacant at night, people obey an unannounced curfew. Because there are no Vietnamese around, American men look smaller to me, and their bones less huge, but everyone appears more sickly than I remembered.

When a taxi driver first said to me, "Have a nice day," I thought he sensed what a sad and scrambled presence sat in his backseat. Not at all. Others who have never looked at me pick up this odd litany and everywhere—even blown up on the chests of small boys in T-shirts—is that mocking empty yellow face reminding us to smile and enjoy.

At a party on Seventy-second Street, a man notices the G.I. watch on my wrist which I bought in Saigon on the black market. On the back of the watch are the words: "wrist watch nonmaintanable." They always pleased me. He asks if he can buy one at Hunting World. I advise him to go to Fort Dix and raise his right hand. He moves away.

Reprinted by permission of International Famous Agency. First appeared in *Esquire* Magazine. Copyright © 1973 by Gloria Emerson.

I have always had the reputation of being a nervous kind of woman. Nonmaintanable.

New York: No one else is uneasy about forgetting the names of fire support bases in Vietnam. I used to recite them in alphabetical order, lacking worry beads and remembering no poetry or interesting prayers. There were lots of B's: Bastogne, Beverly, Birmingham, Brown, Bruiser, Buttons. My favorite names were Fire Bases Siberia, Schwartz, Uplift and Love. And there was even a fire base called Lonely. A rather stupid American company commander once wanted to name a fire base after Nixon. It would have been overrun in one day. So he was persuaded to name it after his wife instead.

A long time ago I didn't know a fire base was for artillery. I thought it was where soldiers put out fires.

Walking by Bloomingdale's—hoping to remember what it was I should have wanted to buy—I found a group of blacks trying to raise money for a drug rehabilitation center. They are shaking tin cans in front of women whose minds were on towels and bathing suits. One black is watching it all, with the air of an unhopeful adviser. I know where he has been. Yes, he says, he was in Vietnam. Pleiku 1966. Six entire years ago, six springs behind us. He is surprised I know the names: Pleiku, Kontum, Dak To, Ben Het.

Wow, he says. Wow, I say. Those names.

"I didn't mind Pleiku much," he tells me. I tell him how for the last three years in Vietnam the G.I.'s wrote F.T.A.—Fuck the Army—on their helmets. He says he never saw any of that stuff on television. I swear it was so.

A loud upper-class braying interrupts us. It is recognition from a friend—a female Peabody—who is pushing her elderly, handsome mother in a wheelchair. The old woman looks at the blacks shaking their cans, and mumbling to the shoppers.

You are back, the friend shouts. The man of Pleiku 1966 backs off and I cannot hold him any longer. I agree that I am back. I am told how well I look—a tiny bit too thin perhaps, but I was never plump. We laugh at that. The friend tells me her mother is like Lazarus, quite able to rise and walk if she so wishes. The mother remembers me, understands that I have been gone for two years.

"How did you like living in Bangkok?" she asks.

New York: If you have been in Vietnam for a long time, start talking to yourself. No one has been paying attention to the war. Yes, yes, it is dreadful, they say. A horrible mistake. Some people ask me questions, mostly women. "What did you eat?" and "What did you wear?" they say. A very pleasant woman—whose eyes fill up easily with tears—wants to know what I wore to officers' dances. (American men have always kept silent on wars so women know nothing.)

And what many people want to know, and try delicately to find out, is did I ever get close enough to the fighting to see (italics) real dead (unitalics). Real white dead, of course. It is no good at all trying to describe it to them. How brave of you, they say.

It costs twenty-two dollars to have my hair washed in a place on Sixty-fifth Street where the water is very hot. I do not know why, except Mrs. Paley comes here too, but she is washed in a private room. Under the dryer I write letters to friends in Saigon while the woman next to me skips over the stories of the seige of An Loc in *The New York Times*. Very Dear Luong, Wear a flak jacket. Don't go ahead and die without me there. Dear Craig Dear. Be careful of Highway Thirteen. Don't go on Route One. My Dear Tom and Hoa. My heart is with you, my heart is with you.

At the Radio City Post Office on the West Side, there is a little hand-lettered sign that says in red letters: "Smile. God Loves You." It is not out of the question that an old Army chaplain has run amok and is now lettering these commands. I ask the lady with the blonde waxy curls and silver eyelids to, please, tell me who made the sign.

"A man goes around doing them," she says.

I buy the stamps for my A.P.O. 96243 letters.

"He is told to do it," she adds. Neither of us is smiling. The letters to Saigon are stamped, and leave me.

Cambridge: Harvard Square slightly sickens me. So does the Yard. There are hundreds of young men. They remind me of their surrogates in Vietnam in 1970 and 1971. It is odd not to see the green combat fatigues that reminded me of laundry bags. But Harvard is not Long Binh or Chu Lai or Cam Ranh. Jane Fonda can come here and Bob Hope would be stoned.

Dear Mrs. Hobbs, I have been with the 1st of the 5th and seen your son John in Quang Tri on his track and he says please do not worry about him. (You were right to worry, Mrs. Hobbs, forgive me for lying to you.)

I move around Cambridge totally ill at ease, for I feel I am surrounded by cheats. Would Hobbs have liked it here?

But the memory of his long, thin face is held and clamped down and it is a fat boy in a Cambridge bookstore who makes me smile and lets me remember the G.I. who wanted to go through the war in his underpants. He was very tan except for his legs. And the tan was all he had to take home, the only proof that something normal had happened to him after all. I never knew what he did except unload choppers in a mean hot patch of land where the Vietnamese had left or been thrown away.

The boy really fretted about his tan. They wouldn't let him work without his pants.

"My legs look like milk bottles," he said.

On Mount Auburn Street I eat lunch with some students no older than Hobbs had been. They do not ask me questions about the war, or even about the Vietnamese. There is nothing left to tell. They talk to me about the war while I eat most of the sandwiches and no one notices a thing.

Cambridge to Concord: David has a tiny apartment with Lillian and its only failure is a cursed plant growing out of the helmet he wore in Vietnam for years.

It is a crooked and weary plant of a curious color, poisoned by its steel house. Lillian has made a tunafish salad and I hold it in my lap as we drive to Concord. Our picnic is in the graveyard where Emerson and Thoreau and Alcotts are buried. It is a splendid place whose stones were carefully, slowly put up in honor and love. No hasty work here. The Vietnamese put paper money, paper food, paper clothing and even paper bicycles on the Buddhist graves of their dead, hoping these gifts will help them in their heaven. I could leave a Kleenex on the grave of Emerson but decide against it.

It is our Thirty Years War: David and I talk about Vietnam as we never had time to do in Saigon or on helicopters or following armies. There is a light grey curse on all of us, we agree on this. I tell him that P.—who always seemed so unmoved by the war, and the ruin, and the futility—had told me a fearful story.

"It was in 1967, maybe 1966, and P. was flying a chopper over a fire-free zone when the door gunner saw two Vietnamese in a rice paddy."

Lillian is told that in Vietnam if you were a Vietnamese in the wrong place at the wrong time you were killed, and a fire-free zone meant only V.C. stayed in it.

"And P. who wore earphones heard the gunner and the pilot decide to go down and get the dinks, blow them away, and they were in a fine mood about it. But what really scared P.—he said it was the worst moment of the war, that he had never been so afraid of (italics) something (un-italics)—was when the chopper was almost on top of the two Vietnamese, and you know the wind it blows up, and the noise, and there was the gunner pointing his 50-caliber machine gun right at them, and P. saw that they wouldn't look up before they died. The gunner was angry when he saw long black streaks of hair down their backs—Christ, they were women—but P. saw how they could hardly keep standing up, were holding on to each other, and yet they never raised their heads."

David lay down to hide his face in the grass and Lillian is not sure she understands the point of it. She is older than the door gunner was, but she cannot picture it, any of it, and she had already heard so much.

"Lillian, they wouldn't look up," I heard myself repeating.

Houston: In the airport, waiting for the flight to New York, I count sixteen men carrying, not suitcases, but lumpy dark plastic bags so their plastic clothes will not wrinkle. An Airman First Class says he was in Vietnam and, feeling a loopy expansiveness, a need to find someone who will reassure me that what I saw was really there, we talk of the Phu Cat Air Force Base in Binh Dinh province. It looked like a chunk of suburban California with a 10,000-foot runway. The man is unmoved to learn that it has been turned over to the Vietnamese. Vietnam was something that happened to him but is not happening to him now. He never thinks about it, he says, or reads a story about it.

He wants to get up and buy a Coke, but I do not stop talking. I tell him how only a few months ago I went back to Phu Cat—a ghost base now—and that the Vietnamese commander had big problems maintaining such a huge, fancy place.

"And you know what he said—he said his biggest problem was keeping all that grass mowed," I said. "All that Air Force grass."

"I never did care for them people," the man said. "I hope we took the lawn mowers with us."

Philadelphia: My sister is a kind and gentle woman who forgives me my violence. She does not agree that I should keep up a sense of outrage about the war because she wants me to be calm and happy.

"That's a lot of shit," I say—all that Vietnam language in her kitchen. We have our fifth cup of coffee. I try to make her laugh by describing the sign on an American base in Vietnam. It said, "Will the last person to leave the tunnel please turn out the light?" She smiles to please me.

New York: I have a Zippo lighter from the *Constellation,* one of the aircraft carriers whose pilots used to bomb North Vietnam. Denis gave it to me as a good-bye present. It is a strange gift for I choose never to go on the carriers, never to talk to the pilots.

The Zippo is engraved with the words of an A-1 pilot flying over North Vietnam on February 19, 1971, as he tried to find out whether a downed U.S. crew was still alive, still there.

"Give me voice or give me beeper," the pilot kept saying in a flat tired voice from a corner of Kansas. Denis heard him.

There may be no other sentence in our language that cuts me as much. A man could say it to his wife at breakfast. I could write it to Charles whom I have not seen in twelve years. It only means: "Tell me if you are really alive."

But people read it on the lighter and they do not get it, not at all.

"What is a beeper?" they ask. As if they could not guess.

Brooklyn: They were our restless, obsessed historians and they are dead. But their photographs show us all too well how Vietnam punished us while we were punishing the Vietnamese. The photographs are on exhibit at the Brooklyn Museum and I know them all. One of the museum guards stands with his back to Larry Burrows' photograph—that terrible, dark photograph—of wounded G.I.'s at a medical field station. I ask him what he thinks of the photographs. It is not certain at first whether he is able to understand what I am saying.

"I haven't seen them," the guard said. All right. They knew this would happen. They were always talking to the deaf.

New York: The Army doctors in Vietnam always looked so young. Dr. S., my eye doctor on Madison Avenue, is old. He looks like a calm and manicured Marc Chagall who wears lovely Italian shoes. The war is over for him because his nephew was not drafted three years ago. I try to tell him, very simply, that the bombing is wrong but he wants me to stop moving my head.

"You mean it really doesn't do any good," Dr. S. says, in the manner of a man who has not really gotten his money's worth but keeps on paying anyway.

Brooklyn: There is a man who delivers newspapers in Brooklyn I would like to meet but never will. He is Lou Singer of L & LC Delivery. He read a book of war poems, *Winning Hearts and Minds*—published by the 1st Casualty Press[1]—and he has really read them. This spring, he put a note with each newspaper he delivered.

"Dear Customer,

"I've read the book of poems reviewed here and was so impressed that I felt everyone I could reach should know about it. If interested please use order form on back of tear sheet." Also attached to the note is a reprint of John Seelye's review in *The New York Times Book Review.*

Honor Singer of L & LC Delivery. Read Rottmann, Barry and Paquet who edited the book and have poems in it. I meet Rottmann in the Brooklyn house that was the 1st Casualty Press. He is a Missouri boy, tight-lipped, suspicious of us all. Rottmann was a First Lieutenant with the 25th Infantry Division in Cu Chi. But we have nothing to say to each other. His Vietnam is not my Vietnam. I never tell him that I think he is a fine poet. Rottmann would think I was gushing. An Easterner's gush.

To build a gook stretcher, all you need is:
Two helicopters
Two long, strong ropes,
And one elastic gook.

New York: I have ten copies of *Winning Hearts and Minds.* There are nine copies to give away. There is no one to give them to. Maybe Singer has a big family who would like them.

[1] 1st Casualty Press, publisher of *Winning Hearts and Minds, War Poems by Vietnam Veterans,* is now at P.O. Box 518, Coventry, Conn. 06238.

New York: I am wired to my dreams of Indochina. Now, I have one for daytime. I rent a light aircraft and fly over the house of Ambassador Ellsworth Bunker if he ever quits Saigon and returns to his homestead near Townshend, Vermont. I will have 15,000 leaflets to drop on him, his house, his wife, his dog and his barn.

"This is a V.C. hamlet. Your allies are going to destroy it so you will be free of the enemy. You have fifteen minutes to leave your home. Do not stay here or you will be killed."

Run Bunker run.

The night dream has only come back once since my return. I am running, of course. But I have been wounded in the right leg so I cannot run fast enough. There is a U.S. helicopter trembling heavily before it takes off. The North Vietnamese are behind me. I am within a few feet of the helicopter but it rises without me. The door gunner is grinning, and he sticks one hand out, making the V-sign but jabbing his fingers upwards in a kind of fuck-you way. I am alone.

And I have forgotten how to say in Vietnamese: "I am against the war. I am a friend of all the Vietnamese people." The N.V.A. see me.

New York: On Seventy-ninth Street, there is now a Chinese restaurant where I used to drink coffee at the counter in a dim Schrafft's where the voices of Ireland asked me if I wanted coffee cake or a glass of water. There seems to be no convenient place to buy stamps. Cigarettes are only sold in machines. I walk slowly now, remembering how Luong once said to me in Saigon that we could not ask the Vietnamese to hurry. Why not?

"There are no rush words in Vietnamese," he said.

A. is going to Washington to demonstrate against the bombing. She is going to lie down on a floor in the Capitol building to symbolize the dead of Indochina. There is a plan for the demonstrators to dig a hole as big as a bomb crater to show people what a bomb does. I suggest that they lie down inside U.S. Army plastic green body bags but A. and I are not sure if you can breathe inside them. No one I ever knew who ended up in a body bag could breathe anyway. The longest man always looked so little inside a body bag.

"We are going to get busted," A. says. She is a good woman and she knows it is better to do something than simply mourn. I decide not to go to Washington. I am a prisoner of a war, so I sleep instead.

New York: They have dug out the shrapnel in Luong's spine so he is back at work in the Saigon office of *The New York Times.* He was wounded at Dong Ha, standing up to take a picture. Luong-Capa, Luong-Cartier-Bresson, Luong-Larry Burrows. He writes me and I can do nothing for one day except read the letter, fold it, unfold it, read it:

"Today eighteen years ago this country was cut in two. And today is the day of the 151st session of the Paris peace talks . . . and the only agreement that the warring parties ever reached so far is the shape of the conference table; and this morning at the regular briefing for the Vietnamese press Colonel Hien gave the following casualty figures of the past week: *Friendly* 837 K.I.A. (up 5%), 2367 W.I.A. and 321 M.I.A.; *enemy* 2871 K.I.A. (down 14%), 43 captured, etc. And also today we received a bad [sic] news from Quang Tri that two journalists were confirmed dead and one missing.

"And still no further words on the fate of poor Alex Shimkin. Also today Mr. Ruyet and the Song Than daily called me and asked me to make money contribution to their campaign of collecting the remains of thousands of people killed along Route One above My Chanh, and burying them.

"This is a day in the life of Nguyen Ngoc Luong (I just stole the title of some Soviet writer's novel)."

Ah, Luong, living under that sky, nothing should surprise you. Be ready now for *a* bad news every day. I wish I could send you new eyeglasses, and a small black pig because you always wanted to raise pigs you said, and a flak jacket to your ankles. But all I can send you is love and tears.

For Discussion

1. Describe Emerson's reactions upon returning to New York.
2. What does Emerson miss seeing and hearing in the United States?
3. Emerson reports the remarks of other people without comment. How then does she reveal her feelings?
4. Describe your reaction to the incident in the rice paddy.
5. What purpose does Emerson have for including the incidents of the Air Force grass, her conversation with her sister, and the Zippo lighter inscription?
6. Discuss the logic for Emerson's daydream. Does a similar logic exist for the night dream?
7. Explain Emerson's decision not to take part in the Washington, D.C., protest. Does it surprise you? Why or why not?
8. Examine Emerson's response to Luong's letter. What makes it so effective?
9. Discuss the various literary techniques used in this essay.
10. Try to identify the style of this essay. What gives the writing its strong impact?

RICHARD GOLLANCE

I'm Proud
To Be a Sissie

Richard Gollance is on the staff of the Gay Community Services in Los Angeles. He produces a weekly program for the non-commercial radio station KPFK-FM. This article describes a frequently encountered aspect of the recent liberation movements: "coming out," the open acknowledgment of homosexuality.

"Gay" men have had to work out problems and find answers that their "straight" brothers will be facing as the influence of the women's liberation movement affects more and more heterosexual relationships. The rigid conception which saw the male as forceful, competent, intelligent, and unsentimental and the female as weak, supportive, intuitive, and sentimental is eroding. "We do not want to imitate men and take over their power. We want to humanize all of society," Gloria Steinem said recently. I have seen men's consciousness-raising groups, inspired by the feminists' challenges, hurl as much anger, confusion, and regret in discussing what is expected of them and what is denied them as you would expect from a similar gathering of women. These males want to be able to feel emotions, to treat both women and men with tenderness and perception, to be able to loosen up, but they don't know how to go about it. They won't be able to make those changes while they cling to their stereotype male roles.

Like most boys, I was aware of my father's awesome schedule and responsibilities. He got up very early in the morning, before the rest of us, to take the Long Island Railroad to work, spent long hard hours walking from loft to loft to see customers around New York's garment district, and came home at night so exhausted that he often fell asleep in front of the television set. What amazed me was that he spent almost all his time and effort on a job that he admitted he didn't like very much.

After I went to work myself, I realized that my father was in no small minority. Most jobs mean nothing. When a man's value revolves around how well he can outsmart other men and increase his earning power, the only way he can survive is by emotionally desensitizing himself until his joy of living is channeled through his successful competitions.

It is hard for me to imagine ever living like that. I can't examine whether or not I'm jeopardizing my control and power whenever I make a decision. I've stopped worrying about whether or not I'm a Real Man. I like to dance, and sometimes when I'm walking along the beach, I'll dance right there. Sometimes I visit my friend Donna, who is "straight," and we play with finger nail polish, painting designs on each other's nails. (It started when she was in a rush and did her own nails while we were talking; the colors looked like so much fun that I had to try it myself.) I have a bright red scarf I like to wear around my head, like a gypsy. Maybe I'll sew this evening, or go for a motorcycle ride in the mountains this afternoon, or write a few scenes for a play I'm working on. I don't consider whether my voice is deep enough or my presence authoritative enough. I don't have to do a mini-size version of the He-Man Strut or feel apologetic for being mini-size. And I won't surrender my life to an office. I work part-time, just enough to support myself and that's all. Any other work I do will have to be meaningful to me.

This is a new freedom for me. Gentleness, introversion, slightness, or emotionality are dangerous in a boy, a sure sign that he may not be capable of meeting his male duty in the grown-up world. When I was very young, sometimes I played with dolls, or cried, or painted. I don't remember when the first pressures to change all that started, but gradually the agony of being made fun of and being called a "fairy" became the most horrible part of my life. Any situation could suddenly turn on me and leave me shattered. And my secret guilt about being homosexual intensified the need to hide and reconstruct the incorrect parts of my personality. As much as I tried, I never fully escaped the threat of imminent humiliation. What hurts most now is realizing that my quest for masculinity and normality always involved restricting myself, never exploring or expanding myself. I wasted so much time and energy doing things I didn't enjoy. I remember my adolescence as a time of being constantly on guard.

There is no legitimate way for a boy in the suburbs to avoid baseball in the spring. Without raising a fuss, I would try out for the Little League, and every year wind up in the outfield of a third-string team where I couldn't do much harm. For encouragement, my parents would come to all the games, and at any family gathering, an uncle or a cousin was sure to ask my batting average, how my team was doing, what position I played: Was I a hero? Meals were rescheduled to accommodate practices, and buying a mitt was an event.

There was an annual ritual I became familiar with. It would start with my coach looking at me strangely after I threw a ball a few times. The routine: he would take me aside and ask me to have a catch with him, and I knew what was coming. He would try to be tactful (but make me realize, at the same time, that it was a serious problem) and say something, like "You're not following through when you throw the ball. You're doing it all wrong, like a girl."

The coach would then try to teach me the right way but, realizing me hopeless, would finally give up. I knew I was stuck in the outfield forever. Eventually I found an illegitimate way to avoid baseball in the spring. For several years I got sick for a few weeks every April or May. I dreaded the end of winter.

I finally discovered a spring sport. Distance running doesn't really require talent as much as it requires drive and a monumental need to prove something. Why else would you go around and around a track several miles a day and subject yourself to a grueling regimen whose only pleasure is the possibility of winning a race perhaps once a week? Why else go to bed early when all the next day promises is more timed laps and more calisthenics? I had that monumental need. Even after I established that I could be athletic and after I grew to hate the meaningless, repetitive exertion, I still continued. At last I had something to prove my precarious identity.

Every circumstance, every action demanded second-guessing. When I heard a sarcastic wolf-whistle as I walked in the school halls, I fashioned a grotesque walk that had virtually no wiggle in it. When I dated, the strong certainty and the impenetrable protectiveness I worked so hard to convey precluded any human communication and made the evening a torture. When I dressed, when I sat down and crossed my legs, when I carried a package, when I was angry at someone, when I chose books or magazines, or which classes to take, I always had to figure out if I were doing it the right way for a boy.

The details of my high school years may be singular, but few "gay" men escape similar traumas. It is hard for me to relate to a world where men distrust and battle other men and take women as their earned reward. Just desiring to love and be close to another man contradicts what men should be and how they are supposed to treat each other. "Straight" boys rarely experience such direct challenges to their socialization. They may vaguely resent what is expected of them, but scholarship, hero-worship, and prospective wealth and power are well-nigh irresistible.

Until about a year ago (I "came out" at seventeen; I'm twenty-three now), I wasn't able to accept being anything less than the strong one, the aggressor. I was afraid of being put down again for acting like a girl. While gay liberation helped me learn to like myself, the influence of feminists finally helped me transcend the contradictions between my needs and my fears. Intellectually, I could understand that by rejecting any feminity in myself as unworthy, I was downgrading women. That was acceptable rhetoric. But acting on it took time. I was only convinced, step by step, as I felt the exhilaration of recovering those carefully lost parts of myself and seeing the shared delight of my friends, feminists and gay men, as I kept exploring. It was the first time I was given some reassurance about myself; perhaps my natural instincts weren't impossible after all. I didn't feel I had to stand outside and guard myself. It was a relief to lose that terrible self-consciousness.

When I go to bed with another man, we are each physically capable of being passive or active. For a long time, sex produced a subtle competition: who would give in? I could not ease up enough to enjoy being sexually passive; it was a defeat with a reward—closeness—that made it worth continuing nonetheless. Since I have relaxed and stopped thinking of sex as something akin to rape and plunder, the sensual pleasure has become dominant, and my bed adventures have lost that edgy strain of competition. One man is not the victor and the other the victim.

If a "gay" man can recognize the implications of his sexuality, he can be personally freed in a day-to-day way. He doesn't have to demand control over all his encounters; his variable sexual experiences should relax him to react spontaneously. These are lessons "straight" men can learn from their "gay" brothers, but only when they do not fear being submissive. Feminist pressure to equalize male-female relations suggests a new freedom for men to meet their momentary needs rather than their assumed responsibilities. The real crisis for heterosexual men will be whether they see this as a positive or a negative challenge.

Some confused males are still living in my father's world and are still stuck with their boyhood models: the spartan athlete, the fast-drawing gunslinger, the omnipotent billy-clubbed policeman, the blood-and-guts soldier, the computerized fast-talking executive, the remote intellectual, the awesome scientist, the unapproachable President of the United States. Life is still the great challenge for men to beat. All pleasures are to be withheld for future security. Men are enemies and women booty. If they ever shed their hard, masculine mechanisms, society and its life-denying institutions would cave in, from government to private enterprise, from the military to public education. But imagine for a moment what could replace it. Men and women wouldn't have to fit into slots. They could slide and explore and grow.

For Discussion

1. In what ways does Gollance differ from his father in behavior and attitude?
2. Discuss whatever meaning the following quotations have for you:
    a. "I've stopped worrying about whether or not I'm a Real Man."
    b. "Gentleness, introversion, slightness, or emotionality are dangerous in a boy, a sure sign that he may not be capable of meeting his male duty in the grown-up world."
    c. "It is hard for me to relate to a world where men distrust and battle other men and take women as their earned reward."
    d. ". . . my bed adventures have lost that edgy strain of competition."
3. How did the feminist movement help Gollance to "come out"? What important realizations were implicit in his coming out?
4. Gollance speaks of those lessons that "straight" men can learn from their "gay brothers." Beyond this, what lessons might anyone learn from Gollance's liberation?

ARTHUR EGENDORF, JR.

Art Thou Really So Different from Anyone Else?

As more facts about the origins of the Indochina war are made public, the question of amnesty becomes more complex. The following essay, by Arthur Egendorf, Jr., was published in a collection of articles edited by Murray Polner: *When Can I Come Home? A Debate on Amnesty for Exiles, Anti-war Prisoners and Others* (1972). Egendorf is a Vietnam veteran, having served in Military Intelligence in Vietnam.

> Wie viel bist du von andern unterschieden?
> Erkenne dich, leb mit der Welt in Frieden.
>
> Art thou really so different from anyone else?
> Get to know thyself, and live with the world in peace.
> —GOETHE, *Faust*

"Hell no, we won't go." First it sounded silly. Then embarrassing. Finally that cry became an outright threat. Spilling their guts out in protest over an issue that could only be decided by heads of state, they refused to recognize how ludicrous they were and how futile their indignance. Just kids, incapable of accepting what they were, they demanded a voice they didn't deserve. That made it harder on others their age who were engaged in the struggle to be recognized through achievement rather than disruption: a vague but growing pressure to take some stand when there wasn't enough information or understanding to decide. What made them so certain of their course when there were probably good arguments on all sides? In rejecting so much, what sustained their sanity in the midst of anomie and disbelief? There was the faint suspicion that they knew something that the rest of us didn't. But all that I, a nineteen-year-old college student, could say of them for sure was that they were different. That was 1964.

"Why don't you tell them to shove it?" was a friend's question when notice from my draft board arrived three years later. A full answer was impossible; only, "Because . . . I can't do that." With college over, graduate school didn't have any immediate appeal. Europe did. Going away entailed certain risks with the draft, but they could be handled, like anything else. The notice followed me to Germany, after almost a year of my being abroad. The clamor over the war at home was less than a distant rumble, since an energetic study of French and German had left me no time to read American publications. My goals and reactions were unchanged from what they had been years before. There was an indulgent family, bent on respectability, that had to be pleased, a well-ingrained drive for accomplishment to placate, and a yearning to fit into a proud tradition in which men of honor pit themselves against fate without wincing.

Going to jail was out of the question, permanent exile unthinkable. The thought of using influence or subterfuge to avoid service reeked of dishonor. While the arguments supporting the war had already become dubious, it was impossible to believe that a great nation's leaders could be altogether wrong. And although the prospect of being in the infantry was extremely distasteful, it *had* to be that the Army needed men with talent and initiative for constructive purposes. It was these thoughts that I had in mind on the way to an Army recruiter in Munich. I enlisted, signing up for a total of three years, in order to guarantee my placement in the Army Intelligence "Area Studies" program.

The military provided a flight home to begin Basic Training. It was the summer of 1967. During the first few unpleasant weeks, solace came from my belief that those, like myself, who were courageous enough to withstand the ordeal of duty in troubled times would eventually be rewarded. There were many for whom the Army was the first brush with life outside of school. I felt stronger than they, having already been away for a year and accustomed to loneliness. The realization didn't come until sometime later that the toughness was also a drawback. It made me resistant to a new, upsetting thought, one that others seemed to have understood from the outset. Many of the men in training were there by default. It was not something they wanted to do, but they had simply not taken the trouble to avoid it. The resisters on the outside were still another breed. Yet their distinctiveness was no longer so ineffable. It became clearer with time that they were the fortunate few who had developed a commitment to their own ideals when others, like many of us in training, were still in doubt.

Intelligence school was an unexpected shock. What had been advertised as "Area Studies" was actually espionage. It was too late to back out. I had made a commitment. But inarticulate instructors, simplistic lesson plans, and an incredibly dogmatic approach to history, politics, and human behavior made it all seem like rank idiocy. Our instructions for finding good agents: "Get the man who is ideologically motivated, hates Communists, has a healthy fear of American power, and wants to get in Uncle Sam's good graces. But make sure he's beholden to you too. Get him to take your money and your booze, or else you'll never be able to control him." And it was through these means that we were to collect the information on which sound policy was to be based.

It appeared that I had allowed myself to be deceived into joining an effort that was inevitably doomed to failure by its own distorted and preconceived version of truth. Suddenly, the radical rhetoric that had been so easy to dismiss as misguided and irresponsible years before, provided the only logic adequate to deal with this new situation. Reading newspapers and magazines assiduously, I cheered each new demonstration and case of draft resistance. Theirs was the more difficult ordeal. Belief in some eventual reward for dutiful submission palled before an increasing awareness that rewards were absurd: The resisters were simply right.

Friends outside the service wrote occasional letters. It was hard to understand their reticence and distant tone. In private thoughts, I could concede that my initial decision to join the service was based on misconceptions. The Army experience was senseless. But I revolted at my friends' vague indictments of my complicity. Only excuses and consolations came to mind: I was the class radical; I at least could speak from first-hand knowledge and not from mere speculation; I had an obligation to fulfill. Those reactions grew out of a new sense of vulnerability and precariousness. If I acted on my true feelings, the Army might remove me from the comforts of the Intelligence corps and send me to the infantry, even to jail. Once let loose, the desperation might even lead me to become a lifelong fugitive. And so, in spite of what I felt, self-preservation became the abiding concern. They could make me a spy, but I would do them one better. To save myself, I would dissimulate and hold my real self in abeyance.

A year in Saigon destroyed the last remnants of doubt. Intelligence knew none of the answers to the important questions. Gruff, haughty American officials living with their concubines in Saigon villas, disdainful G.I.s, and massive resentment among the Vietnamese for the clumsy and disruptive foreigners shattered any hope that we were there to help them. Inside knowledge of intrigue, corruption, and a tottering regime founded on repression devastated the myth of our building a viable, representative political structure. Only the claims of a few honest men in the military, that we were there to maintain our control of the situation, rang true. And that admission simply bolstered the polemics of the enemy. We were fighting a nasty, aggressive, imperialistic war. How disappointing that I had to go so far to find out what others had known long before without ever having been away.

"If I were Vietnamese, I would be with the Vietcong." It didn't matter that I said those words to Army officers, who were willing to stake their lives on the fight with the enemy, or to Saigon aristocrats, some of whom I genuinely liked even though I knew they were likely candidates for V.C. assassination. I still spied for a cause I couldn't believe in, with the relish of a successful double deceiver delicately balancing conflicting loyalties. There were men dying not too far away, and I didn't want to be with them. There was also the year left to serve after Vietnam to consider. Only a good performance could win me a place in another safe haven, so I did the job better than most. The calculation worked. Returning to the United States in April 1969, in the midst of a crippling colitis attack, I was given a privileged job in Washington.

A few months afterward, I met and talked for a few minutes with a man I knew. But I couldn't place him. It took three days to remember who he was, that he had taken me to lunch several times in Saigon. Other names, places, and events were even harder to remember. The forgetting seemed almost purposeful, and with that sudden insight, the dam cracked, without breaking. At work, I was supposed to read reports from spies using American companies for cover (always with the consent of the company president). There was advice to give: whether a fifty-year-old agent should seduce a twenty-year-old Japanese teletype operator so that he could force her to supply him with the information she transmitted at her job. And a constant demand for shrewd deception: How can official records throughout the government be put to better use, altering some to make our agents' cover more convincing, and appropriating others for leads to more "human resources." I tried to have nothing to do with it all. Ideas and slogans culled from underground newspapers at night became the rhetoric for the next day's conversations at the office. They couldn't send me back to Vietnam, so there was no fear in telling everyone what I felt. Yet I stuck it out, going to work every morning and taking my pay, in spite of the conflicts.

Ever since I enlisted, the only plan for what to do after the Army was a return to Europe. In Washington the basis for the plan changed. It was no longer to go back to something I had started, but rather to get away from the nightmare I was in. "Why go to Germany?" asked an uncle. My answer: "That's where the Nazis are . . . I'm a Nazi, and that's where I belong." Yet the day the Army released me in May 1970, I couldn't leave the country. The upheaval and disruptions of the previous three years had developed their own logic, and I couldn't escape it. An emotional breakdown followed. After months of putting the pieces back together, I found my way to Vietnam Veterans Against the War.

As monumental change follows unsettling change, new pat answers replace the ones discarded . . . up to a point. After time and reflection on the latest shift, doubts return, to the point where the flux appears clearly rooted in a few inescapable truths. From the time I entered the military, it became increasingly obvious that the heroes of this war were those who fought it in the streets of American cities, or in the courts, or in jails, or by leaving the country rather than lend their support. Certainly there are distinctions among them. Men who went jail or left the country because of their public stand faced different consequences than the ones who used a psychiatrist's diagnosis to avoid the draft. But the distinctions are irrelevant. Whatever the personal cost, all of them, exiles, deserters, and resisters of every stripe, answered the call to fight a senseless war with the most appropriate response—an outright refusal.

It is hard to imagine any dissenting minority that has been so dramatically and unequivocally vindicated by the course of history as those who refused to fight in Vietnam. If the legal authorities in the United States cease to persecute the resisters, so much the better. They will only be recognizing the absurdity of punishing individuals for the foresight that was so clearly lacking within the government and major sections of the larger society during a period of meaningless suffering for millions of Vietnamese and Americans. Those who said "no" to the war should receive an apology, not just a pardon; they should be granted a place of honor, not amnesty.

While that conclusion is indisputable to me, it was only reached through anguished reflection. In fact, this essay is extremely difficult to write. There is a strong urge to forget past pain, to gloss over personal shortcomings, and to carry on as if the war didn't happen and I had taken no part in it. What comes to mind now are vivid recollections of the distressing process through which an ex-Army spy eventually began to face his own bitter errors in judgment head on. The realizations came very slowly at first, followed by an anxious groping for some understanding of why different alternatives hadn't been chosen. But it was only after the struggle made its impact that the hidden despair, once brought to light, began to subside, and I could start feeling whole again . . . braced with a cautious hope that I wouldn't make the same mistaken choices again.

Given the trauma experienced by one man, it is unlikely that the wounds caused by an entire society's errors will heal in any simple fashion. Historians claim that the nation has not been so divided since the Civil War. It is a time when people judge others and themselves more by their allegiances than by personal qualities. And the greater the polarities, the greater the desire in many of us to bridge the gaps and obscure the issues that separate us. But there is no way to escape the judgment that the war has been a colossal mistake. Whatever ruse people may employ to hide from the past, it is certain that many others here and elsewhere in the world and especially the war's victims, the Vietnamese, will not forget.

A mistake of such proportions is a crime. And the crimes of a nation that calls itself democratic are the responsibility of all its citizens, a notion that the resisters have embraced most fittingly. But that the war has dragged on in spite of their efforts indicates that the responsibility is shared unevenly. Ultimately, it resides with the Presidents, their advisers, and military officials who have had the power to end the war or substantially alter its course had they chosen to do so. But that still doesn't exonerate the individual voter and soldier.

As a young man I look forward to the day when passions will subside and the war in Vietnam is relegated to history. Toward that end, amnesty must be reserved for the true criminals, the principals in the crime and everyone associated with it. I am thinking of amnesty in the largest sense. There is a need to establish a new consensus on which citizens can accept each other and come together, after which it is no longer necessary to defend past roles in order to live in the present. *But the forgiveness can only follow a clear understanding of what and whom there is to forgive.* First, an entire nation must come to grips with the painful lessons that the war has to teach.

Hopefully, more people will come to realize that unquestioned deference to higher authorities has been a self-serving cop-out: The deferent have been able to avoid answering troublesome questions for themselves. In the end, it has also been self-defeating. We have delegated responsibility for the life and death of millions to men who gained power through unrelenting attention to their own self-interest with the delusionary expectation that once in office, they would act with the wisdom of philosophers. The most perceptive and sensitive individuals can be trapped by a need to preserve their tenure in office, incapable of correcting mistakes even after they are recognized. In Vietnam, what began as a measured display of U.S. force, a military exercise for limited political objectives, has become the longest war in our history. Three times as many explosives have been dropped, and almost half as many men called into military service as during the entire course of World War II. And through it all, the bulk of Americans have been waiting in silence until the men whose job it is to decide call for an end.

It is not enough that military tribunals sit in judgment on men like Lieutenant William Calley. His conviction, based on the ruling that he acted as a sane and free agent at the time of his crime, is more of a reflection of our own perverted standards of normality than of any real justice. Such trials are travesties when a case involving the murder of a Vietnamese spy is dismissed for fear of disclosing espionage *modus operandi,* and of bringing embarrassment to the government; and when the misfeasance of the highest officials has yet to be brought seriously into question.

Nor is it reasonable to expect our legal system to deliver a lasting verdict on the guilt or innocence of those who initiated and conducted the war, for it has stubbornly refused to rule on the legality or the constitutionality of the war itself. Many legal technicalities have been raised that even cast doubt on the appropriateness of the Nuremburg decisions as a precedent for war crimes trials after Vietnam. But there are other questions yet to be answered before proceedings based on the Nuremburg precedent could convene. Did the original trials actually lead to a greater understanding of the moral issues involved? Or was their usefulness canceled out by the resentment they evoked of the unjustifiable self-righteousness of the adjudicators? After Vietnam, what party or individual has the jurisdiction and the "clean hands" to set itself up as a judge? In any case, there can be little doubt that legal judgments alone cannot convey the essential message, for even the lessons of Nuremburg were lost on one of the principal parties to its decisions, the United States.

The most crucial postwar task entails more than removal of the officials responsible for the war from office, and the assignment of guilt. The widespread attitudes that made the war possible must change. A substantial portion of the population presently favors the men on trial for atrocities, not because, as some maintain, they did not bear ultimate responsibility for their acts, but because they were only doing their duty. Some of those same people do not see the war as a hideous error, but as a worthwhile cause subverted by elements within the United States. It is difficult to imagine that such minds will be changed by making martyrs out of misguided leaders. And any effort to try war criminals on a massive scale will undoubtedly be misconstrued as an attempt to establish pacifism as a national creed, undermining the institutions that enable a nation to defend itself.

There will inevitably be more investigations and trials. So there should be. But they must be conducted in such a manner to make clear that the judgments apply to more than the limited group that can be brought under scrutiny. There should be no illusions that the evil throughout society is expiated by punishing a few individuals. Nor should there be any support given to the idea that a few scapegoats have to be sacrificed to pacify the most rabid faction. The indictments must indicate how sincere, conscientious people, in and out of office, can be blinded to the implications of their acts . . . by fear, by intimidation, and by their own struggle to maintain the tenuous security afforded them by a restricted vision that excludes intrusive, disturbing truths. When that lesson is understood, when the citizenry at large shows a willingness to accept their share of responsibility for a national catastrophe, it will be time to open a new chapter on amnesty.

In the lines at the head of this essay, the goddess of truth says to a headstrong and immoderate Faust, "Art thou really so different from anyone else? Get to know thyself and live with the world in peace." In the aftermath of an unjust war, the greatest imperative is not to decide whom to punish or whom to pardon. Rather, it is contained in the goddess' exhortations to Faust. The insensitivity of this willful and excessive nation has shielded it from the suffering caused to others by its efforts to transform the world according to its own fantasies. Now its people, and particularly its leaders, must learn to develop the self-knowledge, the sense of shared interest with all humans beings, to live with the world in peace.

For Discussion

1. Discuss and evaluate Egendorf's reasons for joining the Army.
2. Trace the stages in Egendorf's changing position toward the Vietnam conflict.
3. Who, according to Egendorf, are the heroes of the Vietnam War? How do they differ from traditional war heroes?
4. What does Egendorf mean by "amnesty in the largest sense"? Do you agree with his viewpoint? Why or why not?
5. What difficulties does Egendorf foresee in attempting to punish guilt for war crimes?
6. Whom does Egendorf hold responsible for the Vietnam War?
7. How does Goethe's quotation at the beginning apply to the content of the the whole essay?
8. How do Egendorf's views relate to those of Robert McAfee Brown (in "The Impassioned NO")? Of Leo Tolstoy (in this section)?

```
NO                    NO    NO NO NO NO           NO NO
   NO              NO       NO                  NO        NO
      NO        NO          NO                NO
         NO  NO             NO                NO
            NO              NO NO NO            NO
            NO              NO                    NO NO
            NO              NO                        NO
            NO              NO                          NO
            NO              NO                NO        NO
            NO              NO NO NO NO          NO NO
```

—Nicholas C. Lindsay

THE
IRONIC
NO

We are all in the same pot, we are all guilty, or innocent, depending on whether we take the frog's view or the Olympian view.

HENRY MILLER
Letter to Mr. J. Hirsch

The ironic writer plays with his subject and reader. By deliberately distorting his material or placing his reader in an unexpected or novel position to it, he manipulates his reader into recognizing a new dimension of experience, into seeing in a way he never saw before. When this art of manipulation is used to ridicule human weakness, stupidity, or cruelty, it is called *satire*. When it is not used for purposes of ridicule, the larger term *irony* is employed. But whether it is comic or not, irony always involves a disparity or tension between what appears to be true and what is true, between what is said and what is actually meant, between what is pretended and what is real.

Like the discursive writer, the ironic writer makes an appeal to our minds. He wants the reader to see beneath the surface appearance of

men's behavior and to recognize, through laughter or shock, the contradictions between what men say they are and what they really are.
He does this by using various ironic "arts": invective (abusive language),
sarcasm (caustic or bitter distortion of one's meaning with an intent to
injure or strike back), hyperbole (exaggeration or overstatement), under-
statement (saying less than one means), and Socratic irony (pretended
ignorance or innocence while exposing someone else's pretense). All of
these methods are used to throw the reader off balance, to confound or
surprise him into seeing the subject under ridicule—which may be the
reader himself.

Most of us do not like to be laughed at. For this reason, the satirist
often "tricks" his reader by setting up a situation in which the reader is
unknowingly led to adopt a point of view different from his customary
one, thus making him laugh at what he would ordinarily find offensive
or threatening. As Henry Miller says, the satirist tries to make the
reader see himself as he is—from "the frog's view"—and not as he would
like to see himself—from "the Olympian view." This often unflattering
picture of humanity can be disagreeable, even when it is funny. But in a
sense the satiric writer is perhaps the most flattering of all writers because he depends upon the reader's sense of humor in its broadest
application—his ability to laugh even "when it hurts," even when what
he is laughing at turns out to be his most cherished beliefs.

By its very nature, all satire is dissent, and in its objection to and
exposure of human folly, it has great social value. Furthermore, it enables
the writer to vent his anger in a communicable form and to channel his
strong feeling in a way which might otherwise be less constructive. For
these reasons, irony can be a healthful and humanizing experience; it is
a positive way of attacking social ills. And when the reader shares in it,
he benefits.

The essays which follow are excellent examples of varied ironic voices.
Some of the writers will shock you; others will make you laugh; still
others will do both. But each writer will be trying to make you see his
protest in an original and often surprising way.

JONATHAN SWIFT

A Modest Proposal

For Preventing the Children of
Poor People in Ireland from Being
a Burden to Their Parents or Country,
and for Making Them Beneficial
to the Public

Born in Ireland in 1667 of English parents, Jonathan Swift graduated from Trinity College, Dublin, and was ordained as an
Anglican priest, taking a parish near Dublin. His ambition, however, led him to England to seek a career in public affairs. Despite brilliant success as a political writer, he never received
public award and finally, in 1713, accepted an appointment as
Dean of Saint Patrick's Cathedral in Dublin, a position he held
until his death in 1745. Although Swift wrote serious and satirical
verse, he is best known for his prose satires. *Gulliver's Travels*,
The Battle of the Books, *The Tale of a Tub*, as well as the following selection, published in 1729, illustrate the logic and brilliance of his satire.

It is a melancholy object to those who walk through this great town
or travel in the country, when they see the streets, the roads, and cabin
doors, crowded with beggars of the female-sex, followed by three, four,
or six children, all in rags and importuning every passenger for an alms.
These mothers, instead of being able to work for their honest livelihood,
are forced to employ all their time in strolling to beg sustenance for their
helpless infants, who, as they grow up, either turn thieves for want of
work, or leave their dear native country to fight for the Pretender in
Spain, or sell themselves to the Barbadoes.[1]

I think it is agreed by all parties that this prodigious number of chil-

---

[1] As indentured servants in order to pay for their emigration to a colony. [Ed.]

dren in the arms, or on the backs, or at the heels of their mothers, and frequently of their fathers, is in the present deplorable state of the kingdom a very great additional grievance; and therefore whoever could find out a fair, cheap, and easy method of making these children sound, useful members of the commonwealth would deserve so well of the public as to have his statue set up for a preserver of the nation.

But my intention is very far from being confined to provide only for the children of professed beggars; it is of a much greater extent, and shall take in the whole number of infants at a certain age who are born of parents in effect as little able to support them as those who demand our charity in the streets.

As to my own part, having turned my thoughts for many years upon this important subject, and maturely weighed the several schemes of other projectors, I have always found them grossly mistaken in their computation. It is true, a child just dropped from its dam may be supported by her milk for a solar year, with little other nourishment; at most not above the value of two shillings, which the mother may certainly get, or the value in scraps, by her lawful occupation of begging; and it is exactly at one year old that I propose to provide for them in such a manner as instead of being a charge upon their parents or the parish, or wanting food and raiment for the rest of their lives, they shall on the contrary contribute to the feeding, and partly to the clothing, of many thousands.

There is likewise another great advantage in my scheme, that it will prevent those voluntary abortions, and that horrid practice of women murdering their bastard children, alas, too frequent among us, sacrificing the poor innocent babes, I doubt, more to avoid the expense than the shame, which would move tears and pity in the most savage and inhuman breast.

The number of souls in this kingdom being usually reckoned one million and a half, of these I calculate there may be about two hundred thousand couples whose wives are breeders; from which number I subtract thirty thousand couples who are able to maintain their own children, although I apprehend there cannot be so many under the present distresses of the kingdom; but this being granted, there will remain an hundred and seventy thousand breeders. I again subtract fifty thousand for those women who miscarry, or whose children die by accident or disease within the year. There only remain an hundred and twenty thousand children of poor parents annually born. The question therefore is, how this number shall be reared and provided for, which, as I have already said, under the present situation of affairs, is utterly impossible by all the methods hitherto proposed. For we can neither employ them in handicraft or agriculture; we neither build houses (I mean in the country) nor cultivate land. They can very seldom pick up a livelihood by stealing till they arrive at six years old, except where they are of towardly parts; although

I confess they learn the rudiments much earlier, during which time they can however be looked upon only as probationers, as I have been informed by a principal gentleman in the county of Cavan, who protested to me that he never knew above one or two instances under the age of six, even in a part of the kingdom so renowned for the quickest proficiency in that art.

I am assured by our merchants that a boy or a girl before twelve years old is no salable commodity; and even when they come to this age they will not yield above three pounds, or three pounds and half a crown at most on the Exchange; which cannot turn to account either to the parents or the kingdom, the charge of nutriment and rags having been at least four times that value.

I shall now therefore humbly propose my own thoughts, which I hope will not be liable to the least objection.

I have been assured by a very knowing American of my acquaintance in London, that a young healthy child well nursed is at a year old a most delicious, nourishing, and wholesome food, whether stewed, roasted, baked, or boiled; and I make no doubt that it will equally serve in a fricassee or a ragout.

I do therefore humbly offer it to public consideration that of the hundred and twenty thousand children, already computed, twenty thousand may be reserved for breed, whereof only one fourth part to be males, which is more than we allow to sheep, black cattle, or swine; and my reason is that these children are seldom the fruits of marriage, a circumstance not much regarded by our savages, therefore one male will be sufficient to serve four females. That the remaining hundred thousand may at a year old be offered in sale to the persons of quality and fortune through the kingdom, always advising the mother to let them suck plentifully in the last month, so as to render them plump and fat for a good table. A child will make two dishes at an entertainment for friends; and when the family dines alone, the fore or hind quarter will make a reasonable dish, and seasoned with a little pepper or salt will be very good boiled on the fourth day, especially in winter.

I have reckoned upon a medium that a child just born will weigh twelve pounds, and in a solar year if tolerably nursed increaseth to twenty-eight pounds.

I grant this food will be somewhat dear, and therefore very proper for landlords, who, as they have already devoured most of the parents, seem to have the best title to the children.

Infant's flesh will be in season throughout the year, but more plentiful in March, and a little before and after. For we are told by a grave author, an eminent French physician,[2] that fish being a prolific diet, there are more children born in Roman Catholic countries about nine months after

---

[2] Rabelais.

Lent than at any other season; therefore, reckoning a year after Lent, the markets will be more glutted than usual, because the number of popish infants is at least three to one in this kingdom; and therefore it will have one other collateral advantage, by lessening the number of Papists among us.

I have already computed the charge of nursing a beggar's child (in which list I reckon all cottagers, laborers, and four fifths of the farmers) to be about two shillings per annum, rags included; and I believe no gentleman would repine to give ten shillings for the carcass of a good fat child, which, as I have said, will make four dishes of excellent nutritive meat, when he hath only some particular friend or his own family to dine with him. Thus the squire will learn to be a good landlord, and grow popular among the tenants; the mother will have eight shillings net profit, and be fit for work till she produces another child.

Those who are more thrifty (as I must confess the times require) may flay the carcass; the skin of which artificially dressed will make admirable gloves for ladies and summer boots for fine gentlemen.

As to our city of Dublin, shambles may be appointed for this purpose in the most convenient parts of it, and butchers we may be assured will not be wanting; although I rather recommend buying the children alive, and dressing them hot from the knife as we do roasting pigs.

A very worthy person, a true lover of his country, and whose virtues I highly esteem, was lately pleased in discoursing on this matter to offer a refinement upon my scheme. He said that many gentlemen of this kingdom, having of late destroyed their deer, he conceived that the want of venison might be well supplied by the bodies of young lads and maidens, not exceeding fourteen years of age nor under twelve, so great a number of both sexes in every county being now ready to starve for want of work and service; and these to be disposed of by their parents, if alive, or otherwise by their nearest relations. But with due deference to so excellent a friend and so deserving a patriot, I cannot be altogether in his sentiments; for as to the males, my American acquaintance assured me from frequent experience that their flesh was generally tough and lean, like that of our schoolboys, by continual exercise, and their taste disagreeable; and to fatten them would not answer the charge. Then as to the females, it would, I think with humble submission, be a loss to the public, because they soon would become breeders themselves: and besides, it is not improbable that some scrupulous people might be apt to censure such a practice (although indeed very unjustly) as a little bordering upon cruelty; which, I confess, hath always been with me the strongest objection against any project, how well soever intended.

But in order to justify my friend, he confessed that this expedient was put into his head by the famous Psalmanazar, a native of the island Formosa, who came from thence to London above twenty years ago, and in conversation told my friend that in his country when any young person happened to be put to death, the executioner sold the carcass to persons of quality as a prime dainty; and that in his time the body of a plump girl of fifteen, who was crucified for an attempt to poison the emperor, was sold to his Imperial Majesty's prime minister of state, and other great mandarins of the court, in joints from the gibbet, at four hundred crowns. Neither indeed can I deny that if the same use were made of several plump young girls in this town, who without one single groat to their fortunes cannot stir abroad without a chair, and appear at the playhouse and assemblies in foreign fineries which they never will pay for, the kingdom would not be the worse.

Some persons of a desponding spirit are in great concern about that vast number of poor people who are aged, diseased, or maimed, and I have been desired to employ my thoughts what course may be taken to ease the nation of so grievous an encumbrance. But I am not in the least pain upon that matter, because it is very well known that they are every day dying and rotting by cold and famine, and filth and vermin, as fast as can be reasonably expected. And as to the younger laborers, they are now in almost as hopeful a condition. They cannot get work, and consequently pine away for want of nourishment to a degree that if at any time they are accidentally hired to common labor, they have not strength to perform it; and thus the country and themselves are happily delivered from the evils to come.

I have too long digressed, and therefore shall return to my subject. I think the advantages by the proposal which I have made are obvious and many, as well as of the highest importance.

For first, as I have already observed, it would greatly lessen the number of Papists, with whom we are yearly overrun, being the principal breeders of the nation as well as our most dangerous enemies; and who stay at home on purpose to deliver the kingdom to the Pretender, hoping to take their advantage by the absence of so many good Protestants, who have chosen rather to leave their country than to stay at home and pay tithes against their conscience to an Episcopal curate.

Secondly, the poorer tenants will have something valuable of their own, which by law may be made liable to distress, and help to pay their landlord's rent, their corn and cattle being already seized and money a thing unknown.

Thirdly, whereas the maintenance of an hundred thousand children, from two years old and upwards, cannot be computed at less than ten shillings a piece per annum, the nation's stock will be thereby increased fifty thousand pounds per annum, besides the profit of a new dish introduced to the tables of all gentlemen of fortune in the kingdom who have any refinement in taste. And the money will circulate among ourselves, the goods being entirely of our own growth and manufacture.

Fourthly, the constant breeders, besides the gain of eight shillings sterling per annum by the sale of their children, will be rid of the charge of maintaining them after the first year.

Fifthly, this food would likewise bring great custom to taverns, where the vinters will certainly be so prudent as to procure the best receipts for dressing it to perfection, and consequently have their houses frequented by all the fine gentlemen, who justly value themselves upon their knowledge in good eating; and a skillful cook, who understands how to oblige his guests, will contrive to make it as expensive as they please.

Sixthly, this would be a great inducement to marriage, which all wise nations have either encouraged by rewards or enforced by laws and penalties. It would increase the care and tenderness of mothers toward their children, when they were sure of a settlement for life to the poor babes, provided in some sort by the public, to their annual profit instead of expense. We should see an honest emulation among the married women, which of them could bring the fattest child to the market. Men would become as fond of their wives during the time of their pregnancy as they are now of their mares in foal, their cows in calf, or sows when they are ready to farrow; nor offer to beat or kick them (as is too frequent a practice) for fear of a miscarriage.

Many other advantages might be enumerated. For instance, the addition of some thousand carcasses in our exportation of barreled beef, the propagation of swine's flesh, and improvement in the art of making good bacon, so much wanted among us by the great destruction of pigs, too frequent at our tables, which are no way comparable in taste or magnificence to a well-grown, fat, yearling child, which roasted whole will make a considerable figure at a lord mayor's feast or any other public entertainment. But this and many others I omit, being studious of brevity.

Supposing that one thousand families in this city would be constant customers for infants' flesh, besides others who might have it at merry meetings, particularly weddings and christenings, I compute that Dublin would take off annually about twenty thousands carcasses, and the rest of the kingdom (where probably they will be sold somewhat cheaper) the remaining eighty thousand.

I can think of no one objection that will possibly be raised against this proposal, unless it should be urged that the number of people will be thereby much lessened in the kingdom. This I freely own, and it was indeed one principal design in offering it to the world. I desire the reader will observe, that I calculate my remedy for this one individual kingdom of Ireland and for no other that ever was, is, or I think ever can be upon earth. Therefore let no man talk to me of other expedients: of taxing our absentees at five shillings a pound: of using neither clothes nor household furniture except what is of our own growth and manufacture: of utterly rejecting the materials and instruments that promote foreign luxury: of curing the expensiveness of pride, vanity, idleness, and gaming in our women: of introducing a vein of parsimony, prudence, and temperance: of learning to love our country, in the want of which we differ even from Laplanders and the inhabitants of Topinamboo:[3] of quitting our animosities and factions, nor acting any longer like the Jews, who were murdering one another at the very moment their city was taken: of being a little cautious not to sell our country and conscience for nothing: of teaching landlords to have at least one degree of mercy toward their tenants: lastly: of putting a spirit of honesty, industry, and skill into our shopkeepers; who, if a resolution could now be taken to buy only our native goods, would immediately unite to cheat and exact upon us in the price, the measure, and the goodness, nor could ever yet be brought to make one fair proposal of just dealing, though often and earnestly invited to it.

Therefore I repeat, let no man talk to me of these and the like expedients, till he hath at least some glimpse of hope that there will ever be some hearty and sincere attempt to put them in practice.

But as to myself, having been wearied out for many years with offering vain, idle, visionary thoughts, and at length utterly despairing of success, I fortunately fell upon this proposal, which, as it is wholly new, so it hath something solid and real, of no expense and little trouble, full in our own power and whereby we can incur no danger in disobliging England. For this kind of commodity will not bear exportation, the flesh being of too tender a consistence to admit a long continuance in salt, although perhaps I could name a country which would be glad to eat up our whole nation without it.

After all, I am not so violently bent upon my own opinion as to reject any offer proposed by wise men, which shall be found equally innocent, cheap, easy, and effectual. But before something of that kind shall be advanced in contradiction to my scheme, and offering a better, I desire the author or authors will be pleased maturely to consider two points. First, as things now stand, how they will be able to find food and raiment for an hundred thousands useless mouths and backs. And secondly, there being a round million of creatures in human figure throughout this kingdom, whose sole subsistence put into a common stock would leave them in debt two millions of pounds sterling, adding those who are beggars by profession to the bulk of farmers, cottagers, and laborers, with their wives and children who are beggars in effect; I desire those politicians who dislike my overture, and may perhaps be so bold to attempt an answer, that they will first ask the parents of these mortals whether they would not at this day think it a great happiness to have been sold for food at a year old in the manner I prescribe, and thereby have avoided such a perpetual scene of misfortunes as they have since gone through by

[3] A district in Brazil.

the oppression of landlords, the impossibility of paying rent without money or trade, the want of common sustenance, with neither house nor clothes to cover them from the inclemencies of the weather, and the most inevitable prospect of entailing the like or greater miseries upon their breed forever.

I profess, in the sincerity of my heart, that I have not the least personal interest in endeavoring to promote this necessary work, having no other motive than the public good of my country, by advancing our trade, providing for infants, relieving the poor, and giving some pleasure to the rich. I have no children by which I can propose to get a single penny; the youngest being nine years old, and my wife past childbearing.

For Discussion

1. The irony of the essay arises from our recognition that there is a difference between Swift himself and the Speaker who makes the proposal. The two different voices address two different audiences and actually make two different arguments. Describe the voices, the audiences, and the arguments.
2. How does the Speaker's language reveal his personality?
3. The Speaker's argument cannot be destroyed by pointing to any fallacies in reasoning or lack of supporting evidence. On what grounds, then, *can* one argue with his proposal?
4. What does this argument do that any good argument should do?
5. Of what purpose are the grisly arithmetic and other special details?
6. What advantages other than economic does the Speaker propose?
7. Archibald MacLeish has said that the purpose of poetry is to make "facts felt." Discuss the essay in the light of this idea.
8. In this essay murder is disguised as humanitarianism. What evidences of similar arguments can you find in contemporary life?
9. What reasons might you have for placing this essay in "The Impassioned NO"? "The Discursive NO"?

ELIZABETH CADY STANTON

Declaration of Woman's Rights

Elizabeth Cady Stanton (1815–1902) felt keenly the Victorian assumption of male superiority and the helplessness of women. Despite her brilliance, she was not permitted to attend college, and, despite her training in law, could not take examinations or set up practice. Married in 1840 (with the word "obey" omitted from the ceremony), she moved to Seneca, New York, where she and some associates called together the first Woman's Rights Convention in 1848. The following "Declaration," adopted at that convention, was widely ridiculed, and many who had signed later withdrew their names. Stanton, along with Susan B. Anthony, is the author of the classic *History of Woman's Suffrage.*

When, in the course of human events, it becomes necessary for one portion of the family of man to assume among the people of the earth a position different from that which they have hitherto occupied, but one to which the laws of nature and of nature's God entitle them, a decent respect to the opinions of mankind requires that they should declare the causes that impel them to such a course.

We hold these truths to be self-evident: that all men and women are created equal; that they are endowed by their Creator with certain inalienable rights; that among these are life, liberty, and the pursuit of happiness; that to secure these rights governments are instituted, deriving their just powers from the consent of the governed. Whenever any form of government becomes destructive of these ends, it is the right of those who suffer from it to refuse allegiance to it, and to insist upon the institution of a new government, laying its foundation on such principles, and organizing its powers in such form, as to them shall seem most likely to effect their safety and happiness. Prudence, indeed, will dictate that goverments long established should not be changed for light and transient causes; and accordingly all experience hath shown that mankind are more disposed to suffer, while evils are sufferable, than to right themselves by abolishing the forms to which they were accustomed. But when a long train of abuses and usurpations, pursuing invariably the same object evinces a design to reduce them under absolute despotism, it is their duty to throw off such government, and to provide new guards for their future security. Such has been the patient sufferance of the women under this government, and such is now the necessity which constrains them to demand the equal station to which they are entitled.

The history of mankind is a history of repeated injuries and usurpations on the part of man toward woman, having in direct object the establishment of an absolute tyranny over her. To prove this, let facts be submitted to a candid world.

He has never permitted her to exercise her inalienable right to the elective franchise.

He has compelled her to submit to laws, in the formation of which she had no voice.

He has withheld from her rights which are given to the most ignorant and degraded men—both natives and foreigners.

Having deprived her of this first right of a citizen, the elective franchise, thereby leaving her without representation in the halls of legislation, he has oppressed her on all sides.

He has made her, if married, in the eye of the law, civilly dead.

He has taken from her all right in property, even to the wages she earns.

He has made her, morally, an irresponsible being, as she can commit many crimes with impunity, provided they be done in the presence of her husband. In the covenant of marriage, she is compelled to promise obedience to her husband, he becoming, to all intents and purposes, her master—the law giving him power to deprive her of her liberty, and to administer chastisement.

He has so framed the laws of divorce, as to what shall be the proper causes, and in case of separation, to whom the guardianship of the children shall be given, as to be wholly regardless of the happiness of women—the law, in all cases, going upon a false supposition of the supremacy of man, and giving all power into his hands.

After depriving her of all rights as a married woman, if single, and the owner of property, he has taxed her to support a government which recognizes her only when her property can be made profitable to it.

He has monopolized nearly all the profitable employments, and from those she is permitted to follow, she receives but a scanty remuneration. He closes against her all the avenues to wealth and distinction which he considers most honorable to himself. As a teacher of theology, medicine, or law, she is not known.

He has denied her the facilities for obtaining a thorough education, all colleges being closed against her.

He allows her in Church, as well as State, but a subordinate position, claiming Apostolic authority for her exclusion from the ministry, and, with some exceptions, from any public participation in the affairs of the Church.

He has created a false public sentiment by giving to the world a different code of morals for men and women, by which moral delinquencies which exclude women from society, are not only tolerated, but deemed of little account in man.

He has usurped the prerogative of Jehovah himself, claiming it as his right to assign for her a sphere of action, when that belongs to her conscience and to her God.

He has endeavored, in every way that he could, to destroy her confidence in her own powers, to lessen her self-respect, and to make her willing to lead a dependent and abject life.

Now, in view of this entire disenfranchisement of one-half the people of this country, their social and religious degradation—in view of the unjust laws above mentioned, and because women do feel themselves aggrieved, oppressed, and fraudulently deprived of their most sacred rights, we insist that they have immediate admission to all the rights and privileges which belong to them as citizens of the United States.

In entering upon the great work before us, we anticipate no small amount of misconception, misrepresentation, and ridicule; but we shall use every instrumentality within our power to effect our object. We shall employ agents, circulate tracts, petition the State and National legislatures, and endeavor to enlist the pulpit and the press in our behalf. We hope this Convention will be followed by a series of Conventions embracing every part of the country.

For Discussion

1. Why do you think the decision was made to model this "Declaration" after the Declaration of Independence?
2. An editorial written after the convention at which the "Declaration" was accepted called the "Declaration" a ridiculous parody upon the Declaration of American Independence. Do you agree? Explain.
3. Compare this "Declaration" to the original Declaration of Independence and discuss the importance of the changes and substitutions.
4. Is *mankind* an appropriate word to encompass both men and women? Explain.
5. What are the laws of nature and of nature's God to which the "Declaration" appeals? Contrast this idea with the widely held opinion that religion prescribes the supportive role of the wife.

6. Which of the grievances of women are no longer relevant? Which remain a problem?

7. With which of these grievances do you agree or disagree? Are there any you would add?

8. What do you think of the accusation, made at the time of the convention, that women who attend such meetings, write resolutions, make speeches, and work in women's committees are neglecting their more appropriate duties?

9. At the time of its adoption, the "Declaration" seemed threatening, for men would have to change their positions in society as women changed theirs. What changes have occurred? What are some of the threats men still feel?

10. What constitutes the ironic impact of this piece?

MARK TWAIN

The War Prayer

"The War Prayer" is an example of Twain's later work, in the
vein of *The Mysterious Stranger, The Damned Human Race,*
"The Man Who Corrupted Hadleyburg," and other darkly
satiric works. (See the introduction to "Reflections on Religion"
for biographical information on Twain.)

It was a time of great and exalting excitement. The country was up in
arms, the war was on, in every breast burned the holy fire of patriotism;
the drums were beating, the bands playing, the toy pistols popping, the
bunched firecrackers hissing and spluttering; on every hand and far down
the receding and fading spread of roofs and balconies a fluttering wilderness of flags flashed in the sun; daily the young volunteers marched down
the wide avenue gay and fine in their new uniforms, the proud fathers
and mothers and sisters and sweethearts cheering them with voices
choked with happy emotion as they swung by; nightly the packed mass
meetings listened, panting, to patriot oratory which stirred the deepest
deeps of their hearts and which they interrupted at briefest intervals
with cyclones of applause, the tears running down their cheeks the while;
in the churches the pastors preached devotion to flag and country and
invoked the God of Battles, beseeching His aid in our good cause in out-
pouring of fervid eloquence which moved every listener. It was indeed a
glad and gracious time, and the half-dozen rash spirits that ventured to
disapprove of the war and cast a doubt upon its righteouness straightway
got such a stern and angry warning that for their personal safety's sake
they quickly shrank out of sight and offended no more in that way.

Sunday morning came—next day the battalions would leave for the
front; the church was filled; the volunteers were there, their young faces
alight with martial dreams—visions of the stern advance, the gathering

momentum, the rushing charge, the flashing sabers, the flight of the foe, the tumult, the enveloping smoke, the fierce pursuit, the surrender!—then home from the war, bronzed heroes, welcomed, adored, submerged in golden seas of glory! With the volunteers sat their dear ones, proud, happy, and envied by the neighbors and friends who had no sons and brothers to send forth to the field of honor, there to win for the flag or, failing, die the noblest of noble deaths. The service proceeded; a war chapter from the Old Testament was read; the first prayer was said; it was followed by an organ burst that shook the building, and with one impulse the house rose, with glowing eyes and beating hearts, and poured out that tremendous invocaton—

> God the all-terrible! Thou who ordainest,
> Thunder they clarion and lightning thy sword!

Then came the "long" prayer. None could remember the like of it for passionate pleading and moving and beautiful language. The burden of its supplication was that an ever-merciful and benignant Father of us all would watch over our noble young soldiers and aid, comfort, and encourage them in their patriotic work; bless them, shield them in the day of battle and the hour of peril, bear them in His mighty hand, make them strong and confident, invincible in the bloody onset; help them to crush the foe, grant to them and to their flag and country imperishable honor and glory—

An aged stranger entered and moved with slow and noiseless step up the main aisle, his eyes fixed upon the minister, his long body clothed in a robe that reached to his feet, his head bare, his white hair descending in a frothy cataract to his shoulders, his seamy face unnaturally pale, pale even to ghastliness. With all eyes following him and wondering, he made his silent way; without pausing, he ascended to the preacher's side and stood there, waiting. With shut lids the preacher, unconscious of his presence, continued his moving prayer, and at last finished it with the words, uttered in fervent appeal, "Bless our arms, grant us the victory, O Lord our God, Father and Protector of our land and flag!"

The stranger touched his arm, motioned him to step aside—which the startled minister did—and took his place. During some moments he surveyed the spellbound audience with solemn eyes in which burned an uncanny light; then in a deep voice he said:

"I come from the Throne—bearing a message from Almighty God!" The words smote the house with a shock; if the stranger perceived it he gave no attention. "He has heard the prayer of His servant your shepherd and will grant it if such shall be your desire after I, His messenger, shall have explained to you its import—that is to say, its full import. For it is like unto many of the prayers of men, in that it asks for more than he who utters it is aware of—except he pause and think.

"God's servant and yours has prayed his prayer. Has he paused and taken thought? Is it one prayer? No, it is two—one uttered, the other not. Both have reached the ear of Him Who heareth all supplications, the spoken and the unspoken. Ponder this—keep it in mind. If you would beseech a blessing upon yourself, beware! lest without intent you invoke a curse upon a neighbor at the same time. If you pray for the blessing of rain upon your crop which needs it, by that act you are possibly praying for a curse upon some neighbor's crop which may not need rain and can be injured by it.

"You have heard your servant's prayer—the uttered part of it. I am commissioned of God to put into words the other part of it—that part which the pastor, and also you in your hearts, fervently prayed silently. And ignorantly and unthinkingly? God grant that it was so! You heard these words: 'Grant us the victory, O Lord our God!' That is sufficient. The *whole* of the uttered prayer is compact into those pregnant words. Elaborations were not necessary. When you have prayed for victory you have prayed for many unmentioned results which follow victory—*must* follow it, cannot help but follow it. Upon the listening spirit of God the Father fell also the unspoken part of the prayer. He commandeth me to put it into words. Listen!

"O Lord our Father, our young patriots, idols of our hearts, go forth to battle—be Thou near them! With them, in spirit, we also go forth from the sweet peace of our beloved firesides to smite the foe. O Lord our God, help us to tear their soldiers to bloody shreds with our shells; help us to cover their smiling fields with the pale forms of their patriot dead; help us to drown the thunder of the guns with the shrieks of their wounded, writhing in pain; help us to lay waste their humble homes with a hurricane of fire; help us to wring the hearts of their unoffending widows with unavailing grief; help us to turn them out roofless with their little children to wander unfriended the wastes of their desolated land in rags and hunger and thirst, sports of the sun flames of summer and the icy winds of winter, broken in spirit, worn with travail, imploring Thee for the refuge of the grave and denied it—for our sakes who adore Thee, Lord, blast their hopes, blight their lives, protract their bitter pilgrimage, make heavy their steps, water their way with their tears, stain the white snow with the blood of their wounded feet! We ask it, in the spirit of love, of Him Who is the Source of Love, and Who is the ever-faithful refuge and friend of all that are sore beset and seek His aid with humble and contrite hearts. Amen.

(*After a pause*) "Ye have prayed it; if we still desire it, speak! The messenger of the Most High waits."

It was believed afterward that the man was a lunatic, because there was no sense in what he said.

For Discussion

1. List the assertions about war which are stated or implied in the first two paragraphs. What mood is created?
2. Look at the language of both prayers. How does the phrasing of each determine the audience's response? What generalizations about the nature of communication can be inferred from your analysis?
3. Twain said, "The difference between the right word and the almost right word is the difference between real lightning and a lightning bug." Find examples of Twain's use of the "right" word.
4. As closely as you can, describe Twain's ironic technique. What adjective best describes the tone of Twain's irony? How is it reflected in the last sentence?
5. In the light of "The War Prayer," what meaning would the word "patriotism" have for Twain? What does it mean to you?

Epigrams

Epigram is defined in Webster's New World Dictionary as "any terse, witty, pointed statement, often antithetical." The epigrams which follow provide excellent examples, although Bierce referred to his as saws, or sayings, and Shaw called his principals[s] or rule[s] of conduct or statement[s] of a general truth." The three authors of the epigrams, all born during the mid-nineteenth century, all reflect the purpose of the satirist— to expose folly to ridicule and to attack vice in all its guises. Thus, a common intent links the mysterious Ambrose Bierce, who, after a career as a journalist and short story writer, disappeared from the world in 1914; Oscar Wilde, the playwright, poet, and critic whose trial and imprisonment as a homosexual led him to live out his life abroad (d. 1900); and George Bernard Shaw, a leading Fabian socialist, vegetarian, and pamphleteer, whose extraordinary career as a playwright spanned sixty years (d. 1950).

AMBROSE BIERCE

A penny saved is a penny to squander.
A man is known by the company that he organizes.
A bad workman quarrels with the man who calls him that.
A bird in the hand is worth what it will bring.
Better late than before anybody has invited you.
Example is better than following it.
Half a loaf is better than a whole one if there is much else.
Think twice before you speak to a friend in need.

What is worth doing is worth the trouble of asking somebody to do it.
Least said is soonest disavowed.
He laughs best who laughs least.
Speak of the Devil and he will hear about it.
Of two evils choose to be the least.
Strike while your employer has a big contract.
Where there's a will there's a won't.

OSCAR WILDE

A thing is not necessarily true because a man dies for it.
Men always want to be a woman's first love. That is their vanity. Women have a more subtle instinct about things: What they like is to be a man's last romance.
When one is in love one begins by deceiving oneself. And ends by deceiving others. That is what the world calls a romance.
A cynic is a man who knows the price of everything and the value of nothing.
. . . Duty is what one expects from others, it is not what one does oneself.
Education is an admirable thing, but it is well to remember from time to time that nothing that is worth knowing can be taught.
The tragedy of old age is not that one is old, but that one is young.
Selfishness is not living as one wishes to live, it is asking others to live as one wishes to live.
Sometimes the poor are praised for being thrifty. But to recommend thrift to the poor is both grotesque and insulting. It is like advising a man who is starving to eat less.
Anybody can sympathize with the sufferings of a friend, but it requires a very fine nature to sympathize with a friend's success.
As one reads history . . . one is absolutely sickened, not by the crimes that the wicked have committed, but by the punishments that the good have inflicted.
An idea that is not dangerous is unworthy of being called an idea at all.
Only the shallow know themselves.
A sentimentalist is simply one who desires to have the luxury of an emotion without paying for it.
Experience is the name every one gives to their mistakes.
There is no such thing as a moral or an immoral book. Books are well written or badly written. That is all.

GEORGE BERNARD SHAW

Do not do unto others as you would that they should do unto you. Their tastes may not be the same.

The best brought-up children are those who have seen their parents as they are. Hypocrisy is not the parent's first duty.

The vilest abortionist is he who attempts to mould a child's character.

Criminals do not die by the hands of the law. They die by the hands of other men.

Assassination on the scaffold is the worst form of assassination, because there it is invested with the approval of society.

Property, said Proudhon, is theft. This is the only perfect truism that has been uttered on the subject.

If you strike a child, take care that you strike it in anger, even at the risk of maiming it for life. A blow in cold blood neither can nor should be forgiven.

The love of fairplay is a spectator's virtue, not a principal's.

The man with toothache thinks everyone happy whose teeth are sound. The poverty-stricken man makes the same mistake about the rich man.

In an ugly and unhappy world the richest men can purchase nothing but ugliness and unhappiness.

Hell is paved with good intentions, not bad ones.

Those who minister to poverty and disease are accomplices in the two worst of all the crimes.

Those who understand evil pardon it; those who resent it destroy it.

Beware of the man who does not return your blow; he neither forgives you nor allows you to forgive yourself.

If you begin by sacrificing yourself to those you love, you will end by hating those to whom you have sacrificed yourself.

From *Man and Superman*, "Maxims for Revolutionists" by George Bernard Shaw. Reprinted by permission of The Society of Authers, on behalf of the Bernard Shaw Estate.

For Discussion

1. Which of the epigrams do you think are true? Which seem merely clever?
2. Which of these three writers seems the most optimistic? Explain.
3. Pick three of your favorite epigrams and explain what human follies are being ridiculed.
4. Where do we presently find epigrams?
5. Discuss the requirements necessary for writing good epigrams.
6. What constructive values can you see operating in these epigrams?

D. H. LAWRENCE

Benjamin Franklin

The following essay is illustrative of Lawrence's interest in personality as a reflection of culture. (See the introduction to "Sex Versus Loveliness" for biographical information on Lawrence.)

The Perfectibility of Man! Ah heaven, what a dreary theme! The perfectibility of the Ford car! The perfectibility of which man! I am many men. Which of them are you going to perfect? I am not a mechanical contrivance.

Education! Which of the various me's do you propose to educate, and which do you propose to suppress?

Anyhow I defy you. I defy you, oh society, to educate me or to suppress me, according to your dummy standards.

The ideal man! And which is he, if you please? Benjamin Franklin or Abraham Lincoln? The ideal man! Roosevelt or Porfirio Diaz?

There are other men in me, besides this patient ass who sits here in a tweed jacket. What am I doing, playing the patient ass in a tweed jacket? Who am I talking to? Who are you, at the other end of this patience?

Who are you? How many selves have you? And which of these selves do you want to be?

Is Yale College going to educate the self that is in the dark of you, or Harvard College?

The ideal self! Oh, but I have a strange and fugitive self shut out and howling like a wolf or a coyote under the ideal windows. See his red eyes in the dark? This is the self who is coming into his own.

The perfectibility of man, dear God! When every man as long as he remains alive is in himself a multitude of conflicting men. Which of these do you choose to perfect, at the expense of every other?

Old Daddy Franklin will tell you. He'll rig him up for you, the pattern American. Oh, Franklin was the first downright American. He knew what he was about, the sharp little man. He set up the first dummy American.

At the beginning of his career, this cunning little Benjamin drew up for himself a creed that should "satisfy the professors of every religion, but shock none."

Now wasn't that a real American thing to do?

"That there is One God, who made all things."

(But Benjamin made Him.)

"That He governs the world by His Providence."

(Benjamin knowing all about Providence.)

"That He ought to be worshiped with adoration, prayer, and thanks-giving."

(Which cost nothing.)

"But—" But me no buts, Benjamin, saith the Lord.

"But that the most acceptable service of God is doing good to men."

(God having no choice in the matter.)

"That the soul is immortal."

("You'll see why, in the next clause.)

"And that God will certainly reward virtue and punish vice, either here or hereafter."

Now if Mr. Andrew Carnegie, or any other millionaire, had wished to invent a God to suit his ends, he could not have done better. Benjamin did it for him in the eighteenth century. God is the supreme servant of men who want to get on, to *produce*. Providence. The provider. The heavenly storekeeper. The everlasting Wanamaker.

And this is all the God the grandsons of the Pilgrim Fathers had left. Aloft on a pillar of dollars.

"That the soul is immortal."

The trite way Benjamin says it!

But man has a soul, though you can't locate it either in his purse or his pocketbook or his heart or his stomach or his head. The *wholeness* of a man is his soul. Not merely that nice comfortable bit which Benjamin marks out.

It's a queer thing, is a man's soul. It is the whole of him. Which means it is the unknown him, as well as the known. It seems to me just funny, professors and Benjamins fixing the functions of the soul. Why the soul of a man is a vast forest, and all Benjamin intended was a neat back garden. And we've all got to fit in to his kitchen garden scheme of things. Hail Columbia!

The soul of man is a dark forest. The Hercynian Wood that scared the Romans so, and out of which came the white-skinned hordes of the next civilization.

Who knows what will come out of the soul of man? The soul of man is a dark vast forest, with wild life in it. Think of Benjamin fencing it off!

Oh, but Benjamin fenced a little tract that he called the soul of man, and proceeded to get it into cultivation. Providence, forsooth! And they think that bit of barbed wire is going to keep us in pound forever? More fools them.

This is Benjamin's barbed wire fence. He made himself a list of virtues, which he trotted inside like a grey nag in a paddock.

1. *Temperance.* Eat not to fullness; drink not to elevation.
2. *Silence.* Speak not but what may benefit others or yourself; avoid trifling conversation.
3. *Order.* Let all your things have their places; let each part of your business have its time.
4. *Resolution.* Resolve to perform what you ought; perform without fail what you resolve.
5. *Frugality.* Make no expense but to do good to others or yourself—i.e., waste nothing.
6. *Industry.* Lose no time, be always employed in something useful; cut off all unnecessary action.
7. *Sincerity.* Use no hurtful deceit; think innocently and justly, and, if you speak, speak accordingly.
8. *Justice.* Wrong none by doing injuries, or omitting the benefits that are your duty.
9. *Moderation.* Avoid extremes, forbear resenting injuries as much as you think they deserve.
10. *Cleanliness.* Tolerate no uncleanliness in body, clothes, or habitation.
11. *Tranquility.* Be not disturbed at trifles, or at accidents common or avoidable.
12. *Chastity.* Rarely use venery but for health and offspring, never to dullness, weakness, or the injury of your own or another's peace or reputation.
13. *Humility.* Imitate Jesus and Socrates.

A Quaker friend told Franklin that he, Benjamin, was generally considered proud, so Benjamin put in the Humility touch as an afterthought. The amusing part is the sort of humility it displays. "Imitate Jesus and Socrates," and mind you don't outshine either of these two. One can just imagine Socrates and Alcibiades roaring in their cups over Philadelphian Benjamin, and Jesus looking at him a little puzzled, and murmuring: "Aren't you wise in your own conceit, Ben?"

"Hence forth be masterless," retorts Ben. "Be ye each one his own master unto himself, and don't let even the Lord put his spoke in." "Each man his own master" is but a puffing up of masterlessness.

Well, the first of Americans practiced this enticing list with assiduity, setting a national example. He had the virtues in columns, and gave himself good and bad marks according as he thought his behavior deserved. Pity these conduct charts are lost to us. He only remarks that Order was his stumbling block. He could not learn to be neat and tidy.

Isn't it nice to have nothing worse to confess?

He was a little model, was Benjamin. Doctor Franklin. Snuff-colored little man! Immortal soul and all!

The immortal soul part was a sort of cheap insurance policy.

Benjamin had no concern, really, with the immortal soul. He was too busy with social man.

1. He swept and lighted the streets of young Philadelphia.
2. He invented electrical appliances.
3. He was the center of a moralizing club in Philadelphia, and he wrote the moral humorisms of Poor Richard.
4. He was a member of all the important councils of Philadelphia, and then of the American colonies.
5. He won the cause of American Independence at the French Court, and was the economic father of the United States.

Now what more can you want of a man? And yet he is *infra dig*, even in Philadelphia.

I admire him. I admire his sturdy courage first of all, then his sagacity, then his glimpsing into the thunders of electricity, then his commonsense humor. All the qualities of a great man, and never more than a great citizen. Middle-sized, sturdy, snuff-colored Doctor Franklin, one of the soundest citizens that ever trod or "used venery."

I do not like him.

And, by the way, I always thought books of Venery were about hunting deer.

There is a certain earnest naïveté about him. Like a child. And like a little old man. He has again become as a little child, always as wise as his grandfather, or wiser.

Perhaps, as I say, the most complete citizen that ever "used venery."

Printer, philosopher, scientist, author and patriot, impeccable husband and citizen, why isn't he an archetype?

Pioneer, Oh Pioneers! Benjamin was one of the greatest pioneers of the United States. Yet we just can't do with him.

What's wrong with him then? Or what's wrong with us?

I can remember, when I was a little boy, my father used to buy a scrubby yearly almanack with the sun and moon and stars on the cover. And it used to prophesy bloodshed and famine. But also crammed in corners it had little anecdotes and humorisms, with a moral tag. And I used to have my little priggish laugh at the woman who counted her chickens before they were hatched, and so forth, and I was convinced that honesty was the best policy, also a little priggishly. The author of these bits was Poor Richard, and Poor Richard was Benjamin Franklin, writing in Philadelphia well over a hundred years before.

And probably I haven't got over those Poor Richard tags yet. I rankle still with them. They are thorns in young flesh.

Because although I still believe that honesty is the best policy, I dislike policy altogether; though it is just as well not to count your chickens before they are hatched, it's still more hateful to count them with gloating when they *are* hatched. It has taken me many years and countless smarts to get out of that barbed wire moral enclosure that Poor Richard rigged up. Here am I now in tatters and scratched to ribbons, sitting in the middle of Benjamin's America looking at the barbed wire, and the fat sheep crawling under the fence to get fat outside and the watchdogs yelling at the gate lest by chance anyone should get out by the proper exit. Oh America! Oh Benjamin! And I just utter a long loud curse against Benjamin and the American corral.

Moral America! Most moral Benjamin. Sound, satisfied Ben!

He had to go to the frontiers of his State to settle some disturbance among the Indians. On this occasion he writes:

We found that they had made a great bonfire in the middle of the square; they were all drunk, men and women quarreling and fighting. Their dark-colored bodies, half naked, seen only by the gloomy light of the bonfire, running after and beating one another with fire-brands, accompanied by their horrid yellings, formed a scene the most resembling our ideas of hell that could well be imagined. There was no appeasing the tumult, and we retired to our lodging. At midnight a number of them came thundering at our door, demanding more rum, of which we took no notice.

The next day, sensible they had misbehaved in giving us that disturbance, they sent three of their counselors to make their apology. The orator acknowledged the fault, but laid it upon the rum, and then endeavored to excuse the rum by saying: "The Great Spirit, who made all things, made everything for some use; and whatever he designed anything for, that use it should always be put to. Now, when he had made rum, he said: 'Let this be for the Indians to get drunk with.' And it must be so."

And, indeed, if it be the design of Providence to extirpate these savages in order to make room for the cultivators of the earth, it seems not improbable that rum may be the appointed means. It has already annihilated all the tribes who formerly inhabited all the seacoast. . . .

This from the good doctor, with such suave complacency is a little disenchanting. Almost too good to be true.

But there you are! The barbed wire fence. "Extirpate these savages in order to make room for the cultivators of the earth." O, Benjamin Franklin! He even "used venery" as a cultivator of seed.

Cultivate the earth, ye gods! The Indians did that, as much as they needed. And they left off there. Who built Chicago? Who cultivated the earth until it spawned Pittsburg, Pa.?

The moral issue! Just look at it! Cultivation included. If it's a mere choice of Kultur or cultivation, I give it up.

Which brings us right back to our question, what's wrong with Benjamin, that we can't stand him? Or else, what's wrong with us, that we find fault with such a paragon?

Man is a moral animal. All right. I am a moral animal. And I'm going to remain such. I'm not going to be turned into a virtuous little automaton as Benjamin would have me. "This is good, that is bad. Turn the little handle and let the good tap flow," saith Benjamin and all America with him. "But first all extirpate those savages who are always turning on the bad tap."

I am a moral animal. But I am not a moral machine. I don't work with a little set of handles or levers. The Temperance-silence-order-resolution-frugality-industry-sincerity-justice-moderation-cleanliness-tranquillity-chastity-humility keyboard is not going to get me going. I'm really not just an automatic piano with a moral Benjamin getting tunes out of me.

Here's my creed, against Benjamin's. This is what I believe:

"That I am I."

"That my soul is a dark forest."

"That my known self will never be more than a little clearing in the forest."

"That gods, strange gods, come forth from the forest into the clearing of my known self, and then go back."

"That I must have the courage to let them come and go."

"That I will never let mankind put anything over me, but that I will try always to recognize and submit to the gods in me and the gods in other men and women."

There is my creed. He who runs may read. He who prefers to crawl, or to go by gasoline, can call it rot.

Then for a "list." It is rather fun to play at Benjamin.

1. *Temperance.* Eat and carouse with Bacchus, or munch dry bread with Jesus, but don't sit down without one of the gods.
2. *Silence.* Be still when you have nothing to say; when genuine passion moves you, say what you've got to say, and say it hot.
3. *Order.* Know that you are responsible to the gods inside you and to the men in whom the gods are manifest. Recognize your superiors and your inferiors, according to the gods. This is the root of all order.

4. *Resolution.* Resolve to abide by your own deepest promptings and to sacrifice the smaller thing to the greater. Kill when you must, and be killed the same: the *must* coming from the gods inside you, or from the men in whom you recognize the Holy Ghost.

5. *Frugality.* Demand nothing; accept what you see fit. Don't waste your pride or squander your emotion.

6. *Industry.* Lose no time with ideals; serve the Holy Ghost; never serve mankind.

7. *Sincerity.* To be sincere is to remember that I am I, and that the other man is not me.

8. *Justice.* The only justice is to follow the sincere intuition of the soul, angry or gentle. Anger is just, and pity is just, but judgment is never just.

9. *Moderation.* Beware of absolutes. There are many gods.

10. *Cleanliness.* Don't be too clean. It impoverishes the blood.

11. *Tranquility.* The soul has many motions, many gods come and go. Try to find your deepest issue, in every confusion, and abide by that. Obey the man in whom you recognize the Holy Ghost; command when your honor comes to command.

12. *Chastity.* Never "use" venery at all. Follow your passional impulse, if it be answered in the other being; but never have any motive in mind, neither off-spring nor health nor even pleasure, nor even service. Only know that "venery" is of the great gods. An offering-up of yourself to the very great gods, the dark ones, and nothing else.

13. *Humility.* See all men and women according to the Holy Ghost that is within them. Never yield before the barren.

There's my list. I have been trying dimly to realize it for a long time, and only America and old Benjamin have at last goaded me into trying to formulate it.

And now I, at least, know why I can't stand Benjamin. He tries to take away my wholeness and my dark forest, my freedom. For how can any man be free, without an illimitable background? And Benjamin tries to shove me into a barbed-wire paddock and make me grow potatoes or Chicagoes.

And how can I be free, without gods that come and go? But Benjamin won't let anything exist except my useful fellow-men, and I'm sick of them; as for his Godhead, his Providence, He is Head of nothing except a vast heavenly store that keeps every imaginable line of goods, from victrolas to cat-o-nine tails.

And how can any man be free without a soul of his own, that he believes in and won't sell at any price? But Benjamin doesn't let me have a soul of my own. He says I am nothing but a servant of mankind—

galley-slave I call it—and if I don't get my wages here below—that is, if Mr. Pierpont Morgan or Mr. Nosey Hebrew or the grand United States Government, the great US, US OR SOMEOFUS, manages to scoop in my bit along with their lump—why, never mind, I shall get my wages HEREAFTER.

Oh, Benjamin! Oh Binjum! You do NOT suck me in any longer.

And why oh why should the snuff-colored little trap have wanted to take us all in? Why did he do it?

Out of sheer human cussedness, in the first place. We do all like to get things inside a barbed-wire corral. Especially our fellow-men. We love to round them up inside the barbed-wire enclosure of FREEDOM, and make 'em work. *"Work, you free jewel, WORK!"* shouts the liberator, cracking his whip. Benjamin, I will not work. I do not choose to be a free democrat. I am absolutely a servant of my own Holy Ghost.

Sheer cussedness! But there was as well the salt of a subtler purpose. Benjamin was just in his eyeholes—to use an English vulgarism meaning he was just delighted—when he was at Paris judiciously milking money out of the French monarchy for the overthrow of all monarchy. If you want to ride your horse to somewhere you must put a bit in his mouth. And Benjamin wanted to ride his horse so that it would upset the whole apple-cart of the old masters. He wanted the whole European apple-cart upset. So he had to put a strong bit in the mouth of his ass.

"Henceforth be masterless."

That is, he had to break in the human ass completely, so that much more might be broken, in the long run. For the moment it was the British Government that had to have a hole knocked in it. The first real hole it ever had: the breach of the American rebellion.

Benjamin, in his sagacity, knew that the breaking of the old world was a long process. In the depths of his own under-consciousness he hated England, he hated Europe, he hated the whole corpus of the European being. He wanted to be American. But you can't change your nature and mode of consciousness like changing your shoes. It is a gradual shedding. Years must go by, and centiures must elapse before you have finished. Like a son escaping from the domination of his parents. The escape is not just one rupture. It is a long and half-secret process.

So with the American. He was a European when he first went over the Atlantic. He is in the main a recreant European still. From Benjamin Franklin to Woodrow Wilson may be a long stride, but it is a stride along the same road. There is no new road. The same old road, become dreary and futile. Theoretic and materialistic.

Why then did Benjamin set up this dummy of a perfect citizen as a pattern to America? Of course he did it in perfect good faith, as far as he knew. He thought it simply was the true ideal. But what we *think* we do is not very important. We never really know what we are doing. Either we are materialistic instruments, like Benjamin or we move in the gesture of creation, from our deepest self, usually unconscious. We are only the actors, we are never wholly the authors of our own deeds or works. IT is the author, the unknown inside us or outside us. The best we can do is to try to hold ourselves in unison with the deeps which are inside us. And the worst we can do is to try to have things our own way, when we run counter to IT, and in the long run get our knuckles rapped for our presumption.

So Benjamin contriving money out of the Court of France. He was contriving the first steps of the overthrow of all Europe, France included. You can never have a new thing without breaking an old. Europe happens to be the old thing. America, unless the people in America assert themselves too much in opposition to the inner gods, should be the new thing. The new thing is the death of the old. But you can't cut the throat of an epoch. You've got to steal the life from it through several centuries.

And Benjamin worked for this both directly and indirectly. Directly, at the Court of France, making a small but very dangerous hole in the side of England, through which hole Europe has by now almost bled to death. And indirectly in Philadelphia, setting up this unlovely, snuff-colored little ideal, or automaton, of a pattern American. The pattern American, this dry, moral utilitarian little democrat, has done more to ruin the old Europe than any Russian nihilist. He has done it by slow attrition, like a son who has stayed at home and obeyed his parents, all the while silently hating their authority, and silently, in his soul, destroying not only their authority but their whole existence. For the American spiritually stayed at home in Europe. The spiritual home of America was and still is Europe. This is the galling bondage, in spite of several billions of heaped-up gold. Your heaps of gold are only so many muck-heaps, America, and will remain so till you become a reality to yourselves.

All this Americanizing and mechanizing has been for the purpose of overthrowing the past. And now look at America, tangled in her own barbed wire, and mastered by her own machines. Absolutely got down by her own barbed wire of shalt-nots, and shut up fast in her own "productive" machines like millions of squirrels running in millions of cages. It is just a farce.

Now is your chance, Europe. Now let Hell loose and get your own back, and paddle your own canoe on a new sea, while clever America lies on her muck-heaps of gold, stranged in her own barbed-wire of shalt-not ideals and shalt-not moralisms. While she goes out to work like millions of squirrels in millions of cages. Production!

Let Hell loose, and get your own back, Europe!

For Discussion

1. How does Lawrence immediately set himself at odds with Franklin?
2. Contrast Lawrence's and Franklin's ideas of the soul. Discuss the metaphors used to illustrate each. How does Lawrence's metaphor fit his idea of "mystery" in "Sex Versus Loveliness"?
3. Discuss Lawrence's objection to honesty as the best policy.
4. What purpose does the illustration of the Indian uprising serve?
5. Discuss Lawrence's creed in terms of its value to the individual. To society.
6. What analysis does Lawrence make of Franklin's negotiations with France?
7. What do you think is at the heart of Lawrence's dislike of Franklin?
8. What does Lawrence find to admire in Franklin?
9. What is Lawrence's focus in the final paragraphs? What other dimension does this add to the purpose of the satire?
10. Locate descriptive phrases in which the word choice reveals Lawrence's attitude toward Franklin.
11. Make an argument for including this piece in "The Impassioned NO"· "The Reflective NO."

H. L. MENCKEN

The Politician

H. L. Mencken was born in Baltimore in 1880. After graduation from high school at sixteen, he began newspaper work at the Baltimore *Evening Herald,* becoming managing editor at the age of twenty-five. In 1906, he joined the staff of the Baltimore *Sun,* where he maintained staff relations until 1941, in the meantime launching *The American Mercury* with George Jean Nathan, an association that was to last nine years. An iconoclastic critic and a celebrated stylist, Mencken exerted a powerful influence on the press of the nation during the first half of this century. Perhaps our greatest satirical journalist, he continually attacked the *"boob*oisie," a term which he used to epitomize American middle-class values. His linguistic study, *The American Language*, is probably his best-known work, but the force of his personality can be strongly noted in his six volumes of *Prejudices*, where this essay appears in Volume IV.

Half the sorrows of the world, I suppose, are caused by making false assumptions. If the truth were only easier to ascertain, the remedy for them would consist simply of ascertaining it and accepting it. This business, alas, is usually impossible, but fortunately not always: now and then, by some occult process, half rational and half instinctive, the truth gets itself found out and an ancient false assumption goes overboard. I point, in the field of the social relations, to one which afflicted the human race for millenniums: that one, to wit, which credited the rev. clergy with a mysterious wisdom and awful powers. Obviously, it has ceased to trouble all the superior varieties of men. It may survive in those remote marches where human beings go to bed with the cows, but certainly it has vanished from the cities. Asphalt and the apostolic succession, indeed, seem to be irreconcilable enemies. I can think of no clergyman in any great American city today whose public dignity and influence are much above those of an ordinary Class I Babbitt. It is hard for even the most diligent and passionate of the ancient order to get upon the first pages of the newspapers; he must make a clown-show, discreditable to his fraying cloth, or he must blush unseen. When bishops begin launching thunderbolts against heretics, the towns do not tremble; they laugh. When elders denounce sin, sin only grows more popular. Imagine a city man getting a notice from the ordinary of his diocese that he had been excommunicated. It would trouble him far less, I venture, than his morning *Katzenjammer*.

The reason for all this is not hard to find. All the superior varieties of men—and even the lowest varieties of city workmen are at least superior to peasants—have simply rid themselves of their old belief in devils. Hell no longer affrights and palsies them, and so the magic of those who profess to save them from it no longer impresses them. That profession, I believe, was bogus, and its acceptance was therefore a false assumption. Being so, it made men unhappy; getting rid of it has delivered them. They are no longer susceptible to ecclesiastical alarms and extortions; *ergo*, they sleep and eat better. Think of what life must have been under such princes of damnation as Cotton Mather and Jonathan Edwards, with even bartenders and metaphysicians believing in them! And then compare it to life under Bishop Manning and the Rev. Dr. John Roach Straton, with only a few half-wits believing in them! Or turn to the backwoods of the Republic, where the devil is still feared, and with him his professional exterminators. In the country towns the clergy are still almost as influential as they were in Mather's day, and there, as everyone knows, they remain public nuisances, and civilized life is almost impossible. In such Neolithic regions nothing can go on without their consent, on penalty of anathema and hell-fire; as a result, nothing goes on that is worth recording. It is this survival of sacerdotal authority, I begin to believe, and not hookworm, malaria or the event of April 9, 1865, that is chiefly responsible for the cultural paralysis of the late Confederate States. The South lacks big cities; it is run by its country towns—and in every country town there is some Baptist *mullah* who rules by scaring the peasantry. The false assumption that his pretensions are sound, that he can actually bind and loose, that contumacy to him is a variety of cursing God—this false assumption is what makes the yokels so uneasy, so nervous, and hence so unhappy. If they could throw it off they would burn fewer Aframericans and sing more songs. If they could be purged of it they would be purged of Ku Kluxry too.

The cities got rid of that false assumption half a century ago, and have been making cultural progress ever since. Somewhat later they got rid of its brother, to wit, respect for government and, in particular, respect for its visible agents, the police. That respect—traditional, and hence irrational—had been, for years, in increasingly unpleasant collision with a great body of obvious facts. The police, by assumption austere and almost sacrosanct, were gradually discovered to be, in reality, a pack of rogues and but little removed, save by superior impudence and enter- prise, from the cut-throats and purse-snatchers they were set to catch. When, a few decades ago, the American people, at least in the big cities, began to accept them frankly for what they were—when the old false assumption of their integrity and public usefulness was quietly aban- doned and a new and more accurate assumption of their roguery was adopted in its place—when this change was effected there was a mea- surable increase, I believe, in the public happiness. It no longer astonished anyone when policemen were taken in evildoing; indignation therefore abated, and with it its pains. If, before that time, the corps of Prohibition enforcement officers—*i.e.*, a corps of undisguised scoundrels with badges —had been launched upon the populace, there would have been a great roar of wrath, and much anguished gnashing of teeth. People would have felt themselves put upon, injured, insulted. But with the old false assump- tion about policemen removed from their minds, they met the new on- slaught calmy and even smilingly. Today no one is indignant over the fact that the extortions of these new *Polizei* increase the cost of potable alcohol. The false assumption that the police are altruistic agents of a benevolent state has been replaced by the sound assumption that they are gentlemen engaged assiduously, like the rest of us, in finding meat and raiment for their families and in laying up funds to buy Liberty Bonds in the next war to end war. This is human progress, for it increases human happiness.

So much for the evidence. The deduction I propose to make from it is simply this: that a like increase would follow if the American people could only rid themselves of another and worse false assumption that still rides them—one that corrupts all their thinking about the great business of politics, and vastly augments their discontent and unhappi- ness—the assumption, that is, that politicians are divided into two classes, and that one of those classes is made up of good ones. I need not argue, I hope, that this assumption is almost universally held among us. Our whole politics, indeed, is based upon it, and has been based upon it since the earliest days. What is any political campaign save a concerted effort to turn out a set of politicians who are admittedly bad and put in a set who are thought to be better? The former assumption, I believe, is always sound; the latter is just as certainly false. For if experience teaches us anything at all it teaches us this: that a good politician, under democracy, is quite as unthinkable as an honest burglar. His very existence, indeed, is a standing subversion of the public good in every rational sense. He is not one who serves the common weal; he is simply one who preys upon the commonwealth. It is to the interest of all the rest of us to hold down his powers to an irreducible minimum, and to reduce his compensation to nothing; it is to his interest to augment his powers at all hazards, and to make his compensation all the traffic will bear. To argue that these aims are identical is to argue palpable nonsense. The politician, at his ideal best, never even remotely approximated in practice, is a necessary evil; at his worst he is an almost intolerable nuisance.

What I contend is simply that he would be measurably less a nuisance if we got rid of our old false assumption about him, and regarded him in the cold light of fact. At once, I believe, two-thirds of his obnoxiousness would vanish. He would remain a nuisance, but he would cease to be a swindler; the injury of having to pay freight on him would cease to be complicated by the insult of being rooked. It is the insult and not the injury that makes the deeper wounds, and causes the greater permanent damage to the national psyche. All of us have been trained, since infancy, in putting up with necessary evils, plainly recognized *as* evils. We know, for example, that the young of the human species commonly smell badly; that garbage men, bootblacks and messenger boys commonly smell worse. These facts are not agreeable, but they remain tolerable because they are universally assumed—because there is no sense of having been tricked and cozened in their perennial discovery. But try to imagine how distressing fatherhood would become if prospective fathers were all taught that the human infant radiates an aroma like the rose—if the truth came constantly as a surprise! Each fresh victim of the deception would feel that he had been basely swindled—that his own child was somehow bogus. Not infrequently, I suppose, he would be tempted to make away with it in some quiet manner, and have another—only to be shocked again. That procedure would be idiotic, admittedly, yet it is exactly the one we follow in politics. At each election we vote in a new set of politicians, insanely assuming that they are better than the set turned out. And at each election we are, as they say in the Motherland, done in.

Of late the fraud has become so gross that the plain people begin to show a great restlessness under it. Like animals in a cage, they trot from one corner to another, endlessly seeking a way out. If the Democrats win one year, it is a pretty sure sign that they will lose the next year. State after state becomes doubtful, pivotal, skittish; even the solid South begins to break. In the cities it is still worse. An evil circle is formed. First the poor taxpayers, robbed by the politicians of one great party and then by those of the other, turn to a group of free-lance rogues in the middle ground—nonpartisan candidates, Liberals, reformers or whatnot: the name is unimportant. Then, flayed and pillaged by these gentry as they never were by the old-time professionals, they go back in despair to the latter, and are flayed and pillaged again. Back to Bach! Back to Tammany! Tammany reigns in New York because the Mitchel outfit was found to be intolerable—in other words, because the reformers were found to be even worse than the professionals. Is the fact surprising? Why should it be? Reformers and professionals are alike politicians in search of jobs; both are trying to bilk the taxpayers. Neither ever has any other motive. If any genuinely honest and altruistic politician had come to the surface in America in my time I'd have heard of him, for I have always frequented newspaper offices, and in a newspaper office the news of such a marvel would cause a dreadful tumult. I can recall no such tumult. The unanimous opinion of all the journalists that I know, excluding a few Liberals who are obviously somewhat balmy—they all believed, for example, that the late war would end war—is that, since the days of the national Thors and Wotans, no politician who was not out for himself, and for himself alone, has ever drawn the breath of life in the United States.

The gradual disintegration of Liberalism among us, in fact, offers an excellent proof of the truth of my thesis. The Liberals have come to grief by fooling their customers, not merely once too often, but a hundred times too often. Over and over again they have trotted out some new hero, usually from the great open spaces, only to see him taken in the immemorial malpractices within ten days. Their graveyard, indeed, is filled with cracked and upset headstones, many covered with ribald pencilings. Every time there is a scandal in the grand manner the Liberals lose almost as many general officers as either the Democrats or Republicans. Of late, racked beyond endurance by such catastrophes at home, they have gone abroad for their principal heroes; losing humor as well as hope, they now ask us to venerate such astounding paladins as the Hon. Béla Kun, a gentleman who, in any American state, would not only be in the calaboose, but actually in the deathhouse. But this absurdity is only an offshoot of a deeper one. Their primary error lies in making the false assumption that some politicians are better than others. This error they share with the whole American people.

I propose that it be renounced, and contend that its renunciation would greatly rationalize and improve our politics. I do not argue that there would be any improvement in our politicians; on the contrary, I believe that they would remain substantially as they are today, and perhaps grow even worse. But what I do argue is that recognizing them frankly for what they are would instantly and automatically dissipate the indignation caused by their present abominations, and that the disappearance of this indignation would promote the public contentment and happiness. Under my scheme there would be no more false assumptions and no more false hopes, and hence no more painful surprises, no more bitter resentment of fraud, no more despair. Politicians, in so far as they remained necessary, would be kept at work—but not with any insane notion that they were archangels. Their rascality would be assumed and discounted, as the rascality of the police is now assumed and discounted.

Machinery would be gradually developed to limit it and counteract it. In the end, it might be utilized in some publicly profitable manner, as the insensitiveness to filth of garbage men is now utilized, as the reverence of the clergy for capitalism is now utilized. The result, perhaps, would be a world no better than the present one, but it would at least be a world more intelligent.

In all this I sincerely hope that one one will mistake me for one who shares the indignation I have spoken of—that is, for one who believes that politicians can be made good, and cherishes a fond scheme for making them so. I believe nothing of the sort. On the contrary, I am convinced that the art and mystery they practice is essentially and incurably anti-social—that they must remain irreconcilable enemies of the common weal until the end of time. But I maintain that this fact, in itself, is not a bar to their employment. There are, under Christian civilization, many necessary offices that demand the possession of anti-social talents. A professional soldier, regarded realistically, is much worse than a professional politician, for he is a professional murderer and kidnaper, whereas the politician is only a professional sharper and sneak-thief. A clergyman, too, begins to shrink and shrivel on analysis; the work he does in the world is basically almost indistinguishable from that of an astrologer, a witch-doctor or a fortune-teller. He pretends falsely that he can get sinners out of hell, and collects money from them on that promise, tacit or express. If he had to go before a jury with that pretension it would probably go hard with him. But we do not send him before a jury; we grant him his hocus-pocus on the ground that it is necessary to his office, and that his office is necessary to civilization, so-called. I pass over the journalist delicately; the time has not come to turn state's evidence. Suffice it to say that he, too, would probably wither under a stiff cross-examination. If he is no murderer, like the soldier, then he is at least a sharper and swindler, like the politician.

What I plead for, if I may borrow a term in disrepute, is simply *Realpolitik, i. e.*, realism in politics. I can imagine a political campaign purged of all the current false assumptions and false pretenses—a campaign in which, on election day, the voters went to the polls clearly informed that the choice before them was not between an angel and a devil, a good man and a bad man, an altruist and a go-getter, but between two frank go-getters, the one, perhaps, excelling at beautiful and nonsensical words and the other at silent and prehensile deeds—the one a chautauqua orator and the other a porch-climber. There would be, in that choice, something candid, free and exhilarating. Buncombe would be adjourned. The voter would make his selection in the full knowledge of all the facts, as he makes his selection between two heads of cabbage, or two evening papers, or two brands of chewing tobacco. Today he chooses his rulers as he buys bootleg whiskey, never knowing precisely what he is getting, only certain that it is not what it pretends to be. The Scotch may turn out to be wood alcohol or it may turn out to be gasoline; in either case it is not Scotch. How much better if it were plainly labeled, for wood alcohol and gasoline both have their uses—higher uses, indeed, than Scotch. The danger is that the swindled and poisoned consumer, despairing of ever avoiding them when he doesn't want them, may prohibit them even when he does want them, and actually enforce his own prohibition. The danger is that the hopeless voter, forever victimized by his false assumption about politicians, may in the end gather such ferocious indignation that he will abolish them teetotally and at one insane swoop, and so cause government by the people, for the people and with the people to perish from this earth.

For Discussion

1. What examples of false assumptions does Mencken discuss in the first three paragraphs?
2. Explain the false assumptions that Americans hold about politicians.
3. What assumptions does Mencken provide as alternates? To what extent do you agree that these are valid?
4. According to Mencken, how would a more "realistic" attitude affect politics and politicians?
5. What would happen if American society discarded its false assumptions regarding politicians, press, police, and clergy? What changes would have to be made?
6. Although Mencken was writing in the early 1920s, many present day political observers have noted a similar "gradual disintegration of Liberalism among us." Discuss Mencken's reasoning in regard to this trend and try to account for its existence today.
7. Identify the following allusions:
   a. Babbitt
   b. Katzenjammers
   c. Cotton Mather
   d. Buncombe
8. What point is Mencken making in his analogy of bootleg whiskey? How valid is his point?
9. Locate sentences which illustrate ironic epigram, irreverent broadside, or hyperbole (for example, the sentence in paragraph three beginning "The police . . .").
10. How does Mencken create irony?

HENRY MILLER

The Staff of Life

The only formal education Henry Miller received, apart from two months at New York City College, was in public schools in Brooklyn, where he was born in 1891. The rest of his impressive and varied knowledge was acquired through reading and travel. In 1930 he went to Paris where his controversial career began with his first novel, *Tropic of Cancer* (1934), banned in the United States, along with many later books, until recent court decisions reversed the restrictions. Despite the long-existing ban, Miller continued to be widely read all over the world. First praised by the "beat" generation, whose prophet he unwillingly became, he now enjoys an enthusiastic following, even in the "academy," where he was ignored for so long. Famous for his realistic and surrealistic descriptions of his expatriate days in Paris, Miller wrote on subjects ranging from oriental philosophy to recipes—all with an equal hilarity, zest, and erudition. "The Staff of Life," now an American classic, develops the idea expressed in Ecclesiastes: "Eat thy bread with joy and drink thy wine with a merry heart."

Bread: prime symbol. Try and find a good loaf. You can travel fifty thousand miles in America without once tasting a piece of good bread. Americans don't care about good bread. They are dying of inanition but they go on eating bread without substance, bread without flavor, bread without vitamins, bread without life. Why? Because the very core of life is contaminated. If they knew what good bread was they would not have such wonderful machines on which they lavish all their time, energy and affection. A plate of false teeth means much more to an American than a loaf of good bread. Here is the sequence: poor bread, bad teeth, indigestion, constipation, halitosis, sexual starvation, disease and accidents,

the operating table, artificial limbs, spectacles, baldness, kidney and blad-
der trouble, neurosis, psychosis, schizophrenia, war and famine. Start with
the American loaf of bread so beautifully wrapped in cellophane and
you end on the scrap heap at forty-five. The only place to find a good
loaf of bread is in the ghettos. Wherever there is a foreign quarter there
is apt to be a good bread. Wherever there is a Jewish grocer or delicatessen you are almost certain to find an excellent loaf of bread. The dark
Russian bread, light in weight, found only rarely on this huge continent,
is the best bread of all. No vitamins have been injected into it by laboratory specialists in conformance with the latest food regulations. The
Russian just naturally likes good bread, because he also likes caviar and
vodka and other good things. Americans are whiskey, gin and beer
drinkers who long ago lost their taste for food. And losing that they
have also lost their taste for life. For enjoyment. For good conversation.
For everything worth while, to put it briefly.

What do I find wrong with America? Everything. I begin at the beginning, with the staff of life: bread. If the bread is bad the whole life is
bad. Bad? Rotten, I should say. Like that piece of bread only twenty-four
hours old which is good for nothing except perhaps to fill up a hole.
Good for target practice maybe. Or shuttlecock and duffle board. Even
soaked in urine it is unpalatable; even perverts shun it. Yet millions are
wasted advertising it. Who are the men engaged in this wasteful pursuit?
Drunkards and failures for the most part. Men who have prostituted
their talents in order to help further the decay and dissolution of our
once glorious Republic.

Here is one of the latest widely advertised products: Hollywood Bread.
On the red, white and blue cellophane jacket in which it is wrapped, this
last word in bread from the American bakeries, it reads as follows:

BAKED WITH
whole wheat flour, clear wheat flour, water, non-diastatic malt, yeast, salt,
honey, caramel, whole rye flour, yeast food, stone ground oatmeal, soya
flour, gluten flour, barley flour, sesame seed, and a small quantity of dehydrated (water free) vegetables including celery, lettuce, pumpkin, cabbage,
carrots, spinach, parsley, sea kelp, added for flavor only.

The only thing missing from this concoction is powdered diamonds.
How does it taste? Much like any other American product. Of course,
this is a reducing bread of which one should eat two slices a day three
times a day and not ask how it tastes. Grow thin, as in Hollywood, and
be thankful it doesn't taste worse. That's the idea. For several days now
I have been trying to get a whiff of some of those ingredients—sea kelp
especially—which were included "for flavor only." Why they were not
added for health too I don't know. Naturally all these delicious-sounding

items amount to about one ten-thousandth part of the loaf. And on the second day, stale, flat and unprofitable, this marvelous new bread is no more attractive to the palate or the stomach than any other loaf of American bread. On the second day it is good for replacing a missing tile on the roof. Or to make a scratchboard for the cat.

The second day! If the first is given to creation, to light, let us say, the second (in America) is given up to garbage. Every second day is garbage day in America. I know because I have had lots to do with garbage. I've hauled it, for pay, and I've eaten it upon necessity. I learned to distinguish between one kind of bread and another by salvaging dry crusts from the garbage can. I don't know which is worse—the day of creation, when everything turns to gas and bilge, with its concomitants dandruff, constipation, halitosis, false teeth, artificial limbs, psychic impotency, and so on, or the second day, given up to garbage, when all creation turns out to be nothing but a mirage and a disillusionment. It has been said, and I have no doubt it is true, that the garbage accumulated by one big American city would feed certain of the little countries of Europe handsomely. I know no quicker way to kill off the warring nations of Europe than to feed them our garbage. The pygmies might thrive on it, possibly even the Chinese coolie, who is supposed to thrive on anything, but I cannot see the Danes, the Swiss, the Swedes, the Greeks, the Albanians, or the Austrians thriving on it. No Sir. I would sooner feed them buzzards than the left-overs from the American table. Already, with our canned food products, our cold storage meat, our dehydrated vegetables, we have brought about a tremendous deterioration in these sturdy people of Europe. From these to the machine and thence to war is but a step. Then, famine, plague, pestilence, dung heaps. And monuments, of course. All sorts of monuments. Done by second or third rate artists.

The care and affection which once was bestowed on the human body now goes to the machines. The machines get the best food, the best attention. Machines are expensive; human lives are cheap. Never in the history of the world was life cheaper than it is to-day. (And no pyramids to show for it either.) How natural, then, that the staff of life should be utterly without value. I begin with bread and I shall end with bread. I say we make the foulest bread in all the world. We pass it off like fake diamonds. We advertise it and sterilize it and protect it from all the germs of life. We make a manure which we eat before we have had time to eliminate it. We not only have failed God, tricked Nature, debased Man, but we have cheated the birds of the air with our corrupt staff of life. Everytime I fling the stale bread over the cliff I beg forgiveness of the birds for offering them our American bread. Perhaps that is why they are not singing any more as they used to when I was a child. The birds are pining and drooping. It's not the war, for they have never participated in our carnages. It's the bread. The stale, flat, unprofitable bread of the second day. It shortens their wing-span, weakens their umbrella-ribs, reduces the scope of their swoop, blunts their beaks, deteriorates their vision, and finally—it kills their song! If you don't believe me, ask any ornithologist. It's a known fact. And how Americans love facts!

Another fact. . . . Food, when it is not enjoyed, kills. The best diet in the world is useless if the patient has no appetite, no gusto, no sensuality. On the whole, Americans eat without pleasure. They eat because the bell rings three times a day. (I omit mention of the clay eaters of the South and other poor whites who live on rats, snakes, and cow-dung.) They don't eat because they love food. To prove it you have only to shove a glass of whiskey before them. See which they reach for first! And now, with vitamins and all the other life-savers, food has become even less important. Why bother trying to squeeze a bit of life out of our worn-out products of the soil. Why pretend? Throw anything down the hatch to stop the gnawing and swallow a dozen vitamins. That way you'll make sure you've had your proper dose of the vital essentials. Should the vitamins fail, see a surgeon. From there to the sanitarium. And from there to the nut-house—or the dung heap. Be sure to get a Hollywood funeral. They're the loveliest, the duckiest, the most sanitary, the most inspiring. And no more expensive than ordinary ground burial. You can, if you like, have your dear lost one propped up in a natural reclining position, her cheeks rouged, a cigarette to her lips, and a phonograph record talking to you just as she once talked to you in life. The most wonderful fake imaginable. Jolly, what? O death, where is thy sting? What's more, she can be kept that way for an unspeakably long period; the cigarette is guaranteed not to rot away before the lips or the buttocks. You can come back and have a second, a third, a twenty-fifth look at the beloved. Still smoking a cigarette. Or you can have her reading a book, the *Iliad*, say, or the *Bhagavad Gita*—something uplifting like that.

I remember when I used to be served a slice of homemade bread with butter and sugar smeared over it. Glorious days! That bread really had a taste. *Schmecht gut, nichtwahr? Yah! Sehr gut. Wunderbar. Ausgezeichnet.* With a piece of bread like that I used to sit and read *Pinocchio* or *Alice Through the Looking Glass* or Hans Christian Andersen or *The Heart of a Boy*. Mothers had time in those days to make good bread with their own hands, and still do the thousand and one things which motherhood demands of a woman. To-day they haven't time to do anything, and hardly a bloody mother in the bloody land knows how to bake a loaf of bread. Mother gets up early now to work in an office or a factory. She's busy doing nothing all day, which is to say, earning a living. Earning a living has nothing to do with living. It's the belt line to the grave, without a transfer or a stopover. A one-way passage via the frying pan and the cookerless cooker. A child is an accident—bad rubber goods or else too much drink and recklessness. Any way, it's there and it has to be fed. You don't bake bread for accidents, do you? And why bother to produce milk from the breast when the cows are working over-time for the dairy companies of America?

Day by day the morons, epileptics and schizoids multiply. By accident, like everything else. Nothing is planned in America except improvements. And all improvements are for the machine. When a plenum is reached war is declared. Then the machine really gets going. War is a Roman Holiday for the machine. Man becomes even less than nothing then. The machine is well fed. The food products become plastics and plastics are what make the world go round. Better to have a good steering wheel than a good stomach. In the old days an army advanced on its stomach; now it advances in tanks or spitfires or super-fortresses. Civilians never advance. Civilians always rot and help make insurance companies richer.

But bread. . . . Let's not forget, it's bread we want—and children that are not accidents brought about by defective rubber or bathtub gin. How to get it? Bread, I mean. By putting a monkey wrench in the machine. By going backwards on all fours, like giraffes with broken necks. By praying for life now and not hereafter. By exercising freedom and not inventing four, five or six freedoms won by the slaughter and starvation of twenty or thirty millions. Begin today by baking your own bread. First of all you need a stove. A wood or coal stove. Not a gas range. Not an electric apparatus. Then let the flies in. Then roll your sleeves up and get your hands in the dough. Lick your fingers. Never mind if you lose your job. Eat your bread first, then maybe you won't want to work in an office or a factory. Life begins with bread. And a prayer. Not a begging prayer, but a prayer of thanks. Don't bless the block-busters. Bless God for his favors—air, water, sun, moon. God wants you to enjoy the bread of life. He never meant you to go out all day working at a job you loathe so that you can buy a loaf of store bread wrapped in cellophane. God gave us germs as well as air and water and sun. Germs attack only what is already rotting. Man is rotting in every fibre of his being: that is why he is a prey to germs. And that is why he is allergic to everything that is for his own good.

Before Communism was there was Communion and before that there was God and God said let there be light and there was light. And what a glorious light it was. It lasted for aeons, and then came the scientific age and darkness fell upon the land everywhere. Now everything can be proved backwards and out of existence and instead of soaring with our own wings or on the backs of our giant birds we make things of metal and plastics which spread havoc and destruction in their wake. We throw bones to the dogs and eat the dogs instead of the bones. Not one step has been taken towards improving the flow of milk from the mammary glands. Only mothers and wet nurses give milk, whereas with time and experimentation every one could give milk and the food problem would be solved for eternity. We wouldn't even need to sit down to eat: now and then a step-ladder might be necessary, but nothing more. Why hasn't any one thought of that? Is it so improbable? Ants have their own milk cows—how did that happen? Anyway, with human milk the universal food, with manna falling from heaven, and nectar and ambrosia for dessert, think what a lot of work would be eliminated. Think too of the gratitude the animals would show, once they got on to the new scheme of things. All we would need, men and animals, would be one huge grass plot. No more dairy companies, no more containers, no more bottles, plates, knives and forks, spoons, pots, pans, stoves. The solution of the food problem would throw a monkey wrench into the entire economic and social system; our mores would change, our religions would disappear, our money become valueless. One can hardly imagine what the cause for war would then be, though doubtless a good excuse will always be found.

Outside of the foreign quarters, then, take it for granted that there is no good bread to be had. Every foreign group has introduced into our life some good substantial bread, even the Scandinavians. (Excepting the English, I should add, but then we hardly think of them as foreign, though why we shouldn't I don't know, for when you think of it the English are even less like us than the Poles or Latvians.) In a Jewish restaurant you usually have a basket filled with all kinds of bread from which to choose. In a typical American restaurant, should you ask for rye, whole wheat or any other kind of bread but the insidious unwholesome, and unpalatable white, you get white bread. If you insist on rye bread you get whole wheat. If you insist on whole wheat you get graham bread. Once in a great while you come upon nut bread; this is always a sheer accident. Raisin bread is a sort of decoy to lure you into eating unpalatable, perfidious and debilitating white bread. When in doubt go to a Jewish restaurant or delicatessen; if necessary, stand up and eat a sandwich made of sour rye, sweet butter, pastrami and pickle. A Jewish sandwich contains more food value than an eighty-five cent meal in the ordinary American restaurant. With a glass of water to wash it down you can walk away feeling fit. Don't sit down and eat a Jewish meal, because the Jews are bad cooks despite their great concern about food, which amounts to a neurosis. It is curious, though, how the desire to survive has made the Jews keen about preserving the staff of life. It is even more curious that they are just as much riddled with disease as the other members of the community—more so, in fact, judging purely from personal observation. They not only have all the physical ailments which other white peoples are heir to but they have all the mental and nervous ailments. Often they have everything at once, and then they concentrate upon food with even greater acuity and despair. It is only when they become revolutionary that they begin to lose interest in food. The real American, on the other hand, though totally unrevolutionary at heart, seems born with an indifference to food. One can serve a white American food which would make an Igorote turn up his nose. Americans can eat garbage, provided you sprinkle it liberally with ketchup, mustard, chili sauce, tabasco sauce, cayenne pepper, or any other condiment which destroys the original flavor of the dish. On the other hand, olive oil which the French eschew when preparing salads because it has too strong a flavor, Americans hardly ever use in their salads. Nothing on God's earth is more uninviting, more anaemic, than the American salad. At its best it is like refined puke. The lettuce is a joke: even a canary would refuse to touch it. This concoction, mind you, is usually served before the meal, together with the coffee which is cold by the time you are ready to drink it. The moment you sit down at a table in the ordinary American restaurant, the moment you begin scanning the menu, the waitress asks you what you wish to drink. (If by chance you should say "cocoa" the whole kitchen would be thrown out of gear.) To this question I usually counter with another: "Do you have anything but white bread?" If the answer is not a flat No, it is: "We have whole wheat," or "We have graham bread." Whereupon I usually mumble under my breath: "You can stick that up your ass! When she says: "What did you say?" I reply, "Do you have rye bread by any chance?" Then, before she can say no, I launch into an elaborate explanation of the fact that I don't mean by rye bread the ordinary rye bread, which is no better than white, graham, or whole wheat, but a succulent, tasty, dark, sour rye such as the Russians and the Jews serve. At the mention of these two suspect nationalities a scowl spreads over her face. While she is saying in her most sarcastic voice that she is sorry but they do not have that kind of rye bread or any rye bread, for that matter, I begin asking about the fruit, what kinds of fruit, fresh fruit, they have on hand, knowing damned well that they haven't any. Nine times out of ten her answer will be: "We have apple pie." ("Stick it up your ass!") "I beg your pardon?" she says. "Yes, fruit . . . you know, the kind that grows on trees . . . apples, pears, bananas, plums, oranges . . . something with skin on it that you peel. "Whereupon a light dawns and she hastens to interpolate: "Oh, but we have apple sauce!" ("Fuck your apple sauce!") "I beg pardon?" Here I look leisurely round the room, surveying the shelves, the counter, the pie plates. Finally, resting my gaze upon a bowl of artificial fruit, I exclaim with glee: "Like that over there, *only real!*"

Sometimes, upon scanning the menu and knowing that it will only give me a belly-ache, I ask immediately if they can serve me a large bowl of fresh fruit. Here, incidentally, let me call attention to the dishes of mixed fruit prepared early in the morning which stand rotting in disgusting sweet canned juices until lunch or dinner hour. In the Automat type of restaurant one sees the counter piled with these vile stews. These, like the salads mentioned a moment ago, and like the pies fabricated by the wholesale bakers (who are probably responsible for more deaths than all our wars put together), and peculiar to the American temperament. There is not the least food value in any of them. The salad is at its worst when served in one of those delightful little inns run by spinsters in villages of imaginary charm, such as one is supposed to find in Vermont, Maryland, or Connecticut. Here everything looks immaculate and is immaculate, and therefore without value, without flavor, without joy. One suddenly feels like a canary which has been castrated and can no longer warble or differentiate between seed and salad. Beginning with this obscene salad one just knows that the meal is going to end with a charming little dessert such as prune whip or vanilla ice cream. To ask for a grape or a herring in one of these places is like committing sacrilege. There are certain things you must never ask for in an American restaurant. Never. One is good sour rye such as the Russians and the Jews make. Another is a cup of strong coffee. (Exceptions: French and Italian restaurants, and Louisiana. In Louisiana you can get a cup of coffee that is like liquid dynamite. But it tastes good; it has chicory in it. And chicory is excellent, despite all opinion to the contrary.) A third is cheese. A fourth is grapes. A fifth is nuts. Never have I seen a bowl of assorted and uncracked nuts put on the table in an American restaurant. Now and then, rarely, very rarely, one sees nuts in an American home. Usually, however, they are there as decoration. The fruit likewise. Fruit and nuts belong on the sideboard for the children, when there are any, to nibble at. The mixed fruit, or fruit salad, as they have the impudence to call it in America, reaches the height of abomination in the arm-chair Automat type of restaurant. Have you ever noticed the derelicts who frequent these eating places, sitting in the show window munching their lunch or dinner? Is there any more lugubrious sight on earth? (The corollary to it is the cheap traveling salesman type of hotel where all day long the weary commercial traveler sits in an enormous leather armchair staring vacantly out on the street. This is the type who gets orders for useless commodities which the American slave toils his ass off to accumulate, which he sells to his own kind and pretends thereby that he is earning an honest living. This is the type that votes the Democratic or Republican ticket year in and year out, in lean years and fat years, in war and in peace, and is always complaining that business is bad. This is the most traveled man in the world, and yet he knows nothing, absolutely nothing, and brags about it. This is the type who when you mention China says immediately—"coolies." If there is any more ignominious coolie than the traveling salesman I have yet to know him. The fact that he reads the "Digest" or some compilation of facts gives him the illusion that he is informed and a useful member of society.)

But it's the pie that takes the cake. The pie is at its worst in the Greek restaurant, often called "New York Café," and encountered in every village and hamlet throughout the length and breadth of the land. In fact, everything is at its worst in this type of eating place. But it's here that the pie becomes positively obsessive. Often there is nothing to offer the weary traveler but pie. There they stand, row upon row of pie plates, all filled with gangrene and arsenic. The crust looks like scurf and is scurf, usually of the finest rancid grease made by the Criscomaniacs of America. Here and there one can detect in a whole pie a piece of fruit, such as apple or peach; it is surrounded by a clot of phlegm swimming in a mess of undefinable paste. The pie of apple or peach is sourish, bilious, gaseous, having no more resemblance to the apple or peach in its native state than corn whiskey has to corn on the cob. The Greek proprietor delights in serving white Americans this unholy dish; he despises them for eating it, but, canny business man that he is, he believes in giving them what they ask for. He himself has a totally different cuisine, a damned good one, too, I must say, if you ever make a friend of him and get invited to his home. On his table you will see olives, real olives, okra, olive oil, fruits of all kinds, nuts, rice, vine leaves, the tenderest lamb imaginable, wines of all kinds, including retsina, and cognac, Greek cognac, and other delicacies.

Let us digress here a moment. . . . How is it that Americans, composed of nothing but foreign nationalities, living amongst people accustomed to the most varied cuisines, people who have made an art of cooking from time immemorial, continue to be the worst cooks in the world, continue to open one foul restaurant after another? Explain it, if you can. To me it's an enigma. The more mixed becomes the blood in our veins, the more American we become. And by American I mean the more set, crass, conservative, prejudiced, stupid, narrow-minded, unexperimental and unrevolutionary. In every big city we have Chinese, Italian, French, Hungarian, Russian, German, Swedish restaurants. Do we learn anything from these skilled restaurateurs? No, not a thing. We go our way, serving pies, mixed fruit salads, hamburgers, baked beans, steak and onions, vicious veal cutlets, whether breaded or unbreaded, and so on. Has any one ever had a good stew in an American restaurant? The peasants of Europe have thrived on stews for centuries. Here a stew means a couple of spoonfuls of superannuated meat swimming in a tiny pool of grease and bilge with bloated potatoes as a garniture. One hasn't begun to eat when the meal is over. It's an imaginary stew at the best. And the most imaginary part of it is the vegetables without which no stew is complete: leeks, carrots, turnips, onions, celery, parsley, and so on. If you find a tiny piece of any other vegetable than the potato you are indeed a lucky individual.

All right, steak then! Steak is the great American dish. Steak and onions. Fine. Nothing better, I say. Where can you get it? I mean without paying $2.50 per person! The first and only time I got the real flavor of steak was when I passed through Denver. Up till then I never knew what a real steak tasted like. The meat companies are for convincing us that meat from the refrigerator, meat that has been on ice several years, is the best meat of all. The whole world is being shipped and fed this cold storage meat, thanks to Armour & Co. and their subsidiary hog-butchers. In France I used to eat *filet de boeuf* practically every other day. It cost, for one person, a good portion, mind you, from twelve to eighteen cents, at the rate of exchange prevailing in the late thirties. It was delicious meat, and I knew how to prepare it (Americans as a rule know only how to spoil a good piece of meat in cooking it). When I came to America, in 1940, I went to the butcher one day and asked for my customary *filet de boeuf*. A piece for two people came to $1.10, so help me God. I couldn't believe my ears. And this was in a cheap butcher shop on Third Avenue, New York. Christ only knows what it would have cost in the Park Avenue neighborhood. I took it home and I fried it. I did everything just as I used to at the Villa Seurat. I had wine with it too, the best I could buy for $1.25 the bottle. I also had grapes and nuts, and a salad prepared with the best olive oil. I had several kinds of cheese, including roquefort and camembert. Despite all precautions the meal didn't taste the same. There was something lacking. As a matter of fact, all the essentials were lacking. A piece of lettuce grown in America is like a piece of lettuce grown in France only in looks and name. American fruit, the most sensational looking fruit in the world (barring the tropics), is practically tasteless compared to the sicklier looking European fruits. American cheeses look delicious, and God knows the Kraft Brothers have tickled them up inordinately, but they do not have the flavor of the cheeses they are made to imitate. A stale piece of Camembert in a dirty French restaurant is worth a whole box of beautiful looking fresh Camembert put out by the crafty cheese-makers of Wisconsin. The flat Dutch cheeses are of course still more flat and tasteless when you eat them in America, being as they are the product of the most pampered cows in all the world. Wines, even when they are good, and in the realm of ordinary table wines America makes some of the best, do not taste as good as in Europe, perhaps because the atmosphere, the violence, the tempo of American life destroys whatever blessing wine confers.

Wine with the meal, in America, produces the wrong result. What is required, when attempting to digest American food, is strong spirits—whiskey, gin, cocktails. The correct procedure is to get soused beforehand; this enables one to eat without noticing how vile the food is. It gets one flushed and excited, and the food is forgotten. It makes one argumentative, which aids in bringing on indigestion, dyspepsia, flatulence, constipation, hemorrhoids, and finally the operating table. Whichever road you take, in America, you always wind up at the surgeon's door. If you buy an automobile it's the surgeon you have to reckon with eventually. If you take a good-paying job, it's the surgeon who will bleed you to death. If you economize and eat in armchair restaurants, or the Greek restaurants (where American food is served—not the real Greek restaurant), you meet the surgeon sooner or later, generally sooner. If you take to the soil and live the outdoor life, you first must have all your teeth pulled out and plates inserted. Farmers have about the worst teeth of all, even worse than factory workers. They have all the physical ailments, too, and are often as not undernourished. Farmers die of inanition in the midst of plenty. There isn't anything you can do, in America, by way of earning a living whereby you can escape dire taxation, disease, accident, misery and humiliation. At the end of every road stands the surgeon, who is for Americans what Nemesis was for the Greeks. The whole culture of America springs from two lunatics: the Marquis de Sade and Sacher Masoch. Justice, always retributive, is apotheosized by the surgeon. His henchmen are the dentists. If you have an ache or pain never mention it to the dentist, or he will immediately extract all your teeth. Nowadays even cowboys are proud of their false teeth. Scarcely any hardworking American, however splendid his physique, is without plates or bridges after forty. Hardly any normal American has a full head of hair after forty. Hardly any American over twenty-one, whether he works hard or takes it easy, is without eye-glasses. Almost every American suffers from hemorrhoids. Practically every American over forty has a bad heart. Cancer, syphilis, arthritis, tuberculosis, schizophrenia are so prevalent that we accept them as part of the bargain—i.e., the American way of life. Nearly every family boasts of one moron among its members, one lunatic, one drunkard, one pervert. All the food advertisements boast of the vitamin contents of their products. All the medicaments advertised boast of their cure for every thing under the sun. It is obvious that our foods lack the proper vitamins, just as it is obvious that in employing these health foods so rich in vitamins we nevertheless are afflicted with all the diseases known to man. We die young, mortgaged to the hilt, insolvent, despite all the insurance policies issued by all the insurance companies whose tentacles reach into every avenue of commercial and industrial life. It is also evident that, despite the fact this is the land of opportunity where freedom reigns, where every one has the right to worship and the right to vote for the wrong candidate, that the zest for life is so low that less than one child per family is now produced, except among certain Indian tribes, certain religious communities, certain strata of poor whites, and among the Negroes as a whole. Even the Jews, known for their big families as well as their good bread, are beginning to have less children—in America. And when the Jew loses his desire to perpetuate his own kind there must indeed be something seriously wrong with the national life. In the poorest countries of Europe the Jews still remain fertile; here, with everything in his grasp, except recognition by the Gentiles, he withers away. Only among the American Indians, and there only in certain tribes, is the population on the increase. It is said that this is due in part to the practice of polygamy. And here we touch another tender subject, one almost as potent as bread. I mean the fear among native white Americans of indulging in any other form of marriage but that sponsored by the Christian churches. Why not polygamy? Why not polyandry? Why not any kind of marriage, including love marriages? With polygamy the Mormons were fast on the way to building an empire. Nobody can say that the Mormons are, or ever were, an undesirable element in the great American community. They were and still are one of the few communities in this country where poverty is relatively unknown. They produce less criminals than other parts of the country— and less morons, and less idiots, and less trouble of any nature. And God knows they were never, never more immoral than the other members of the community. On the contrary, they were not only more law-abiding, more peaceful, more prosperous, more social-minded and far-visioned than the other communities of America, but they were absolutely more moral in the strictest sense of the word, that is, in the sense that they actually practiced what they preached.

But to get back to bread. . . . Today the mailman brought three kinds of bread: Italian bread, a milk loaf, and pumpernickel. (No sour rye, of course, no corn bread.) The bread comes from Monterey, the nearest town, which is fifty miles away. In Monterery there is no Jewish grocer or delicatessen, worse luck. In Monterey there are Mexicans, Portuguese and Filipinos, but who gives a damn what these poor devils eat? The Mexicans have their tortillas, the Portuguese their garlic, and the Filipinos . . . well, among other things they have all our bad habits. Nobody in Monterey has a good slice of bread to eat. Nor in Carmel either, unless it's Robinson Jeffers, and that would be a sacramental bread. Just outside of Carmel lives Edward Weston, the photographer. And that leads me to speak of another kind of bread: photographic bread. Have you ever noticed that even the photographic bread tastes poorly? Have you ever seen a piece of bread photographed by our advertising maniacs which you would like to bite into? I haven't. Edward Weston could undoubtedly make you the most wonderful photographic bread conceivable—*but could you eat it?* The bread you hang on your wall is not the bread you want to eat at table. Even a piece of bread by Man Ray would prove unpalatable, particularly if he just happened to be reading his favorite author, the Marquis de Sade. Sacher Masoch might have made a good bread, if he had lived long enough. It has a Kosher sound, *Sacher Masoch*. But in the long run I have a feeling it would make one morbid and introspective, this Sacher Masoch bread.

I have now found that the only way to eat our most unwholesome, unpalatable and unappetizing American bread, the staff of our unsavory and monotonous life, is to adopt the following procedure. This is a recipe, so please follow instructions to the letter.

To begin with, accept any loaf that is offered you without question, even if it is not wrapped in cellophane, even if it contains no kelp. Throw it in the back of the car with the oil can and the grease rags; if possible, bury it under a sack of coal, *bituminous coal*. As you climb up the road to your home, drop it in the mud a few times and dig your heels into it. If you have a dog with you, let him pee on it now and then. When you get to the house, and after you have prepared the other dishes, take a huge carving knife and rip the loaf from stem to stern. Then take one whole onion, peeled or unpeeled, one carrot, one stalk of celery, one huge piece of garlic, one sliced apple, a herring, a handful of anchovies, a sprig of parsley, and an old toothbrush and shove them into the disemboweled guts of the bread. Over these pour first a thimbleful of kerosene, a dash of Lavoris and just a wee bit of Clorox; then sprinkle guts liberally with the following—molasses, honey, orange marmalade, vanilla, soy bean sauce, tabasco sauce, ketchup and arnica. Over this add a layer of chopped nuts, assorted nuts, of course, a few bay leaves (whole), some marjoram, and a stick of licorice cut into fine pieces. Put the loaf in the oven for ten minutes and serve. If it is still lacking in taste whip up a chili con carne piping hot and mix bread well with it until it becomes a thick gruel. If this fails, piss on it and throw it to the dog. But under no circumstances feed it to the birds. The birds of North America are already on the decline, as I pointed out earlier. Their beaks have become dull, their wingspan shortened; they are pining and drooping, moulting in season and out. Above all, they no longer sing as they used to; they make sour notes, they bleat instead of tweeting, and sometimes, when the fogs set in, they have been heard to cackle and wheeze.

For Discussion

1. What specific qualities in American bread are characteristic of American society? Look at the adjectives chosen to describe the bread.
2. Analyze Miller's palate. What specific American foods does he hate? What evidence can you cite that American taste is moving farther from—or nearer to—his liking?
3. What does Hollywood bread symbolize? Hollywood funeral? Photographic bread?
4. Look at the digressions on foreign ghettos, Greek restaurants, and ordinary American restaurants. What does each contribute?
5. What purpose do the numerous references to machines serve?
6. In what ways is this essay dated? In what ways not?

7. Find examples of hyperbole and invective. Look at the sections charting the sequence of bread leading to famine.
8. Sarcasm is a kind of irony. Find examples which illustrate Miller's mastery of this art. (Also see Mencken in this section.)
9. Look up the word "paean." How does this essay qualify as a paean?
10. What relationship does Miller establish with the reader? How does he do it?
11. Miller's attitude toward his subject becomes more apparent when portions of the essay are read aloud. Listen to the last paragraph. What is its tone, and how is it consistent with that of the whole essay?

DICK GREGORY

America Is
My Momma

Dick Gregory, born in 1932, one of the first black satirists, has
entertained in night clubs, on television and radio; has lectured
to college audiences; and has campaigned for the Presidency
of the United States as a peace candidate. Gregory's social
satire is available on recordings as well as in his books, which
include *From the Back of the Bus, Nigger, What's Happening?,
Write Me In!,* and *The Shadow That Scares Me,* from which the
following selection is taken.

> And the tongue is a fire. . . . With it we bless the Lord and Father,
> and with it we curse men, who are made in the likeness of God.
> From the same mouth come blessing and cursing. My brethren,
> this ought not to be so.　　　　　　　　　　　　—James 3:6, 9–10

The Apostle James describes well what I have experienced in the church
all my life. The tongue, the words we say or sing and do not mean, and
the verses of scripture we interpret to fit our own prejudices, stains the
whole body and sets on fire the cycle of nature. The same words are used
to praise God and to curse men; to justify evil and to condemn it.

A popular song in the church is "The Battle Hymn of the Republic."
Really listen to the words of that song and you will realize that very few
people have the right to sing it. The day a person does decide to sing it
should be the last day of his life. That is what the words of the song
imply: "As He died to make men holy, let us die to make men free." If
the Enforcer swept through the church today and said, "Put up or shut
up," I only know about five folks who could sing that song and mean it.
And three of them are already dead.

"As He died to make men holy, let us die to make men free." We do just the reverse. We will try to *kill* to make men free. But the song doesn't say that. It says, "Let us *die* to make men free." This refusal to live by our words makes a laughingstock out of the church, Good Friday, and Easter. Another song which amuses me is "Onward, Christian Soldiers." Church folks seem to think a Christian soldier is a Marine who prays. When you sing, "Onward, Christian Soldiers," you are not *really* talking about a man who will follow the cause of right to his death.

The church today has become a sick comedy. I tell my own kids to go to church only as a form of entertainment. The church is in such sad condition today that I cannot justify their attendance for any other reason. If my momma had told me that the church was a form of entertainment, I could have understood those old sisters sitting in the front pew of my church looking so evil. We never had a picture of the Devil in my house; only pictures of Jesus. But if we had a picture of the Devil, I'm sure it would have looked like one of those front pew sisters.

TAKE A PROSTITUTE TO CHURCH

The church is supposed to be so pure, much more pure than the nightclub. Yet I can take a prostitute to the nightclub with me and nobody will automatically assume I have been sleeping with her. It isn't strange to see a prostitute in a nightclub and she is welcome. My wife can walk into the nightclub with a pimp and nobody will assume she has been sleeping with him. But I defy you women to pick up an old wino out of the gutter on your way to church some Sunday and bring him along with you to hear the message of God. When you arrive, just listen to the sisters whisper.

And you men, I defy you to invite the town prostitute some Sunday morning, "Sister, would you like to come with me to church and hear my minister?" If she accepts the invitation, the minute you walk in the front door people will start whispering that you must have been with her all night. This is the church. It doesn't happen in a nightclub, a pool hall or a tavern. It makes me think they put the crosses on the wrong buildings.

WHY JUDAS?

When I was a kid, I used to ask my momma why the church accused a Jew of killing Christ. In Sunday school they taught me that all Judas did was *kiss* Christ. I asked, "Momma, if you kiss me on the cheek and Daddy takes a gun and pulls the trigger on me, who are they going to get for murder?" Momma answered, "Daddy, of course." That bothered me, because I could not understand why the Good Book kept accusing the kisser. Why not get that Roman soldier's name; the one with the nails and the hammer. He is the real killer. Just as it is today, nobody ever wants to accuse the man with the gun.

Of course, Momma knew her Bible and she had an explanation. She said, "They didn't know what Jesus looked like and if Judas hadn't kissed him, he couldn't have been arrested. That is why Judas gets blamed for killing Christ." The story I learned in Sunday school did not say that Christ was invisible. He walked out in the open every day. Thousands of people saw him and heard him teach. Two thousands years later we have his picture on the wall and claim to know what he looked like. We don't have pictures of Judas.

So I said to Momma, "Do you mean to tell me that the king and the queen, who own the Army, the Navy, the CIA, and the secret police, were so stupid that they didn't know what the boss looked like but they could recognize his helper?" If you can believe that, you can believe anything. The power structure had enough sense to know that if Jesus had lived he would have hurt them. But they didn't know what he looked like. Even as a child that explanation didn't make sense to me.

When you start twisting the words of the Bible around, the church and the whole world are in trouble. The Christian soldiers are pictured on the front page of the newspaper with their heads bowed worshiping with the chaplain immediately after a good kill. The Christian soldier prays to his God. His buddy on the other side of the firing line, called the "enemy," prays to his God. And they are both praying at the same time! Man really puts God on the spot on the front line of the battlefield.

If I was silly enough to go to war, I would give God better treatment than that. I wouldn't take a Bible to battle with me and I wouldn't pray. My last prayer would be just before I shipped out. I would tell God, "Okay, Brother. I am going to do for myself for about four or five years. You'll hear from me when I get back."

When I was a kid, religion made con-men out of everyone in our house. I flatly refused to pray the Lord's Prayer. It just did not make sense to pray to God, "Give us this day our daily bread," when sometimes there was six months' food supply in the pantry. I used to listen to my momma pray. She would start out with the Lord's Prayer. Since everything is really covered in that prayer, she should have stopped while she was ahead. But she would start improvising. She would pray, "Bless the sick and shut-in," which she knew she wasn't going to visit, and then she would start her thirty-minute beg. "Lord, you know the rent is due, the bills have to be paid; and if you will just do *this* for me, let me tell you what I'll do for *you.*"

Hearing a prayer like that used to make me wonder who God is.

Momma would always try to work out deals with Him. But at the end of every prayer, Momma would always give God a cop-out: "Lord, let not my will but thine be done." Next week the rent still would be due and Momma would say, "I guess the Lord knew what He was doing." On those church radio services I heard prayers which were even safer. I heard a woman pray, "Lord, thank you for all the good you have done to me and the evil too." That *really* made me wonder who God is. It is a vicious God whom you have to thank for wrong.

I finally came to the conclusion that I couldn't go to school and to church too. At school I would be taught to prove everything to the *n*th degree. When I asked questions in church, looking for proof, the minister would say, "What's wrong with you, boy?" So I decided if I had to go to church, I would make some money at it. Back in the 1940s when I was a kid, my church used to take up a special collection every Sunday for African missionary work. The church didn't even have a back wall in it yet and there was much more work to do on the building, so I knew the money was not going to Africa. I used to sneak back and wipe out that collection every Sunday. It was the only way I could justify spending my time in church when they wouldn't explain things to me.

JOSEPH AND MARY AT THE HILTON

I never could understand the story of Christmas. People used to weep and wail every year over the fact that "there was no room for Mary in the inn." Every Christmas the innkeeper took a beating in my church for the way he treated poor Mary and Joseph. But Mary was pregnant. Suppose Mary and Joseph came back today and walked into the lobby of the Conrad Hilton and said to the desk clerk, "This is Mary and I am Joseph. We're not married, but let me tell you about this dream we had." You know they would be thrown out immediately. The dream might be legitimate, but you don't tell the desk clerk about it and then get mad because he doesn't believe you. You can't go into a hotel today with a pregnant woman to have a baby. Nor can you check into the hospital just to have a place to sleep. It is just the reverse. You go to the hospital to have the baby and go to the hotel to read the Bible—there is one in every room. The government has taken the Bibles out of the schools, but it left them in the hotel rooms. So maybe the government knows which place is more hip.

My momma could never understand how white folks could twist the words of the Bible around to justify racial segregation. Yet she could read the Ten Commandments, which clearly say, "Thou shalt not kill," and still justify eating meat. Momma couldn't read the newspaper very well, but she sure could interpret the Word of God. "God meant you shouldn't kill people," she used to say. But I insisted, "Momma, he didn't say that. He said, 'Thou shalt not kill.' If you leave that statement alone, a whole lot of things would be safe from killing. But if you are going to twist the words about killing to mean what you want them to mean, then let white folks do the same thing with justifying racial segregation."

"You can't live without eating meat," Momma would persist. "You'd starve." I couldn't buy that either. You get milk from a cow without killing it. You do not have to kill an animal to get what you need from it. You get wool from the sheep without killing it. Two of the strongest animals in the jungle are vegetarians—the elephant and the gorilla. The first two years are the most important years of a man's life, and during that period he is not involved with eating meat. If you suddenly become very ill, there is a good chance you will be taken off a meat diet. So it is a myth that killing is necessary for survival. The day I decide that I must have a piece of steak to nourish my body, I will also give the cow the same right to nourish herself on human beings.

There is so little basic difference between animals and humans. The process of reproduction is the same for chickens, cattle, and humans. If suddenly the air stopped circulating on the earth, or the sun collided with the earth, animals and humans would die alike. A nuclear holocaust will wipe out all life. Life in the created order is basically the same and should be respected as such. It seems to me the Bible says it is wrong to kill—period.

If we can justify *any* kind of killing in the name of religion, the door is opened for all kinds of other justifications. The fact of killing animals is not as frightening as our human tendency to justify it—to kill and not even be aware that we are taking life. It is sobering to realize that when you misuse one of the least of Nature's creatures, like the chicken, you are sowing the seed for misusing the highest of Nature's creatures, man.

IF YOU HAD TO KILL YOUR OWN HOG

Animals and humans suffer and die alike. If you had to kill your own hog before you ate it, most likely you would not be able to do it. To hear the hog scream, to see the blood spill, to see the baby being taken away from its momma, and to see the look of death in the animal's eye would turn your stomach. So you get the man at the packing house to do the killing for you. In like manner, if the wealthy aristocrats who are perpetrating conditions in the ghetto actually heard the screams of ghetto suffering, or saw the slow death of hungry little kids, or witnessed the strangulation of manhood and dignity, they could not continue the killing. But the wealthy are protected from such horror. They have people to do the killing for them. The wealthy profit from the daily murders of ghetto life but they do not see them. Those who immerse themselves in the daily life of the ghetto see the suffering—the social workers, the police, the local merchants, and the bill collectors. But the people on top never really see.

By the time you see a piece of meat in the butcher shop window, all of the blood and suffering have been washed away. When you order a steak in the restaurant, the misery has been forgotten and you see the finished product. You see a steak with butter and parsley on it. It looks appetizing and appealing and you are pleased enough to eat it. You never even consider the suffering which produced your meal or the other animals killed that day in the slaughterhouse. In the same way, all the wealthy aristocrats ever see of the black community is the finished product, the window dressing, the steak on the platter—Ralph Bunche and Thurgood Marshall. The United Nations or the Supreme Court bench is the restaurant and the ghetto street corner is the slaughterhouse.

Life under ghetto conditions cuts short life expectancy. The Negro's life expectancy is shorter than the white man's. The oppressor benefits from continued oppression financially; he makes more money so that he can eat a little better. I see no difference between a man killing a chicken and a man killing a human being, by overwork and forcing ghetto conditions upon him, both so that he can eat a little better. If you can justify killing to eat meat, you can justify the conditions of the ghetto. I cannot justify either one.

Every time the white folks made my momma mad, she would grab the Bible and find something bitter in it. She would come home from the rich white folks' house, after they had just called her "nigger," or patted her on the rump or caught her stealing some steaks, open her Bible and read aloud, "It is easier for a camel to pass through the eye of a needle than for a rich man to get into Heaven." When you get involved with distorting the words of the Bible, you don't have to be bitter. The same tongue can be used to bless and curse men.

THE LORD KNEW THERE WOULD BE NEEDLES

When Momma used to curse the rich white folks with the judgment against rich men, I used to try to point out the contradictions. "Momma," I would say, "they didn't have needles when the Bible was written." And she would say, "The Lord knew they would one day." Now I thought it was terribly unfair to write something that couldn't possibly be understood for a few thousands years. So I used to prod Momma for more answers. "What about those people at the time of Christ? How were they supposed to understand the Bible?" That just wasn't Momma's immediate problem. "They ain't here now," she would say. Then I would try to explain that the eye of a needle was an arch in the old Arabian cities and when a camel came through, the bigger the load the more the camel would have to stoop to get through. The rich man had more trouble getting through the eye because his load was bigger than the poor man's. But Momma wouldn't listen. She wanted *all* rich men cursed, because of what one rich man had just done to her.

Momma always had the Bible under her arm. If she was flat broke and found a nickel on the street, she would fall on her knees and say, "Thank God!" But on payday, if she found a dollar, she wouldn't even think to thank Him, because finding money didn't mean anything when there was already money in her purse. Even though the Bible clearly says, "Thou shalt not steal," Momma could always justify stealing from the white folks' pantry. She knew her kids were hungry and she used to try to justify her stealing to us. "If I didn't steal, you would starve to death. The white folks aren't paying me enough anyway." It is so easy for people to justify what they want to believe. Sophisticated Negroes today who are embarrassed by the rioting and looting in the ghetto can still justify their grandma raiding the white folks' pantry for survival. The ghetto brother is fighting for survival also. If you can justify one kind of stealing, you can justify any manifestation of theft that suits your particular fancy. But right is right and wrong is wrong.

If the same Negroes who are embarrassed by the rioting and looting in the ghetto picked up the newspaper one morning and read that the First National Bank of Kansas City was held up by five well-dressed, collegiate-looking Negroes pulling off the biggest bank robbery in history, they would not be embarrassed. They would wink at each other that morning at work and talk about how clever those cats were in Kansas City. But a Brooks Brothers suit does not change the complexion of looting. You cannot justify stealing because the thieves were brilliant and looked respectable, any more than you can justify stealing as necessary for survival. "Thou shalt not steal" means that stealing is wrong. The Bible goes further in talking about how man should treat his fellow man. It clearly condemns the conditions of life which cause a man to steal for survival. But stealing itself is still wrong. When the same tongue can bless one man's stealing and curse another man's stealing, all hell breaks loose, to paraphrase the Epistle of James!

ILLEGITIMATE PARENTS

My momma and my church always taught me that illegitimacy is something wrong. My society tells me that it is something "colored." Society is forever reminding me of the rate of illegitimacy in Negro neighborhoods. Statistically this is true. Negro women in America represent 20 percent of the illegitimacy rate and white women represent 2 percent. But if Negroes could ever get their hands on that white man's abortion credit card, those statistics would change.

But if illegitimacy is wrong and colored, then Christ was colored and a sinner. Because the story in the Good Book clearly shows that He was illegitimate. Either church folks should admit that Christ Himself shared in the wrong or they should stop slandering the ghetto mother. The only way for the current church attitude to be consistent with the Bible is to interpret the Christmas story this way: Illegitimacy is wrong, unless the illegitimate child ends up being the religious boss—the Son of God. You cannot bless one illegitimate birth and curse another one. The Apostle James said, "From the same mouth come blessing and cursing. My brethren, this ought not to be so." He was speaking to both church and society.

In America, we have a habit of cursing the underdog and branding the defenseless. The term "illegitimate child" is a contradiction. All children are the product of the same sexual act. The legitimate result of that sexual act is the birth of a child. The child born out of wedlock is the natural product of an illegitimate sexual act. Yet the statistics speak of "illegitimate children" and not "illegitimate mothers and fathers." We curse the underdog and brand the defenseless.

America's obsession with the Negro crime rate is another example of cursing the underdog and branding the defenseless. Billions of dollars made from dope, gambling, and prostitution are stolen from the greatness of America and all by white men. There are no Negroes in the Cosa Nostra. Just as there are very few Negro cops. At the time of the Watts riot, for example, there were fifty-one hundred cops in Los Angeles. Only 205 were Negro. And there were only four Negro cops in the 77th Precinct which is responsible for law enforcement in the Watts section of Los Angeles. In the history of the Los Angeles Police Department, a Negro had never been graduated above the rank of lieutenant.

When you speak of a Negro crime rate, you are really talking about a "Negro-arrested-by-the-police-and-convicted" rate! Go into any traffic court and you will see twice as many Negroes as whites. When I consider the population proportion, I refuse to believe that Negroes do twenty-eight times more speeding than white folks. America must ask herself the question: what would the white crime rate look like if the overwhelming majority of cops were Black Muslims?

"RELIEF" OR "FOREIGN AID"?

America curses the underdog on relief. "Relief" has become a dirty word in this country. An atmosphere has been created where people are ashamed to be on relief. If relief embarrasses or shames America, let it be called foreign aid. America is never embarrassed to send money all over Europe, for health projects and the like, and it is nothing but relief. A white man once asked me about the shame of the increasing number of colored folks on the relief rolls. I asked him, "Do you know any Africans on relief?" He answered, "No." So I said, "Then why didn't you leave us over there?"

I personally feel that all Negroes in this country should be on relief, regardless of their income. Relief is like my coming into your barn and stealing a horse. I put him in my stable. When the stolen horse gets hungry, I have to feed him. I would have to be a fool to come by your house and demand oats. Nor should the horse be expected to feed himself or be embarrassed that he is hungry. When a man decides to steal, he must accept the consequences of his theft. Relief is America paying her just dues for theft. It is the theft which is shameful, not the dues. I am tired of America balancing her wrongs by cursing my natural rights.

The irony is that the "curse" is really the "blessing." Having been on relief for twenty years, I have a personal resentment against it and wish that relief would be eliminated. Five minutes after my momma received her relief check, it was in the hands of that Right Wing bigot. He owned the business where Momma spent her money. Some seventeen million dollars a month is spent on relief in the state of Illinois. Though white folks curse relief, in all honesty the State of Illinois has to bless it. If relief were terminated, in ten months' time it would cost the State of Illinois $170 million. Knock that kind of revenue out of a state's economy and it is doomed.

WHEN THE STATE KILLS

We speak of separation of church and state. I personally believe that the state has completely taken over the church. Even if you accept my momma's interpretation of "Thou shalt not kill" as covering only *human* life, the church is a long way from converting the state. The state is still allowed to kill the man who has killed. We still allow capital punishment in America. But two wrongs do not make a right. Have you ever stopped to consider who leads the condemned man to the killer? The minister or the priest! The state has completely taken over the church and uses it as a moment of final comfort for those whom the state would kill. I have often wondered what the clergyman says to the condemned man at the last moment before the execution. "Is there anything more I can do for you, son?" I would tell him, "Yes, Father. Stand here next to the electric chair and hold my hand." My Baptist preacher was always putting his foot in his mouth. I can just hear him saying to the condemned man as they are strapping him into the electric chair, "Well, son this is as far as I go. I really don't know what to say, but more power to you."

Capital punishment is a disgrace. For the church to allow it to continue is an even greater disgrace. It is wrong for the church to tell me I should not kill and still be unwilling to make the same demand of the state. The greatest contradiction of all is for the clergyman to be present at the hour of the state's vengeance. If that same clergyman would go all the way and jump into the electric chair just once, it would end capital punishment immediately. Such an act would be a "sit-in" to end killing.

One of the most sacred acts of a Christian society is the act of marriage. Yet it is possible to bypass the church completely and get married by city hall. If you do go to the church to get married, you had better get things straight with city hall first.

A friend of mine was getting married and I was to be the best man. When we got to city hall, the old Justice of the Peace was sitting in his office surrounded by all those soldiers with their pregnant girls. And he was tired of it all. When my friend, his bride, and I walked into the office, the Justice never even looked up. He just mumbled his formalities and ended up with, "I now pronounce you man and wife." Then he looked up for the first time and told *me* to kiss the bride. That is how sacred marriage is in society today.

I cannot help but question how anything as sacred as marriage can depend upon the payment of a ten-dollar fee. If you went to city hall, got married, kissed your bride, and then told the Justice, "I'm not paying you," he probably would say, "Then it doesn't count." And you would not be married. Marriage has become that automatic and commercial and yet people wonder about the breakdown of the family.

President Johnson, backed by the statistics and findings of the Moynihan Report, has said that a breakdown of the family is responsible for the plight of the Negro in America. He is absolutely correct. America is my momma. And my momma was America to me. Since the United States Constitution is the farthest thing from the Negro in America, it is the last thing to be blamed for his plight. State, city, and county governments are closer, but they are still distant. My momma, as head of the family, was the only authority my America allowed me to touch. When my momma stole food from white folks, and justified it as necessary for survival, I did not blame the system. I did not blame a country where the black man is denied his constitutional rights; where Momma was stripped of her womanhood and Daddy of his manhood. I blamed Momma for stealing.

We got on the bus or streetcar and Momma always put my age back. The only thing a poor ghetto kid has is his God-given birthday. I was robbed of that. As Momma was robbed of her womanhood and Daddy of his manhood, I was robbed of my childhood. As a child, I didn't blame the system; I blamed Momma.

AMERICA WAS MOMMA'S MOMMA

Now that I am a man, I have "given up childish ways." I realize that America is my momma and America was Momma's momma. And I am going to place the blame for injustice and wrong on the right momma. Even today, when I leave my country to appear on television and make other public appearances in foreign countries, I find it difficult to speak of the injustices I experience in this country. Because America is my momma. Even if Momma is a whore, she is still Momma. Many times I am asked if I would go to war if drafted. I always answer, "Yes, under one condition; that I be allowed to go to the front line without a gun. Momma is worth dying for, but there is nothing worth killing for. And if I ever change my opinion about killing, I will go to Mississippi and kill that sheriff who spit in my wife's face."

America is my momma. One Fourth of July, I want to go to the New York harbor and talk to Momma—the Statue of Liberty. I want to snatch that torch out of her hand and take her with me to the ghetto and sit her down on the street corner. I want to show her the "tired, the poor, the huddled masses yearning to breathe free." I want to show Momma what she has been doing to her children. And Momma should weep. For the grief of the ghetto is the grief of the entire American family.

For Discussion

1. What purpose does the biblical quotation at the beginning serve?
2. Why does Gregory object to the "Christian soldier"? Would Mark Twain agree? (See "War Prayer" and "Reflections on Religion.")
3. What specific accusations does Gregory level against the church? Is he irreligious?
4. Discuss Gregory's demonstration of the "forked tongue" in regard to
   a. prostitution
   b. theft
   c. illegitimacy
   d. relief
   e. capital punishment
5. What is Gregory's purpose in using recollections of his childhood, particularly of his religious training?
6. Gregory's objections to killing are developed in several ways. Discuss these objections and comment on the strength of his arguments.

7. How valid are the analogies of the ghetto owner to the meat eater and the welfare recipient to the stolen horse?
8. Identify and discuss each of the "momma's" Gregory develops.
9. Gregory's use of contradictions and pairings of opposites reveal his ironic voice, which for the most part is humorous. How does his tone change in the final section?
10. Discuss Gregory's use of colloquialism in his paraphrasing of biblical stories.

JERRY FARBER

The Student as Nigger

Jerry Farber has become a familiar name among college students, principally for the following controversial essay, which was widely read in underground editions before it was included in a book of the same title, written by Farber, containing this and other works. Like Kunen and other younger writers, Farber has been a spokesman for a new generation of dissenters from traditional educational philosophy. He is now on the English faculty at California State University, San Diego.

Students are niggers. When you get that straight, our schools begin to make sense. It's more important, though, to understand why they're niggers. If we follow that question seriously enough, it will lead us past the zone of academic bullshit, where dedicated teachers pass their knowledge on to a new generation, and into the nitty-gritty of human needs and hang-ups. And from there we can go on to consider whether it might ever be possible for students to come up from slavery.

First let's see what's happening now. Let's look at the role students play in what we like to call education.

At Cal State L.A. where I teach, the students have separate and unequal dining facilities. If I take them into the faculty dining room, my colleagues get uncomfortable, as though there were a bad smell. If I eat in the student cafeteria, I become known as the educational equivalent of a niggerlover. In at least one building there are even restrooms which students may not use. At Cal State, also, there is an unwritten law barring student-faculty lovemaking. Fortunately, this anti-miscegenation law, like its Southern counterpart, is not 100 percent effective.

Students at Cal State are politically disenfranchised. They are in an academic Lowndes County. Most of them can vote in national elections —their average age is about 26—but they have no voice in the decisions which affect their academic lives. The students, are, it is true, allowed to have a toy government of their own. It is a government run for the most part by Uncle Toms and concerned principally with trivia. The faculty and administrators decide what courses will be offered; the students get to choose their own Homecoming Queen. Occasionally, when student leaders get uppity and rebellious, they're either ignored, put off with trivial concessions, or maneuvered expertly out of position.

A student at Cal State is expected to know his place. He calls a faculty member "Sir" or "Doctor" or "Professor"—and he smiles and shuffles some as he stands outside the professor's office waiting for permission to enter. The faculty tell him what courses to take (in my department, English, even electives have to be approved by a faculty member); they tell him what to read, what to write, and, frequently, where to set the margins on his typewriter. They tell him what's true and what isn't. Some teachers insist that they encourage dissent but they're almost always jiving and every student knows it. Tell the man what he wants to hear or he'll fail your ass out of the course.

When a teacher says "jump" students jump. I know of one professor who refused to take up class time for exams and required students to show up for tests at 6:30 in the morning. And they did, by God! Another, at exam time, provides answer cards to be filled out—each one enclosed in a paper bag with a hole cut in the top to see through. Students stick their writing hands in the bags while taking the test. The teacher isn't a provo; I wish he were. He does it to prevent cheating. Another colleague once caught a student reading during one of his lectures and threw her book against the wall. Still another lectures his students into a stupor and then screams at them in a rage when they fall asleep.

Just last week, during the first meeting of a class, one girl got up to leave after about ten minutes had gone by. The teacher rushed over, grabbed her by the arm, saying "This class is NOT dismissed!" and led her back to her seat. On the same day another teacher began by informing his class that he does not like beards, mustaches, long hair on boys, or capri pants on girls, and will not tolerate any of that in his class. The class, incidentally, consisted mostly of high school teachers.

Even more discouraging than this Auschwitz approach to education is the fact that the students take it. They haven't gone through twelve years of public school for nothing. They've learned one thing and perhaps only one thing during those twelve years. They've forgotten their algebra. They're hopelessly vague about chemistry and physics. They've grown to fear and resent literature. They write like they've been lobotomized. But, Jesus, can they follow orders! Freshmen come up to me with an essay and ask if I want it folded and whether their name should be in the upper right hand corner. And I want to cry and kiss them and caress their poor tortured heads.

Students don't ask that orders make sense. They give up expecting things to make sense long before they leave elementary school. Things are true because the teacher says they're true. At a very early age we all learn to accept "two truths" as did certain medieval churchmen. Outside of class, things are true to your tongue, your fingers, your stomach, your heart. Inside class, things are true by reason of authority. And that's just fine because you don't care anyway. Miss Wiedemeyer tells you a noun is a person, place or thing. So let it be. You don't give a rat's ass; she doesn't give a rat's ass.

The important thing is to please her. Back in kindergarten, you found out that teachers only love children who stand in nice straight lines. And that's where it's been at ever since. Nothing changes except to get worse. School becomes more and more obviously a prison. Last year I spoke to a student assembly at Manual Arts High School and then couldn't get out of the goddamn school. I mean there was NO WAY OUT. Locked doors. High fences. One of the inmates was trying to make it over a fence when he saw me coming and froze in panic. For a moment, I expected sirens, a rattle of bullets, and him clawing the fence.

Then there's the infamous "code of dress." In some high schools, if your skirt looks too short, you have to kneel before the principal, in a brief allegory of fellatio. If the hem doesn't reach the floor, you go home to change while he, presumably, jacks off. Boys in high school can't be too sloppy and they can't even be too sharp. You'd think the school board would be delighted to see all the spades trooping to school in pointy shoes, suits, ties and stingy brims. Uh-uh. They're too visible.

What school amounts to, then, for white and black kids alike, is a 12-year course in how to be slaves. What else could explain what I see in a freshman class? They've got that slave mentality: obliging and ingratiating on the surface but hostile and resistant underneath.

As do black slaves, students vary in their awareness of what's going on. Some recognize their own put-on for what it is and even let their rebellion break through to the surface now and then. Others—including most of the "good students"—have been more deeply brainwashed. They swallow the bullshit with greedy mouths. They honest-to-God believe in grades, in busy work, in General Education requirements. They're pathetically eager to be pushed around. They're like those old grey-headed house niggers you can still find in the South who don't see what all the fuss is about because Mr. Charlie "treats us real good."

College entrance requirements tend to favor the Toms and screen out the rebels. Not entirely, of course. Some students at Cal State, L.A. are expert con artists who know perfectly well what's happening. They want the degree or the 2-S and spend their years on the old plantation alternately laughing and cursing as they play the game. If their egos are strong enough they cheat a lot. And, of course, even the Toms are angry down deep somewhere. But it comes out in passive rather than active aggression. They're unexplainably thick-witted and subject to frequent spells of laziness. They misread simple questions. They spend their nights mechanically outlining history chapters while meticulously failing to comprehend a word of what's in front of them.

The saddest cases among both black slaves and student slaves are the ones who have so thoroughly introjected their masters' values that their anger is all turned inward. At Cal State these are the kids for whom every low grade is torture, who stammer and shake when they speak to a professor, who go through an emotional crisis every time they're called upon during class. You can recognize them easily at finals time. Their faces are festooned with fresh pimples; their bowels boil audibly across the room. If there really is a Last Judgment, then the parents and teachers who created these wrecks are going to burn in hell.

So students are niggers. It's time to find out why, and to do this, we have to take a long look at Mr. Charlie.

The teachers I know best are college professors. Outside the classroom and taken as a group, their most striking characteristic is timidity. They're short on balls.

Just look at their working conditions. At a time when even migrant workers have begun to fight and win, college professors are still afraid to make more than a token effort to improve their pitiful economic status. In California State colleges the faculties are screwed regularly and vigorously by the Governor and Legislature and yet they won't offer any solid resistance. They lie flat on their stomachs, with their pants down, mumbling catch phrases like "professional dignity" and "meaningful dialogue."

Professors were no different when I was an undergraduate at UCLA during the McCarthy era; it was like a cattle stampede as they rushed to cop out. And in more recent years, I found that my being arrested in sit-ins brought from my colleagues not so much approval or condemnation as open-mouthed astonishment. "You could lose your job!"

Now, of course, there's the Vietnamese war. It gets some opposition from a few teachers. Some support it. But a vast number of professors who know perfectly well what's happening are copping out again. And in the high schools, you can forget it. Stillness reigns.

I'm not sure why teachers are so chickenshit. It could be that academic training itself forces a split between thought and action. It might also be that the tenured security of a teaching job attracts timid persons who are unsure of themselves and need weapons and the other external trappings of authority.

At any rate teachers ARE short of balls. And, as Judy Eisenstein has eloquently pointed out, the classroom offers an artificial and protected environment in which they can exercise their will to power. Your neighbors may drive a better car; gas station attendants may intimidate you; your wife may dominate you; the State Legislature may shit on you; but in the classroom, by God, students do what you say—or else. The grade is a hell of a weapon. It may not rest on your hip, potent and rigid like a cop's gun, but in the long run it's more powerful. At your personal whim—any time you choose—you can keep 35 students up for nights and have the pleasure of seeing them walk into the classroom pasty-faced and red eyed carrying a sheaf of typewritten pages, with title page, MLA footnotes and margins set at 15 and 91.

The general timidity which causes teachers to make niggers of their students usually includes a more specific fear—fear of the students themselves. After all, students are different, just like black people. You stand exposed in front of them, knowing that their interests, their values and their language are different from yours. To make matters worse, you may suspect that you yourself are not the most engaging of persons. What then can protect you from their ridicule and scorn? Respect for Authority. That's what. It's the policeman's gun again. The white bwana's pith helmet. So you flaunt that authority. You wither whisperers with a murderous glance. You crush objectors with erudition and heavy irony. And, worst of all, you make your own attainments seem not accessible but awesomely remote. You conceal massive ignorance—and parade a slender learning.

The teacher's fear is mixed with an understandable need to be admired and to feel superior, a need which also makes him cling to his "White supremacy." Ideally, a teacher should minimize the distance between himself and his students. He should encourage them not to need him . . . eventually or even immediately. But this is rarely the case. Teachers make themselves high priests of arcane mysteries. They become masters of mumbo-jumbo. Even a more or less conscientious teacher may be torn between the need to give and the need to hold back, the desire to free his students and the desire to hold them in bondage to him. I can find no other explanation that accounts for the way my own subject, literature, is generally taught. Literature, which ought to be a source of joy, solace and enlightenment, often becomes in the classroom nothing more than a source of anxiety—at best an arena for expertise, a ledger book for the ego. Literature teachers, often afraid to join a real union, nonetheless may practice the worst kind of trade-unionism in the classroom; they do to literature what Beckmesser does to song in Wagner's "Meistersinger." The avowed purpose of English departments is to teach literature; too often their real function is to kill it.

Finally, there's the darkest reason of all for the master-slave approach to education. The less trained and the less socialized a person, the more he constitutes a sexual threat, and the more he will be subjugated by institutions such as penitentiaries and schools. Many of us are aware by now of the sexual neurosis which makes white men so fearful of integrated schools and neighborhoods and which makes the castration of Negroes a deeply entrenched Southern folkway. We should recognize a similar pattern in education. There is a kind of castration that goes on in schools. It begins, before school years, with parents' first encroachment on their children's free unashamed sexuality and continues right up to the day when they hand you your doctoral diploma with a bleeding, shriveled pair of testicles stapled to the parchment. It's not that sexuality has no place in the classroom. You'll find it there but only in certain perverted and vitiated forms.

How does sex show up in school? First of all, there's the sado-masochistic relationship between teachers and students. That's plenty sexual, although the price of enjoying it is to be unaware of what's happening. In walks the teacher in his Ivy League equivalent of a motorcycle jacket. In walks the teacher—a kind of intellectual rough trade—and flogs his students with grades, tests, sarcasm and snotty superiority until their very brains are bleeding. In Swinburne's England, the whipped school boy frequently grew up to be flagellant. With us the perversion is intellectual but it's no less perverse.

Sex also shows up in the classroom as academic subject matter—sanitized and abstracted, thoroughly divorced from feeling. You get "sex education" now in both high school and college classes: everyone determined not to be embarrassed, to be very up to date, very contempo. These are the classes for which sex, as Feiffer puts it, "can be a beautiful thing if properly administered." And then, of course, there's still another depressing manifestation of sex in the classroom: the "off-color" teacher, who keeps his class awake with sniggering sexual allusions, obscene titters and academic innuendo. The sexuality he purveys, it must be admitted, is at least better than none at all.

What's missing, from kindergarten to graduate school, is honest recognition of what's actually happening—turned-on awareness of hairy goodies underneath the petti-pants, the chinos and the flannels. It's not that sex needs to be pushed in school; sex is push enough. But we should let it be, where it is and like it is. I don't insist that ladies in junior high lovingly caress their students' cocks (someday, maybe); however, it is reasonable to ask that the ladies don't, by example and stricture, teach their students to pretend that those cocks aren't there. As things stand now, students are psychically castrated and spayed—and for the very same reason that black men are castrated in Georgia: because they're a threat.

So you can add sexual repression to the list of causes, along with vanity, fear and will to power, that turn the teacher into Mr. Charlie. You might also want to keep in mind that he was a nigger once himself and has never really gotten over it. And there are more causes, some of which are better described in sociological than psychological terms. Work them out. It's not hard. But in the meantime what we've got on our hands is a whole lot of niggers. And what makes this particularly grim is that the student has less chance than the black man of getting out of his bag. Because the student doesn't even know he's in it. That, more or less, is what's happening in higher education, And the results are staggering.

For one thing damn little education takes place in the schools. How could it? You can't educate slaves; you can only train them. Or, to use an even uglier and more timely word, you can only program them.

I like to folk dance. Like other novices, I've gone to the Intersection or to the Museum and laid out good money in order to learn how to dance. No grades, no prerequisites, no separate dining rooms, they just turn you on to dancing. That's education. Now look at what happens in college. A friend of mine, Milt, recently finished a folk dance class. For his final exam, he had to learn things like this: "The Irish are known for their wit and imagination, qualities reflected in their dances, which include the jig, the reel and the hornpipe." And then the teacher graded him A,B,C,D, or F, while he danced in front of her. That's not education. That's not even training. That's an abomination on the face of the earth. It's especially ironic because Milt took that dance class trying to get out of the academic rut. He took crafts for the same reason. Great, right? Get your hands in some clay? Make something? Then the teacher announced that a 20-page term paper would be required—with footnotes.

At my school we even grade people on how they read poetry. That's like grading people on how they fuck. But we do it. In fact, God help me, I do it. I'm the Adolph Eichmann of English 323. Simon Legree on the poetry plantation. "Tote that iamb! Lift that spondee!" Even to discuss a good poem in that environment is potentially dangerous because the very classroom is contaminated. As hard as I may try to turn students on to poetry, I know that the desks, the tests, the IBM cards, their own attitudes toward school and my own residue of UCLA method are turning them off.

Another result of student slavery is equally serious. Students don't get emancipated when they graduate. As a matter of fact, we don't let them graduate until they've demonstrated their willingness—over 16 years—to remain slaves. And for important jobs, like teaching, we make them go through more years, just to make sure. What I'm getting at is that we're all more or less niggers and slaves, teachers and students alike. This is a fact you want to start with in trying to understand wider social phenomena, say, politics, in our country and in other countries.

Educational oppression is trickier to fight than racial oppression. If you're a black rebel, they can't exile you; they either have to intimidate you or kill you. But in high school or college, they can just bounce you out of the fold. And they do. Rebel students and renegade faculty members get smothered or shot down with devastating accuracy. In high school, it's usually the student who gets it; in college, it's more often the teacher. Others get tired of fighting and voluntarily leave the system. This may be a mistake, though. Dropping out of college for a rebel, is a litle like going North, for a Negro. You can't really get away from it so you might as well stay and raise hell.

How do you raise hell? That's a whole other article. But just for a start, why not stay with the analogy? What have black people done? They have, first of all, faced the fact of their slavery. They've stopped kidding themselves about an eventual reward in the Great Watermelon Patch in the sky. They've organized; they've decided to get freedom now, and they've started taking it.

Students, like black people, have immense unused power. They could, theoretically, insist on participating in their own education. They could make academic freedom bilateral. They could teach their teachers to thrive on love and admiration, rather than fear and respect, and to lay down their weapons. Students could discover community. And they could learn to dance by dancing on the IBM cards. They could make coloring books out of the catalogs and they could put the grading system in a museum. They could raze one set of walls and let life come blowing into the classroom. They could raze another set of walls and let education flow out and flood the streets.They could turn the classroom into where it's at—a "field of action" as Peter Marin describes it. And, believe it or not, they could study eagerly and learn prodigiously for the best of all possible reasons—their own reasons.

They could. Theoretically. They have the power. But only in a very few places, like Berkeley, have they even begun to think about using it. For students as for black people, the hardest battle isn't with Mr. Charlie. It's what Mr. Charlie has done to your mind.

For Discussion

1. What are the connotations of the word "nigger"?
2. This essay follows a clear pattern of organization. Analyze the main divisions.
3. The student-nigger analogy is the basis of Farber's argument. In what specific ways does he develop this analogy? Discuss each point of comparison.
4. What specific criticism does Farber make of faculty. Of administration? Of students?
5. How valid is Farber's observation about the slave mentality—"obliging

and ingratiating on the surface but hostile and resistant underneath"—as it applies to students?

6. How does your own experience contradict or support Farber's characterization of the teacher as timid? As tyrannical? As sadistic?

7. Discuss the teaching of literature as Farber describes it. How might his criticism be applied to other subjects?

8. What is Farber saying about the place of sex in the school? What do you think should be its proper place?

9. In what ways is the black man better off than the student-nigger?

10. Does Farber's criticism of education extend to what is being taught as well as how it is being taught? Explain.

11. Discuss Farber's use of invective, obscenity, and hyperbole. How does each affect the force of his argument? The logic of his argument?

12. What does Farber's language say about his attitude toward his subject and his audience?

13. Analogies are never conclusive as arguments and are valid only insofar as they point to essential likenesses. Perhaps by constructing other analogies you can gain insight into the validity of Farber's comparison. Consider, for example, "The Child as Nigger," "The Patient as Nigger," "The Laborer as Nigger," "The Wife as Nigger."

JUDY SYFERS

Why I Want a Wife

This brief essay has been widely discussed since its publication in the spring, 1972, issue of *Ms.*, the first national magazine to focus exclusively on feminist concerns. Ms. Syfers says of herself: "I am a middle-class and very nearly middle-aged, unemployable housewife with two female children. I therefore have ample reason for anger, but I feel it important to stress that the problems of an American wife stem from the fact that we live in a society which is structured in such a way as to profit only a few at the expense of the many. And as long as we women tolerate such a capitalist system, all but a privileged few of us must necessarily be exploited as workers and as wives."

I belong to that classification of people known as wives. I am A Wife. And, not altogether incidentally, I am a mother.

Not too long ago a male friend of mine appeared on the scene from the Midwest fresh from a recent divorce. He had one child, who is, of course, with his ex-wife. He is obviously looking for another wife. As I thought about him while I was ironing one evening, it suddenly occurred to me that I, too, would like to have a wife. Why do I want a wife?

I would like to go back to school so that I can become economically independent, support myself, and, if need be, support those dependent upon me. I want a wife who will work and send me to school. And while I am going to school I want a wife to take care of my children. I want a wife to keep track of the children's doctor and dentist appointments. And to keep track of mine, too. I want a wife to make sure my children eat properly and are kept clean. I want a wife who will wash the children's clothes and keep them mended. I want a wife who is a good nurturant attendant to my children, arranges for the schooling, makes sure that they have an adequate social life with their peers, takes them to the park, the zoo, etc. I want a wife who takes care of the children when they are sick, a wife who arranges to be around when the children need special care, because, of course, I cannot miss classes at school. My wife must arrange to lose time at work and not lose the job. It may mean a small cut in my wife's income from time to time, but I guess I can tolerate that. Needless to say, my wife will arrange and pay for the care of the children while my wife is working.

I want a wife who will take care of *my* physical needs. I want a wife who will keep my house clean. A wife who will pick up after my children, a wife who will pick up after me. I want a wife who will keep my clothes clean, ironed, mended, replaced when need be, and who will see to it that my personal things are kept in their proper place so that I can find what I need the minute I need it. I want a wife who cooks the meals, a wife who is a *good* cook. I want a wife who will plan the menus, do the necessary grocery shopping, prepare the meals, serve them pleasantly, and then do the cleaning up while I do my studying. I want a wife who will care for me when I am sick and sympathize with my pain and loss of time from school. I want a wife to go along when our family takes a vacation so that someone can continue to care for me and my children when I need a rest and a change of scene.

I want a wife who will not bother me with rambling complaints about a wife's duties. But I want a wife who will listen to me when I feel the need to explain a rather difficult point I have come across in my course of studies. And I want a wife who will type my papers for me when I have written them.

I want a wife who will take care of the details of my social life. When my wife and I are invited out by my friends, I want a wife who will take care of the babysitting arrangements. When I meet people at school that I like and want to entertain, I want a wife who will have the house clean, will prepare a special meal, serve it to me and my friends, and not interrupt when I talk about the things that interest me and my friends. I want a wife who will have arranged that the children are fed and ready for bed before my guests arrive so that the children do not bother us. I want a wife who takes care of the needs of my guests so that they feel comfortable, who makes sure that they have an ashtray, that they are passed the hors d'oeuvres, that they are offered a second helping of the food, that their wine glasses are replenished when necessary, that their coffee is served to them as they like it. And I want a wife who knows that sometimes I need a night out by myself.

I want a wife who is sensitive to my sexual needs, a wife who makes love passionately and eagerly when I feel like it, a wife who makes sure that I am satisfied. And, of course, I want a wife who will not demand sexual attention when I am not in the mood for it. I want a wife who assumes the complete responsibility for birth control, because I do not want more children. I want a wife who will remain sexually faithful to me so that I do not have to clutter up my intellectual life with jealousies. And I want a wife who understands that *my* sexual needs may entail more than strict adherence to monogamy. I must, after all, be able to relate to people as fully as possible.

If, by chance, I find another person more suitable as a wife than the wife I already have, I want the liberty to replace my present wife with another one. Naturally, I will expect a fresh, new life; my wife will take the children and be solely responsible for them so that I am left free.

When I am through with school and have acquired a job, I want my wife to quit working and remain at home so that my wife can more fully and completely take care of a wife's duties.

My God, who *wouldn't* want a wife?

For Discussion

1. What is your immediate response to this essay? Hostility? Empathy? Why?
2. Which of the jobs Syfers wishes done by her wife should be shared by men? Which should not? What other jobs do you think wives should be expected to do?
3. Which satiric jibes at husbands are justified? Which are not?
4. What does the author achieve through repetition?
5. What ironic techniques does Syfers use? For what audience is she writing?

APPENDIX

Thematic Contents

Subject Contents

Rhetorical Contents

INDEX OF
AUTHORS AND TITLES